The Journey to Rome

Conversion Literature by Nineteenth-Century American Catholics

Christine M. Bochen

Garland Publishing, Inc.
New York & London
1988

LIBRARY OF CONGRESS CATALOGING-IN-PUBLICATION DATA

Bochen, Christine M.
  The journey to Rome : conversion literature by nineteenth-century American catholics / Christine M. Bochen.
    p. cm. -- (The Heritage of American Catholicism)
  Originally presented as the author's thesis (Ph. D.--Catholic University of America) under the title: Personal narratives by nineteenth-century American Catholics.
  Bibliography: p.
  ISBN 0-8240-4086-4 (alk. paper)
1. Converts, Catholic--United States--Biography--History and criticism. 2. Converts, Catholic--United States--History--19th century. 3. Autobiography. 4. Conversion--History of doctrines--19th century. I. Title. II. Series.
BX4668.15.B63 1988   88-15610
248.2'42'0973--dc19   CIP

DESIGN BY MARY BETH BRENNAN

PRINTED ON ACID-FREE, 250-YEAR-LIFE PAPER.
MANUFACTURED IN THE UNITED STATES OF AMERICA

To My Mother,
Jane Bochen,
and
To the Memory of My Father,
Stanley J. Bochen
(1914-1973)

TABLE OF CONTENTS

PREFACE

Throughout this century, students of religion have devoted considerable attention to the study of religious experience of individuals, in particular to their conversions. Curiosity about the dynamics of religious conversion has been especially intense among students of nineteenth-century America.[1] But to date, studies have focused on conversion as experienced within the setting of evangelical Protestantism. With the exception of Jay P. Dolan's examination of conversions to Roman Catholicism occurring at Catholic missions or revivals, research on the subject of conversion to Roman Catholicism has not advanced far beyond the documentation of the fact of conversion offered by nineteenth-century authors.[2] Recent interest in the

---

[1]William James, The Varieties of Religious Experience (New York: Longmans, Green & Co., 1902; reprint ed., with an introduction by Reinhold Niebuhr (New York: Collier Books, 1961) reflected a concern with conversion. See pp. 160-210. Early empirical studies concentrated on the differences between sudden and gradual conversions. See Edwin Starbuck, "A Study of Conversion," American Journal of Psychology 9 (1897-98):268-308; The Psychology of Religion (Chicago: University of Chicago Press, 1916); E. T. Clark, The Psychology of Religious Awakening (New York: Macmillan, 1929). Some recent studies which stress the primacy of conversion within nineteenth-century evangelical Protestantism are: Dickson D. Bruce, Jr., And They All Sang Hallelujah: Plain Folks Camp Meeting Religion (Knoxville: The University of Tennessee Press, 1974) and John B. Boles, The Great Revival, 1787-1805: The Origins of the Southern Evangelical Mind (Lexington: The University of Kentucky Press, 1972).

[2]Jay P. Dolan, Catholic Revivalism and the American Experience (Notre Dame: University of Notre Dame Press, 1978), especially pp. 134-137; 142-143. Early essays on the subject of conversion to Roman Catholicism during the nineteenth century include Richard H. Clarke,

i

experience of Catholic people in nineteenth-century America reveals
a growing conviction among Roman Catholic scholars that the story
of American Catholicism will not be told fully until studies explore
what it meant and what it means to be a Catholic in America. James
Hennesey describes this task as the writing of "people-history."[3] This
dissertation is intended to be a contribution in that direction.

This dissertation examines accounts of religious conversion
contained in the personal narratives of nineteenth-century American
converts to Roman Catholicism. Given their newly acquired status as
members of an unpopular religious minority, a number of converts
recorded their conversion stories in an effort to justify becoming
Catholic and to defend the teaching and practice of their Church.
These narratives constitute a literary genre which is a distinctive
form of autobiographical writing -- distinctive in that conversion to
Roman Catholicism is clearly the focus of the narrative, determining
what elements of the life story to include and what elements to
exclude. A study of these autobiographical writings illuminates
understanding of the conversion experience in nineteenth-century
America. In contrast to the dominant Protestant understanding of
conversion as a tumultuous event, converts to Roman Catholicism

---

"Our Converts," American Catholic Quarterly Review 18 (1893):539-561;
19 (1894):112-138; John Gilmary Shea, "Converts -- Their Influence
and Work in this Country," American Catholic Quarterly Review 8 (1883):
509-529. But these essays are descriptive rather than analytic:
they shed light on the fact of conversion but do little to inform the
reader regarding the dynamics of the experience itself.

[3] James Hennesey, "Dimensions of American Catholic Experience,"
Catholic Mind 73 (1975):18-26. Jay P. Dolan's Catholic Revivalism
and The Immigrant Church: New York's Irish and German Catholics,

described the process of conversion as one of prolonged and extensive self-examination and careful scrutiny of the Christian creed.

The dissertation begins with an examination of the shape and style of nineteenth-century American Protestantism as a context for conversion to Roman Catholicism. Particular attention is given to Protestantism's denominational character and its evangelical cast, both of which established the necessity and centrality of the conversion experience. Conversion was critical to evangelical Christianity: a sudden and dramatic change of heart was viewed as the essential beginning of the Christian life. Narrative authors were dissatisfied with Protestantism as they had experienced it; they rejected both the tactics and the objectives of evangelism.

Chapter Two briefly recounts the history of the Roman Catholic Church in America during the nineteenth century as it pertains to the phenomenon of conversion to Catholicism. Despite the Church's minority status and the strong anti-Catholic sentiment which prevailed during the century, conversion to Roman Catholicism occurred at a vigorous rate. The sources of conversion are identified and understandings of conversion among Roman Catholics are discussed.

Chapter Three explores the personal narratives written by nineteenth-century American converts to Roman Catholicism as a form of spiritual autobiography in the attempt to identify similarities and differences between the narratives and the spiritual autobiographies written by Puritans and Quakers in England and in America during the

1815-1865 (Baltimore: Johns Hopkins University Press, 1975) are prime examples of a concern with "people-history."

seventeenth and eighteenth centuries. The narratives are identified,
the criteria for including works in this study set forth, and the
distinctive characteristics of conversion narratives discussed.

Chapter Four consists of a description and analysis of the
personal narratives written by John Thayer, Stephen Cleveland Blythe,
Daniel Barber, Isaac T. Hecker, Orestes Brownson, Joshua Huntington,
Levi Silliman Ives, Augustine Hewit, Clarence C. Walworth, William
Richards, B. W. Whitcher, and Charles Warren Stoddard. The life of
each author is briefly sketched, the structure and content of his
narrative reviewed, and his conversion examined. Chapter Four concludes
with a summary of some motifs which recur in the body of narratives.

Chapter Five sets forth the major finding of this dissertation:
for the narrative authors, conversion was a matter of mind and heart.
Although they emphasized the rational appeal of the Catholic faith, they
also found Catholicism aesthetically pleasing. Conversion to Roman
Catholicism was essentially a process of inquiry and reflection and
thus differed from the sudden, dramatic event, experienced by converts
within the Protestant revival setting. Becoming a Catholic was an
expression of faith: these Christians were impelled by their faith
to join the Roman Church, which attracted them with its doctrinal
uniformity, its polity, and its piety. The narratives offer evidence
that Roman Catholicism appealed to the converts as "heart religion."

I am grateful to my readers, Dr. William M. Shea, Dr. William
Cenkner, and Dr. Roger Cummins, for their assistance in the completion
of this dissertation. I owe a special word of thanks to Dr. Shea for
his helpful suggestions and for the encouragement he so generously gave.

CHAPTER I

THE SHAPE AND STYLE OF NINETEENTH-CENTURY

AMERICAN PROTESTANTISM: A CONTEXT FOR CONVERSION

Change -- adaptive and innovative -- characterized the experience

of Americans in the nineteenth century. Migration westward continued

to recast geographical boundaries and the very existence of the

frontier aroused a sense of adventure and exploration.[1] Between 1815

and 1860, some five million immigrants settled in the United States

transforming the complexion of society itself. Another ten million arrived

between 1860 and 1890[2]. In the latter half of the century, unprecedented

numbers of natives and immigrants flocked to urban areas as the

factory began to replace the farm as the cornerstone of the economy.

Immigration, urbanization, and industrialization permanently altered

the character of life.

The impact of these three movements was especially apparent

in widespread concern with reforming the quality of life. Rapid social

change had disrupted America's equilibrium and created a host of problems,

such as overcrowding, poverty, and labor abuses. Reformers mobilized to

---

[1]Sidney E. Mead argues that the very existence of the frontier
was a formative factor in the American experience. Open spaces emphasized the existence of social space -- space for free action and
experimentation in styles of life and belief. The Lively Experiment:
The Shaping of Christianity in America (New York: Harper & Row, 1963),
pp. 1-15.

[2]Edwin Scott Gaustad, A Religious History of America (New York:

uproot these social evils. Other longstanding causes, such as temperance, the abolition of slavery, the achievement of women's rights,
and the reform of prisons and hospitals, also aroused their zeal.[3]

Religious ferment and enthusiasm were marks of the century as
well. Population shifts, first in the direction of the wilderness,
then toward the city, made innovation in religious structures and
evangelizing techniques imperative. Nineteenth-century American
Protestants exhibited great vitality and fervor in shaping new patterns
of religious response. Existing religious groups were revitalized in
the process of adapting to the needs of the frontier and city; churches
strove to "win" the West and redeem the city. The formation of revival
groups, voluntary associations, and reform societies represented the
most common modes of adaptation among the Protestant denominations.
Those denominations which responded most creatively and aggressively
to the requirements of the times realized the largest increase in
membership. Methodists and Baptists experienced phenomenal growth because they developed evangelical tactics well-suited to the frontier.
Revivalists also rose to the challenges of evangelizing city-dwellers.

New sects emerged with striking frequency during the century,
another clear sign of a growing religious fervor. Each sect fashioned

----

Harper & Row, 1974), p. 202. See pp. 202-226 for a discussion of the
impact of immigration upon American life.

[3]Timothy L. Smith, Revivalism and Social Reform in Mid-
Nineteenth-Century America (Nashville: Abingdon Press, 1957). For
a brief but helpful summary of reform movements in nineteenth-
century American, see Sydney E. Ahlstrom, A Religious History
of the American People (New Haven: Yale University Press, 1972),
pp. 637-647.

a response to the world as the members of the sect perceived it. A
variety of theological and ideological tenets informed these sects:
the belief that perfect sanctification was possible, the expectation
of an imminent millenium, and the certainty that salvation could be
experienced through life in the community. Impulses toward perfection-
ism, adventism, communitarianism, spiritualism, and revivalism interacted
in diverse ways in each sect to produce a distinctive religious vision
and way of life.[4] Joseph Smith, Mother Ann Lee, William Miller, Ellen
G. White, and John Humphrey Noyes attracted enthusiastic followers.

One aspect of religious ferment was particularly outstanding:
the emphasis on the religious experience of the individual person,
on his conversion.[5] Indeed, the nineteenth century may accurately
be described as a "century of conversion" by reason of its singular
accent on the primacy of experiential religion and the necessity of
personal rebirth. The emphasis on conversion in nineteenth-century
American religion was clearly in evidence within the major Protestant
denominations as well as in the emergent sects. Personal experiences
of conversion prompted shifts in affiliation from one body to another.
Conversions were not simply confined to Protestant and sectarian ranks;
the Roman Catholic Church attracted converts as well.

---

[4]The Rise of Adventism: Religion and Society in Mid-
Nineteenth-Century America, ed. Edwin Scott Gaustad (New York: Harper &
Row, 1974) explores the forces at work in the origin of American sects.
Bryan Wilson's Religious Sects (New York: McGraw Hill Book Co., 1970)
explores the relationship between world views and varieties of
sectarian response.

[5]The meaning of "religious conversion" is ambiguous. The term
is used to refer to the movement from unbelief to belief, the
experience of rebirth or regeneration, spiritual awakening, a change
from one religious belief system or tradition to another, and a shift

4

The dynamics of conversion to Roman Catholicism among nineteenth-century Americans is the specific focus of this study. Its primary sources are accounts of conversion contained within personal narratives written by converts to Roman Catholicism.[6] Because these converts came from the ranks of the Protestant denominations and the Episcopal Church, it is fitting to begin with a description of the shape and style of American Protestantism in the nineteenth century, particularly of its denominational structure and of its revivalistic activity.[7] Moreover, since the narratives of converts to Roman

---

in denominational affiliation. Specific meanings of conversion in nineteenth-century American Protestantism and Roman Catholicism are explored in detail below and in the chapters which follow.

[6]The conversion narratives include An Account of the Conversion of the Reverend Mr. John Thayer, Lately a Protestant Minister, At Boston in North-America, Who embraced the Roman Catholic religion at Rome, on the 25th of May, 1783; Written by Himself. (Baltimore: William Goddard, 1788); An Apology for the Conversion of Stephen Cleveland Blythe, to the Faith of the Catholic, Apostolic and Roman Church. Respectfully Addressed to Protestants of Every Denomination. (New York: Printed by Joseph Desnoues, 1815); Catholic Worship and Piety Explained and Recommended, in sundry letters, to a very near friend, and others. By Daniel Barber, A.M. And not so long since a Minister of the Protestant Episcopal Church in Claremont, State of New Hampshire (Washington City: E. De Krafft Press, 1821); Levi Silliman Ives' The Trials of a Mind in its Progress to Catholicism: A Letter to His Old Friends (Boston: Patrick Donahue, 1854); Isaac T. Hecker's Questions of the Soul (New York: D. Appleton & Co., 1855); Orestes A. Brownson's The Convert; Or, Leaves From My Experience (New York: D. & J. Sadlier, 1857); Joshua Huntington's Gropings After Truth; A Life Journey from New England Congregationalism to the One Catholic and Apostolic Church (New York: The Catholic Publication Society, 1868); B.W. Whitcher's Story of a Convert, as Told to His Former Parisioners (New York: P. O'Shea, 1875); Augustine F. Hewit's "How I Became a Catholic," Catholic World 46 (1887):32-43; William Richards' On the Road to Rome, and How Two Brothers Got There (New York: Benzinger Brothers, 1895); Charles Warren Stoddard's A Troubled Heart and How It Was Comforted At Last (Notre Dame, Ind.: "Ave Maria" Office, 1895); Clarence E. Walworth's Oxford Movement in America; or, Glimpses of Life in an Anglican Seminary (New York: The Catholic Book Exchange, 1895).

[7]This chapter focuses on the broad contours of the Protestant

Catholicism suggest that dissatisfaction with the tenor of evangelical
Christianity was a significant factor in eventual conversion to Rome,
this first chapter considers a major thrust of evangelical Christianity:
its emphasis on the centrality of religious conversion as the foundation
for a Christian life.[8]

The Shape of Protestantism in Nineteenth-Century America

The distinctive shape of nineteenth-century American Protestantism
was rooted in its denominational structure. The denomination is "a
voluntary association of like-minded individuals who are united on the
basis of common beliefs for the purpose of accomplishing tangible and
defined objectives."[9] A primary objective is "the propagation of its
point of view."[10] "Voluntaryism" and pluralism are the most significant
marks of the denominational structure of church polity and inter-church
relations. First, membership is based on free choice. Second, no one
ecclesiastical structure is to be identified with or equated to the true
church.[11] Denominationalism was well-suited to the situation created by
constitutional prohibition of an established church and the consequent
autonomy of the church in relation to the state.

---

experience rather than on the particulars of denominational histories.
In the course of analyzing the accounts of conversion contained in the
narratives that comprise the source material for this dissertation,
I will examine aspects of the American Protestant and Episcopal
experiences germane to the authors' conversions to Roman Catholicism.

[8]Winthrop S. Hudson, American Protestantism (Chicago:
University of Chicago Press, 1961), p. 78.

[9]Sidney E. Mead, "Denominationalism: The Shape of Protestantism
in America," Church History 23 (1954): 291.

[10]Ibid.

[11]Hudson, p. 34.

Voluntaryism

Denominational membership was determined by choice rather than by birth. Because churches were voluntary organizations, they had to rely on their own ability to gather and maintain membership.[12] Voluntaryism presumed that the laity had a variety of options before them: persons were able to choose not to affiliate with any group. Because the churches depended on their ability to attract and sustain membership, the laity exercised considerable influence and power over denominational leaders. The leaders, in turn, developed political acumen and perfected their powers of persuasion as they sought to maintain support and retain their authority.[13] Denominational leaders became particularly sensitive to the divisive potential of doctrinal debates and scrupulously shunned theological discussion. As a result, unity was frequently purchased at the price of fundamentalism and reductionism. Mass evangelism was most successful when the message preached was simple. Therefore, as Sidney Mead suggests, revivalism contributed to a triumph of pietism, a victory of heart over mind and emotion over reason.

Holding revivals became the primary method for gathering and

---

[12]Hudson speaks of the "gathered church" as the prevalent form of church polity even in colonial America. The traditional parish system, sustained by religious "establishment," was impossible in the new land. The image of "gathering" implies the drawing together of those persons committed to common objectives. The centrality of conversion is a logical outgrowth of the "gathered church." Winthrop S. Hudson, Religion in America (New York: Scribners, 1965), pp. 14-16.

[13]Mead observes that "whatever else top denominational leaders may be, they must be denominational politicians." "Denominationalism," p. 300.

In discussing the authority of the clergy in New England during

maintaining church membership. The voluntary status of the churches

required intensive missionary efforts and revivalism was a most

effective missionary tactic. Those denominations that employed

revivalistic measures most successfully experienced the greatest

increase in membership. In addition to their intra-denominational

efforts, denominations became involved in a variety of concerted

national and foreign missionary campaigns that grew out of the fervor

and zeal aroused by revivalism. The nineteenth century witnessed the

founding of the American Bible Society (1816), the American Sunday School

Union (1824), The American Tract Society (1825), and the American

Home Mission Society (1826) -- to name but a few of the earliest

associations.

Pluralism

Denominationalism expressed the pluralistic nature of

Protestantism. Since no single church body was to be identified

with the Church of Christ, diversity was inevitable. Each group

had to identify and demonstrate the unique character of its under-

standing of Christian faith and practice. This was no small task

because the differences among denominations were greatly outnumbered

by the similarities. Sidney Mead suggests that the factor which

---

the colonial era, Hudson notes the origin of a changing clerical role.
"Far removed from the status-giving context of an ordered church life
and dependent upon what support they could enlist among the laity both
for the formation and maintenance of the congregations they served,
the only real authority the clergy possessed was the authority they
could command by their powers of persuasion and the force of their
example." Religion in America, p. 13.

ultimately differentiated one church from another was degree of conformity to the biblical model. The authority of the Bible was a cornerstone of belief in every Protestant body, but the intensity with which a church conformed to the example of the primitive Christian community allowed it to manifest its uniqueness and so to defend its right to exist.[14] This preoccupation with biblical paradigms carried its own hazards: it diminished consciousness of centuries of intervening history and cumulative religious insight, thereby contributing to reductionism and fundamentalism.

Pluralism and voluntaryism encouraged a strong spirit of competition among the denominations by creating a market situation. The metaphor of the marketplace and the correlative image of a set of religious teachings and practices as a "commodity" accurately describe the competitive spirit that developed among the denominations. The market situation modified the roles of clergy and laity. The clerical role was shaped by increasing emphasis upon popular appeal; ministerial effectiveness was measured by observable criteria, e.g. increased membership and impressive conversion tallies. The laity, in turn, exercised the options of selective consumers to choose or refuse the commodity offered. Thus "dynamics of consumer preference" shaped the denominational product.[15] Inter-denominational competition often accentuated trivial differences while substantial doctrinal points

---

[14]Mead, "Denominationalism," p. 297.

[15]Peter L. Berger, The Sacred Canopy: Elements of a Sociological Theory of Religion (New York: Doubleday & Co., 1967), p. 145.

were relativized.[16] Furthermore, the competitive spirit, untempered by
the Gospel, generated divisiveness among the denominations. Jealousy
and bitterness sometimes characterized inter-denominational rivalry.[17]

The denominational cast of Protestantism clearly affected the
understanding of conversion. The denominational principle itself
neutralized any potential claims to primacy on the part of any one
denomination. No denomination was able to claim identity with the
Church of Christ. Logically, then, conversion was likely to be, and
indeed, was defined in experiential rather than sociological categories.
Conversion was understood and experienced primarily as personal rebirth,
rather than as a shift in affiliation. The significant identification
with Christ outweighed the importance of belonging to a particular church
body.

The Style of Protestantism
in Nineteenth-Century America

The denominational shape of Protestantism required a distinctive style of evangelism, designed to arouse religious interest
and awaken congregations to a desire for experiential religion. Above
all, revivalism was an effective technique of mass evangelism, aimed

---

[16]Mead, "Denominationalism," p. 317.

[17]Winfred E. Garrison observes that division among the
denominations "breeds wasteful and sometimes acrimonious rivalry,
diminishes efficiency in pursuit of the common major objectives of
all churches, sets narrow bounds to Christian fellowship, and encourages religious provincialism." "Characteristics of American
Organized Religion," The Annals of the American Academy of Political
and Social Science 256 (1948): 18.

at promoting spiritual awakening or rebirth. The technical aspect of
revivalism is well-developed in the writings of the nineteenth-century
revivalist, Charles Grandison Finney, who saw a good revival as the
product of careful planning and calculated human effort rather than
as a spontaneous eruption of supernatural power. Finney reasoned that
a revival was "the result of the right use of the appropriate means."[18]
God's blessing was, of course, an essential ingredient in a revival,
but Finney argued that man's effort was also an indispensible component
of a successful revival. God ordained that it was the preacher's work
which occasioned the desired effect, namely, the revival of religion.[19]

Revivalism, however, cannot simply be equated with the en-
gineering of mass conversions. In the nineteenth century, it consisted
of more than the methods employed to awaken religious faith and fervor;
it was a mood or spirit that permeated the consciousness of many.
Revivalism expressed the epoch's understanding of human nature, its
frailties and sinfulness, and offered a road to redemption. It portrayed
human nature as weak and vile; only the saving power of Jesus Christ

---

[18] Charles Grandison Finney, Lectures on Revivals of Religion,
ed. William G. McLoughlin (Cambridge, Mass.: The Belknap Press of
Harvard University Press, 1960), p. 13.

[19] Ibid., pp. 13-14. McLoughlin notes the difference of
opinion between Finney and Jonathan Edwards regarding the origin
of revivals (n. 7, p. 13). In A Faithful Narrative of the Surprising
Works of God, Edwards speaks of "a very extraordinary dispensation
of Providence: God has in many respects gone out of, and much beyond
his usual and ordinary way." The Works of Jonathan Edwards, vol. 4:
The Great Awakening, ed. C. C. Goen (New Haven and London: Yale
University Press, 1972), p. 157. Edwards was filled with awe at
the amazing work of God; a century later, religious awakening had
become commonplace and subject to rational explanation.

enabled men to overcome the evils to which human nature was heir.

Furthermore, revivalism exposed the human need for experiential religion

while simultaneously legitimizing public expression of religious

feeling. It aroused the desire for enthusiastic religion and satisfied

that desire by providing a social context in which individuals could

experience the catharsis of conviction and conversion.

Revivalist tactics and techniques reflected a distinctive

theological perspective. The primacy of conversion was the theological

cornerstone of the evangelical Protestant denominations. First, the

revivalist emphasized individual conversion as the primary goal of

Christian ministers. Conversion to Jesus Christ meant salvation. The

revivalist stressed the possibility of perfection as much as he

emphasized the sinfulness of the unconverted. Revivalism was optimistic;

eventually, all Americans would profess faith in Jesus Christ. Such

optimism was consistent with growing American faith in human progress.

Second, conversion was the focal point of revivalist ecclesiology as well.

The Church was defined as the body of persons who had experienced

conversion and that experience was a requirement for full church

membership.

Revivalism was a technique, a spirit, and a theological per-

spective that profoundly affected American society. As a force for

social control and an impetus for reform, it met two diverse social

needs.[20] Revivalism served

...to provide a unifying and self-restraining code of social

-----

[20]William G. McLoughlin, "Revivalism," in The Rise of Adventism, p. 119. See also pp. 120-153.
Revivalism as an impetus to reform is explored in the fol-

and personal conduct for the average man; to organize a vast
array of religious, educational, and related social institutions
(both on the frontier and in the cities) to implement that
code; to encourage the formation of numerous evangelistic,
home missionary, charitable, and benevolent societies to
civilize the wild frontiersman, to assimilate the foreigner,
and to reform the vicious, dangerous, and corrupt masses;
and above all to provide Americans with a sense that their
way of life was God's way for all men.[21]

Revivalism identified the individual's place in the cosmos and in

society, specifying the nature of his relationship with God and

neighbor. For both individual and group, revivalism produced an

ethical system, a code of conduct. Its simple message was easily

converted into a blueprint for action. Clearly, revivalism was a

conservative force for individual, church, and society alike.

Revivalists also stimulated reform movements in nineteenth-century

---

lowing studies: Gilbert H. Barnes, The Anti-Slavery Impulse, 1830-
1844 (New York: D. Appleton-Century Co., 1933); Alice Felt Tyler,
Freedom's Ferment: Phases of American Social History to 1860
(Minneapolis: University of Minnesota Press, 1944); Whitney Rogers
Cross, The Burned-Over District: The Social and Intellectual History
of Enthusiastic Religion in Western New York, 1800-1850 (Ithaca:
Cornell University Press, 1950; reprint ed., New York: Harper &
Row, 1965); Timothy L. Smith, Revivalism and Social Reform in Mid-
19th-Century America (New York: Abingdon Press, 1967); Charles
C. Cole, Jr., The Social Ideas of the Northern Evangelists, 1826-
1860 (New York: Octogon Books, 1966).
        Revivalism as a force for conformity and conservatism is
explored in the following works: John R. Bodo, The Protestant
Clergy and Public Issues, 1812-1848 (Princeton: Princeton Univer-
sity Press, 1954); Charles I. Foster, An Errand of Mercy: The Evan-
gelical United Front, 1790-1837 (Chapel Hill: University of South
Carolina Press, 1960); Clifford S. Griffin, Their Brothers' Keepers:
Moral Stewardship in the United States, 1800-1865 (New Brunswick:
Rutgers University Press, 1960); T. Scott Mijakawa, Protestants
and Pioneers: Individualism and Conformity on the American Frontier
(Chicago: University of Chicago Press, 1964).

[21]McLoughlin, p. 129.

America by exposing a variety of social evils, slavery and intemperance among them, and by identifying appropriate Christian solutions. Revivalism provided a context in which Americans negotiated "crucial turning points" in self-understanding.[22] Both at the beginning of the nineteenth century and at its end, Americans faced critical questions. During the Awakening of 1795-1835, they asked: "What kind of nation is the U.S. to be now that it is free and able, under God, to govern itself?"[23] Later, during the Awakening of 1875-1915, they posed another question: "How can a Christian people reconcile Scripture and science to deal with urban-industrial society?"[24] Effects of revivalism extended far beyond church life.

Revivals: Contexts for Conversion

Revivalistic fervor peaked on three fronts: Kentucky (the initial center of frontier revivalism), New England, and upstate New York. Geographical location, charismatic leadership, theological perspectives, and the religious zeal of residents acted together to create climates in which sudden outbursts of religious excitement became frequent and concern with spiritual matters commonplace.[25] Revivals

---

[22]Ibid., p. 132.

[23]Ibid., p. 151.

[24]Ibid.

[25]Cross analyzes the peculiar blend of diverse factors which made upstate New York fertile ground for revivalistic preachers (passim). A similar interaction of varied influences created a supportive social base for revivals in the South, especially in Kentucky (Boles, passim).

which occurred in these areas were the primary contexts for conversion
in nineteenth-century American Protestantism.

Cane Ridge

Logan County, Kentucky was an unlikely starting place for a
revival, but "through an unusual combination of personality, theology,
time, society, and coincidence...a remarkable outbreak of religious
emotion erupted" there.[26] The happening at Cane Ridge constituted a true
revival. Logan County had experienced a decline in religious fervor,
as had the nation after the Revolutionary War. Preachers in Logan
County acknowledged and lamented that decline and sought to explain
it.[27] Some argued that man's wrongdoing was a source of displeasure
to God; therefore, God was chastening man. Others were more optimistic:
man was surely being prepared for a new and wonderful work of God.
These days of darkness were intended to develop man's trust and
confidence in the Lord. The time of trial and tribulation was a
necessary prelude to deliverance and the moment of deliverance was
proclaimed to be near at hand. Repentance, expressed in prayer and
fasting would prepare persons for God's action. Prophetic themes
abounded. The covenant motif was frequently cited. When Christians
had prepared themselves, God would act.[28]

---

[26]Boles, p. 36.

[27]Ibid., pp. 25-35.

[28]Ibid, p. 32.

Preparation for a religious awakening continued under the inspired preaching of James McGready who arrived in Logan County in 1796. McGready was a gifted revivalist who was able to describe heaven so vividly that his congregation would "almost see its glories and long to be there" and he would "so array hell and its horrors before the wicked, that they would tremble and quake, imagining a lake of fire and brimstone yawning to overwhelm them, and the wrath of God thrusting them down the horrible abyss."[29] McGready offered his hearers only one way in which they might avoid the terrors of damnation: they must be born anew; they must experience conversion.

> In that awful day, when the universe, assembled, must appear
> before the quick and dead, the question brethren, will not be,
> were you a Presbyterian -- a Seceder -- a Covenanter -- a
> Baptist -- or a Methodist; but, did you experience a new birth?
> Did you accept Christ and his salvation as set forth in the
> Gospel?

McGready was heard. In June of 1798, the Gasper River congregation awakened. McGready wrote that the "Lord poured out his spirit in a very remarkable manner."[30] A month later, McGready and John Rankin, one of his North Carolina converts, witnessed a revival at a Gasper River service. Many were so overcome that they fell to the floor:

> ...the power of God seemed to shake the whole assembly.
> Towards the close of the sermon, the cries of the distressed
> arose almost as loud as his preacher's voice. --After the

---

[29] Franceway R. Cossett, The Life and Times of Rev. Finis Ewing, One of the Fathers and Founders of the Cumberland Presbyterian Church (Louisville, 1853), p. 44, cited by Bernard A. Weisberger, They Gathered at the River: The Story of the Great Revivalists and Their Impact upon Religion in America (Boston: Little, Brown & Co., 1958), pp. 23-24.

[30] James McGready, The Posthumous Works of the Reverend and

congregation was dismissed the solemnity increased, till the
greater part of the multitude seemed engaged in the most
solemn manner. No person seemed to wish to go home -- hunger
and sleep seemed to affect nobody -- eternal things were the
vast concern. Here awakening and converting work as to be
found in every part of the multitude; and even some things
strangely and wonderfully new to me.[31]

The revival at Gasper River, the first of the camp-meetings, set the

stage for Cane Ridge.

The Cane Ridge revival was the most sensational outbreak of

enthusiastic religion heretofore experienced in the South. Barton Warren

Stone, who held the pulpit at Cane Ridge, organized the revival which

became a model for other camp-meetings. Thousands of persons gathered

on the slopes of a large hill. Estimates range from twelve to twenty-five

thousand.[32] Presbyterian, Baptist, and Methodist preachers joined

forces, urging their listeners to accept Jesus Christ and experience

the new birth which brings assurance of salvation and escape from the

everlasting fires of hell. Peter Cartwright included a firsthand

account of the events of Cane Ridge in his autobiography:

...the mighty power of God was displayed in a very extraordinary manner; many were moved to tears, and bitter and
loud crying for mercy. The meeting was protracted for weeks.

Pious James M'Gready, Late Minister of the Gospel, in Henderson
Kentucky, ed. James Smith, 2 vols. (Louisville, Kentucky and
Nashville, Tennessee: 1831-1833), 2:71, cited by Boles, p. 40.

[31]Ibid., 1:iv-xvi.

[32]James McGready, "A Short Narrative of the Revival of Reli-
gion in Logan County, in the State of Kentucky, and the adjacent
Settlement in the State of Tennessee, from May 1797, until
September," New York Missionary Magazine 3 (1802): 193, cited by
Boles, pp. 56-57.

Ministers of almost all denominations flocked in from far and
near. The meeting was kept up by day and night. Thousands
heard of the mighty work, and came on foot, on horseback, in
carriages and wagons....Hundreds fell prostrate under the mighty
power of God, as men slain in battle. Stands were erected
in the woods from which preachers of different Churches proclaimed
repentence toward God and faith in our Jesus Christ, and it
was supposed, by eye and ear witnesses, that between one and
two thousand souls were happily and powerfully converted to
God during the meeting. It was not unusual for one, two, three,
and four to seven preachers to be addressing the listening
thousands at the same time from the different stands erected
for the purpose. The heavenly fire spread in almost every
direction. It was said, by truthful witnesses, that at times more
than one thousand persons broke out into loud shouting all at
once. And that the shouts could be heard for miles around.[33]

"Everything acted together -- the size of the crowd, the noise of

simultaneous sermons and hymns, assorted shouts, cries, groans,

and praises, the exhaustion brought on by continual services, the

summer heat -- simply overwhelmed the participants with their beliefs

in providential omnipotence."[34] There was no question but that this

was the work of God.

The revivals brought together Methodists, Presbyterians,

and Baptists. Denominational differences were blurred in the face

of such religious excitement. The denominations were united in their

affirmation of the centrality of conversion as a pre-requisite to

---

[33]Peter Cartwright, Autobiography of Peter Cartwright, with
an Introduction, Bibliography, and Index by Charles L. Wallis
(New York: Abingdon Press, 1956), p. 34. Stone places the number
at twenty to thirty thousand. Barton Warren Stone, The Biography
of Eld. Barton Warren Stone, Written by Himself: with Additions
and Reflections by Elder John Rogers (Cincinatti, 1847; reprint ed.,
New York: Arno Press, 1972), p. 37.

[34]Cartwright, pp. 33-34.

salvation, their commitment to the methods of revivalism, and in their style of pietism. After Cane Ridge, the practical, provincial, and individualistic cast of southern religion was firmly established.[35]

The North:
New England and Western New York

In the North, two areas proved to be especially fertile ground for revivalistic fervor: New England, especially Connecticut, and western New York State which was designated the "Burnt" or "Burned-over district," so furiously did the fires of the spirit burn there.[36]

Enthusiastic religion made its appearance in New England during the eighteenth century. The First Great Awakening revitalized churches suffering from a decline in spirit as well as in numbers. The Awakening altered the style of New England religion by encouraging emotional and experiential religiosity. However, the Great Awakening, with its resurgence of religious vitality, was short-lived. Americans turned their attention and energy to the war effort. Deism, popular among the nation's leaders, emphasized human responsibility and worldly concerns. After the Revolutionary War, America was ripe for another awakening.

The Second Awakening came upon New England in phases, as had the first. Between 1797 and 1801, "refreshing showers" fell from

---

[35]Boles, p. 66.

[36]Ibid., pp. 129-130.

19

Connecticut to New Hampshire.[37] In 1801, Yale was the scene of a

revival prompted by the preaching of its President, Timothy Dwight.

Waves of revivalistic excitement came over the College in 1812-13

and again in 1815. Dwight's influence continued through his students,

especially Nathaniel William Taylor and Lyman Beecher.

New England revivals were distinctive in tone and in theology.

Revivals there were restrained; the absence of hysterical outbursts,

common elsewhere, was seen as a sign God's presence and work. New

Haven Theology, which provided the theoretical base for New England

revivalism, abandoned the long-standing Puritan view of human nature

as perverse and emphasized man's freedom and goodness. Nathaniel

William Taylor, recognized architect of the New Haven Theology,

argued that man is a free agent, who exercises his freedom in the

experience of conversion.[38]

Upstate New York was the third major center of revivalistic

activity. During the winter of 1799-1800, the burned-over district

had been the scene of a revival, so pervasive and memorable as to

merit being called the "Great Revival." It was the culmination of the

religious excitement of several years.[39] A lesser peak was

---

[37]Cross identifies "the Burned-over District as that portion
of New York State lying west of the Catskill and Adirondack Mountains"
(p. 4).

[38]Ahlstrom, p. 416.

[39]Nathaniel William Taylor, Man, a Free Agent without the
Aids of Divine Grace, p. 8, cited by Sidney E. Mead, Nathaniel
William Taylor 1786-1858. A Connecticut Liberal (Chicago: University
of Chicago Press, 1942), p. 111.

experienced in 1807-1808 and religious revivals continued after the
War of 1812. Religious interest and sensitivity grew, fed by the
persistent efforts of New Englanders to evangelize the West.
Western New York State attracted more than its share of "Yankee
Benevolence."[40] Theological perspectives, generated by the New
School Theology took root, affirming the role of human effort in
the redemption of sinners and supporting the reform of the social
order.

In 1830, upstate New York was ready for Charles Grandison
Finney. Finney emerged as the master theoretician and practitioner
of revivalism and became the most articulate spokesman for those
who recognized that revivals required methods rather than miracles.
Finney argued that a revival was "a purely philosophical result
of the right use of any constituted means -- as much so as any other
effect produced by the application of means."[41] Finney was for
all practical purposes a native son of the Burned-over District;
though he had been born in Connecticut, he lived in Oneida County,
New York until he was about twenty. He taught in New Jersey, continued his studies in New England, and eventually settled into the
study of law in Adams, New York. There he became interested in
religious matters. Intrigued by law authors who cited the Mosaic

---

[40]Cross, pp. 9-10. Cross contrasts the gradual peaking of
revivalistic fervor with the suddenness of the Kentucky Revival.
This contrast is oversimplified. Cf. Boles.

[41]The image is suggested by Cross (p. 14).

Institute as the basis of common law, Finney purchased a Bible and
read it in conjunction with his studies. That led to his conversion.

In his Memoirs, Finney recounts the story: the heightening
of interest in salvation, his resolve "to settle the question of his
soul's salvation" once and for all, the realization that salvation
was to be found in Jesus Christ, and an overwhelming sense of
sinfulness -- all of which prepared him to accept Jesus Christ.

> All my feelings seemed to rise and flow out; and the utterance
> of my heart was, "I want to pour my whole soul out to God."
> ...it seemed as if I met the Lord Jesus Christ face to face....
> I received a mighty baptism of the Holy Ghost....the Holy Ghost
> descended upon me in a manner that seemed to go through me,
> body and soul....It seemed like the very breath of God.[42]

Following his conversion, Finney became convinced that he
was called to preach the Gospel and prepared himself for the task
by studying theology. Finney was ordained a "presbygational"
minister, as the "products" of the Plan of Union between Presbyterian
and Congregational Churches were called. The Plan of Union,
established in 1801, was a measure to prevent divisive quibbling among
Calvinists. But Finney showed little interest in debating the
theological subtleties of Calvinism or in preserving Calvinism
in its purity. He denied ever having read the Westminster Confession,
which was accepted as the common confession of faith in the Plan of
Union. Finney's theological views were more compatible with those
of the New Theology or New Haven School, whose proponents included
Nathaniel Taylor and Lyman Beecher. However, Finney's revivalistic

---

[42]Finney, p. 13.

methods met with the opposition of Old and New Calvinists alike.
The emotional excesses, experienced by Finney's congregations,
aroused Old Calvinist opposition. And leading proponents of New England
revivalism, such as Lyman Beecher and Asahel Netterton, feared that
Finney would undermine the potential of evangelism by his excesses.[43]

Despite the controversy engendered by Finney's methods,
there is no question that Finney set the course of northern revivalism
during the nineteenth century. His spirit and vision played a central
role in reshaping the understanding of conversion among American
revivalists. Finney's primary contributions to American religious
history were his recognition that religion is "the work of man" and
his insistence that revivals were the "result of the right use of
the appropriate means" rather than miracles.[44]

Finney's Lectures were more than a "how-to" manual for the
revivalist. His intention was practical: to disseminate what he
had learned through his work as a revivalist. But Finney moved beyond
a description of manifestations and effects to an exploration of the
nature and structure of revivals. Finney's Lectures constitute a
phenomenology of revivalism. His belief that revivals were the work
of man was conducive to a careful exploration of the revival process
for it truly mattered what men did. Revivals were the reasonable
outcome of the use of appropriate means, not the arbitrary manifestations

---

[43] Charles G. Finney, Memoirs of Rev. Charles G. Finney,
Written by Himself (New York: A. S. Barnes & Co., 1876), pp. 19-20.

[44] For a detailed discussion of the controversy between Finney
and Beecher, see McLoughlin, Modern Revivalism, especially pp. 30-64.

of God's whims. Preparing for a revival was like "breaking up the
fallow ground"; an examination of conscience, prayer and faith in its
power, and openness to the Spirit softened the heart, readying it to
receive God's word.[45] Finney argued that preparations for a revival
ought to include "social" prayer as well as "secret" prayer; prayer
meetings brought sinners nearer to conversion.[46] The testimony of
other Christians, by precept and example, was also effective in bringing
sinners to conviction and conversion.

Finney carefully distinguished three types of potential converts:
careless, awakened, and convicted sinners. He identified the approach
best suited for each type. A careless sinner was most likely to be
awakened by the inspiring example of those already converted to Christ.
The awakened but as yet unconverted sinner required immediate and intensive attention. Persons, "awakened by some providential circumstance,
as sickness, a thunderstorm, pestilence, death in the family, disappointment or the like, or by the Spirit of God" were "ready to hear on the
subject of religion with attention and seriousness, and some feeling."[47]
The convicted sinner, who already recognized his guilt, required wise
handling to carry him beyond the anxious state to repentance and
conversion. To meet the needs of potential converts, Finney employed
"new Measures" -- anxious meetings, protracted meetings, and the anxious
seat -- measures which Finney deemed effective and therefore legitimate
and which his opponents criticized and condemned.

---

[45] Finney, Lectures, pp. 9, 13.

[46] Ibid, p. 38.

[47] Ibid., p. 124.

Charles Grandison Finney's contribution to evangelism was twofold: his passionate preaching moved thousands to conviction and conversion and his written reflections provided a systematic base for the methods of evangelical Christianity. Recognizing that conversion was in large part a matter of religious socialization and education, Finney developed effective techniques for mass evangelization.

Denominationalism gave American Protestantism its distinctive shape; revivalism stamped American Protestantism with a characteristic style. Denominationalism rendered voluntary choice a necessary require- ment for church membership; revivalism created the setting in which actual choices were made. But the impact of the denominational structure and revivalistic style extended beyond the sphere of church polity and missionary methodology to the understanding of Christian experience. Both denominationalism and revivalism emphasized the centrality of person- al religious experience in the Christian life. Conversion consisted in the rebirth that occurred when a person abandoned sin and accepted Jesus Christ. Conversion became the prerequisite for church membership. Because the churches depended upon voluntary membership, fostering conversions became their primary objective. Many nineteenth-century Protestants agreed that a well-planned and well-executed revival was the best way to promote the experience of conversion.

Understandings of Conversion
in Nineteenth-Century Evangelical Protestantism

Nineteenth-century evangelical Protestants viewed conversion as the primary religious experience.[49] The goal of conversion was clear

---

[49]The centrality of conversion is reflected in the interest

and forthright: salvation. Salvation meant rebirth, death to the old man and birth of the new man. Rebirth signified inner trans-formation and a corresponding change in social standing: "Conversion gave every convert a new way of looking at the world -- the old life was utterly and completely rejected upon conversion and replaced by a positive response to the Lord's offer of grace."[50]

Conversion experiences of religious leaders, recorded in biographies and autobiographies, functioned as paradigms. First, their accounts testified to the impact of God's grace in their lives. These men were convinced that through the power of God they were led from sinfulness to salvation, from worldliness to a promise of eternity. Their stories inspired others to seek salvation. Second, their written accounts of conversion were normative: they defined the acceptable form of conversion. Popular accounts, such as those of Peter Cartwright and Charles Grandison Finney, conventionalized the conversion experience by expressing the expectations of the community which, in turn, shaped the experience of individual converts.[51]

---

in the phenomenon of conversion in nineteenth-century Protestantism shown by American students of religion such as: Starbuck, Coe, Clark, and, more recently, by Bruce and Boles.

[50] Bruce, p. 122.

[51] Models of conversion put forth in autobiographies have played a part in shaping religious experience in America since the colonial ear. See Edmund Sears Morgan, Visible Saints: The History of a Puritan Idea (New York: New York University Press, 1963), p. 66; William Haller, The Rise of Puritanism (New York: Harper & Row, 1938), pp. 90-91, 127; and Daniel B. Shea, Spiritual Autobiography in Early America (Princeton: Princeton University Press, 1968), passim. These authors discuss the evolution of spiritual writings of an autobiographical nature, including diaries and journals, and indicate their function within the community. Owen C. Watkins traces the Puritan interest in spiritual autobiography to its English roots. The Puritan Experience: Studies

The Structure of Conversion

The conversion experiences related in the autobiographical accounts of nineteenth-century revivalists consisted of three distinct stages: pre-conversion, conviction, and conversion. Prior to conversion, an individual's behavior was "worldly" and "sinful," or so he was likely to characterize it after his conversion. Peter Cartwright confessed to being "a wild, wicked boy" who "delighted in horse-racing, card-playing, and dancing."[52] John Hagerty, a Methodist preacher, recalled that before his conversion he "took much delight in young peoples' company and dancing."[53] Tension commonly characterized this initial stage, as relatives and friends pleaded with the sinner to abandon his old ways.

Conviction consisted in awareness of one's sinfulness. It came "when the tension between one's worldly life and religion could no longer be borne, the religious life having been acknowledged as superior."[54] Usually, a crisis, such as a personal disaster or a confrontation with death (one's own or that of another) precipitated conviction by disrupting a person's system of meaning and value. Jacob Bower had such an experience:

---

in Spiritual Autobiography (New York: Schoken Books, 1972).

[52]Cartwright, p. 31.

[53]John Hagerty to Edward Dromgoole, 19 January 1778, cited by William Warren Sweet, ed., The Methodists, A Collection of Source Materials (Chicago: University of Chicago Press, 1946), p. 125.

[54]Bruce, p. 65.

> Soon we met large companies of Negro-s [sic] , we passed several
> companies, at length we met an old man walking by himself, I
> stopped him and enquired of him, where they were all going so
> early in the morning. The old negro said, "we are all going to
> Beards Town [Kentucky] to see a fellow servant hung to day
> for killing his fellow servant." I started on with this thought,
> how does that man feal [sic] , knowing that he must die to day.
> Suddenly as if some one had asked me. And how do you feal?
> You don't know but that you may die before he does. All of a
> sudden (ah I shall never forget it) as if a book had been oped
> to me, the inside of which I had never seen: I got a sight
> of the wretchedness of my heart -- a cage of every unclean and
> hateful thing. (ah [sic] thought I, here lies the root of
> bitterness, the fountain from which all my sinful actions have
> flowed. My mind & heart have always been enmity against God,
> who is so holy that he cannot allow of no sin, however small
> it may appear in the sight of men. How can I ever be admitted into
> Heaven with such a heart? it is uterly [sic] imposible [sic].
> Lost, lost forever lost.[55]

Cartwright had a sense of impending death just before he experienced

conviction:

> A few minutes after we had put up the horses, and were sitting
> by the fire, I began to reflect on the manner in which I had
> spent the day and evening. I felt guilty and condemned. I
> rose and walked the floor. My mother was in bed. It seemed
> to me, all of a sudden my blood rushed to my head, my heart
> palpitated, in a few minutes I turned blind; an awful impression
> rested on my mind that death had come and I was unprepared to
> die. I fell on my knees and began to ask God to have mercy on
> me.[56]

Finney had a similar experience. The night before he was converted

"a strange feeling" of impending death came over him. "I knew that

if I died I should sink down to hell...".[57]

---

[55] Jacob Bower, "The Autobiography of Jacob Bower: A Frontier
Baptist Preacher and Missionary" in William Warren Sweet, ed., The
Baptists, 1783-1840 (Chicago: University of Chicago Press, 1931), p. 190.

[56] Cartwright, p. 36.

[57] Finney, Memoirs, p. 13.

> Just at this moment I again thought I heard some one approach
> me, and I opened my eyes to see whether it were so. But right
> there the revelation of my pride of heart, as the great difficulty
> that stood in the way, was distinctly shown to me. An overwhelming
> sense of my wickedness in being ashamed to have a human being see
> me on my knees before God, took such powerful possession of me,
> that I cried at the top of my voice, and exclaimed that I would
> not leave that place if all the men on earth and all the devils
> in hell surrounded me. "What!" I said, "such a degraded sinner
> as I am, on my knees confessiong my sins to the great and holy
> God; and ashamed to have any human being, and a sinner like
> myself, find me on my knees endeavoring to make peace with my
> offended God!" The sin appeared awful, infinite. It broke me
> down before the Lord.[58]

The metaphor of being "broken down" before the Lord is as precise

as it is potent: it points to the absence of structure and order that

marks the threshold experience of conviction.

Anxiety, distress, even "agony" accompanied conviction.

Conviction signified a break with one's past that was often enacted

in what might be termed a ritual of separation. For example, Cartwright

asked his father to sell his race-horse and gave his pack of cards to

his mother, who three them into the fire. Breaking with the past

meant severing relationships with friends. Finney retreated to the

woods "feeling that I must be alone, and away from all human eyes and

ears, so that I could pour out my prayer to God."[59] The separation

from one's former life was physical as well as psychological. However,

"it was not a separation into a new life."[60] Rather, the convicted

person found himself in the "betwixt and between," in transition

---

[58]Ibid., p. 16.

[59]Ibid., p. 14.

[60]Bruce, p. 66.

between two ways of life and, in effect, between two different worlds.[61]

In this structureless state, the old self died and descended into darkness.

In contrast, conversion was an ascent from the darkness of hell to

the glorious light of heaven as Cartwright's account reveals:

> To this meeting, I repaired, a guilty, wretched sinner. On
> the Saturday evening of said meeting I went, with weeping
> multitudes, and bowed before the stand, and earnestly prayed
> for mercy. In the midst of a solemn struggle of soul, an im-
> pression was made on my mind, as though a voice said to me,
> "Thy sins are all forgiven thee." Divine light flashed all
> around me, unspeakable joy sprung up in my soul. I rose to my
> feet, opened my eyes, and it really seemed as if I was in heaven;
> the trees, the leaves on them, and everything seemed, and I
> really thought were, praising God. My mother raised the shout,
> my Christian friends crowded around me and joined me in
> praising God; and though I have been since then, in many
> instances unfaithful, yet I have never, for one moment, doubted
> that the Lord did, then and there, forgive my sins and give me
> religion.[62]

God's grace broke through in conversion and as a result all was

transformed: one's relationship to God, one's self and even the

world itself. A sense of assurance replaced the feeling of ambiguity:

> I was more assured of his forgiving love and enjoyed much peace
> in believing I now thought I never should sin more. My mind
> was taken up with God, and convers'd with Him as a Man with
> his Friend. My confidence was unshaken and my hope full of
> immortality.[63]

---

[61] Victor W. Turner's study of rites of passage identified
an intermediate stage, a miminal period during which a person neither
belongs to his old world nor is yet a part of the new. See "Betwixt and
Between: The Liminal Period in Rites de Passage" in Symposium on New
Approaches in the Study of Religion, Proceedings of the American
Ethnological Society, 1964, ed. June Helm (Seattle: University of
Washington Press, 1964), pp. 4-20; The Ritual Process: Structure and
Anti-Structure (Chicago: Aldine, 1969). Turner builds upon the earlier
work of Arnold van Gennep, The Rites of Passage (Chicago: University
of Chicago Press, 1960).

[62] Cartwright, p. 38.

[63] Sweet, 4:126.

Intimacy rather than fear and trepidation characterized the convert's relationship with God.[64]

Finney's account reveals a similar sense of familiarity with the Lord; he testifies that

> ...it seemed as if I met the Lord Jesus Christ face to face.
> ...it seemed to me that I saw him as I would see any other
> man. He said nothing, but looked at me in such a manner as
> to break me right down at his feet....it seemed to me a reality,
> that he stood before me, and I fell down at his feet and poured
> out my soul to him. I wept aloud like a child, and made such
> confessions as I could with my shocked utterance.[65]

Finney experienced "a mighty baptism of the Holy Ghost."

> Without any expectation of it, without ever having the thought
> in my mind that there was any such thing for me, without any
> recollection that I had ever heard the thing mentioned by any
> person in the world, the Holy Spirit descended upon me in a
> manner that seemed to go through me, body and soul. I could
> feel the impression, like a wave of electricity, going through
> and through me. Indeed it seemed to come in waves and waves of
> liquid love; for I could not express it in any other way. It
> seemed like the very breath of God. I can recollect distinctly
> that it seemed to fan me, like unseen wings.[66]

Conversion consisted in a restructuring of the self, in effect the creation of a new self.

The Revival Meeting

Effective use of the techniques of revivalism depended upon a controlled environment in which a person might experience conversion more quickly than if he were left to his own resources. Camp-meetings and protracted meetings created the desired setting. Goals and roles were clearly delineated. All focused on the primary objective

---

[64] Bruce, p. 68.

[65] Finney, Memoirs, pp. 19-20.

[66] Ibid., p. 20.

of conversion and

> ...every aspect of the meeting contributed to that end in one way or another. The organization of the camp-meeting was based upon conversion as one key discriminating attribute, for participants were kept apart on the basis of whether they had received grace. Exhortations were directed at winning souls to the way. Even the patterns of interaction among various groups of participants encouraged those outside the fold to enter in. But the camp-meeting consisted of more than effectively organized methods for bringing on conversions. It was a collective expression of the very idea of conversion.[67]

Participants in the camp-meeting were divided into three groups: sinners, mourners, and converts. Sinners included all who had not yet been converted.[68] Mourners were those sinners who had been awakened and convicted. Preachers and exhorters were determined to awaken the sinner and convert the awakened. In order to facilitate the transition from conviction to conversion, mourners were segregated in the mourners' pen. While there, they were subjected to intense and concentrated exhortation and preaching. Their very presence in the pen symbolized their separation from other members of the congregation. Mourners existed in a liminal state: "betwixt and between all fixed points of classification."[69] Set outside the social system, they suffered a consequent loss of status.

The "anxious seat" was the Northern counterpart to the mourners' pen. This "new measure," introduced by Finney, consisted in "the appointment of some particular seat in the place of meeting, where the

---

[67]Bruce, p. 84.

[68]For a detailed discussion of the structure of the camp-meeting, see Bruce, pp. 69-95. Also see Charles A. Johnson, The Frontier Camp Meeting: Religion's Harvest Time (Dallas: Southern Methodist University Press, 1955) for a discussion of the development of the camp meeting.

[69]Victor W. Turner, "Passages, Margins, and Poverty: Religious Symbols of Communitas," Worship 46 (1972):393.

anxious may come and be addressed particularly, and be made subjects
of prayer, and sometimes conversed with individually."[70] In response to
the criticism of his opponents, Finney outlined the functions of the
anxious seat. He premised his defense on the argument that the "design"
of the seat was "undoubtedly philosophical, and according to the laws of
mind."[71] The individual who was able to publicly acknowledge his condition of sinfulness had already made considerable progress toward conversion. Willingness to take a place on the anxious seat signalled a
person's determination. If he fancied himself a Christian and yet refused
to do "so small a thing as that," he was publicly exposed. The anxious
bench was a test; Finney argued that its function was similar to that
of baptism in apostolic times: separating the sincere from the deluded.
So in addition to its obvious function as a proselytizing device,
the anxious bench served as a tool for discerning the authenticity of
a person's desire to be saved.

Both the mourners' pen and the anxious seat functioned to
identify and isolate the awakened and convicted in order that they
might be encouraged to submit to Jesus Christ. It mattered not what
position one held in the community; one's place in the pen or on the
seat was not determined by social status. All were equal before the Lord;
conversion was all that mattered.

Emotional outbursts and a variety of physical exercises were
ordinary happenings at camp-meetings. Shouting, crying, and falling

---

[70]Finney, Lectures, p. 267.

[71]Ibid.

were the most usual bodily manifestations. More dramatic exercises,
such as dancing, rolling, barking, and jerking occurred with less
frequency.[72] Revivalists generally viewed bodily effects as manifestations of the power of God. That was especially the case in the
South where many participants expected that conversion would effect
"some kind of catalytic state."[73] Such a belief predisposed the
participants to these exercises. The enthusiasm generated by the
crowd, the rhythm of chanted hymns, the shouts and cries, even hunger
and lack of sleep which were inevitable during prolonged meetings,
the pleas, proddings and proclamations of the preacher -- all served to
heighten the susceptibility to emotional outbreaks.

Conversion as a Social Event

Conversion was an event of social significance: it marked
the convert's re-entry into the social structure as a member of
the company of the saved. Conversion altered the person's relationship
to the community: the convert assumed new status and accepted new
responsibilities. Some new converts became preachers, thus assuming
professional roles and corresponding responsibilities vis á vis the
religious community, but all were expected to live in accordance with
the demands of the Gospel. That often meant associating with converted
Christians and severing relationships with sinners; it always meant
adherence to the community's ethic, its definitions of good and

---

[72]A first hand account of these exercises may be found in
Cartwright, pp. 45-47. Also see Johnson, pp. 54-68.

[73]Boles, pp. 53-67.

evil.[74] In the South, revivalists generally defined ethical behavior

in individualistic terms: personal vice and personal virtue. New

converts were to overcome sin in their own lives. "The southern Christian

was taught to accept the world and try to perfect his soul.[75] Save

souls and society will be saved as a consequence. In the North,

revivalists called converts to join forces in the battle against social

evil. Northern revivalism gave impetus to social reform.[76]

The public setting in which conversions occurred emphasized the

social aspect of conversion. Insofar as the setting, whether camp-

meeting or revival, defined expectations and so shaped responses of

participants, the meeting was itself reminder that conversion was much

more than a private matter.

The Ecclesial Dimension of Conversion

The revivals of the early nineteenth century are misunderstood

if viewed as "missions to the heathen." Perry Miller notes that "they

were addressed to those already more or less within the churches,"

to persons already acquainted with the principles and ethos of

---

[74]For a helpful discussion of conversion as a socialization
process, see David O. Moberg, The Church as a Social Institution:
The Sociology of American Religion (Englewood Cliffs: Prentice Hall,
1962), pp. 421-444. Also see Hans L. Zetterberg, "The Religious
Conversion as a Change of Social Roles," Sociology and Social
Research 26 (1952):165.

[75]Boles, p. 195. For a penetrating discussion of the impact
of revivalism on the forming of the "southern mind," see pp. 165-203.

[76]See Smith.

Protestant Christianity.[77] The revivals erupted and continued within
the framework of the existing denominations: Presbyterian, Methodist,
Baptist, and Congregationalist. The denominations were, of course,
reshaped by these revivals. Some were strengthened, others weakened by
resulting schisms, but the revivals did not arise outside existing
churches nor did the revivalists address themselves to persons entirely
ignorant of the Christian message.

Conversion was essential to the prevailing evangelical ecclesiology:
the true church was the society of those who had publicly accepted Jesus
Christ and were saved. In order to achieve the status of full membership
in the Church, an individual had to experience conversion. The specific
denomination to which a person belonged was less important than the
fact that he belonged. Indeed, the denominational structure of American
Protestantism made it possible for church members to move rather freely
from one church to another. Conversion was more significant than
alternation. Alternation means a change in religious affiliation, e.g.
movement from one denomination to another. Conversion implies a more
radical change, in this case, accepting Jesus Christ. Evangelical
Protestantism emphasized the importance of accepting Jesus over the
significance of affiliation with a given denomination. Consequently,
evangelical Protestants were well-disposed toward inter-denominational
cooperation in the common goal of saving souls and they minimized
denominational differences in the effort.

---

[77]Perry Miller, The Life of the Mind in America (New York:
Harcourt, Brace & World, 1965), p. 10.

The emphasis on the experience of conversion determined the
distinctive theological cast of evangelical Protestantism, notably its
fundamentalism. Nineteenth-century evangelical Protestantism exhibited
fundamentalism in two ways. First, the evangelical denominations tended
toward a simple and even simplistic interpretation of the Bible.
Fundamentalism, in this sense, was a by-product of the "religion of the
heart," which left little room for intellectual inquiry. The fervor which
characterized camp-meetings and revivals determined the religious
sensibility of evangelical Protestantism. Anything that nurtured the
simple piety of the congregation was deemed important; all else was
judged worthless and even detrimental. The resulting anti-intellectualism
was pronounced. For example, an educated ministerial force, given to
exploring the intricate and obscure subtleties of doctrinal discourse,
was viewed by many as a distinct liability. Peter Cartwright expressed
this sense in a very practical argument:

> Suppose now, M. Wesley had been obliged to wait for a
> literary and theologically trained band of preachers before
> he moved in the glorious work of his day, what would Methodism
> have been on the Wesleyan connection to-day?
> . . .
> The Presbyterians, and other Calvinistic branches of the
> Protestant Church, used to contend for an educated ministry,
> for pews, for instrumental music, for a congregational or stated
> salaried ministry. The Methodists universally opposed these
> ideas; and the illiterate Methodist preachers actually set the
> world on fire (the American world at least) while they were
> lighting their matches.[78]

The evangelical denominations were fundamentalistic in another

---

[78]Cartwright, pp. 63-64. See Richard Hofstadter, Anti-
Intellectualism in American Life (New York: Knopf, 1963) for a
discussion of the contrast between the educated ministry of
Puritanism and the anti-intellectualism expressed by opponents of
educated ministry in evangelical Protestantism (pp. 55-141).

sense as well: they agreed upon the foundations (or fundamentals)

of the Christian faith. Methodists, Baptists, and Presbyterians shared

belief in man's depravity, his need for salvation, and God's grace as

the condition for man's response of faith.[79] Fundamentalism knew no

geographical boundaries: it was as evident in the North as in the South

as Finney's exhortation suggests. Finney cautioned his hearers against

the danger of ensnaring young converts "by examining them too extensively

or minutely on doctrinal points"; doctrinal examination ought to be limited

to "certain cardinal doctrines of Christianity...embraced in the experience

of every true convert."[80] A "change of heart" was more significant

than a lengthy and "technical" confession of faith. Finney maintained

that under proper questioning, "real converts" would

> ...see clearly those great fundamental points, the divine
> authority of the scriptures, the necessity of the influences
> of the Holy Spirit, the divinity of Christ, the doctrine of
> total depravity and regeneration, the necessity of the
> atonement, justification by faith, and the eternal punishment
> of the wicked.[81]

Conversion offered the assurance of salvation. Spiritual

hymns and choruses consistently expressed the conviction that con-

version secures salvation. The convert's sense of assurance came

from a deep and intense inner conviction that he had been saved.[82]

---

[79]Boles, p. 133.

[80]Finney, Lectures, p. 392.

[81]Ibid., p. 393. McLoughlin observes that Finney's "definition
of the 'great fundamental points' of the gospel became the basis of
evangelism in most denominations during the latter part of the nineteenth
century" (n.3, p. 393).

[82]Bruce, p. 107.

Having rejected this world, the convert was assured of his place in the next. Conversion guaranteed passage to eternity and promised fulfilment in the life to come.

The conversion experience was self-legitimating. The fact that one had experienced conversion according to the prescribed mode was itself a sign that one was saved. Provided that the convert did not slide back to former sinful ways, he could rest in the knowledge that he was saved. In a sense, the camp-meeting or revival was a scene of judgment, marked by a profound sense of finality. Each person was forced to make a decision for or against Jesus Christ. It was a temporal choice with eternal ramifications: heaven or hell, salvation or damnation. But the convert experienced immediate effects of conversion as well. He was transformed here and now by God's grace, grace freely given. Faith constituted the convert's free acceptance of this grace.

Because evangelical Protestantism viewed man's work as a necessary correlate to God's grace, human effort was essential to conversion. The major denominations (Presbyterian, Methodist, Baptist) agreed that both minister and sinner "played a necessary role in the conversion process; the minister by presenting the message and the unbeliever by accepting it."[83] In Finney's words, conversion was the work of God and of man.[84] In likening the change of heart to a "change of mind," Finney departed from the traditional notion of human depravity that characterized popular Calvinism and voiced a basic

---

[83]Boles, p. 136.

[84]Finney, Lectures, pp. 19-23.

tenet of the evangelical Christianity: human beings participated in their own transformations which were not simply effected by the miraculous intervention of God.[85]

The experience of conversion accentuated the final solitariness of a person before the Divine Judge. Conversion-centered theology bred a strong strain of individualism. Although social and ecclesial factors influenced the would-be-convert, conversion was ultimately a private experience which occurred within the inner recesses of the self which others could not enter.

Finally, the experience of conversion was tumultuous, dramatic, and sudden. A review of autobiographical accounts of conversion shows this and descriptions of multiple conversions in revival settings confirm the observation. The concentrated, condensed format for the conversion process, developed in the camp-meeting and revival settings, promoted abrupt transformations. Physical arrangements, such as the mourners' pen and the anxious bench, as well as impassioned preaching, unleashed intense responses. The environment heightened participants' susceptibility to emotional outbursts. Group expectations aroused the imaginations of individuals searching for religious experiences.

The structure of the conversion experience reflected the prevailing theological and ecclesiological perspectives of evangelical Protestantism: its stress on the authority of the Bible, its belief in the direct relationship between God and man (a relationship facilitated by preaching but not controlled by minister or clergyman), its conviction that conversion assured salvation. The ecclesiology of

---

[85]Ibid., pp. 8-9.

evangelical Protestantism was straightforward: the church was the body of those who had experienced conversion by accepting Jesus Christ.

The emphasis on the primacy and centrality of conversion was both the source and the product of the distinctive character of evangelical Protestantism. The stress on personal religious experience informed the style of revivalism while also necessitating the development and perfection of revivalist techniques.

The highly-charged revivalistic context in which conversions occurred and the abrupt and tumultuous nature of the experience appealed to scores of Americans. But others were alienated and repelled by the tenor of revivalism. Among the latter were some who converted to Roman Catholicism. Accounts of conversion, written by a number of these converts reveal that they were repelled by the tactics of revivalism and the understanding of conversion in nineteenth-century evangelical Protestantism.

The Roman Catholic Church in America was highly suspect. Roman Catholics were feared and despised; Catholicism aroused ridicule and hostility. Nevertheless, converts were drawn to the Church of Rome where they found what they had not been able to find in the evangelical atmosphere of the Protestant denominations. The phenomenon of conversion to Roman Catholicism in nineteenth-century America is the subject of the next chapter.

CHAPTER II

CONVERSIONS TO NINETEENTH-CENTURY

AMERICAN CATHOLICISM

The Roman Catholic Church was an unlikely end to an American's religious quest during the nineteenth century. Anti-Catholic sentiment was pervasive and vigorous. A number of factors contributed to the antipathy toward the Roman Catholic Church in America: its despised immigrant population, its loyalty to Rome, and its generally suspect status as a religious and cultural minority. Nevertheless, the Roman Catholic Church attracted a substantial number of converts during the nineteenth century, among whom were men who detailed their journeys to Rome in personal narratives of conversion.[1]

This chapter focuses upon the phenomenon of conversion to nineteenth-century American Catholicism, beginning with a brief account of the history of the Roman Catholic Church in America as it pertains to the nineteenth-century conversions. Estimates of the number of conversions and identification of their sources follow. The chapter concludes with a discussion of the ways in which nineteenth-century Roman Catholics understood conversion.

---

[1]Stephen Cleveland Blythe, Daniel Barber, Levi Silliman Ives, Orestes A. Brownson, Isaac T. Hecker, Joshua Huntington, B. W. Whitcher, Augustine F. Hewit, William Richards, Charles Warren Stoddard, and Clarence E. Walworth wrote narratives of conversion during the nineteenth century. John Thayer had written the first such narrative at the end of the eighteenth century.

The Roman Catholic Church in
Nineteenth-Century America: Change and Growth

The decisive factor in the history of the Roman Catholic
Church in nineteenth-century America was its minority status, which
affected the internal affairs of the Church as well as its relationship
to American society.   Both its foreign ties and its massive immigrant
population cast Roman Catholicism as a cultural and religious alternative
to the prevailing Protestant ethos.   Protestants perceived Catholicism
as a threat and Catholics were faced with the difficult task of
demonstrating that Roman Catholicism and Americanism were compatible.

Roman Catholicism's Minority Status

Roman Catholics had constituted a numerical minority since
America's founding.   In 1776, Catholics comprised but a miniscule
fraction of the American population -- about 25,000 in a total of
3,000,000.[2]   But the number of Catholics increased steadily.   In
1850, the Catholic population was estimated at 3,500,000 or one-
seventh of the population.   In 1890, the official census of the
United States numbered the entire population at 62,885,548; by that
year, the Catholic population was estimated at 12,000,000.[3]   By 1850,
Roman Catholics constituted the largest single religious group,
larger than any of the Protestant denominations.[4]   The Catholic
population grew primarily through immigration and through natural

---

[2]Clarke, p. 541.

[3]Ibid.

[4]Gaustad, The Rise of Adventism, p. xiii.

increase; however, conversions contributed significantly to the growth of the Catholic Church. Writing in 1893, Richard H. Clarke estimated the number of converts and their descendents since the signing of the Declaration of Independence to be 700,000 persons.

Even as the Catholic population grew numerically, Roman Catholicism continued to represent a cultural minority. Protestantism continued to exert the strongest influence upon the national ethos. The influence of Protestantism was not confined to the formal impact of the churches. The theological perspectives and ethical guidelines that originated in institutional structures informed the American spirit. American Protestantism was not simply a system of religious beliefs and practices; it generated a constellation of values and meanings that was fundamental to American life. For example, the American spirit of optimism gained support from the conviction that human action mattered, a tenet espoused by nineteenth-century Protestant revivalists such as Charles Grandison Finney. Revivals of religion were possible and successful because persons were believed capable of restructuring their lives with the aid of God's grace. Belief in the value of human effort also laid the foundation for a burgeoning reform spirit among American Protestants who maintained that man had the capacity to transform the social order.

American culture was unmistakenly Protestant. Will Herberg maintains that "the contours of American Protestantism" shaped American life from the very beginning.[5] Sidney Ahlstrom suggests that American

---

[5]Will Herberg, Protestant -- Catholic -- Jew: An Essay in American Religious Sociology, rev. ed. (New York: Doubleday & Co., 1960), p. 81.

Protestantism reigned as a "quasi-establishment," especially between 1815 and 1860. During this period, Protestantism informed America's popular culture: its moral attitudes and basic teachings were honored by lawmakers, and dominated newspapers and textbooks."[6] Ahlstrom argues that the values which are operative in a society's educational system express the fundamental perspectives of a culture. The fact of "a Protestant America" persisted throughout the nineteenth century. Winthrop Hudson observes that America "seemed so indelibly Protestant that in the end, it was confidently believed, all minority goups would be either assimilated or Americanized."[7]

Early Attitudes Toward Roman Catholicism

The strength and pervasiveness of the Protestant culture inevitably affected the manner in which Protestants viewed Catholics, especially as their number swelled through immigration. Protestants perceived Catholicism as incompatible with American values and as a threat to the very foundations of American life. Such a view nourished intense hatred of all things and persons Catholic.

Although Catholics were the target of Protestant antipathy from the time of their arrival in the colonies, anti-Catholicism had not always been as vociferous or widespread as it became by mid-century. Anglo-Catholic families of high social standing had dominated an earlier phase of Catholic history. The Carrolls were

---

[6]Ahlstrom, p. 556.

[7]Hudson, p. 126. This hope was not to be realized; the twentieth century witnessed the emergence of what Hudson calls "Post-Protestant America."

such a family; they were aristocrats who enjoyed prestige and respect
not accorded to the Catholic population at large. Apparently, neither
the Carrolls nor their countrymen deemed the family's affiliation with
the Roman Catholic Church as incompatible with loyalty and service to
America. Charles Carroll signed the Declaration of Independence and served as a member of the United States Congress. He came to prominence
when he voiced opposition to Robert Eden, the governor of Maryland.
Using the pseudonym of "first Citizen," Carroll participated in a
published debate with the governor's defender, Daniel Dulaney. Dulaney
attacked Carroll's religious affiliation. In response, Carroll argued
that his religious beliefs did not interfere with his standing as an
American: "What my speculative notions of religion may be, this is
neither the place nor the time to disclose; my political principles
ought only to be questioned on the present occasion."[8] Catholicism and
Americanism were not in conflict: church and state were separate spheres
of action.

Nor did John Carroll, the first bishop of the Catholic Church
in America, see any opposition between loyalties to Church and
country. His reasoning echoed that of his cousin. John Carroll
maintained that the affairs of church and state and the work of
churchmen and statesmen ought not to be casually mixed. A draft of a
letter written before he travelled to Canada as an emissary of the
first Continental Congress reveals that he was well aware of "the risk

---

[8]Kate Mason Rowland, The Life of Charles Carroll of Carrollton,
1737-1832 with His Correspondence and Public Papers, 2 vols. (New
York: G. P. Putnam's Sons, 1898), 1:285.

he ran in thus mingling religion and politics."[9] Carroll wrote that
he had "observed that when the ministers of religion, leave the duties
of their profession to take a busy part in political matters, they
generally fall into contempt, and sometimes even bring discredit to the
cause in whose service they are engaged.[10] Although Bishop John
Carroll's views regarding church-state relations were conservative,
he remained confident that the Roman Catholic Church in America would
prosper.

The very fact that Carroll was tapped for public service
reveals that he was esteemed by his non-Catholic countrymen. And as
long as Anglo-Saxon American Catholics like the Carrolls represented
the Church, the respect accorded them as individuals reflected on the
Church as a whole.

Growing Anti-Catholic Sentiment

Native Anglo-Saxon American Catholics were destined to steer
the course of the Roman Catholic Church in America for only a few
decades. Soon the influx of immigrants recast American Catholicism by
shifting the balances of power within the Church and permanently altering
the complexion of American Catholicism. The masses of Catholic
immigrants unleashed a violent outbreak of anti-Catholicism. In the
face of immigrant waves, the Church was compelled to redefine
itself as well as to re-examine its relationship to American society.

Between 1815 and 1866, some 2,720,000 Catholic immigrants

---

[9]Peter Guilday, The Life and Times of John Carroll (Westminster, Md.: The Newman Press, 1954), p. 96.

[10]Cited by Guilday, p. 97.

arrived in the United States; the largest numbers came from Ireland and Germany respectively.[11] The immigrants flocked to urban areas, areas which were already beginning to experience problems of overcrowding, poverty, and disease that were the by-products of industrialization. The new immigrant work force competed with native Americans for jobs and so threatened an already tottering economic balance. Their very number made the immigrants appear a threat to Protestants; as a result of immigration, the Roman Catholic Church had become larger than any single Protestant denomination. Their foreignness set the aliens apart as a different and dangerous breed of people who huddled together in their own enclaves and resisted assimilation.

The influx of immigrants aroused latent anti-Catholicism. At its roots, anti-Catholic sentiment was a legacy of the Reformation. Many Protestants looked upon Roman beliefs and practices as so much superstitious mumbo-jumbo, particularly because doctrines and rituals were clothed in the language and customs of an alien culture. Enlightenment thought informed yet another brand of anti-Catholicism which portrayed Catholicism as the embodiment of the irrational.[12] Furthermore, there had been a strain of anti-Catholic feeling in America since the colonial era. Colonial hostility toward Catholics mirrored English intolerance for Catholicism. Anti-Catholic feeling increased noticeably after 1830. Early nineteenth-century Protestant revivals aroused missionary zeal, thereby intensifying anti-Catholic feeling. Thomas T.

---

[11] New Catholic Encyclopedia, s.v. "United States of America," by J. T. Ellis.

[12] Ahlstrom, p. 556.

McAvoy theorizes that "the fervent appeals of some orators to seaboard

Protestants to check the growth of Roman Catholicism in the West" aggravat-

ed the situation of the Catholic Church. While seeking enthusiastic

support for the missions, preachers depicted Roman Catholicism as "the

enemy of faith and culture."[13]

Anti-Catholic sentiment imbued nineteenth-century culture.

The average Protestant American of the 1850's had been trained
from birth to hate Catholicism; his juvenile literature and school
books had breathed a spirit of intolerance; his illicit dips as
a youth into the parentally condemned but widely read Ned Buntline
tales had kept his prejudice alive; his religious and even his
secular newspapers had warned him of the dangers of Popery; and
he had read novels, poems, gift books, histories, travel accounts,
and theological arguments which confirmed these beliefs. Only
the unusually critical reader could distinguish between truth
and fiction in this mass of calumny; more were swept away to a
hatred of Catholicism which endured through their lives.[14]

Ray Billington suggests that literary campaigns most effectively

mobilized anti-Catholic feeling.

Conflicts over trusteeism, Irish rioting, lawlessness and disorder, foreign pauperism, school controversies, a political
Popery -- all these were important in fomenting a spirit of
intolerance among the people. But had not a legion of writers
made this growing sentiment the basis of an effective literary
campaign, the No-Popery crusade would have been far less fruitful.[15]

Catholics responded defensively to the Protestant attack

in their own publications. The Catholic press launched its counter-

_____

[13]Thomas T. McAvoy, A History of the Catholic Church in the
United States (Notre Dame: University of Notre Dame Press, 1969),
p. 133. Also see Donna Merwick, Boston Priests, 1848-1910: A Study
of Social and Intellectual Change (Cambridge: Harvard University Press,
1973). Merwick notes that the "evangelists of 'the second Great
Awakening' intermittently attacked Romanism from 1828-1834" (p. 5).

[14]Ray Allen Billington, The Protestant Crusade 1800-1860: A
Study of the Origins of Nativism (New York: Rinehart, 1938), p. 345.

[15]Ibid.,

attack with "vigorous appeals to reason."[16] Faced with gross mis-

representations of its doctrine, the Catholic press concentrated on

exposing and explaining Catholic teaching. But it was difficult, if

not impossible, to respond to the flood of incendiary "horror literature"

that fired the popular imagination.[17] The anti-Catholic writers employed

every genre -- from children's book to novel, play, and poem -- spanning

a variety of themes: the evils of Rome, the immorality of convent life,

the licentiousness of the Roman clergy, Jesuit political conspiracies,

the anguish suffered by converts to Roman Catholicism who tried to

retrace their steps. In the end, Romanism emerged as a vile and corrupt

force.

Propagandists had three objectives:

> ...first, to show that Catholicism was not Christianity, but an
> idolatrous religion, the ascendency of which would plunge the
> world into infidelity; secondly, that Popery was by nature ir-
> reconcilable with the democratic institutions of the United
> States and was determined to insure its own existence by
> driving them out; and thirdly, that the acceptance of the moral
> standards of the Catholic Church would be suicidal to the best
> interests both of Protestantism and the nation. It was about
> these principal contentions that most of the arguments were
> built.[18]

The numerous acts of violence provoked by anti-Catholic antipathy

testify to the success of the propaganda campaigns. One such oc-

currence was the burning of an Ursuline convent in Charleston in 1834.

---

[16]Paul J. Foik, Pioneer Catholic Journalism (New York: The United States Catholic Historical Society, 1930), p. x.

[17]Ahlstrom, p. 560. Rebecca Theresa Reed's Six Months in a Convent (Boston, 1835) and Maria Monk's Awful Disclosures of the Hotel Dieu Convent of Montreal or the Secrets of Black Nunnery Revealed (New York, 1836) represented the genre of "horror literature" at its worst.

[18]Billington, p. 351.

50

The pastoral letters written by the American Catholic hierarchy during the 1830's document the official Catholic response to the anti-Catholic hostilities. The Pastoral Letter of 1833 detailed the breadth of the attack:

> Not only do they assail us and our institutions in a style of vituperation and offense, misrepresent our tenets, vilify our practices, repeat the hundred times refuted calumnies of days of angry and bitter contention in other lands, but they have even denounced you and us as enemies to the liberties of the republic, and have openly proclaimed the fancied necessity of not only obstructing our progress, but of using their best efforts to extirpate our religion.[19]

The bishops counseled Catholics not to respond violently but rather to re-dedicate themselves to faithful service to God and country in order that they might "sustain that edifice of rational liberty in which we find such excellent protection."[20]

The persecution of the Catholic Church in America remained a principal theme of the Pastoral Letter for 1837. The letter lamented the tragic state of affairs:

> ...That day has gone by, when every American citizen could truly say, that whatever may be the religious opinion which he entertained, or whatever the form of worship which he followed, he enjoyed in full freedom the opportunity of securing for himself what he vindicated for others, the communion with his God in that way which his conviction or his taste might prefer.[21]

The violence exemplified by the destruction of the Ursuline Convent, the injustice promoted by the Massachusetts legislature in its con-

---

[19]"The Pastoral Letter of 1833" in The National Pastorals of the American Hierarchy, 1792-1919, ed. Peter Guilday (Washington: National Catholic Welfare Council, 1923), p. 78.

[20]Ibid.

[21]"The Pastoral Letter of 1837" in The National Pastorals, p. 81.

sideration of relief for those injured in that tragedy, the gross

misrepresentation of Catholic life and thought in Protestant literature --

all were viewed by the American hierarchy as representing not simply

a threat to Catholics but as constituting a threat to the American values

of freedom and democracy.[22]

A later wave of anti-Catholic sentiment gave rise to the nativist

Know-Nothing Party which added political clout to anti-Catholic prejudice.

The Know-Nothings mobilized to fight the alledged conspirary of popery in

America. They saw themselves as defending America against foreign

domination.

Anti-Catholic sentiment forced the Church to defend itself against

the accusations and insinuations of those who feared and despised Romanism

and popery. However, the defensiveness of the Church was tempered by a

growing confidence in its ability to survive and even thrive in the

American setting. The pastoral letters of the 1830's summarize this

twofold position of the Church: guarded and cautious but also resolute

and assured.

Emergence of an "Immigrant Church"

The immigrant population affected the internal affairs of

the Church as surely as it altered the Church's place in society. The

Church faced the challenge of serving the spiritual needs of a changing

constituency. The ways of the immigrants were as alien to fellow

[22]"The Pastoral Letter of 1837" cites the judgment of the
Massachusetts State Legislature: "That Catholics acknowledging, as
they do, the supremacy of a foreign potentate or power, could not
claim under the government the protection as citizens of the Common-
wealth, but were entitled only to our countenance and aid so far as the
rite of national hospitality might serve to dictate" (The National

Catholics as they were to non-Catholics. Immigrants soon outnumbered
native Catholics and the Catholic Church in America became the church
of the immigrants.

The Catholic Church dealt with both social and religious needs
of the immigrants. Social needs were met within the framework of a
familiar religious tradition. The Roman Catholic Church functioned as a
place of refuge for immigrants. In Will Herberg's terms, it provided
"the primary context of self-identification and social location."[23]
The Church facilitated the immigrant's gradual accomodation to American
society. National churches, which emerged in immigrant neighborhoods,
eased the immigrants' assimilation into American society. Organized
on the basis of language rather than geography, national parishes
represented "the intitutionalized attempt of an immigrant group to
preserve the religious life of the old country."[24] Neighborhood
churches offered the security of a familiar cultural atmosphere
in which persons were able to adjust gradually to the customs of
American life. The Church symbolized permanence and security and so
reduced the trauma of relocation for many.

The Church was a symbol of continuity; it provided immigrants
"with a measure of social security and it helped them live as they
had lived in the old country, within the cycle of fall, repentance,

---

Pastorals, p. 90).

[23]Herberg, p. 39. Also see Herberg, "Religion and Culture
in Present-Day America," in Roman Catholicism and the American Way of
Life, ed. Thomas T. McAvoy (Notre Dame: University of Notre Dame Press,
1960), pp. 4-19.

[24]Dolan, The Immigrant Church, p. 21.

confession, forgiveness and hope."[25]   Immigrant religion was a

bulwark of stability, even when religious practice was minimal and

religious faith lukewarm. A common religious faith, even one nominally

affirmed, bonded people together and so promoted social cohesion.

Precisely because the Church was a refuge in a foreign environment,

it appeared as the last stronghold of permanent values, values which

were difficult to abandon. Concern with stability, natural among persons

uprooted from the place of their origin, promoted defensiveness and

resistance to change.[26] The immigrant church exhibited a strong

tendency toward conservatism, even as its members strained to accomodate

themselves to the American context.[27]

Immigrants aroused considerable antipathy among native Catholics.

Antagonism toward foreign-born bishops surfaced at mid-century in the

discussion preceeding the naming of a successor to Samuel Eccleston,

Archbishop of Baltimore. The discussion revealed a pocket of "nativist"

feeling.[28]

---

[25]Hennesey, p. 23.

[26]Hennesey describes this dependence on the past: "The immigrant
church clung to what it knew as tradition. It was suspicious of change.
I doubt many of the immigrants ever head of Jacques Bossuet, but they
would wholeheartedly accept his dictum: 'There is no difficulty about
recognizing false doctrine' we can add here customs, lifestyle. It is
recognized at once, whenever it appears, merely because it is new" (p.
23).

[27]See John J. O'Brien, The Renewal of American Catholicism
(New York: Paulist Press, 1972), pp. 80-108. O'Brien cites Philip
Gleason's image of the Church as "institutionalized immigrant." See
Contemporary Catholicism in the United States, ed. Philip Gleason
(Notre Dame: University of Notre Dame Press, 1969), pp. 3-32.

[28]McAvoy, p. 178. See pp. 163-178 for an exposition of the
tensions at work within the Church.

Orestes A. Brownson, a convert to Catholicism, issued a forceful nativist criticism of the Catholic immigrants. Although he despised the anti-Catholic prejudice of the Protestant nativists, he was also a staunch Americanist and highly critical of immigrants who, in his estimation, advanced the cause of anti-Catholicism by their behavior. It was his hope that these immigrants, particularly the Irish (who constituted the largest mass), would quickly be Americanized.[29] Brownson echoed the thoughts of numerous native Catholics who found the immigrants as unacceptable as did Protestants. The manners and customs of the foreigners, again particularly those of the Irish, repulsed natives. The Irish were boisterous and raucous and their ways were a shock to native Americans.[30] In the eyes of many, the Irish were a liability to church and country; they were uneducated, illiterate paupers.

Tensions most frequently surfaced at the parish level, where

---

[29] For a discussion of Brownson's nativism, see Thomas T. McAvoy, "Orestes A. Brownson and American History," Catholic Historical Review 40 (1954): 262-265. Brownson found himself in a rather unique position. "The Know-Nothings he charged with un-Americanism since they discriminated against the Irish because they were Catholic and because they were poor; the Irish he criticized for their isolation from the majority culture and their persistence in their Irish nationalism" (p. 263). McAvoy documents Brownson's change of mind on this issue in later years when he "pleaded with the Irish to remain Irish because he now saw them in their fidelity to the Church and in their faith in persecution generally, a needed contribution to American life" (p. 264).
His earlier position might well be explained in terms of his "racism." McAvoy remarks that Brownson was "a believer in Anglo-Saxon political and cultural institutions, and most English-speaking people felt some of the supremacy of English imperialism in the world of the nineteenth century: (p. 265).

[30] For a survey of the response of native-Catholics to the immigrants, see Willard E. Wright, "The Native American Catholic, the Immigrant, and Immigration," in Roman Catholicism and the American Way of Life, pp. 211-224. Also see James P. Shannon, "The Irish Catholic Immigration," in Roman Catholicism and the American Way of Life, pp. 204-210.

struggles frequently erupted between the "old" Catholics and the
"new." Controversies centered on the nationality of the priest to be
assigned to the parish, the language to be used in preaching, the observance of saints' days, or even the name of the parish.[31] Because the
conflicts were not always resolved at local levels, they occasionally
escalated to issues of national concern. The "Memorial," presented in
Rome in 1891, is a case in point. Peter Paul Cahensly proposed a
division of the American Catholic Church along ethnic rather than
geographical lines. He argued that such re-organization would counter
losses among the immigrants. Cahensly's "Memorial" was rejected; Roman
Catholic churchmen recognized its divisive potential.

Although the Catholic hierarchy resisted a formal division
of the Church along ethnic lines, they made a constant effort to
accomodate the Church to meet the needs of the immigrants, particularly
through national parish structures. The national parish served a dual
function: it preserved the national heritage of its membership while
it simultaneously drew those members into the communion of the Roman
Catholic Church.

Catholics of all ethnic groups were bound together by a common
struggle and a common faith. In his study of parish life in German
and Irish communities in New York City, Jay P. Dolan observes that
"Catholics built a citadel in the city and walled themselves off from
a hostile Protestant environment."[32]

---

[31] Oscar Handlin, The Uprooted: The Epic Story of the Great
Migration that Made the American People (Boston: Little, Brown, & Co.,
1951), p. 135.

[32] Dolan, The Immigrant Church, p. 44.

Nineteenth-century Catholics were united by their common efforts to resist Protestant pressure for conformity and by a life centered in the parish. Explicitly religious activites such as attendance at mass and devotions and reception of sacraments, as well as participation in parish associations, drew members of a parish together. Involvement in the sacramental and social life of the local parish strengthened ties with the Church as a whole and thus affirmed the solidarity of Catholics of all ethinic groups.

By mid-century, the Roman Catholic Church in America had undergone a radical transformation. Immigration accounted for the phenomenal growth in numbers as well as change in constituency. By 1850, the Roman Catholic Church was the largest religious body in the United States. Immigrant Catholics outnumbered native Catholics. As a result the complexion of the Church changed, radically transforming the Church's relations with American society as well as its internal life.

Conversions to Roman Catholicism in Nineteenth-Century America

As the Roman Catholic Church grew in size and took on the complexion of an immigrant church, anti-Catholic sentiment grew more intense. Fear, hostility, even hatred were common reactions to the Church. In such a milieu, one would expect prospects of attracting converts to be poor. But such was not the case. Conversions to Roman Catholicism did occur and in considerable numbers and this, despite the fact that the social cost of conversion was high. Conversion to Roman Catholicism was more than a redefinition of ecclesiastical allegiance; social ramifications of this act were serious. Converting to Roman Catholicism meant identifying with a social minority and by the 1830's with the religion of the immigrants.

Conversions to Roman Catholicism contributed to the growth of
the Church in America during the nineteenth century, although the number
of conversions hardly matched the increase through immigration or the
constant rate of natural increase. It is not the number of conversions
that prompts this study: that any conversions occurred in the predominantly Protestant culture with its vehement antipathy toward
Catholicism is a phenomenon which invites scrutiny.

Estimates of the numbers converting to Roman Catholicism during
the nineteenth century vary somewhat. In 1893, Richard Clarke estimated
the "convert element" in America since the signing of the Declaration of
Independence at 700,000.[33] The "convert element" consisted of those
converts and their descendants who remained Catholic. Clarke extrapolates
the figure of 700,000 from a published tally of 700 prominent converts
to the Roman Catholic Church:

> Estimating the number of converts from July 4, 1776, to the
> present time and the descendants of deceased converts within
> that time still remaining Catholics, upon the basis of this
> 700 distinguished names being one-twentieth of the whole,
> we would now have the converts of today and the descendants
> of all converts since the Declaration of Independence, amounting
> to 700,000.[34]

Clarke's mathematical skill is questionable; his estimate is the product
of speculation rather than computation. He goes on to state that the
700,000 constitute twenty per cent of the total Catholic population in
1893, or twenty per cent of 14,000,000. This product is accurate, but

---

[33] Clarke, pp. 541-542.

[34] Ibid., p. 542. Clarke uses a previously published list, his
own memory, and available data to compile a roster of more than 730
converts (pp. 543-550).

the portion of the total population designated as the convert element is still arbitrary.

Later estimates of convert numbers are move conservative. Gerald Shaughnessy's classic study of immigration and Catholic growth in the United States between 1790 and 1920 estimates that the number of converts averaged one or one and one-half converts per priest per year. However, Shaughnessey acknowledges that his estimate is generous for the early years, given the circumstances in which the Church found itself: "the generally despised condition of Catholics, the poverty of the Church and the consequent lack of appeal to those who might feel called to seek instruction and entrance into the fold."[35] Shaughnessy's figures are estimates of actual convert numbers rather than of the "convert element":

---

[35]Gerald Shaughnessy, Has the Immigrant Kept the Faith? A Study of Immigration and Catholic Growth in the United States, 1790-1920 (New York: The Macmillan Co., 1825; reprint ed., New York: Arno Press, 1969), p. 71.

Period	Estimated Number of Conversions	Number of clergy (in the first and last year of period)
1790-1820	5,000	34- 150
1820-1830	6,000	150- 232
1831-1840	9,600*	232- 482
1841-1850	18,000	482- 1,800
1851-1860	30,000	1,800- 2,235
1861-1870	40,000	2,235- 3,780
1871-1880	70,000	3,780- 6,000
1881-1890	85,000	6,000- 9,168
1891-1900	125,000	9,168-11,987

*The estimate of conversions during this decade varies from page to page. On p. 123, Shaughnessy offers a figure of 9,400. On p. 125, he estimates the figure at 9,600. The larger number is used in calculating the total.

According to Shaughnessy, nineteenth-century conversions numbered 388,600, an impressive figure, especially if the circumstances of the American context are taken into account. Even during the years, 1830 to 1840, when there was extreme anti-Catholic bigotry, there were nearly ten thousand conversions. The number of conversions increased in the following decade despite a persistent undercurrent of anti-Catholicism in the country. Shaughnessy suggests that anti-Catholicism actually encouraged conversions to Roman Catholicism:

> ...anti-Catholic riots and demonstrations served to weld the members of the Church into a sturdier, more aggressive and more enthusiastic body, while at the same time, the advertising thus given to the Church undoubtedly helped in many cases to bring about the numerous conversions of the period, of which not a few occurred in cultured circles.[36]

Even the Know-Nothing party was unable to stunt the growth of the Catholic Church. The 1850's witnessed a "notable" accession of converts, "due as well to the backfiring of the Know-Nothing attacks as to the effect of the Oxford movement."[37] During the period, 1831-1860, peak years of anti-Catholic bigotry, Roman Catholicism gained some 57,400 converts.

The estimates of total nineteenth-century conversions to Roman Catholicism offered by church historian John Tracy Ellis are in fundamental agreement with Shaughnessy's calculations. Ellis' estimate of the total number of conversions for the period 1815-1900 is 388,600; Shaughnessy's estimate for 1820-1900 is 388,600. Ellis calculates conversions between 1815-1866 to have totalled 103,600 and conversions

---

[36]Ibid., pp. 130-131.

[37]Ibid., p. 143.

between 1870-1900 to have totalled 280,000.[38]

Protestant historians Sydney Ahlstrom and Edwin Scott Gaustad rely on conversion statistics used by Roman Catholic scholars. Ahlstrom notes that between 1813 and 1893 converts to Roman Catholicism may have numbered 700,000.[39] He refers his reader to a study of Brownson's apologetics by George K. Malone.[40] Malone cites Clarke's rough estimate of the "convert element." Ahlstrom observes that "such figures reveal an important fact of American religious life," even if exaggerated or "almost balanced by an equally large defection from the church."[41] Gaustad notes that immigrants accounted for half the increase of 10 million in Catholic membership between 1850 and 1900; "the remaining 5 million members came from natural propagation and new adherents." Gaustad cites Shaughnessy's study as his reference, noting that the work is "indispensable."[42]

Some conversions occurred under the aegis of the parish mission, a phenomenon that Jay P. Dolan calls the "Catholic revival."[43] The Paulists recorded some 2,935 conversions occurring under their auspices from 1858-1900; the Redemptorists counted 4,322 converts

---

[38]New Catholic Encyclopedia, s.v. "United States of America," by J. T. Ellis.

[39]Ahlstrom, p. 548.

[40]George K. Malone, The True Church: A Study of the Apologetics of Orestes Augustus Brownson (Mundelein, Ill.: St. Mary of the Lake Seminary, 1957), p. 2.

[41]Ahlstrom, p. 548.

[42]Edwin Scott Gaustad, Historical Atlas of Religion in America (New York: Harper & Row, 1962), pp. 108, 110.

[43]Dolan, Catholic Revivalism.

from 1840 to 1890.[44] Conversions to Roman Catholicism were considered

a sign of success during a parish mission even though the primary

purpose of the meeting was to re-convert Roman Catholics who had

sinned and strayed. Mission preachers called baptized believers to

a "second conversion," a return to the state of grace.[45] Even if

the figure of more than 380,000 converts counted by Shaughnessy and

endorsed by Ellis is only a rough estimate of nineteenth-century con-

versions to Roman Catholicism, conversions occurring during revivals

account for only a fraction of the total number as the tally of

conversions at St. Paul's Church in New York City shows. Of the total

number of 1675 conversions occurring between 1860 and 1900, only 61 took

place during the course of the 10 missions held in that parish.[46]

The Sources of Conversions
to Roman Catholicism

Richard H. Clarke, a late nineteenth-century observer of the

conversions to Roman Catholicism, considered it "a significant fact that

few converts have been made by the Catholic Church in the country from

the ranks of infidelity, atheism, deism, and other schools rejecting

Christianity."[47] Or to state the observation positively, most converts

---

[44]Ibid., p. 143. Paulist and Redemptorist priests were most
successful in parish mission work.

[45]Dolan, Catholic Revivalism, p. 104.

[46]Ibid., p. 135. Dolan notes that a total of sixty-one
converts was not "a very significant achievement considering the
large mission crowds, but it does underline the predominantly
Catholic dimension of parish revivals during this period."

[47]Clarke, p. 542.

to Roman Catholicism were formerly members of the Protestant denominations or the Episcopal Church. Whether this is indeed significant depends on how one interprets the data.

It is noteworthy that the proportion of church members in the American population was quite modest throughout the nineteenth century. In 1800, the total had risen to twenty-five percent; the great majority, seventy-five percent, were unchurched.[48] The percentage of religiously affiliated Americans continued to rise during the second half of the century but the increase gradual and moderate; in 1900, less that forty percent of the population claimed religious affiliation.[49] Converts to Roman Catholicism generally came from the smaller segment of the American population that was already churched. Likewise, the majority of those who experienced conversion at Protestant revivals were already Christians, at least nominally so. It is possible then that conversion to Roman Catholicism and conversion as experienced during Protestant revivals presumed an existing concern with religion and most especially with salvation. Personal tensions are likely to be resolved through conversion if "these tensions are already seen in a religious light."[50] Therefore, it is hardly surprising that the Roman Catholic Church drew

---

[48]Gaustad, The Rise of Adventism, p. xiii. By 1960, the number of "churched" Americans grew to sixty percent (Gaustad, Historical Atlas of Religion in America, p. 45).

[49]Gaustad, Historical Atlas of Religion in America, Figure 130: "Percentage of National Population with Religious Affiliation," p. 168.

[50]John Wilson, Religion in American Society: The Effective Presence (Englewood Cliffs: Prentice-Hall, 1978), p. 116. Wilson notes that "only a fraction of the converts to sects are former non-believers" and that "this is true even of sects that appeal to the 'unchurched.'"

converts from the Christian churches. Roman Catholicism naturally attracted those who were interested in religion, persons already acquainted with Christianity and given to exploring the implications of its teaching and its practice. The majority of converts, most especially those who wrote about their experiences, recalled ways in which Protestant thought and practice had shaped their early religious histories. And in the nineteenth century, few Protestants escaped exposure to the spirit and tactics of evangelical Christianity. The major denominations, Methodist and Baptist, were evangelical churches and numerous Episcopalians, Lutherans, Presbyterians, and Congrega-tionalists were evangelicals as well. Moreover, converts to Roman Catholicism had been affected by the more subtle but nevertheless effective presence of Protestant Christianity in America. Protestant Christianity provided the symbols and motifs through which Americans expressed their identity: the metaphor of the chosen people, the values which cele-brated the worth of human effort, and the sense of optimism that supported belief in the possibility of personal conversion and social growth. Converts to Roman Catholicism experienced religion as a powerful force in their lives long before they became converts.

Converts to Roman Catholicism came from the entire spectrum of Protestant denominations and the Episcopal Church as well as from "every known religious name and creed."[51] The largest number of

---

[51]"The Philosophy of Conversion," The Catholic World 4 (1868): 459. The author of this unsigned essay suggests that "full as often" converts came "from no name and creed at all." Existing statistical data does not support that assertion.

prominent converts were High Church Episcopalians.[52] A substantial

number were Episcopal clergymen; some were subsequently ordained to

the Roman Catholic priesthood and became influential Roman Catholic

clergymen.[53] However, the predominance of former Episcopalians in

Roman Catholic clerical circles ought not be permitted to obscure the

fact that converts came to the Roman Catholic Church from a variety

of denominations and sects. The popular practice of listing the names

of prominent converts in Catholic publications reveals the diverse

religious backgrounds of converts, while also announcing that the

Roman Catholic Church attracted converts and that these converts were

respectable citizens.[54]

Episcopalians and Lutherans yielded the largest number of

converts to Roman Catholicism. In his study of the American convert

movement, Edward J. Mannix maintains that the largest number came

from the Lutheran Church.[55] The Mercersburg movement encouraged

the conversion of numerous German Lutherans between 1820 and 1850.[56]

The Episcopal Church was a second major source of converts. Others were

---

[52]J. G. Shea, p. 517. Ahlstrom observes that they were "dissatisfied by the evangelization of the Protestant Episcopal Church
and...were carried forward by the implications of their own arguments on
apostolic succession and 'valid' ordination" (p. 548).

[53]The number of Episcopal clergymen who converted to Roman
Catholicism from 1817 to 1867 has been estimated at forty-one. ("The
Philosophy of Conversion," p. 459).

[54]For examples of such lists see J. G. Shea, pp. 509-529; Clarke,
pp. 542-550; Edward J. Mannix, The American Convert Movement (New York:
The Devin-Adair Co., 1923), pp. 108-112.

[55]Mannix, p. 120.

[56]J. G. Shea, p. 523.

formerly Methodists, Presbyterians, Congregationalists, Campbellites, and Baptists.[57] A random sampling at St. Paul's Parish in New York City reveals that Episcopalians and Lutherans, respectively, yielded the largest number of converts. Those at St. Paul's totalled 1675 from 1860 to 1900; the sample numbered 337. Thirty-five percent of the converts were formerly Episcopalians and thirteen percent former Lutherans.[58]

In brief, most converts to Roman Catholicism were already Christians and the largest number Episcopalians and Lutherans. Interest in religion, the desire to discover the true faith, and a strong attraction to Roman ritual drew them to the Roman Catholic Church. But in order to ascertain more specific motives for conversion, it is necessary to examine personal statements, such as those contained in the narratives of conversion.

Some Distinctive Characteristics of Conversion to Roman Catholicism

Conversions to Roman Catholicism differed from conversions within evangelical Protestantism in several ways. The evangelical experience of conversion was generally a sudden, intensely emotional experience which occurred within a social setting designed to induce a change of heart. Conversion to Roman Catholicism was generally a gradual process,

---

[57]Mannix, p. 120.

[58]Dolan, Catholic Revivalism, p. 135; n. 61, p. 230. The proportion of Episcopalians and Lutherans was similar in conversions which occurred in the context of the parish missions. Dolan notes that of the sixty-one conversions which occurred during the ten missions held at St. Paul's, thirty percent of the converts were Episcopal and nineteen percent were Lutheran.

often involving lengthy deliberation over particular articles of faith. For the evangelical, the important thing was <u>that</u> one believed and accepted Jesus. For the Roman Catholic, <u>what</u> was believed and what must be believed were also important. As a technique and as a perspective, revivalism required simplicity; the preacher made a clear and direct plea to his hearers: accept Jesus. Spiritual transformation was essential to conversion and of course, the experience of being born again affected a person's status; conversion fixed one's place in the community. The social effects of conversion within evangelical Christianity were positive: the convert gained status even if conversion resulted in a change in affiliation. The denominational structure of Protestantism insured that Protestants would pay little attention to what sociologists describe as alternation.

Conversion to Roman Catholicism also involved spiritual rebirth but with one major difference: the convert experienced a loss of status. The freedom of movement within Protestantism did not extend to easy exchange of members with the Roman Catholic Church. Becoming a Roman Catholic in nineteenth-century America meant losing one's place as a member of the religious and social establishment. Conversion was radical: the convert assumed a new identity, within and without.

The Mission Convert

Conversions which occurred at parish missions or Catholic revivals reveal some other major differences in the ways in which conversion was experienced within Protestantism and within Roman Catholicism. I speak of both the revitalization of piety experienced by lapsed Catholics and the conversions experienced by seeking

Protestants who made their way to Rome. The latter were few in number; most Protestants approached the Church privately and singly. The Catholic mission combined sacramental ritual and gospel evangelism to produce "a sacramental evangelism."[59] The repentant sinner was expected to seal his change of heart with reception of the sacrament of Penance. Walter Elliott, a Paulist priest and mission preacher, argues that the sacrament of confession made a crucial difference between Protestant and Catholic revivals:

> In a revival there is sudden repentance; in excitement, perhaps frenzy. With Catholics it is in patient searching of the heart done with calm deliberation. In one case a man judges his own heart and approves his own motives; in the other a learned and discreet officer of the Church tests and approves his dispositions in addition to his own judgment, administering warnings drawn from the past and exacting guarantees for the future. Protestant conversion is done in a hurry, in excitement, without any act of humility, done in the vanity of self-judgment, done without reparation for the past and without provisions for the future. No wonder such a change of heart is notoriously uncertain.[60]

Elliott's statement is obviously biased. Nevertheless, Elliott sheds light on an important aspect of the Roman Catholic experience of conversion: its sacramental character. Reception of the sacraments of Penance and Eucharist was a visible sign of repentance. Reception of sacraments signalled a revitalization of piety; in fact, the number of communions received during a mission was a favored way of gauging its success.[61]

Mission preachers had two goals: to inspire and to teach.

---

[59]Ibid., p. 112.

[60]Walter Elliott, Archives of the Paulist Fathers, Elliott Sermons, Sacrament of Penance, cited by Dolan, p. 107.

[61]Dolan, p. 108.

They were to move sinners to repent and experience a metanoia: the "conversion sought was not a lifeless, ritualized act but a radical decision for Jesus rooted in total repentance."[62] But instruction was also important; instructional talks were a regular component of the mission schedule. Dolan points out that these talks were "aimed at preparing people for a proper sacramental conversion and little else."[63] But mission talks had another purpose: to meet the needs of non-Catholics as well as Catholics. Passionist mission records reveal preachers' concern with matters of Catholic doctrine and practice. A public press notice of an upcoming mission described its purpose this way: "It will be the aim of the Fathers to explain matters of Catholic faith and to revive and direct the fervor of Catholic piety."[64] An article in the Clarion Daily Democrat testified that clear explanations of "some of the peculiar tenets of that Church" had indeed been given.[65]

Initial instruction was accomplished through "controversial sermons" which

> ...examined fundamental points of Catholic faith -- for example, the marks of the true Church, the proofs for the doctrine of the Holy Eucharist and the forgiveness of sins. Sometimes the non-Catholics themselves requested discourse on specific topics. In every case the invitation was given well in advance to interest as many Protestants as possible. Occasionally the missionary stayed after the close of the mission precisely to dis-

---

[62]Ibid., p. 106.

[63]Ibid., p. 111.

[64]Mission Record, Pittsburgh Monastery Archives, ff. 44v; 45r, cited by Cassion J. Yuhaus, Compelled to Speak (Westminster, Md.: Newman Press, 1967), p. 281.

[65]Mission Record, ff. 46v; 47r, cited by Yuhaus, p. 282.

cuss points of Catholic faith for the benefit of other non-Catholic denominations.[66]

The instructional emphasis shows that mission preachers were concerned about convert-making even though the primary goal of the mission was to bring lapsed Catholics back to the Church. But the didactic cast also suggests that the experience of the mission convert may not have differed radically from that of the convert who came to the Church after a personal search and struggle. For both, conversion was more than a passing emotional experience. All converts were expected to learn and accept the teachings of the Church and to publically acknowledge their commitment in the profession of faith and in the reception of the sacraments.

Roman Catholic Understandings of
Conversion

A Roman Catholic's view of conversion was to a large extent a product of his attitude toward Protestantism and his response to some fundamental theological issues of the day. Two divergent, even contradictory, views of conversion emerge in nineteenth-century discussions: the conservative understanding of conversion as a radical renunciation of Protestantism and the liberal view of conversion to Roman Catholicism as a fulfilment of Christian faith. In each case, the perspective on conversion is part of a larger network of attitudes and ideas regarding true religion.

Conservative Catholics were generally suspicious and defensive in their dealings with Protestants and so likely to look upon

---

[66]Yuhaus, pp. 279-280.

conversion as requiring condemnation and rejection of the errors
of Protestantism. Liberal Catholics, more open and tolerant in their
relations with Protestants, looked upon conversion to Roman Catholicism
as a natural development in the Christian life; Protestantism nurtured
values consonant with Catholicism.[67] Those who feared for the safety
of the Church in what they judged to be a hostile environment viewed
Protestantism as a menace to the Roman Catholic Church. But Catholics
who were optimistic about the future of the Church in America had no
reason to fear Protestantism.

The way in which a Catholic resolved key theological issues
shaped his view of conversion. Positions on three vigorously debated
issues were central; these issues included the nature of true religion,
the nature of the Church, and the role of human effort in discovering
religious truth. Liberal and conservative patterns emerged in the
discussion which these topics engendered and proponents of each
perspective came to understand conversion differently.

What is the true religion? Does Protestantism share in any
of the constitutive elements of true religion? Some Catholics maintained
that Protestantism possessed some elements of "true religion." For
example, Richard Clarke argued that the Protestant denominations
functioned as "nurseries of conversions" insofar as they were
"promoters of some beautiful features of Christian truth."[68] The

---

[67] For an informative discussion of the contrasting Roman Catholic
attitudes toward Protestantism, see Robert D. Cross, The Emergence
of Liberal Catholicism in America (Cambridge: Harvard University Press,
1958), especially pp. 22-50.

[68] Clarke, p. 542.

"love of religious antiquity and episcopacy" expressed by Episcopalians,
the "ardent advocacy of the principle of ecclesiastical authority"
manifested by Presbyterians, the "intense culture of the personality
of God and of the Saviour" nourished by the Methodists, the "hatred of
Erastianism and opposition to what they took to be idolatry" maintained
by the Puritans, and the "zeal against mere formal religion exhibited
by Evangelicals" -- all these demonstrated the manner in which the
Protestant denominations laid the foundation for eventual conversion
to Catholicism.[69] In each case, non-Catholic Christians already
experienced a dimension of true religion which was to be found in its
fullness in the Roman Catholic Church. Roman Catholics, who shared
Clarke's view, saw the passage from the Episcopal Church or any of the
Protestant denominations to the Roman Catholic Church as natural progress
toward the fullness of faith. Conservative Catholics denied that
Protestantism possessed any element of the true religion whatsoever.
True religion, they maintained, was simply co-terminous with the Roman
Catholic Church.[70]

The issue of what constitutes true religion was posed more
directly in the question: what is the church? Or to put the question
another way: are the Roman Catholic Church and the true Church of
Christ one and the same? Conservatives argued that the true Church of
Christ was identical with the Roman Catholic Church. Consequently,
outside the Church there is no salvation, as Michael Mueller pointedly

---

[69]Ibid.

[70]For an example, see Thomas S. Preston, "American Catholicity,"
American Catholic Quarterly Review 16 (1891):396-408.

stated in the sub-title of The Catholic Dogma, which was indeed a
manifesto of the conservative position.[71]

Liberals responded that although the Church of Christ was
unquestionably present in the Roman Catholic Church in its fullness,
non-Catholic Christians perceived the Christian truth in part and so
belonged to the "soul" of the Church.[72] Conversion to Roman Catholicism
perfected their earlier perceptions of truth and moral value. In fact,
a person's Protestant experience prepared him for conversion. Walter
Elliott wrote that "one truth calls for another and helps the mind to
receive it"; persons "are partly converted by coming to believe any
Catholic truth."[73] Elliott, himself a Paulist, expressed the position
of fellow-convert-priests who "felt the continuity of their religious
aspirations" and therefore "resented any implication that in their
Protestant days they had been beyond the pale of salvation."[74]

Conservatives, on the other hand, pictured conversion as a total
break with past religious history. Robert D. Cross offers a helpful
summary of that position:

> To Catholics, conversion means the profession of faith,
> by a former nonbeliever, in the supernatural authority of the
> Church as the authorized representative of God in all matters
> concerning salvation. Because conservatives were convinced
> that the average non-Catholic possessed little religious truth,
> did not respect the supernatural, and was determined to attack
> the Church rather than obey it, they visualized conversion as

---

[71]Michael Mueller, The Catholic Dogma: Out of the Church There
Is No Salvation (New York: Benzinger Brothers, 1888).

[72]Cross, p. 56.

[73]Walter Elliott, "Half-Converts," The Catholic World 63
(1896):431-432.

[74]Cross, p. 56.

a dramatic, intense remaking of man's whole life, a spiritual
death and transfiguration. When a man finally became aware
of his desperate need of the Church, he would expect and desire
truths in sharp contrast with everything he had believed before.
A man would enter the Church because it offered unity instead
of pluralism, absolute dogma instead of an unqualified liberty
of opinion, a deep devotionalism instead of an arid rationalism.[75]

What is the role of human effort in the process of conversion?
Does human effort encourage or impede conversion. Or is it simply
superfluous to the conversion process?[76] Responses to these questions
also reflected two distinct theological perspectives. Conservatives
generally saw little value in work aimed directly at promoting
conversions. Human effort was most effectively exerted in the spiritual
realm: prayer was the most effective work.[77] Even the most carefully
reasoned arguments were detrimental: overtures at dialogue, initiated in
the hope of exposing the truth of Catholicism, led to a dilution of
Catholic belief. "The temptation to dilute Catholic doctrine springs
from the desire to make it appear reasonable and to facilitate the
return of wanderers to the true fold."[78] Such watering-down of Catholic
teaching endangered the integrity of Roman Catholicism.

Liberal Catholics applauded and encouraged efforts to promote

---

[75]Ibid., p. 59.

[76]See Cross (pp. 58-69) for a summary of the discussion of these
issues in the Catholic press.

[77]The power of prayer in effecting conversions is lauded by F. G.
Lentz, "The Conversion of the American People," The Catholic World 55
(1892):884-887. Lentz's argument for the urgency of prayer is based on
his belief that "if the Catholics of America do not endeavor to cast this
devil out of their non-Catholic fellow-countrymen, he will ultimately take
possession of themselves" (p. 885).

[78]A. F. Hewit, "Pure vs. Diluted Catholicism," American Catholic
Quarterly Review 20 (1895):463.

conversions which they considered to be a vital dimension of the Church's
apostolate. They formulated guidelines for the task. First, potential
converts among Protestants ought to be approached as they are, that is,
as those who are "in perfectly good faith, sincerely seeking the truths
of religion, and honestly striving, just as Catholics do, to conform
their lives to their belief."[79] Though membership in a sect may
be heretical, a Protestant's "good faith" unites him with Catholics
and allows for fruitful encounter and dialogue.[80] An attitude of
reconciliation should characterize the encounter: "it is better to
imitate Him who 'breaketh not the bruised reed nor quencheth the smoking
flax,' and to hold towards them, not the weapons of controversy, but the
arms of the Good Shepherd."[81] Second, working for conversions
requires the use of reason and intellect. The potential convert ought
to be aided in discovering the logical consequences of beliefs already
held and truths already perceived. God's grace builds on nature; honest
and intelligent instruction was demanded. The Roman Catholic faith ought
to be made to appear reasonable and its compatibility with American
values ought to be accented. Catholicism ought to be presented as a
universal rather than a provincial faith:

> It was extremely important, the liberals believed, that
> potential converts be confronted with Catholic doctrines and
> practices only in purest form, stripped of the personal, local,

---

[79] Alfred Young, A Plea for Erring Brethren," The Catholic World
50 (1889):358. See also Walter Elliott, "The Human Environment of
the Catholic Faith," The Catholic World 43 (1886):463-470; J. J. Keane,
"The Reunion of Christendom," American Catholic Quarterly Review 13
(1888):304-314.

[80] Young, p. 358.

[81] Keane, p. 310.

and racial accretions which too often were mistaken by Protestant and Catholic alike for the essence of the faith.[82]

Theological positions which surfaced during the discussion of these issues supported two models of conversion: conversion as the fulfillment of the Christian faith and conversion as the radical disavowal of the convert's religious past. In both cases, the model of conversion was rooted in a comprehensive understanding of the Roman Catholic experience and a correlative view of Catholic-Protestant relations.

The nineteenth was a decisive century for the Roman Catholic Church in America: its constituency and complexion changed radically as did its place in American society. At the beginning of the century, the Church was an insignificant religious minority; by mid-century, it was the largest religious body in the United States. At century's end, the Roman Catholic Church was able to look back with pride and confidence, knowing that it had weathered the widespread antipathy of non-Catholics and withstood the numerous internal conflicts that were by-products of rapid growth and a changing population. And despite these difficulties, the Church attracted an impressive number of converts, more than 380,000. Most came from the Episcopal and Lutheran Churches and other Protestant denominations; some even came from the ranks of the unchurched.

How did they come? What were they looking for? What did they find? These questions are difficult to answer with generalizations. Individual accounts offer the best clues to what it meant to become a Roman Catholic. Such accounts are contained in the small body of

---

[82]Cross, p. 62.

narratives written by ninteenth-century converts. These narratives constitute a distinctive form of spiritual autobiography and provide a framework for understanding the dynamics of conversion to Roman Catholicism.

CHAPTER III

PERSONAL NARRATIVES OF CONVERSION:

A DISTINCTIVE FORM OF SPIRITUAL AUTOBIOGRAPHY

Personal narratives of conversion written by nineteenth-century
American converts to Roman Catholicism constitute a distinctive form
of spiritual autobiography. The unique character of these narratives
is especially apparent when the narratives are viewed in relation to
the genre of spiritual autobiography. Then similarities and differences
in focus and breadth of content and structure and in the intent of the
authors emerge with clarity.

Spiritual Autobiography:
A Brief History of the Development of the Genre

The history of spiritual autobiography began with Augustine's
Confessions, written at the end of the fourth century.[1] The Confessions was a culmination of an autobiographical tradition that was
conceived and developed in antiquity. Contrary to popular opinion,
Augustine's Confessions did not represent the emergence of an entirely
new literary genre but rather the flowering of an already existent
literary tradition.[2] The difference between the Confessions and the

---

[1]Augustine of Hippo, Confessions, trans. Vernon J. Bourke
(Washington: The Catholic University of America Press, 1953).

[2]George Misch, A History of Autobiography in Antiquity, 2 vols.
(Cambridge: Harvard University Press, 1951).

works which preceded it is a difference of perspective and depth:
"Augustine was the first to probe deeply into the psyche, to substitute
self-observation for observation of the world, and to feel that the
story of self alone was important enough to sustain a lengthy narrative."[3] Augustine's conversion to Christianity prompted introspection
and self-examination; he focused upon the profound changes wrought
within him by God's grace. The experience in the garden at Milan
transformed him completely; he died to his old self and experienced
the pain of rebirth. In it all, Augustine discerned the constant
work of God, especially as he reviewed his life in the light of his
conversion. Augustine used "God's latterly discovered plan as a con-
trolling idea, to give retrospective force to the raw data of his remembered experience."[4]

Centuries passed before Augustine's concern with the inner
life became commonplace. It was not until the seventeenth and eighteenth centuries that spiritual autobiography emerged as a popular
literary mode. Two factors in the social and religious milieu
fostered the development of spiritual autobiography. Historians of
European culture agree that "something like a mutation in human
nature took place" in the late sixteenth and early seventeenth centuries.[5] The result was the emergence of a new personality type: the

---

[3]Robert Scholes and Robert Kellogg, The Nature of Narrative
(New York: Oxford University Press, 1966), p. 79.

[4]M. H. Abrams, Natural Supernaturalism: Tradition and
Revolution in Romantic Literature (New York: W.W. Norton & Co.,
1971), p. 85.

[5]Lionel Trilling, Sincerity and Authenticity (Cambridge:

"individual," defined by a newly discovered "inner space," a belief
in his own worth, and a sense of privacy. The age widened options
and choices available to persons, while simultaneously increasing the
pressure upon the individual to choose.

> This was most apparent in respect of political and religious
> controversies, but many other areas of life were beginning to
> offer a new range of possibilities. Changing views about
> science and man's relationship to nature; social mobility;
> exploration and travel; and the wider circulation of news, ideas
> and information: all challenged existing habits of thought
> and traditional loyalties.[6]

Decisiveness rather than acceptance of the inevitable became requirements of the time and "the fact that decisions had to be taken, or
were at least now seen to be possible, led inescapably to self-assess-
ment and increasing self-awareness."[7]

Recognition of the "individuality" of each person was a by-
product of the Renaissance. "The subtle set of differences whereby
any individual is distinguished from every other individual" was "not
perceived as an 'accidental' variation from the norm, or as a dis-
countable matter, but as a matter of great importance."[8] Each life
was unique. The Renaissance also contributed to the development of
historical consciousness: man's horizon shifted "from eternity to

---

Harvard University Press, 1972), p. 19.

[6]Owen Watkins, The Puritan Experience: Studies in Spiritual
Autobiography (New York: Shocken Books, 1972), p. 227.

[7]Ibid.

[8]Karl J. Weintraub, "Autobiography and Historical Consciousness," Critical Inquiry 2 (1975-76): 838.

time."[9] With that shift came the awareness that each person's self

was a "unique and unrepeatable form of being human" and that each person

has "the perceived task in life to 'fulfill,' to actualize this very

specific individuality."[10]

The visual arts and literature reflected this new individualism:

the self-portrait and autobiography celebrated the newly acquired sence

of individual importance. Heightened concern with sincerity, traced

by Lionel Trilling and Henri Peyre, testified to a growing recognition

of the integral relation between art and life, between the artist's

work and his lived experience.[11] Sincerity demanded continuing self-

scrutiny and introspection and was simultaneously the product of such

effort. It is neither accidental nor surprising that the coming of

age of the "individual" paralleled the rise of autobiography. Con-

sciousness of the self and the struggle for sincerity awakened the

autobiographical impulse. The genre of autobiography and its cognate

forms provided a most appropriate forum for self-examination and self-

revelation.

The Reformation reinforced this emphasis on the self. Reformers

stressed the direct nature of the relationship between God and man;

that relationship was no longer seen a mediated by the institutional

---

[9]Margaret Bottrall, Every Man a Phoenix: Studies in Seventeenth-century Autobiography (London: John Murray, 1958), p. 162.
Also see Weintraub, pp. 821-848.

[10]Weintraub, p. 839.

[11]Henri Peyre, Literature and Sincerity (New Haven: Yale
University Press, 1963). Peyre focuses on the concern with sincerity
in French literature but he also comments on parallel developments
in seventeenth and eighteenth-century England. In England, sincerity

Church. Responsibility for salvation was set squarely upon the shoulders of the individual believer. "The Reformation age...swept away the clutter, pursued simplicity of vision, and directed the gaze of the worshipper towards that which truly mattered."[12] What mattered was within: religion of the heart and will. In his study of the Reformation, Owen Chadwick concludes that by the mid-seventeenth century, "the chief need...appeared to be morality, the chief problem of theology the course and growth of the good life."[13] The focus upon the interior life naturally developed into a concern with life as lived, with the manner in which religious ideals were translated into action. Inevitably, the self became the object of careful scrutiny. A conviction of sinfulness often awakened an acute sense of guilt that was aggravated by uncertainty regarding the state of one's soul.

Puritan Autobiography

Puritan spirituality, in particular, vividly accented the agonies of the interior life: the Puritans "liberated men from the treadmill of indulgences and penances, but cast them on the iron couch of introspection."[14] John Bunyan's Grace Abounding to the Chief of Sinners testifies to the anguished soul-searching experienced in the

---

had "a religious connotation" due to the "potent influence" of Puritanism (p. 35).

[12]Owen Chadwick, The Reformation (Baltimore: Penguin Books, 1964), pp. 443-444.

[13]Ibid., p. 444.

[14]Perry Miller as cited by Ahlstrom, p. 128. Ahlstrom does not specify the source of the quotation.

atmosphere created by English Puritanism.[15] Once the drama of

salvation was relocated in the human heart, that heart could not escape

the agony of battle, smarting no less for its spirituality. Such

intense spiritual experience impelled Bunyan and others who followed

his example to take pen in hand and retrace the strategies of the

powers of darkness and light which vied for their souls.

In England, increasing consciousness of the self and in-

dividualism in the religious quest encouraged the writing of

spiritual autobiographies. In his study of seventeenth-century

British autobiography, Ivan Dean Ebner observes that between 1600

and 1640 only three or four autobiographies were written in each

decade. "But during the forties and the fifties, the number

doubled, and doubled once more during the sixties, continuing at

that level until the close of the century."[16] By the end of the

century, there were more than one hundred British autobiographies

in existence.[17] Ebner attributes the increase in number after 1640

to the individualism encouraged by the Puritans. Puritanism em-

phasized the value of human effort and the worth of the life well

lived. Spiritual autobiographies were "the product of a Puritan

conviction that the highest art a man could practice was the art

---

[15]John Bunyan, Grace Abounding to the Chief of Sinners and
The Pilgrim's Progress from World to that which is to come, ed.
Roger Sharrock (London: Oxford University Press, 1966).

[16]Ivan Dean Ebner, "Seventeenth-century British Autobiography:
The Impact of Religious Commitment" (Ph.D dissertation, Stanford
University, 1965), pp. 5-6.

[17]Ibid., p. 7.

of living."[18]

Bunyan's Grace Abounding is a classic example of British spiritual autobiography. It has been characterized as a "psychology of conversion" and so it is.[19] Grace Abounding is a "relation of the merciful work of God upon my Soul."[20] The quest for peace and salvation shaped the autobiography as it shaped Bunyan's life. In the light of this concern with his spiritual condition, all other details of family life and social setting appeared to be unimportant, even meaningless. References to his background and his parents are limited to two brief paragraphs. Then Bunyan quickly moves on to recount his anguished memory of the temptations that tormented him during his childhood years. A sense of guilt, a conviction of sinfulness, and a fear of damnation dominated his thought and emotions from the earliest years of his life. The content of Grace Abounding reflects Bunyan's belief that everything fades in importance in the face of the cosmic clash between good and evil, re-enacted on a microcosmic scale in the heart of man. Good and evil, salvation and damnation, heaven and hell define the dualistic universe which Bunyan inhabited. The dynamics of conversion -- sinfulness, guilt, despair, doubt, and finally conviction -- inform the narrative.

Bunyan's Grace Abounding was one such narrative among many. Ebner lists some seventy-four seventeenth-century British

---

[18]Watkins, p. 1.

[19]Ebner, p. 17.

[20]Bunyan, p. 7.

autobiographies written by Baptists, Independents, Anglicans, Roman Catholics, Ranters, Muggletarians, and Presbyterians.[21] In each case, the theology of the author determined the focus of his autobiography and the extent of his concern with conversion.[22]

Journals of the Friends

Theology's influence upon the content of autobiography is well illustrated in the writings of Friends.[23] The basic tenet of Quaker belief, that God was within each person and immediately present to him, aroused the autobiographical impulse. Because George Fox and his followers believed that they could apprehend God's truth directly, they naturally turned their attention inward. Belief in the "inner Light" established the primacy of the interior life. Conversion occurred when a person recognized and submitted to the Light. The stark simplicity of Quaker piety was an expression of the belief that what was essential to the religious life was within man. Neither the church nor the Bible were final authorities; truth and power were to be found through personal experience.

Autobiographical writings of Friends took the form of tes-

---

[21]Ebner, pp. 238-243.

[22]Ebner's thesis is that seventeenth-century English autobiographies may be classified according to the religious commitments of their authors (pp. 233-237).

[23]Autobiographical works written by members of the Society of Friends will be referred to as "Quaker" writings. Though the designation, Quaker, was originally used in a derogatory sense, it is now commonplace to use the term to designate the literature written by the Friends.

timonies or confessional tracts and journals. Testimonies were
brief, pointed accounts of conversion. The typical testimony was
"simple and practical, and involved no 'windy doctrine.'"[24] The
effectiveness of the testimony as an evangelizing tool derived from
the inherent authority of the author's experience. Quaker testimonies "were not complete life histories, but conversion stories
with just enough detail of the writer's outward life to explain
his inward development."[25] They were usually written shortly after
conversion and expressed the sense of resolution and peace that
accompanied conversion.[26]

Testimonies or confessional tracts ranged from four to sixty
pages in length. The confessional tracts were conventional in form
and in content. The tracts included

> ...first, the writer's earliest intimations of God, and of reli-
> gious questioning; second, an earnest endeavor to ascertain
> from the variety of prevailing teachings -- Anglican, Presby-
> terian and Puritan -- an adequate basis for a religious life;
> next, a record of the writer's first knowledge of the Quakers
> or of the Publisher of Truth who "convinced" him; fourth, the
> struggle in the individual soul against surrender; fifth, the
> final submission, and last, the entry into the activities and
> the defense of the Society.[27]

---

[24]Watkins, p. 161. Watkins' discussion of Quaker testimonies,
their content, and their use is helpful. See pp. 160-181.

[25]Ibid., p. 182.

[26]Ibid., p. 184.

[27]Luella M. Wright, The Literary Life of the Early Friends:
1650-1725 (New York: Columbia University Press, 1932; reprint ed.,
New York: AMS Press, 1966), p. 201.

Some forty confessional tracts were published before 1680.[28]

Quaker journals were more extensive and detailed than were the testimonies, a fact which suggests that written records were kept with some regularity.[29] Journals recounted the experiences of persons living in the Light. In her study of early Quaker writings, Luella M. Wright defines the Quaker journal as "an account, written at first hand, of the personal and religious life of one who became so identified with the Quaker group after he had once surrendered himself to its teachings, that his memories expressed the aims and beliefs of the Society."[30] A journal was "published posthumously at the discretion of surviving Friends who submitted it to the Morning Meeting for approval and censorship."[31] Journals of Friends who had traveled widely in their preaching ministry were likely to be published because other Friends were interested in those whom they had known. The circulation of the journals contributed to the cohesiveness of a growing Quaker community by

---

[28]Ibid., p. 202. Wright points out that it is sometimes difficult to distinguish confessional tracts from journals. The principle of distinction which she employs is this: accounts are designated as confessions "when the period of conviction to Friends' principles dominated other interests" (p. 203).

[29]Watkins, p. 186.

[30]Wright, p. 156. Wright observes that more than twenty-five typical Quaker journals were in print before 1725 and "more than twenty others written by Friends whose youth and maturity belong to the period under study." In addition, approximately eight other assorted personal accounts, some complete and some fragmentary, were written by Quakers during the same period (p. 160).

[31]Watkins, p. 187.

providing models of spiritual accomplishment to be imitated.[32]
The journals were an outgrowth of what Wright calls the "group mind"
and simultaneously informed the "mind" of the community: "Through
the religious confession and the autobiography proper, the Friends
evolved a means for expressing their emotional life and their religious experiences, and also a means for communicating to their constituency and outsiders Quaker ideas of practical Christianity."[33]

The experiences of George Fox were of special interest to
his followers. His <u>Journal</u> testified to the work of the Lord in
his life:

> And when all my hopes in them and in all men were gone, so that
> I had nothing outwardly to help me, nor could tell what to do,
> then, Oh then, I heard a voice which said, "There is one, even
> Jesus Christ, that can speak to thy condition", and when I heard
> it my heart did leap for joy. Then the Lord did let me see
> why there was none upon the earth that could speak to my condi-
> tion, namely that I might give him all the glory; for all are
> included under sin, and shut up in unbelief as I had been, that
> Jesus Christ might have the pre-eminence, who enlightens, and
> gives grace, and faith, and power. Thus, when God doth work
> who shall let it? And this I know experimentally.[34]

From that point, all that Fox did was based on the assurance that

Christ had opened and transformed him:

> ...the Lord did gently lead me along....Christ it was who had
> enlightened me, that gave me his Light to believe in, and gave
> me hope, which is himself, revealed himself in me, and gave me his
> spirit and gave me his grace, which I found sufficient in the
> deeps and in weakness.[35]

---

[32]Ibid.

[33]Wright, p. 193.

[34]George Fox, The Journal of George Fox, ed. John L. Nickolls
(Cambridge: Cambridge University Press, 1952) p. 1.

[35]Ibid., pp. 11-12.

Fox believed that all that was essential to the spiritual life was given at the moment of conversion. There was no progress in the spiritual life. All that was required was a constant effort to live in response to the Inner Voice.

The structure of a journal was an appropriate format for Quaker autobiography. Journal format permitted the author to acknowledge the presence of God in the commonplace occurences of daily life.

There was little departure from the conventional style and content of the best known journals of George Fox and his contemporaries: John Burnyeat, William Caton, and Stephen Crisp. However, Wright contends that the genre was already well-established before 1689: "Every phase of life and thought, portrayed in these four pioneer journals -- the home environment, religious crises, psychopathic states, adoption of Quaker tenets, imprisonment, domestic affairs, travels in the ministry, -- all had previously found expression in Quaker literature before 1689."[36] Consequently, the origins of the genre of Quaker journals cannot simply be ascribed to George Fox, though his thinking dominated the "group mind" of the Society of Friends.[37]

Differences in theologies accounted for the essential differences between Quaker journals and Puritan autobiographies. Quaker theology affirmed the basic goodness of man and expressed

---

[36]Wright, p. 193.

[37]Ibid., p. 196.

deep trust in man's ability to discern God's will for him. Puritan
theology pictured the spiritual life as a struggle to overcome the
powers of evil. The Puritan belief in God's absolute sovereignty
precluded confidence in man's ability to discern the mind of God.
The typical Quaker journal described a life lived in the Light;
the ordinary Puritan autobiography told of a constant struggle to
glimpse the light and to remain within its blaze.

Spiritual Autobiography in America

Spiritual autobiography was a popular literary genre among
Puritans and Quakers in seventeenth and eighteenth century America.[38]
The forces that accounted for the popularity of the genre in England were also present in America: a concern with the self and
theological perspectives that encouraged introspection and soul-
searching.

American Puritan Writings

Typical seventeenth-century American Puritan narratives
tended more "toward formalistic recitation and mechanical pattern"
than did their English counterparts.[39] Seventeenth-century New

---

[38] Daniel B. Shea's Spiritual Autobiography in Early America
(Princeton: Princeton University Press, 1968) is especially useful
in assessing the nature and function of spiritual autobiography
in early Protestant America. Shea explores the genre of spiritual
autobiography in America before 1800. In particular, he examines
representative Puritan and Quaker narratives. Shea's work com-
plements that of Watkins and Ebner who explore the spiritual autobiography in seventeenth-century England.

[39] Ibid., p. 90.

Englanders lacked the "impulsiveness and wild fluctuation of emotion" that characterized a John Bunyan.[40] The conventional form of the early narratives was due in large part to the fact that the narratives were composed to satisfy requirements for church membership. New England Puritans stipulated that an applicant for church membership give an account of his "experience of grace."[41] The congregations of Massachusetts, Connecticut, New Haven, and Plymouth insisted on public evidence that the person petitioning for membership was "elect of God."[42] Daniel B. Shea argues that these

> ...narratives hardly deserve to be considered as autobiography
> not simply because their subject matter is restricted, nor even
> because their vocabulary is uniform and impersonal, but because
> their authors' designated purpose was to convince the elders
> that the presence of grace was evident in their experience.
> ...The autobiographical act is reduced to testifying that one's
> experience has conformed, with allowable variations, to a cer-
> tain pattern of feeling and behavior.[43]

Nevertheless, these narratives do serve a purpose: they are "the only appropriate measure of independence and originality in the genre."[44] Furthermore, these early narratives, as simplistic as they were, laid the groundwork for an American tradition of valuing reflection on the spiritual life.

---

[40] Ibid.

[41] Ibid., p. 91

[42] The Puritan Tradition in America 1620-1730, ed. Alden T. Vaughn (Columbia: University of South Carolina Press, 1972), pp. 92-93.

[43] D. B. Shea, p. 91.

[44] Ibid.

The striking feature of American Puritan autobiography was an adherence to certain literary conventions. Puritan piety determined what was essential to an account of the spiritual life and autobiographers readily complied with prevailing standards. The result was what Shea has called the "textbook conversion."[45] With studied regularity, autobiographers recounted their sinfulness in youth, an experience of illumination, usually provoked by preaching, and finally, conviction and repentance. This pattern of Puritan experience was repeated in hundreds of accounts.[46] Faith did not rule out doubt and backsliding, and autobiographers recorded their life-long struggle against the powers of darkness and their frequent "tremblings of heart" and "plunges."[47]

Puritan autobiography testified that the power of Divine Providence was manifested in the author's life as clearly as it was manifested in the life of the community. Thomas Shepherd includes a list of "good things" he received from the Lord: being itself, health, care, deliverance from "that profane and wicked town" where he was born and lived.[48] What followed was an inclusive catalogue of God's acts in Shepherd's behalf. Such confession satisfied Shepherd's need to acknolwedge God's hand in his life.

---

[45]Ibid., p. 92. Also see p. 100.

[46]Morgan, p. 72.

[47]D. B. Shea, p. 108.

[48]God's Plot: The Paradoxes of Puritan Piety, Being the Autobiography and Journal of Thomas Shepherd, ed. Michael McGiffert (Amherst: The University of Massachusetts Press, 1972), pp. 7-74.

Puritans strove to demonstrate that God was truly present and active in the day-to-day events of their lives. Sometimes the result was forced and oversimplified, as was the case with John Dane's Declaration of Remarkable Providences.[49] A more skilled writer, such as John Winthrop, expressed his belief in the providential acts of God through carefully reasoned theological argumentation. Winthrop tells the story of his spiritual life while simultaneously setting forth his conviction that faith precedes justification, that faith is the free gift of God, "even though man must reach out his hands to receive it...."[50]

"The autobiographical search for self, the self that would endure in the life of grace, very often has a quite public purpose."[51] This was clearly the case among Puritans whose autobiographies were intended to be a matter of public record. Autobiography was unlike diary or journal in that autobiography was written in order that it might be read. The diary was "a device for personal meditation and analysis" which "would fail of its purpose if the writer could not bring himself to view his most abhorrent self," but the auto-biography was "public in nature, setting forth an exemplary position."[52]

---

[49] John Dane, A Declaration of Remarkable Providences in the Course of My Life (Boston, 1854). For a detailed discussion of the content and style of Dane's narrative, see D. B. Shea, pp. 126-138.

[50] D. B. Shea, p. 106.

[51] Ibid., p. 118.

[52] Ibid., p. 142.

The Puritan describes himself differently in diary and autobiography:

> ...the diary is an effort in self-discovery, the unretouched
> reflection of the Puritan seen in isolation; the autobiography
> asserts an important, meaningful relationship between an in-
> dividual life and the lives of other Puritans by presuming that
> the author can find himself some kernel of wisdom or insight
> which may be imparted to his fellow Pilgrims. The subject of
> the autobiography thus no longer perceives himself as totally
> separated from the world; rather he places himself into a social
> context so that others may, by observing him and his life, dis-
> cover something about themselves.[53]

The diary records the insights of the present moment; the autobiography reflects upon the past: "What was lonely self-discovery
for the diarist becomes in the autobiography a general illustration
of God's grace and a specific proof of the worthiness of the author
to belong to God's community on earth."[54]

Spiritual autobiography was intended to edify readers, even
if those readers were only the children of the author. The author's
desire to inspire and instruct readers shaped the content and form
of the autobiographies. And "however violent the struggle they
recited," success marked their outcomes; whatever the idiosyncracies
of the author and his experiences, these were hidden beneath conventional patterns.[55] Above all else, the autobiographer was concerned with testifying to God's providential presence in his life
and committed to demonstrating that God's grace was the principle

---

[53]Cynthia G. Wolff, "Literary Reflections of the Puritan
Character," Journal of the History of Ideas 29 (1968): 26.

[54]Wolff, p. 26.

[55]D. B. Shea, p. 113.

of order and meaning in his life. Such testimony, it was hoped, would inspire others to acknowledge the power and presence of God.

It is inaccurate, then, to characterize American Puritan spiritual autobiography solely or even primarily as a private religious exercise. Often, the narratives were delivered as part of public ritual, such as a foundation meeting. Frequently, what was happening in the church community encouraged the composition of a narrative. For example, Winthrop's exchanges with Roger Williams and his opposition to Anne Hutchinson prompted him to examine the course of his religious life.[56] Occasionally, the narrative became an organ for technical expositions of questions of grace and justification that had no proper place in the genre of spiritual autobiography. An author's ability to balance self-scrutiny and theological argumentation determined his success as a Puritan autobiographer.

Quaker Journals

Quaker autobiographical writings also fared well in America. In America, as in England, Quaker journals satisfied the needs of both individuals and communities. The drive to self-expression was strong among Quakers: "Reliance upon the inner Light rendered them more introspective than many of their religious contemporaries; the habit of looking upon life as sacramental caused them to consider all acts of importance per se."[57] Their social status as a

---

[56] Ibid., pp. 102-106.

[57] Wright, p. 194.

religious minority in America also prompted Friends to write accounts of their experiences as a defense against the frequent attacks upon their beliefs. In sharing their experiences, they revealed the basic tenets of their belief. And Friends wrote to
edify other Friends, to instruct and to inspire them.

American Quaker autobiography conformed to literary conventions, well-established by 1700. A group mentality and a common set of experiences accounted for the high degree of conformity.
Shea's amusing comment makes the point: "With few exceptions,
Quaker journals were the autobiographical expression of Quaker
ministers, and taken as a whole they display the same tendency toward repetitive experience as might autobiographies of buffalo
hunters or retired generals."[58] The typical Quaker autobiographer
focused upon the process by which he came to submit to the Light
and the influence of the Light in his life subsequently. Regularly,
the authors acknowledged their intention to express gratitude for
God's graciousness toward them by narrating their experiences in
order that others might benefit. Unlike the Puritans, Quakers did
find peace in their religion. Quaker authors were free of the
preoccupation with sin that plagued Puritans.[59]

The Function of Spiritual Autobiography

Spiritual autobiography satisfied several personal objectives. The process of writing deepened the author's self-understand-

---

[58] D. B. Shea, p. 40.

[59] Wright, p. 199.

ing, forcing him to examine his life and determine its source of order and direction. Invariably, he found that religious beliefs provided him with the framework in which he interpreted his experiences. Indeed, religious beliefs often motivated him to write the account of his spiritual life. Autobiography was a confession of faith: the Puritan proclaimed the primacy of God's grace in his life and the Quaker testified to the presence of the Light in his life. Spiritual autobiography contributed to the spiritual growth of the author and that of his readers, who were encouraged to follow his example.

The community discovered paradigms of the spiritual life in these autobiographies. Autobiographies identified the acceptable pattern of the religious struggle and clarified the demands of faith.[60] In this way, autobiographies insured orthodoxy in faith and practice. The dialogue which the autobiographies engendered contributed to the vitality of the religious community: autobiography provided the author with an opportunity to expound his religious views and his readers responded in kind. In this way, spiritual autobiographies fostered the growth of a common religious culture and so promoted social cohesion within the believing community.[61]

---

[60]Morgan, p. 66; William Haller, The Rise of Puritanism (New York: Harper & Row, 1938), pp. 90-91, 127; D. B. Shea, passim; Watkins, pp. 30-31. For a discussion of the function of spiritual autobiography in nineteenth-century evangelical Protestantism, see Bruce, especially pp. 62-64.

[61]The interaction between the author and the community of believers in seventeenth-century England, which Watkins describes, was also evident in America. The authors of spiritual autobiography "knew who they were writing for: their friends and fellow worship-

Puritans and Quakers laid the foundation for the development of spiritual autobiography in America. Both Puritans and Quakers were deeply interested in the spiritual life and in religious experience; both manifested a missionary zeal in attracting adherents; and both recognized the function of autobiographical statements as paradigms of the spiritual life.[62] By 1800, spiritual autobiography was established as an American literary tradition.

Distinctive Characteristics of Spiritual Autobiography

Spiritual autobiography is a personal narrative which focuses upon the author's religious experiences: the awakening of religious sentiments, conversion, and the impact of the newly acquired religious faith upon his life. The "spiritual" component defines the genre's concerns and priorities: events and issues which bear upon salvation and which testify to the workings of

---

pers, all those who took a serious interest in personal religion, and all those on the fringe of church life who had not yet committed themselves. They read one another's stories with intense interest and concern, they discussed the problems of spiritual life and the implications which public debate on such matters had for the reputation of the Church in the world at large. They replied to criticisms and attempted to clear away misunderstandings. Above all they hoped to build one another up in the faith through the painstaking analysis and discussion of personal experience. A cohesive social life and a common culture are implied in all this activity with free interplay between writers and readers, the published material being only a fraction of the ongoing dialogue" (p. 31).

[62] Watkins notes that these factors contributed to the vigor of spiritual autobiography in seventeenth-century England. But these factors have been present during every period and in every social group in which spiritual autobiography has been popular (pp. 28-30).

grace in the life of the individual are central to the narrative,
and all other happenings are insignificant by comparison.

Three elements are essential to autobiography: a sense
of self-scrutiny on the part of the author, a review of a substantial portion of his life, and a deliberate shaping of his past.[63]
Spiritual autobiography requires yet another element: a focus
upon one's religious development. The self is understood in light
of the author's religious beliefs and values.

A sense of self-scrutiny is indispensable to the autobiographer: he must be "an aware self," self-conscious and reflective.[64]
"Autobiography presupposes a writer intent upon reflection on the
inward realm of experience, someone for whom this inner world of
experience is important."[65] The autobiographer must strike the
delicate balance between subjectivity and objectivity: he must be
present to himself as subject while also able to stand outside
himself. A sense of self-scrutiny requires that the author assume
a wholistic view of his life. In doing so, the autobiographer rises
above the narrow limits that characterize the work of the diarist.
The diarist reports the happenings of the day; the autobiographer
reviews countless experiences and events, discerning the pattern
of his life. Because the autobiographer works with a substantial
portion of his life, he must be selective in recounting his ex-

---

[63]Roy Pascal, Design and Truth in Autobiography (Cambridge:
Harvard University Press, 1960), p. 9.

[64]Weintraub, pp. 822-824.

[65]Ibid.

periences, always imposing order upon random happenings. By

shaping the past, he constructs a "coherent story."[66]

How an autobiographer sees his life depends on his stand-

point. Roy Pascal notes that the standpoint

> ...may be the actual social position of the writer, his acknow-
> ledged achievement in any field, his present philosophy; in
> every case it is his present position which enables him to see
> his life as something of a unity, something that can be re-
> duced to order.[67]

Religious faith defines the standpoint of the spiritual autobiographer.

Religion is "a particular sort of perspective, a particular manner

of interpreting experience."[68] Religious patterns are "frames of

perception, symbolic screens through which experience is interpreted;

and they are guides for action, blueprints for conduct."[69] The auto-

biographer who views his life in light of a religious system uses

religion as the ordering principle, the principle governing his

"selection of facts, distribution of emphasis, choice of expression."[70]

The question of grace dominates spiritual autobiography:

"whether or not the individual has been accepted into divine life,

an acceptance signified by psychological and moral changes which the

---

[66]Pascal, p. 9.

[67]Ibid.

[68]Clifford Geertz, Islam Observed: Religious Development
in Morocco and Indonesia (New Haven: Yale University Press, 1968),
p. 96. Also see his "Religion as a Cultural System: in Anthropological
Approaches to the Study of Religion, ed. Michael Banton (London:
Tavistock, 1969), pp. 204-215.

[69]Geertz, Islam Observed, p. 98.

[70]Pascal, p. 10.

autobiographer comes to discern in his past experiences."[71] The
author's concern with grace is not exhausted in a narrative of the
conversion itself; indeed, the conversion experience has not generally been the focal point within Protestant spiritual autobiographies.
Therefore, American Puritan and Quaker autobiographies ought to
be classed as narratives of conversion.[72] Puritan and Quaker authors
were concerned with the spiritual life as a whole, particularly
with the fruits of conversion. The effects of conversion were
deemed more significant than the conversion itself. Puritan theology viewed the spiritual life as an ongoing struggle and so conceived conversion as a beginning rather than an end. Quaker theology stressed the centrality of life lived in response to the Inner
Light; the process by which a Quaker discerned that Light within
himself did not dominate his account. In light of these theological perspectives, it was logical for authors of spiritual autobiographies to "extend the scope of their inquiry to include any experiences and events that might bear on their spiritual condition."[73]
Spiritual autobiography recounts the author's religious experience
during a substantial portion of his life.

The spiritual life is regularly portrayed in the metaphor Bun-

---

[71]D. B. Shea, p. xii.

[72]Ibid., p. xi. The same observation applies to British
spiritual autobiography. Shea would be likely to take issue with
Margaret Bottrall's designation of Bunyan's Grace Abounding as
a "conversion-narrative" on the grounds that Bunyan recounts a
life-long spiritual struggle (Bottrall, p. 4).

[73]D. B. Shea, p. xi.

yan chose: the battle between darkness and light, evil and goodness.
God's grace snatches man from the power of Satan. Grace effects
rebirth and transforms the individual's purpose and direction. The
centrality of grace reflects an emphasis on experiential religion,
an emphasis which favored the development of spiritual autobiography.

Spiritual autobiography is confessional writing in two
distinct senses: it is a personal confessio and it represents
an ecclesiastical confession. On the personal level, spiritual
autobiography reflects the double movement of confession: confessio
peccati and confessio laudis. The author confesses his own sinfulness, weakness, and unworthiness, and praises the Lord who has
forgiven his offenses and blessed him with the gift of faith. Confession provides an outlet for the deeply felt need to acknowledge
one's failures. The genre of spiritual autobiography may be viewed
as a written alternative to oral confession. The writing of spiritual autobiography is for many what it was for Augustine: an act
of repentance and an act of thanksgiving.

Spiritual autobiography is confessional insofar as it reflects a particular communal faith experience. The configuration
of symbols, myths, and doctrines that constitute a given theological perspective provide the framework for the self-examination that
is basic to spiritual autobiography. A primary principle of dif-
ferentiation in spiritual autobiography is that of confessional
commitments. Studies of British and American spiritual autobiographies have shown that two dominant confessional stances, Puritan
and Quaker, produced discernably different autobiographical work.

Ebner has explored additional differences in pattern among the writings of Baptists, Anglicans, and Presbyterians. Each denomination provided authors with a way of looking at reality and a guide for action.

The confessional stance filters reality; it acts as a lens through which reality is perceived. The beliefs and values of the group reflect a distinctive view of the world and of life. The experience of the individual is interpreted according to the conceptual framework provided by the faith community. That framework functions as a principle of order and meaning for the author. The faith community furnishes the writer with models against which he can define his individuality. For example, Puritan theological perspectives provided the believer with both map and measure:

> With a map in his hands that identified the main landmarks, he could plot his own tracks in relation to them in terms that were understandable to himself and to others, and the unique sequence of twists and turns showed that his route was an individual one. The Puritan life-pattern provided him with a stick to measure his growth against, so that the form, proportions, and outline of his spiritual life could be the more clearly discerned.[74]

Spiritual autobiography is social in nature and in purpose. It reflects the religious concerns of the community, its dominant symbols and teachings, and its theological perspectives. The author addresses the community, responding to its needs and interests. Although a spiritual autobiography tells of an intensely personal experience, it is a public statement which serves a function within the community. While strengthening both the author's and the

---

[74]Watkins, p. 56.

readers' commitments to the faith, spiritual autobiography also serves as a proselytizing device by enticing unbelievers to heed the testimony to God's grace.

The autobiographer publicly acknowledges that he shares a view of the world and a blueprint for moral action with other believers. In that sense, he aligns himself with a community, confessing that its symbols and perspectives enhance his self-understanding. He speaks as an individual, to be sure, but as one who is very much a member of the community. In a real sense, spiritual autobiography is a confession of commitment and allegiance to a community of believers.

Seventeenth and eighteenth-century American spiritual auto-biographies shared some fundamental likenesses in focus and structure and in purpose. The autobiographies focused upon the spiritual life as a whole. Theological perspectives and religious beliefs provided the framework in which life experiences were examined and understood. Authors wrote in order to increase their self-understanding as well as to edify their readers. Spiritual autobiography satisfied the author's need for self-expression and the community's longing for models of the life well lived.

Personal Narratives of Conversion

While seventeenth and eighteenth-century spiritual auto-biographers concerned themselves with the spiritual life as a whole, some nineteenth-century authors focused upon conversion. Evangelical revivalists, such as Peter Cartwright and Charles Grandison Finney, wrote accounts which served as paradigms of the conversion experience. Emphasis on conversion in autobiography was a by-product of the centrality of conversion in evangelical piety, theology, and ecclesiology.

Roman Catholic converts also centered on conversion in their autobiographical accounts of religious life. Their convert status no doubt contributed to their preoccupation with conversion. The circumstances which made the Roman Catholic Church in America the object of antipathy and derision also made it likely that Protestants would view becoming a Roman Catholic as a bizarre action at best. The convert's desire to explain and justify his move, coupled with his missionary zeal in wanting to attract others to the Church, motivated him to write an account of his conversion.

Nineteenth-Century Roman Catholic Autobiographical Writings

Louis Kaplan's Bibliography of American Autobiographies includes a total of forty-eight entries under the heading of "Conversions" for 1800-1900.[75] Of these, ten are autobiographical accounts written by converts to Roman Catholicism: Catholic Worship and Piety, Explained and Recommended in sundry letters to a very

---

[75]Louis Kaplan, A Bibliography of American Autobiographies (Madison: The University of Wisconsin Press, 1961). Kaplan lists a total of 6,377 works published up to 1945. He excludes journals, diaries, and collected letters, as well as episodic accounts and works in which the autobiographical element is insignificant. Two subject headings are especially pertinent to this study: "Conversion" and "Religious Experiences." None of the sixty-eight autobiographical writings listed by Kaplan under the latter heading for the nineteenth century was written by a Roman Catholic. This fact suggests that converts to Roman Catholicism were more highly motivated to write narratives of their conversions than Roman Catholics were to render general accounts of their spiritual lives.

near friend, and others. By Daniel Barber, A. M. and not long since
a Minister of the Protestant Episcopal Church in Claremont, State
of New Hampshire; Orestes A. Brownson's The Convert; or Leaves from
My Experience; L. Silliman Ives' The Trials of the Mind in Its
Progress to Catholicism. A Letter to His Old Friends; William
Richards' On the Road to Rome, and How Two Brothers Got There;
Clarence E. Walworth's The Oxford Movement in America; or, Glimpses
of Life in an Anglican Seminary; J. R. Buck's A Convert Pastor's
Autobiography; The Life and Letters of Eliza Allen Starr; Charles
Warren Stoddard's A Troubled Heart and How It Was Comforted At Last;
Leonard Sargent's Pictures and Persons; John Lawson Stoddard's
Rebuilding a Lost Faith.[76]

Wilfred Parsons' bibliography of works written by Catholic
authors and published between 1729 and 1830 includes three additional titles by converts: An Account of the Conversion of the
Rev. John Thayer, lately a Protestant Minister, at Boston, in North
America, Who Embraced the Roman Catholic Religion at Rome, on the
25th of May, 1783; written by himself; An Apology for the Conversion of Stephen Cleveland Blyth, To the Faith of the Catholic, Apostolic and Roman Church. Respectfully addressed to Protestants of
every denomination.; and Elizabeth Seton's Memoirs of Mrs. S****,

---

[76]J. R. Buck, A Convert Pastor's Autobiography (Huntington,
Ind.: Our Sunday Visitor, 1942); The Life and Letters of Eliza Allen
Starr, ed. James J. McGovern (Chicago: The Lakeside Press, 1905);
Leonard Sargent, Pictures and Persons (Washington: St. Anselm's
Priory, 1931); John Lawson Stoddard, Rebuilding a Lost Faith
(New York: F. J. Kennedy, 1923). See above, p. 4, for the facts
of publication for the accounts of Barber, Brownson, Ives, Richards,
Walworth, and C. W. Stoddard.

107

Written by herself. A Fragment of Real History.[77] Other works

bearing titles which suggest an autobiographical cast include:

Joshua Huntington's Gropings After Truth: A Life Journey from

New England Congregationalism to the One Catholic and Apostolic

Church; James Kent Stone's An Awakening and What Followed; Augus-

tine F. Hewit's "How I Became a Catholic"; Issac Hecker's Questions

of the Soul; B. W. Whitcher's The Story of a Convert, as Told to

His Former Parishioners after He Became a Catholic; Peter H.

Burnett's The Path Which Led a Protestant Lawyer to the Catholic

Church and The Reasons of J. J. M. Oertel, Late a Lutheran Minister,

for Becoming a Catholic.[78]

All of the works listed above are autobiographical, at least

in part. But not all of these works are narratives of conversion

and therefore not all are pertinent to this study. Two sets of

criteria determine which works ought to be considered: criteria of

content and of chronology. Generally, the study focuses upon nar-

ratives which chronicle a nineteenth-century conversion and which

were written and published during the nineteenth century. Excep-

---

[77]Elizabeth Seton, Memoirs of Mrs. S**** (Elizabethtown,
N.J.: Issac A. Kollock, 1817). For facts of publication for the
works of Thayer and Blyth, see above, p. 4.

[78]James Kent Stone, An Awakening and What Followed (Notre
Dame: The Ave Maria Press, 1920); Peter H. Burnett, The Path Which
Led a Protestant Lawyer to the Catholic Church (New York: Benzinger
Brothers, 1859); J. J. M. Oertel, The Reasons of J. J. M. Oertel,
Late a Lutheran Minister, for Becoming a Catholic (New York: Patrick
Kavanaugh, 1840). For facts of publication for the work of
Huntington, Stone, Hewit, Hecker and Whitcher, see above, p. 4.
A variety of bibliographic sources were used in order to
compile as complete a list of autobiographical works as possible.

tions are made when they serve the dual purpose of this study: achieving an understanding of the conversion narratives as a distinctive form of spiritual autobiography and broadening knowledge of the nature of the conversion experience of nineteenth-century American converts to Roman Catholicism. Therefore, John Thayer's narrative is treated at some length even though Thayer converted in 1783 and published his account in 1788. Thayer was one of the earliest, well-known American converts to Roman Catholicism and his autobiographical account was the first conversion narrative. The chronological parameters of this study exclude the writings of John Lawson Stoddard and Leonard Sargent. Stoddard's conversion occurred in 1922 and his narrative was published in 1923. Sargent became a Roman Catholic in 1909; his narrative was published by The Benedictine Foundation in 1931 as part of a series of historical monographs. J. R. Buck's autobiography also falls outside the nineteenth-century frame: although Buck's conversion occurred in 1895, his Convert Pastor's Autobiography was not published until

---

Kaplan's Bibliography is indispensable. Brother David's American Catholic Convert Authors: A Bio-Bibliography (Detroit: Walter Romig & Co., 1944) contains useful background information, but I found the information contained there inaccurate in several instances. A series of eleven Master's dissertations, entitled A Survey of Catholic Book Publishing in the United States, 1831-1900 (Washington: The Catholic University of America Photoduplication Service, 1960) and prepared by graduate students at The Catholic University of America, under the direction of Eugene P. Willging and James J. Kortendick, is a checklist of works written and published by Catholics. Two late nineteenth-century essays on American converts were also useful in assembling this list of autobiographical works: J. G. Shea, pp. 509-529; Clarke, 18: 539-561; 19: 112-138. No copy of The Reasons of J. J. M. Oertel has been located.

1942.[79] Kaplan erroneously includes these works in a listing of nineteenth-century autobiographical works.

The essential criterion is content. The critical question is whether a given work may be designated a conversion narrative. The obvious mark of a conversion narrative is its concern with conversion. With one exception, all the autobiographical works written by nineteenth-century converts to Roman Catholicism deal with conversion, explicitly or at lease implicitly. The Memoirs of Mrs. S**** constitutes the single exception. The Memoirs consists of approximately two dozen entries written by Elizabeth Ann Seton. All but two of the entries were made during the five weeks preceding the death of her husband on December 27, 1803. As may be expected, Elizabeth's thoughts fastened upon William's illness, his weakened state, and his impending death, as well as upon the circumstances in which she and the members of her family found themselves. The Setons had travelled to Italy in the hope that the climate there would be favorable to William's health. When they arrived, the entire family was quarantined because authorities feared that William was suffering from yellow fever. The Setons were released from quarantine only a week before William's death. The Memoirs testifies to Elizabeth's inner strength and determination and to her firm, constant faith in God, personal qualities which were well in evidence in her later life as a convert. But the memoirs were written prior to her conversion and do not anticipate it.

------

[79] For biographical information on Sargent, Stoddard, and Buck, see David, pp. 176, 196, 40-41.

Though her conversion contributed to the interest in Elizabeth Seton's life and so prompted publication of the Memoirs,
Seton intended her reflections to be private. Isaac A. Kollack,
publisher of the text, argues that the work was made public because
"on a perusal of the manuscript we were pleased, and struck with
an idea that it would be beneficial if given to the world."[80] The
subject matter of the work and the circumstances surrounding its
publication make it a unique piece in the body of autobiographical
works by nineteenth-century converts to Roman Catholicism, though
not a narrative of conversion.

The remaining works deal with conversion but not all are
conversion narratives. The Life and Letters of Eliza Allen Starr
is an editor's compilation of brief autobiographical sketches, diary
entries, and letters written by Eliza Allen Starr and of letters
written to Starr by frineds (including a considerable number written
by Frances Patrick Kenrick, Archbishop of Baltimore). Starr did
not write an account of conversion intended for the public but she
did describe the gradual process of her conversion in a letter
addressed to her cousins and in a brief autobiographical sketch
she wrote for the Starr family record. Her experience is similar
to that of other converts and so worth citing. In 1845, she heard
Theodore Parker deliver a sermon which shook her confidence in
her religious position:

> ...as sentence after sentence came from the lips of the renowned
> preacher, first a tremor, than an actual chill came over me,

---

[80] Issac A. Kollock, Introduction to Memoirs of Mrs. S****,p. 11.

as with smoothly flowing language, but irresistable logic, I
found him demolishing every foundation-stone of my religious
faith, and even hope. There was nothing left for me but to
find other premises, other starting-points, or forego all the
beautiful intellectual as well as spiritual life which had come
to me as a child from the sacred scriptures; the Old Testament
story of man, the New Testament story of a Child born to save
the world from its sins, Who was crucified, died, rose again
from the dead, ascended into heaven, from whence he will come
to judge the living and the dead -- all this I had believed on[81]
the authority of the Scriptures themselves....

The experience left her with a question: "What authority have I

for the faith that is in me?"[82] She found the answer in the Roman

Catholic Church almost ten years later.

The theme of conversion appears again and again in Starr's

letters, testifying to the centrality of the conversion experience

in her life. The letters which Starr received from Archbishop Peter

Richard Kenrick from the time of her conversion until Kenrick's death

in 1863 attest to her interest in the experience and example of other

converts. Kenrick's letters read like a veritable "Who's Who" of

America's converts to Roman Catholicism. Starr was herself a

prominent convert, respected for her contribution to art education;

she taught art, gave an annual series of lectures on the arts, and

organized the art department at St. Mary's Academy (which later be-

came St. Mary's College). She wrote numerous poems and essays for

The Catholic World, Ave Maria, New York Freeman's Journal, and the

London Monthly, as well as numerous devotional books.[83]

---

[81]Starr, p. 34.

[82]Ibid.

[83]For lists of Starr's publications, see Dictionary of
American Biography; David, pp. 191-192.

Starr was eminently qualified by experience and talent to write a detailed account of her conversion, as was Elizabeth Ann Seton. Both Seton and Starr were women of stature and accomplishment. Yet neither offered a public account of her conversion. Why? It is likely that the position of women in nineteenth-century American Catholicism precluded their participation in the religious controversies of the day. The men who wrote conversion narratives did so to meet social and religious obligations as well as to satisfy personal needs; most participated in the theological and ecclesiastical exchanges of the day. Apparently, neither Seton nor Starr, nor any other women converts, felt the need to justify or explain their conversions. Barred from the arena of religious controversy in pulpit and press, perhaps women were more likely to view religious belief and affiliation as a private matter.[84]

Apologetics, as motive and motif, regularly characterizes conversion narratives. But it is essential to distinguish between works which use the account of conversion to frame or introduce an apologetic treatise and works which center upon conversion. The former are not conversion narratives. Titles can be misleading. For example, both Peter Burnett and Levi Silliman Ives entitled their works in such a way as to suggest that they had described the circumstances of their conversions: The Path Which Led a Protestant Lawyer to the Catholic Church and The Trials of the Mind in

---

[84] It is significant that many women converts achieved prominence in the literary field, as poets and novelists. See David for a list of works written by Roman Catholic converts.

Its Progress to Catholicism. Ives wrote a conversion narrative;
Burnett did not. Ives sought to explain his departure from the
Protestant Episcopal Church to his friends. As he retraced the
process of conversion, he identified and explained articles of
belief that attracted him to Roman Catholicism as well as those
which caused him most difficulty. He wrote about these controversial issues in the first person and so constantly reminded his
readers that he was writing from personal experience. His purpose
was to explain the reasons for his conversion. Burnett briefly
recounted his attraction to Roman Catholic worship, his burgeoning
interest in Catholic thought, and an eighteen-month period of intensive study which culminated in his conversion to Roman Catholicism.[85] This autobiographical section is relegated to the preface
and takes up less than four pages. What follows is a lengthy, detailed apologetic treatise. Burnett's brief autobiographical statement reminds the reader that Burnett was a convert who himself perceived the truth and consistency of Roman Catholic doctrine. However, Burnett's primary intention is to demonstrate the truth of
Roman Catholic teaching. In so doing, he indirectly justified his

---

[85]Burnett, pp. v-viii. Peter Hardemann Burnett (1807-1895)
was born in Nashville, Tennessee. Although he had little formal
education, he read widely. After several of his business ventures
failed, he turned to the study of law and was admitted to the bar
in 1839. A pioneer in spirit and practice, he moved to Oregon where
he served as a member of the territorial legislature. Later, he
became chief justice and governor. Burnett resumed his law practice and was president of the Pacific Bank from 1863-1880. Burnett
converted to Roman Catholicism in 1846. (Dictionary of American
Biography; Dictionary of Catholic Biography; David pp. 42-43.

own conversion to Roman Catholicism. But autobiography remains
subordinate to the task of apologetics. The result of Burnett's
efforts is an apologetic treatise that appears to be a theological
counterpart to the briefs he prepared as a lawyer.

James Kent Stone also prefaced his apologetic treatise,
The Invitation Heeded, with a brief autobiographical account.[86]
But his goal was doctrinal exposition rather than self revelation.
He denied that he was writing to vindicate himself, saying that
he wrote in the hope that others, intrigued by his conversion might
recognize the marks of the 'divine Church.'"[87] Nevertheless, Stone
briefly outlined the experiences which led to his conversion. He began to question his long-standing prejudice against the claims of
the Roman Church; he experienced an intellectual crisis which came
upon him with "terrifying rapidity"; and he resolved to begin an

---

[86]James Kent Stone (1840-1921) was born in Boston; he
graduated from Harvard and studied at the University of Göttingen.
When he returned from Europe, he taught in Dixwell's Latin School
and served in the Union Army. In 1863, he was appointed an
assistant professor in Latin at Kenyon College; he became its
president in 1867. While at Kenyon, he pursued theological studies
and was ordained in the Episcopal Church. In 1868, he became
president of Hobart College. After his wife's death in 1869,
he resigned the presidency of Hobart. Stone entered the Roman
Catholic Church in December, 1869. He joined the Paulists and was
ordained a priest in 1872. After agreeing to the adoption of this
two daughters, he joined the Passionists, taking the name of Father
Fidelis of the Cross. He spent several years in Rome, served
as a missionary in South America, and held numerous positions
of leadership within the order (Dictionary of American Biography;
Dictionary of Catholic Biography; David, pp. 197-198).

[87]Stone, The Invitation Heeded, p. 31.

"impartial investigation."[88] Stone's conversion does not inform
the book; The Invitation Heeded is more appropriately classified
as an apologetic work than as a narrative of conversion.

Some fifty years later, Stone again recalled his conversion.
An Awakening and What Followed consists of an exposition of doctrinal
issues and a memoir of his life as a missionary. But the first
few pages which deal with conversion offer a striking contrast to
his first account. The second parallels and even includes entire
portions of the first but in the course of the second telling, Stone
distinguishes the personal transformation involved in conversion
from the change in affiliation which conversion effects. Stone
describes the personal transformation in mystical language which
identifies the conflict between the vision of something like "the
heavenly Jerusalem" and the voice within which shouted "Shut that
door!".[89] Stone concluded that the cry was either diabolical in
origin or the "cry of alarm from my sub-conscious self."[90] He
settled the conflict with an act of the will: "I made a resolve
-- a simple, intense resolve -- to be true, true to God, true to
my conscience, true to myself. It was all I could do."[91] His
conversion lay in that resolve; it changed his life. He struggled
with the doubts and questions stirred by that experience for more

---

[88]Stone, The Invitation Heeded, pp. 29-30.

[89]Stone, An Awakening and What Followed, p. 1.

[90]Ibid.

[91]Ibid., p. 3.

than a year before he became a member of the Church.[92] Stone's

later reminiscences on conversion are relevant to the study of

nineteenth-century conversion, but the book in which they are con-

tained is not a narrative of conversion.

Several nineteenth-century American converts to Roman

Catholicism wrote and published autobiographical accounts which

may accurately be described as narratives of conversion: Daniel

Barber, Stephen Cleveland Blythe, Isaac T. Hecker, Orestes A.

Brownson, Augustine Hewit, Joshua Huntington, L. Silliman Ives,

William Richards, Charles Warren Stoddard, Clarence E. Walworth,

and B. W. Whitcher. Late in the eighteenth century, John Thayer

published the first such narrative. The narratives exhibit a

common concern with conversion and so stand out as a distinctively

Catholic contribution to the genre of spiritual autobiography.[93]

---

[92]Stone was received into the Roman Catholic Church on
December 8, 1869. His wife died in February of that year and
he resigned the presidency of Hobart College at the end of the
same academic year.

[93]Conversion was also the subject of a series of autobiographical essays which appeared in The Catholic World, beginning in
July, 1887. These brief accounts exhibit the preoccupation with
conversion that characterizes the longer narratives. The typical
essay traces the author's conversion, beginning with a summary
of the author's earlier religious history and ending with a
charting of the path that led him to the Roman Catholic Church.
The essays were generally unsigned and usually bore simple titles,
such as "story of a Conversion" or "History of a Conversion."
For examples, see The Catholic World 45 (1887): 562-564, 708-710;
46 (1888): 559-562, 708-712; 47 (1888): 128-132, 271-274, 418-422;
49 (1889): 547-552; 50 (1889): 260-262; 50 (1890): 839-840.
The titles of somes essays reveal their distinctive thrust, such
as "A Young Girl's Conversion," "The Story of a Colored Man's
Conversion," and "How a Ritualist Became a Catholic (46 [1888] :
843-846; 47 [1888] : 562-565; 46 [1887] : 272-275).
The frequency with which such essays were published in

Characteristics of Conversion Narratives

The personal narratives written by nineteenth-century converts to Roman Catholicism constitute a distinctive form of spiritual autobiography insofar as the narratives focus on the experience
of conversion. Conversion functions as the principle of selection
in these narratives, determining what elements the authors include
and what elements they exclude. Though the number of conversion
narratives is modest (especially when compared with the prodigious
number of spiritual autobiographies brought forward by American
Puritans and Quakers during earlier centuries), their contribution
is impressive. The narratives grant the twentieth-century reader
an inside view of the process of becoming a Catholic in the nineteenth century and an understanding of what it meant to convert,
thereby shedding light on the experience of being an American
Catholic during the past century.

Personal narratives are in some ways similar to and in some
ways different from the prevailing pattern of spiritual autobiography. Like autobiographies, conversion narratives are works of
self-disclosure, characterized by an attempt at self-scrutiny on
the part of the author, an examination of a substantial segment
of his life, and a purposeful shaping of his past. The autobiographer moves beyond mere narration to the extent that he examines
his life, searches for the meaning of his experiences, and begins

---

the latter part of the century is evidence of their popularity and
suggests that they were found to be useful as didactic and inspirational literature. During the period from July, 1887 to March, 1891, twenty-eight conversion essays were published in The Catholic World.

to discern the pattern or principle of order in his existence. And so does the author of the conversion narrative. Autobiography begins with reflection upon the self and ends in revelation as does the narrative of conversion.

Like spiritual autobiography, the conversion narrative centers on the religious life, more specifically on the process of conversion. Life's meaning, order, and purpose emerge in a religious frame. The convert's newly-found beliefs inform the narrative just as they imbue his consciousness. The conversion narrative is a mode of confessional writing as is spiritual autobiography. Authors of conversion narratives confess their unworthiness, profess faith in God, affirm the truth of the Roman Catholic Church, and proclaim commitment to the Church.

A focus on the process of conversion distinguishes the narratives as a particular form of spiritual autobiography. What pertains to conversion is included and what does not is omitted. The authors of conversion narratives generally shun biographical details, choosing instead to concentrate on the conversion process: all that led up to the conversion and all that followed it. What precedes conversion is seen as a preface to it and what follows as its effects. Biographical details are judged to be insignificant unless they bear directly upon the spiritual life or provide the necessary ontext for discussing the spiritual life. William Richards, one of the convert authors, went so far as to say that he would not "inflict" his biography upon his readers.[94]

[94]Richards, p. 19.

What the author chooses to exclude from his narrative is often as telling as the details he includes. References to early religious history are frequently brief and sometimes so general as to be of little assistance in tracing the individual's religious progress. Their brevity reveals the convert's judgment that what really matters is newly-found faith; his past is of minimal concern. Although the narrative is a revealing personal document, it shares this characteristic with all autobiographical writing: it is an interpretation of experience expressed in part by a process of selection and elimination.

Conversion functions as the integrating principle of the narrative. Conversion establishes the author's standpoint, determining his psychological and intellectual horizon. The convert views his life in the light of conversion. It is "the convert" who examines and interprets the past and present and who recounts the history of his conversion. His account is never a mirror image of the happening itself; memory is the product of recollection and interpretation. The past is edited in light of the present; much is either forgotten or repressed. The conversion narrative is not simply about conversion in the sense that conversion is the subject of the narrative; the narrative testifies that conversion reshaped the author's life and radically altered his identity.

Apologia is a central feature of the conversion narratives. Convert authors tried to justify having become Roman Catholic by presenting the conversion as a reasonable course of action to a host of unsympathetic and even hostile readers. By tracing the

gradual and deliberate movement toward Rome, authors sought
to counter the criticism and disapproval of the community and thus
relieve personal pressure, generated by such opposition. Apologia
often turned into apologetic as authors moved from self-justification to a formal defense of the teachings and practices of the
Roman Catholic Church. Defending the Roman Church was indeed an
effective way of justifying the personal choice to become a member;
if the Roman Church was the true Church of Christ, it made sense
to have become a Roman Catholic.

Conversion as an Impetus to
Autobiographical Writing

Becoming a Roman Catholic meant experiencing an inner
transformation and a major shift in affiliation; it was both conversion and alternation and the two movements could not be separated.
When a person came to believe that the Roman Catholic Church was the
true Church, he was impelled to align himself with Roman Catholicism
publically. The narratives often explore the social significance of
conversion, the implications of religious alternation. The cost of
public profession was high; family and friends frequently severed
relationships with the convert. Because they met with widespread
opposition, narrative authors frequently fell prey to polemics,
which detracted from the quality of the narrative as an autobiographical work. Preoccupation with self-justification and exhaustive
attempts at defending the doctrine and ritual of the Church are not
conducive to a refinement of autobiographical consciousness. The
narrative authors generally neglected the inward journey and contented

themselves with retracing their steps to Rome. The very nature of conversion to Roman Catholicism in nineteenth-century America was an obstacle to the degree of self-revelation that characterizes spiritual autobiography at its best.

Converts fared better as a group than did born-Catholics in autobiographical writing. The fact that conversion narratives constitute the primary form of autobiographical writing in nineteenth-century American Catholicism is significant. Born-Catholics apparently did not feel the need to engage in self-justification though some wrote apologetic treatises which explained and defended the tenets of Roman Catholicism.[95] Roman Catholicism did not encourage the turn inward which led Protestants to write spiritual autobiographies, particularly in the seventeenth and eighteenth centuries. The Roman Catholic Church mediated man's relationship with God and dispensed grace; it claimed authority over personal judgment, defined correct teaching, and reserved for itself the right to interpret Scripture. Submission to the Church relieved persons of the countless uncertainties and doubts that plagued those who relied on private judgment. Uncertainty gives rise to self-examination; assurance seldom does. While converts professed that the Roman Catholic Church is the true Church and did so with certitude, they continued to experience tension and conflict which some sought to resolve by writing.

By the end of the century, conversion narratives comprised a

---

[95] For a survey of the apologetic literature written by Catholics in the United States between 1784 and 1858, see Robert Gorman, Catholic Apologetical Literature in the United States (1784-1858), (Washington: The Catholic University of America Press, 1939).

distinctive body of autobiographical writings. The literary conventions governing the narratives were in place: the typical narrative
began with a brief account of the author's religious history, detailed
his progress to Rome, and more often than not, explained some of
the most frequently misunderstood beliefs and practices of the
Church. Conversion narratives served author and readers (whether
they be Catholic or non-Catholic). The author aired his reasons for
becoming a Catholic; the non-Catholic reader achieved some understanding of the conversion and might even follow suit; the Catholic
reader was inspired by the Church's power to survive and thrive
in America as he received instruction regarding some of the essentials of Roman Catholic belief and piety.

CHAPTER IV

PERSONAL NARRATIVES OF CONVERSION:

ANALYSIS OF THE TEXTS

The narratives written by converts to Roman Catholicism yield valuable information regarding the process of becoming a Roman Catholic in nineteenth-century America and provide answers to a variety of questions. What attracted converts to the Roman Catholic Church? To what extent did dissatisfaction with Protestantism or with the Episcopal Church contribute to conversion? What were the obstacles to conversion? What was the experience of conversion like? How did it differ from conversion as experienced in nineteenth-century Protestantism? How did non-Catholics react to the conversion? Why did converts write about their experiences?

Each narrative bears the stamp of its author's individuality: his experience is uniquely his own. But as careful examination of each shows, the narratives share common elements: a focus on conversion, an attempt at self-justification, and explanation and defense of Roman Catholic belief and piety. The analysis of each work will include: a brief sketch of the author's life, a review of the structure and content of his narrative, and a discussion of his conversion experience. The purpose of this analysis is twofold: to gain an understanding of the way in which these authors experienced and perceived conversion to Roman Catholicism and to examine the development and function of the distinctive form of spiritual autobiography which they produced.

123

An Account of the Conversion of the
Reverend Mr. John Thayer

John Thayer was one of the first American converts to Roman

Catholicism and certainly one of the best known. He was also the first

to write a conversion narrative and judging by the numerous editions

published in America and abroad, it was indeed a popular account.[1]

John Thayer was born in Boston, Massachusetts on May 15, 1758

to an established Puritan family living "in easy circumstances."[2]

By his own admission, he was an unethusiastic student until he entered

Yale at the age of sixteen; he was awarded an honorary degree in

---

[1] John Thayer, An Account of the Conversion of the Reverend Mr.
John Thayer, Lately a Protestant Minister, At Boston in North-America, Who
Embraced the Roman Catholic Religion at Rome, on the 25th of May 1783;
Written by Himself, 5th ed. (Baltimore: William Goddard, 1788). The
Baltimore edition, reprinted from the London edition, was the first
printed in America. All references to the text of the narrative pertain
to the Baltimore edition. The 6th edition was printed by Bowen & Howard
of Wilmington, North Carolina in 1789. The narrative was reprinted in
Hartford in 1790 and again in 1832 and in Philadelphia in 1837. Mention
is also made of an 1840 printing in either New Haven or Hartford; no
copy of this edition is extant. Joseph Sabin cites the second
edition printed by J. P. Coughlin, No. 37, Duke Street, near Grovesner-
Square, London and sold by P. Byrne, Grafton-Street, Dublin in 1787 as
the oldest copy in existence. Sabin reports that he was unable to locate
a copy of the first edition. He enumerates five additional editions
reprinted in England, one in Spain, and four in Ireland; all were
in English. In addition, he cites five French and two German translations, along with translations in Latin, Portuguese, and Spanish.
For complete bibliographical information on those editions, see
Bibliotheca Americana: A Dictionary of Books Relating to America,
1934 ed., s.v. "Thayer (John)."

[2] Thayer, p. 3. Biographical sketches of John Thayer appear in
the Dictionary of American Biography, the Catholic Encyclopedia, and
the New Catholic Encyclopedia. Also see Richard H. Clarke, "A Noted
Pioneer Convert of New England: Rev. John Thayer, 1758-1815," American
Catholic Quarterly Review 29 (1904):138-166; Percival Marritt, Sketches
of the Three Earliest Roman Catholic Priest in Boston, (The Publications
of The Colonial Society of Massachusetts, vol. 25; reprint ed.,
Cambridge: John Wilson and Son, 1923), pp. 211-229; Arthur T. Connolly,
"Historical Sketch of the Rev. John Thayer, Boston's First Native-Born
Priest," United States Catholic Historical Magazine 2 (1889):261-273.

1779.[3] He was licensed as a Congregational minister and served as

chaplain under John Hancock, 1780-1781. Late in 1781, he sailed to

France to satisfy his "secret inclination to travel."[4] After a visit

to England, he travelled to Rome, where his desire to learn more about

Roman civilization awakened his interest in Roman Catholicism. His initial

investigation led him to acknowledge that Roman Catholic doctrine was

reasonable; he continued his study of Roman Catholicism and entered the

Church in 1783. John Thayer was ordained four years later after having

completed studies for the priesthood at the Seminary of Saint Sulpice

in Paris. He published the first edition of his narrative that same

year, 1787.

The biographical information contained in Thayer's narrative is

scanty. However, his briefly sketched personal history serves as a

frame for the account of conversion. He includes only that which is

essential to the story of his conversion and so covers the first twenty-

three years of his life in less than a half-page. The record of his

sojourn in Europe is more detailed, since his experiences in Europe

led to his conversion.

Late in 1789, Thayer returned to the United States where his

---

[3]Percival Merritt mentions reports of Thayer's allegedly dis-
graceful dismissal from Yale but argues that the story "appears to be
purely imaginative" since "it is highly improbable that he would have
received an honorary degree in 1779 if he had been dismissed in
disgrace the previous academic year" (p. 212). However, it is
obvious that President Stiles did not esteem Thayer. Stiles alluded
to Thayer's having begun his life in "Impudence, Ingratitude, Lying &
Hypocrisy." Ezra Stiles, Literary Diary, iii. 416, cited by Merritt,
p. 212.

[4]Thayer, p. 4.

narrative had already been in print for a year. Bishop John Carroll
assigned Thayer to assist Father Louis de Rousselet in Boston. It was
not long before Thayer judged that the French priest was ill-suited for
the American mission field. Thayer's letter to Bishop Carroll, written
just a few days after his arrival in Boston, sums up his response to
Rousselet:

> I...wish you to place Mr. Rousselet in another parish as soon
> as possible or he will be in some measure useless here on ac-
> count of his language; seems to be his own desire, as he has
> expressed it to another person tho' not to me....I pray you
> to do this speedily or his long & Tedious [sic] disposition of
> the exercises at chapel might be an obstruction to my zeal &
> to the good which I may produce in this place....I once more
> beg you not to put me in shackles by permitting any priest to
> officiate in the N. England States unless authorized by me.
> In this town especially one priest is sufficient at present.
> My reason for mentioning this so often is the fear lest reli-
> gion, which is at present at an ebb -- shall suffer from some
> intruder.[5]

Thayer went on to detail Rousselet's "long & Tedious" disposition of
chapel exercises. Thayer's letter leaves no doubt that he wanted to
establish himself as pastor of the Roman Catholic Church at Boston.
For his part, Rousselet was equally unimpressed with Thayer and
tried to retain his own following among the small Catholic population.[6]
At first, Thayer was well received by both Catholics and non-Catholics.[7]
But before long, relations between French and English factions became

---

[5]John Thayer to John Carroll, cited by Peter Guilday, The Life
and Times of John Carroll (Westminster, Md.: The Newman Press, 1954),
pp. 422-423.

[6]Laurita Gibson, Some Anglo-American Converts to Catholicism
Prior to 1829 (Washington, D.C.: The Catholic University of America,
1943), p. 112.

[7]Guilday, p. 423.

strained. In 1790, Thayer acquired the lease on the church, thereby dispossessing Rousselet.[8] When one of Rousselet's supporters died while Rousselet was on a mission visit among the Indians, his family requested the service of the Episcopalian, Dr. Samuel Parker, rather than permitting Thayer to preside at the funeral. When he returned, Rousselet offered Mass for the deceased in the Episcopal Church. In 1791, Bishop Carroll went to Boston to settle the dissension. Although the Bishop suspended Rousselet, he did not name Thayer the pastor of the church at Boston. While in Boston, Bishop Carroll wrote: "I am very sorry not to have a clergyman of amiable, conciliatory manners, as well as of real ability."[9] Thayer's "tactless zeal, his uncompromising Puritan spirit, his uneasiness under ecclesiastical restraint, and his egotism" prevented him from accomplishing what he had hoped for -- the conversion of America, beginning with the conversion of Boston.[10] Relieved of his duties in Boston, Thayer travelled about Massachusetts, Rhode Island, New Hampshire, and Connecticut, "lecturing, publishing, discussing and baptizing."[11] In 1793, Bishop Carroll sent Thayer to Alexandria where he attempted to build a church. But his anti-slavery position and his unrestrained zeal quickly destroyed his popularity. Thayer's eagerness "to convert the world overnight and...his devotion to fixed ideals" made it impossible for him to adjust and compromise.[12] Thayer was inflexible:

---

[8] Gibson, p. 114.

[9] Letter of John Carroll, 11 June 1791, cited by Guilday, p. 425.

[10] Dictionary of Catholic Biography, s.v. "Thayer, John."

[11] Gibson, p. 121.

[12] Ibid., p. 122.

the "aggressive Puritan had become the militant Catholic."[13]

Thayer visited towns in Canada, then worked in the Kentucky
missions from 1799 until 1803. But he found that he was unsuited for
mission work and retreated to Limerick, Ireland. Though he did not
return to the United States, he continued to work for the cause of
American missions, urging priests to go to the States, collecting funds
for the American missions, and working toward the founding of a religious
order for women in Boston.[14] He died in Ireland in 1815.

The conventional features of conversion narratives are already
present in Thayer's narrative. The focus is on the experience of conversion. Thayer alludes to his early religious history, identifies the
experiences which contributed to his conversion, and describes the
nature of the conversion event and its aftermath.

Thayer's references to his early religious history are few.
At the beginning of the narrative, he points out that he was brought
up in the Protestant religion, "the only prevailing and almost the only
known in New England," and that he became "a Minister of the Puritan
sect."[15] His references are general. It is clear that he assumed that

---

[13]Ibid., p. 118.

[14]Richard H. Clarke describes Thayer's work for the Church in
Ireland. Clarke's account tends to "canonize" Thayer; he portrays
Thayer as America's first great convert to American Catholicism. Under
Clark's pen, Thayer's limitations become virtues and his failures,
accomplishments: "Father Thayer was not a parish priest by vocation,
temperament, training or habit; he was an exceptional personage, suited
for good and great efforts and noble results, not in the way of the world,
but in the way of the Cross. His saintly character, with its indiosyn-
cracies, perhaps eccentricities, did not harmonize with men of the world"
("A Noted Pioneer Convert," p. 161).

[15]Thayer, pp. 3-4. The prevailing opinion is that although he
was licensed to preach, he was not ordained. Clarke disagrees; he

his readers would be familiar with the religious establishment of New

England. It is also evident that as convert, Thayer considered a more

detailed account to be unnecessary. This early religious experience was

only pre-history: what mattered was his conversion to Roman Catholicism.[16]

Thayer tells nothing more of his early experiences than that he

had acquired a strong antipathy toward Roman Catholicism, which had

been represented to him "in the most odious colours."[17] One incident,

recounted in the narrative, reveals the intensity of Thayer's aversion

to Roman Catholicism. When he became ill during a stay in France,

Thayer's first concern, as he remembered it, was to forbid that any

Catholic priest come near him.[18] Certainly, Thayer's inclusion of this

incident was purposeful: the episode emphasized the vehemence of Thayer's

fear of the Church and his contempt for all persons and things

Catholic. Such "unjust prejudice" was the legacy of Thayer's Puritan

upbringing. The literature of New England was rife with anti-Catholic

sentiment. Sermons, catechisms, and textbooks were replete with

condemnations of "Romanist" evils, as were diaries, pamphlets, and

almanacs.[19] New Englanders denounced the papacy and such Roman Catholic

---

maintains that Thayer was ordained in the Congregational Church ("A
Noted Pioneer Convert," p. 139).

[16]Most biographical accounts of John Thayer simply state that
his family was Puritan. The New Catholic Encyclopedia entry notes
that Thayer's parents were members of the First Church in Boston
and so Unitarians. But it is important to note that Unitarianism
did not emerge as a denomination until the early part of the nineteenth
century.

[17]Thayer, p. 4.

[18]Ibid.

[19]Arthur J. Riley, Catholicism in New England to 1788

practices as the sacraments, veneration of saints and angels, and the
use of images and relics.[20] Priests were viewed with hostility and suspicion: they were described as "sedition-mongers, immoral, avaricious,
ignorant, perverters of dogma."[21] Such thinking undoubtedly affected
Thayer's attitude toward Roman Catholicism and in the light of it,
his eventual conversion to Roman Catholicism appears all the more
astonishing.[22]

All in all, John Thayer's references to his previous religious
affiliation are vague. He speaks of "Protestant" attitudes, "Protestant"
friends, and "Protestant" teachings, frequently contrasting them with
Roman Catholic teaching. He observes that others judge him to be a
"determined Protestant" and he sees himself as one who thinks as
Protestants do.[23] Thayer simply identifies Protestantism with the
"standing order" of New England, that is, with the Congregational
Church. However, he does distinguish between the sectarians (such as
the Anabaptists and the Arminians) and Protestants. Throughout the

---

(Washington, D.C.: The Catholic University of America Press, 1936), p.
307. Riley gives a detailed account of "the moulding and development of
a hostile viewpoint in regard to various aspects of Catholic civilization"
in colonial New England (p. 307). Also see pp. 306-325.

[20]Riley, pp. 312-313.

[21]Ibid., p. 317.

[22]Thayer, p. 5. Clarke discusses the intense anti-Catholic
feeling in the colonies during Thayer's youth. He recalls that during
the colonial period, priests were tolerated only in Pennsylvania and
Maryland. He also points out that the celebration of "Pope Day" expressed anti-Catholic sentiment in ritual form: the Pope was burned in
effigy. Clarke argues that Thayer's early responses to Roman Catholicism
reflected the prevailing attitude of hatred toward Roman Catholics.

[23]Thayer, pp. 6-7.

narrative, Thayer refers to his former religious affiliation and experiences only when such reference serves the primary purpose of his account: telling the story of his conversion to Roman Catholicism.

It is likely that two other experiences affected Thayer's religious development: his time at Yale and his association with Dr. Charles Chauncy. Thayer could hardly have escaped exposure to the spirit of religious enthusiasm and controversy which characterized the atmosphere at Yale. By Thayer's time, churchmen at Yale had overcome their initial hostility toward the preaching of George Whitefield and other itinerant preachers of the Great Awakening and had begun to sympathize with the evangelical movement.[24] But Thayer did not comment on his experiences at Yale in his conversion narrative. Nor did he discuss his work with Dr. Chauncy. It is likely, however, that Dr. Chauncy is the "good teacher" to whom Thayer attributes his success.[25] Chauncy was pastor of Boston's First Church where Thayer's parents worshipped. It is probable that Chauncy mitigated Yale's influence on Thayer. Chauncy argued for the role of reason in religion. In 1743, when the fervor and furor generated by the Great Awakening was at its height, he wrote a critique, Seasonable Thoughts on the State of Religion in New England, in which he took issue with the unrestrained enthusiasm exhibited by the "awakened." Chauncy became an articulate spokesman for the reasonableness of religion, taking issue with the revivalist insistence that an experience of conversion was essential to salvation. His liberal religious thought must have affected the views of his student.

---

[24]Ahlstrom, p. 290.

[25]Thayer, p. 4.

Perhaps, it was because of his association with Chauncy that Thayer became

concerned with the importance of religious argumentation and the role

of reason in deciding religious issues.

The greater part of the narrative consists of an orderly exposition

of Thayer's progress toward Roman Catholicism. Here again Thayer is

highly selective, recording only those experiences which he considers

to be germane to his conversion. And it is always the convert who

selects and interprets his experiences. Thayer sees a hidden force at

work in his life: Divine Providence. Although it was only after his

conversion that he recognized God's grace at work in his life, he

interprets the past in its light. For example, while Thayer travelled to

Europe "to learn the languages which are most in use, and to acquire a

knowledge of the constitution of states, of manners, customs, laws and

government of the principal nations" in order to be of greater service

to his country, he later observes that "the secret designs of Providence"

were preparing "more specious advantages" for him.[26]

During his visits to France and England, he did study the

manners and customs of the peoples. And Providence was constantly

at work. His attitude toward Catholicism improved while he was in

France. Later, the warmth and generosity shown him by Italians in

Rome further reduced his antipathy for Roman Catholicism, leading him

to condemn "the unjust prejudices" which he had absorbed during his

youth.[27]

Intellectual curiosity stimulated Thayer's initial serious

---

[26]Thayer, p. 4.

[27]Ibid., p. 5.

interest in Roman Catholicism. He wanted to learn more about Roman
Catholicism while in Rome as he would have desired to explore "the
Religion of Mahomet" [sic] if he had been in Constantinople.[28] The
sights of Rome excited Thayer's religious imagination. When he beheld
the Pantheon, Thayer "was struck with an idea which appeared...sublime,
and which he thought might furnish the subject of an elegant discourse,
if the Catholic Religion were true."[29] He was intrigued by the fact
that the capital of the pagan world became the capital of the Christian
world: "it was worthy of God, to make the centre of idolatry, the
centre of the true faith."[30] Thayer was so pleased by the idea that he
wished it was true in order that he might preach it from the pulpit.
The idea appears to have been at least as pleasing to the Roman Catholic
priest who recorded it as it was to the Protestant viewing the Pantheon.

Thayer's interest in Catholicism was nurtured by his encounters
with priests with whom he discussed doctrinal issues. What he learned
about the uniformity of Roman Catholic teaching increased his dissatisfaction with Protestantism. Thayer concluded that the Protestant
principle of private judgment, which established each individual as his
own authority, precluded unity of faith. The lack of a "fixed rule of
faith" gave rise to "eternal contradictions of ministers among themselves,
and the frequent variations of each of them in their doctrine."[31] In the
end, the lack of agreement on the essentials of faith leads to "an

---

[28]Ibid., p. 6.

[29]Ibid., p. 5.

[30]Ibid.

[31]Ibid., p. 9.

indifference to all Religion, and saps the very foundation of
Christianity."[32]

The sojourn in Rome transformed Thayer in ways he had not
anticipated:

> ...at first I had only intended to form an exact knowledge of
> the Catholick [sic] doctrine, and I was insensibly come to such
> a state, that I discovered nothing in it but what was reason-
> able. When I began my inquiry, I had not the least suspicion
> that my own sect was false; I already found it deficient, and
> had my doubts, though I was very far from being determined to
> abandon it. The prejudice in which I had been educated had
> still too much influence over my mind, and my heart was not
> yet disposed to make the sacrifice which this change required.
> I thought I had done a great deal by resolving to take with me
> to America the best works of Controversy which had been written
> by Catholicks [sic] and to read them on my return, with a deter-
> mination of then changing my Religion, if after mature reflec-
> tion I could not answer their arguments: for I was resolved
> whatever proof was brought against me, not to make my adjura-
> tion at Rome, for fear of taking a precipitate step.[33]

Thayer makes it clear that conversion was as much an affair of the

heart as it was a matter of the head. The developments which brought

him to the brink of conversion appealed to both head and heart.

First, Thayer came upon a book on the Guardian Angel by Father

Segnery, which awakened Thayer's devotion to his own angel.[34] He

resolved to act in a manner pleasing to his angel, that is, to pre-

serve himself from sin. In retrospect, Thayer concluded that this

resolution removed an obstacle to the graces God would bestow in

conversion.

Thayer's interest in the miracles attributed to the Venerable

---

[32] Ibid.

[33] Ibid., p. 10.

[34] Ibid.

Labre also hastened his conversion. Thayer felt compelled to examine the evidence for the purported cures. After careful investigation, he was unable to discount the "supernatural" nature of the cures and to dispel the thought that he was placing himself in jeopardy by remaining in his sect. The thought plunged Thayer into a "violent state": "Truth appeared to me on every side; but it was combated by all the prejudices which I had sucked in from my infancy."[35] Thayer was, at this point, what William James would a century later call a "divided self":

> I clearly saw that the church of Rome is established on innumerable and unanswerable proofs, and that her replies to the reproaches of Protestants are solid and satisfactory; but I must abjure errors in which I had been brought up, and which I had preached to others. I was a minister in my own sect, and I must renounce my state and fortune: I was tenderly attached to my family and I must incur their indignation: Interests so dear kept me back: In a word, my understanding was convinced, but my heart was not changed.[36]

Reading a book entitled, Manifesto di un Cavaliero Christiano convertito alla Religione Catholica, intensified Thayer's interior struggle and so forced its resolution. The book began with a prayer imploring the enlightenment of the Spirit. Thayer desired that enlightenment and yet feared that he would not receive it. Nevertheless, he brought himself to say the prayer and the result was tumultuous: "the violent agitation of my soul, with the conflicts it had sustained, drew from me an abundance of tears."[37]

---

[35] Ibid., p. 12.

[36] Ibid. See James, pp. 143-159.

[37] Thayer, p. 13.

He read the book and experienced conversion: "God spoke to my
heart, at the same time that he enlightened my understanding, and
gave me strength to surmount the obstacles which had hitherto re-
tarded me."[38] Before he had finished the book in its entirety,
Thayer exclaimed: "My God: I promise to become a Catholick [sic]."[39]
That very day, Thayer announced his intention to become a Catholic,
first to the family with whom he lodged and then in a public announcement to his Protestant friends, who were gathered at a coffee house.
He invited his friends to a public abjuration.

Before his abjuration, he was still troubled by the homage
Catholics paid to the Blessed Virgin and the saints. He resolved
his difficulties through prayer and an act of trust in God. Thayer
argued that if a person acts in good faith, he cannot be deceived in
his choice of religion, especially "when, after exact watchfulness
over his own conduct, after fervent prayer, after long and toilsome
investigation, he determines to embrace it at the expense of all that
is most dear to him on earth, -- family, state, fortune, reputation."[40]
It is an argument which falls back on trust in God's mercy toward the
individual who follows his inner lights, rather than an argument which
one might expect from a newly converted Catholic -- namely, recourse
to the authority vested in the Roman Catholic Church.

Thayer viewed his conversion as a radical transformation:

---

[38] Ibid.

[39] Ibid.

[40] Ibid., p. 15.

What difference between my present and former state! My
thoughts, my taste, my views are wholly changed; I do not know
myself again. As soon as I had taken my determination, I
renounced the profane studies in which I had been hitherto
employed; I left my books half read; I parted with those which
belonged to me. From that time my passions have had little
influence over me; my projects of ambition and settlement in
the world are entirely laid aside. I have no pretensions on
earth: I take no pleasure but in the things of God: I feel
within my heart, a peace which I had bever known; not, as formerly, the deceitful security of a stifled conscience, which
presumes on the mercy of God, without seeing the danger to
which it is exposed: It is the sweet confidence of a child
who finds himself within the arms of a Father, and has reason
to hope that nothing can tear him from them, notwithstanding[41]
the dangers with which he is surrounded.

Thayer was certainly not given to understatement, nor was humility

his strongest virtue. Without hesitation, he attributes radical

changes in personality and demeanor to his conversion. Restraint

in statement or in action did not come easily to John Thayer. Having

tasted the "sweets which are felt at the foot of the Alter," Thayer

did not hesitate to direct his energies to becoming "the instrument

of the conversion" of his countrymen. In a final burst of enthusiasm,

Thayer proclaimed his willingness to seal his faith with blood, certain

as he was that God would grant him the strength for martyrdom.

The reader of Thayer's narrative is left with the picture of

a man intent upon drawing others to his way of thinking. Thayer

believed that America was ripe for the harvest and he was ready to

reap. Thayer's narrative, a public confession of faith in the truth

of Roman Catholic teaching, was meant to aid in that harvest of souls.

Thayer wrote for "the edification of Christians, and for the greater

glory of God" to whom he was "indebted for the light and life of

---

[41]Ibid.

grace."[42]

The narrative reveals Thayer's interior life only in the most general terms. The reader easily glimpses Thayer's dedication. The very existence of the narrative testifies to those qualities. But Thayer does not reveal his inner self. Perhaps he was unable to do so. John Thayer was a complex person whose unrestrained zeal prevented him from achieving success as a Roman Catholic clergymen. It is unlikely that he himself realized why his auspicious beginnings in Boston and elsewhere failed to come to term. He was a man given to action rather than introspection and he was impatient, inflexible, and uncompromising in his religious convictions. In her study of early Anglo-American converts, Sister Laurita Gibson explores the paradox of Thayer's personality:

> The convert is proverbially more demonstrative in his zeal than the born believer. Men who have undergone great mental trials, whose solution of life's problems has been attained at a cost, will not, and perhaps cannot live on the surface of being. The Reverend Mr. Thayer's early religious struggles led him to provoke controversies and to create hostility instead of to stimulate calm and peace.[43]

And his personality "with its idiosyncracies and eccentricities did not harmonize with those of other men."[44] But this complexity of character is not revealed in Thayer's narrative.

The narrative does chart Thayer's progress to the Roman Catholic Church. Intellectual inquiry brought Thayer to the Church and drew

---

[42] Ibid., p. 16.

[43] Gibson, p. 133.

[44] Ibid.

him inside. But Thayer is quick to insist that reason alone does not effect conversion. God acts upon the convert and grants him the strength necessary to make the commitment to the Roman Catholic Church. Thayer's conversion involved a process of study, reflection, and personal struggle. But it also entailed an emotional upheaval. The aftermath was what Thayer perceived to be a radical personal transformation.

Thayer's narrative is important because it is the first. The pattern of Thayer's work reappears in the nineteenth-century narratives with little variation. Such differences as do occur reflect the particular situation in which the author finds himself and his own idiosyncracies.

An Apology for the Conversion of
Stephen Cleveland Blythe, to the Faith of the
Catholic, Apostolic and Roman Church

Stephen Cleveland Blythe's narrative is the sole source of biographical information readily accessible to the contemporary reader.[45] Blythe's name is absent from standard Catholic reference works.[46]

---

[45]An Apology for the Conversion of Stephen Cleveland Blythe, to the Faith of the Catholic, Apostolic and Roman Church. Respectfully Addressed to Protestants of Every Denomination (New York: Joseph Denoues, 1815). The Montreal edition is entitled A Narrative of the Conversion of Stephen Cleveland Blyth [sic], to the Faith of the Catholic, Apostolic and Roman Church, To Which Is Annexed, A Brief Refutation of the Current Objections to Many Articles of Catholic Faith and Discipline (Montreal: Nahum Mower, 1822). References to the text generally pertain to the New York edition. Differences between the texts of the two editions are noted below.

[46]Blythe's name does not appear in the Dictionary of Catholic Biography, the Catholic Encyclopedia, or the New Catholic Encyclopedia, either as Blythe or Blyth (as it is spelled in the Montreal edition). American sources show a preference for the latter spelling, that is,

And references to Blythe among Church historians are sparse. John

Gilmary Shea makes brief mention of Blythe in an essay on American

converts:

> Men of all creeds and of none began to look to the Church as
> the real haven of rest, -- men like Stephen B. Blyth, who
> had examined and studied even Mohammedanism, but found all
> built on hay and stubble, till he came to the true Church
> founded on the rock, the whole system logically coherent,
> worthy of the Most High, and evincing such a knowledge of
> human wants and misteries [sic] that, compared with all others,
> it must be divine.[47]

Shea focuses on Blythe's brief exploration of "Mohammedanism" to

exemplify the variety of religious backgrounds from which converts

came to the Church. But Shea apparently relies on the information

contained in the narrative. Blythe's name is included in Richard H.

Clarke's listing of prominent American converts, but no additional

biographical information appears there.[48]

The historians' apparent neglect of Blythe is understandable.

First, Blythe was not active in the American Catholic Church. He

settled in Montreal shortly after his conversion. In fact, his narra-

tive seems to comprise his entire contribution to the Church in the

United States. Second, he did not remain in the Church; he aposta-

---

Blyth. For the sake of consistency, his name will be spelled as
it appears in the New York edition of the narrative, that is, Blythe
(except in references pertaining to the Montreal edition).

[47] J. G. Shea, p. 516.

[48] Clarke, "Our Converts," p. 543. Clarke cites the New York
edition, published in 1815. He identifies Blythe as a man "who
studied many religious, even mastering Mohammedanism [sic]" (Our
Converts, Part II," p. 133). Clarke does not include Blythe
among the converts whose experiences he describes at greater
length.

tized.[49]

Blythe's Apology consists of two sections. The first is a
brief summary of his life prior to his conversion and a record of
the experiences which culminated in his conversion. The second contains a discussion of the marks which distinguish the Roman Catholic
Church as the true Church and a refutation of charges commonly levelled
against the Church by those outside it.[50] In the Montreal edition, the
text is formally divided into the "Biographical Part" and the "Controversial Part."

The substance of the biographical sections is essentially the
same in both editions. Differences are for the most part confined to
phrasing and appear to be a matter of style. The Montreal edition is
more polished than the earlier American edition. For example, in
the New York edition, Blythe speaks of Bishop Cheverus of Boston as one
who "possessed the language of the country in perfection and thundered
it from the pulpit with the eloquence of a Paul."[51] The Montreal
edition makes the point this way: Mr. Cheverus "had acquired a critical
knowledge of the English language, and preached to the delight and
edification of all who heard him."[52] Another instance of editing occurs
in Blythe's depiction of Harvard College. In the New York edition, he

---

[49]Gorman, p. 36.

[50]Blythe, p. 4.

[51]Ibid., p. 16.

[52]Blyth, p. 21.

remarks that "a general laxity of morals prevailed" at Harvard.[53] In

the Montreal edition, Blythe simply describes Harvard University as

"the first literary Institution, in age and renown, upon the Ameri-

can Continent," noting that John Quincy Adams was his fellow-

student.[54] Perhaps that revision was as much prompted by an eager-

ness to improve the author's status and credibility as by the desire

to achieve a more felicitous style.

The Canadian edition does contain some facts and reflections

which are not found in the American edition but none are essential

to the account of Blythe's conversion.[55] Segments of the narrative

which pertain to Blythe's religious experiences are almost identi-

cal in the two editions.[56] Only one item pertaining to Blythe's

early religious life is recorded in the first edition and omitted

from the second: Blythe's attendance at some revival meetings sponsored

by the Methodists in Salem.[57] Blythe reports that he was not saved.

Perhaps that is why no reference to the meetings appears in the later

edition or maybe Blythe had decided that Canadians were not interested

---

[53]Blythe, p. 5.

[54]Blyth, p. 7.

[55]For example, in the Montreal edition, Blythe speaks of medical
studies (pp. 7-8), his involvement in the theater (p.9), his experiences
in France (pp. 10-11), and his marriage (p. 17); Blythe also introduced
some thoughts on the religion of nature (p. 9) and some observations on
the French Revolution (p. 20) in the Montreal edition.

[56]Compare pp. 7-13 of the New York edition. Both recount Blythe's
search for religious truth in a variety of Protestant sects and in
Islam. There is only one point of difference: in the Montreal edition,
Blythe mentions his early fascination with Theophilanthropy, a version of
Deism popular in France (p. 12).

[57]Blythe, p. 4.

in American religious revivals. The Montreal edition also fails to
mention that Blythe suffered a "melancholy disorder" shortly after his
arrival in Canada.[58]

Finally, the statement of purpose in writing the narrative
differs in the two editions: the first presents the task of writing
the narrative as a matter of personal responsibility; the second,
as a matter of social accountability.

> My conversion to the Catholic Faith, having been a subject of
> remark and speculation, I owe it to truth, as well as to my
> reputation, to impart the motives which prompted this change.
> I have among Protestants, the whole circle of my relatives,
> whose good opinion I highly appreciate. I wish them to recog-
> nize in the following recital, every trait of artless sin-
> cerity, diligent research and cautious deliberation, which
> can justify me to myself and to the impartial world. Happy
> should I be, if in the conviction that I have chosen the better
> part, they would add the ties of religious union to those of
> private friendship.[59]

Self-justification and the desire to convert others initially motivated
Blythe to write the narrative. But the parallel statement in the
revised edition cites the convert's obligation to offer a rational
account of his action as the primary motive for writing the narrative.

> Whenever a Citizen finds it a duty to change his Religion,
> he owes it in deference to public curiosity, so generally ex-
> cited, to impart the motives which prompt his secession from
> his native communion.
> I hasten to acquit myself of this obligation -- and I
> trust that my readers will recognize in the following recital
> of my conversion to the Catholic Faith, every trait of artless
> sincerity, diligent research and cautious deliberation, which
> a measure connected with Salvation should so imperiously re-
> quire. [60]

---

[58]Ibid., p. 20.

[59]Ibid., p. 3.

[60]Blyth, p. 5.

The second parts of both editions of Blythe's narrative are concerned with issues of Catholic teaching and practice. Although some passages appear verbatim in both texts, the two editions are substantially different.[61] In the New York edition, Blythe considers three major points: the marks by which the Roman Catholic Church is identified as the true Church of Christ, a refutation of charges levelled against the Roman Catholic Church (which in part consists of an explanation of teachings and practices frequently misunderstood by non-Catholics [idolatry in the Mass, in the veneration of the Blessed Virgin, saints and angels, in images and relics; the power of the priest to forgive sins; purgatory; the practice of withholding the Eucharistic cup from the laity; the "splendour and magnificence" of the "general economy" and public worship of the Church; use of the Cross; the teaching that out of the Church there is no salvation; and charges concerning the objectionable behavior of some Catholics and Catholic priests as well as the charge that the Church has been inimical to the development of knowledge and culture]), and the errors of Protestantism. Regarding the latter point, Blythe argues that the religious choice comes down to opting for Roman Catholicism or Deism, for faith or reason. The Protestant sects, which lie between the two, are beset by "inconsistencies and incongruences on every side."[62]

---

[61] For example, the section on confession in the Montreal edition (pp. 43-44) corresponds to the discussion of confession in the New York edition (pp. 33-34), as does a good portion of the discussion of purgatory (Montreal edition: pp. 53-54; New York edition: pp. 36-37).

[62] Blythe, p. 60.

Blythe begins the "Controversial Part" of the Montreal edition by observing that it is ironic that anti-Catholic sentiment has indeed contributed to conversions. Converts are struck by the incongruence between the Church as it has been described to them and the Church as it really is and thus they are attracted to it. Blythe makes a personal profession of faith, based on the Nicene Creed, to which he appends articles of faith essential to Roman Catholicism. In the following section, he argues that since the Church is necessary insofar as it makes the saving act of Jesus Christ available to man, the Church must be identifiable. The Church can be known by its marks: it is one, holy, catholic, and apostolic. These marks are not found in the vast array of Protestant sects. Blythe also defends aspects of Catholic doctrine and practice: tradition, sacraments, miracles, the necessity of forms of worship, the use of Latin, the practice of celibacy, and the teaching that outside the Church there is no salvation.

The differences between the apologetic sections of the two editions are not confined to content or structure; they extend to style as well. In the first edition, Blythe engages in simple, popular discussions of Roman Catholic issues. He cites Scripture passages, church fathers, and theologians sparingly. His arguments in defense of Catholic teaching and piety suggest his lack of theological sophistication; his apologetics are homespun, ideal for the layman. But the Montreal edition bears the mark of some careful revision, designed to reinforce the apologetic; references to Scripture are more numerous and the teachings of the Council of Trent are cited with some frequency. The second edition quotes two popular apologists of the

day, namely J. B. Bossuet and R. Challoner, and excerpts selected explanations of Catholic teaching by Dr. Johnson, a renowned Protestant
controversialist, in the attempt to demonstrate the reasonableness
of Roman Catholicism.[63]

A comparison of the two editions raises the question of authorship. Did Blythe himself revise the narrative before it was published
in Montreal? There is some reason to question that he did. First,
it is to be expected that such revision would be acknowledged and
explained or, at least, that the author would take the opportunity
to announce a second edition of his work. Second, there is a noticeable difference in the tone of the two editions. The New York edition
is rough and unrefined; it appears to have been written at a single
sitting. The Montreal edition is cautiously phrased and restrained in
tone. It is possible that the Montreal edition was revised by an
editor who sought to increase its impact as an apologetic work. Such
reasoning accounts for the changes in the biographical section of the
narrative, but it does not itself explain the substantive additions to
the controversial section of the Montreal edition, which surpass the

---

[63]A case in point: "Purgatory (says Dr. Johnson) is a very
harmless doctrine. They (the Catholics) are of the opinion that the
generality of mankind are neither so obstinately wicked as to de-
serve everlasting punishment, nor so good as to merit being admitted
into the Society of Blessed Spirits; and therefore God is graciously
pleased to allow of a middle state,where they may be purified by
certain degrees of suffering. 'There is nothing unreasonable in this,'
-- He adds, 'If it be once established that there are souls in
Purgatory, it is as proper to pray for them, as for our brethren of
mankind who are yet in this life.' In fact, this tenet is so consonant with Reason as well as Scripture, that a vast number of intelligent Protestants have avowed their belief in it" (Blythe, p.
54).

apologetic section of the first edition in scope and depth. A certain resolution of the question of authorship is impossible given the lack of information about Blythe's experiences during the period, 1815-1822. But it appears likely that Blythe revised the narrative in light of his growing concern with apologetic issues. The American edition sets forth the story of his conversion and responds to the questions and criticisms which the newly-converted Blythe viewed most important. Seven years later, his concerns were those of the insider, engaging in an exposition of standard apologetic arguments. A polished narrative was itself a useful apologetic tool. Given Blythe's eventual apostasy, it is possible that his revision of the narrative was an attempt to structure an even more convincing rationale for remaining a Roman Catholic. Blythe tells that he became a member of the Congregation of the Blessed Virgin in 1814 but the date of his apostacy is unknown.

In the course of his Apology, Blythe provides his readers with a brief biographical sketch.[64] Stephen Cleveland Blythe was born in Salem, Massachusetts in 1771. He was baptized in the Episcopal Church. At the age of eleven, he was enrolled at Philips Academy at Andover. In 1786, Blythe began his studies at Harvard. Before the end of his first year, his mother fell ill and Blythe returned to Salem where he began medical studies in 1798.[65]

Four years later, having completed his formal education, Blythe

---

[64]Unless otherwise indicated, all the following references pertain to the New York edition.

[65]Blythe gives the reason for his return in the Montreal edition (p. 7).

moved to Charleston, South Carolina, where he practiced medicine and spent his leisure hours reading and writing poetry. Before long, he succumbed to the temptations that surrounded him and set aside "those solid maxims of piety and prudence" which were part of his New England heritage, abandoning serious reading, prayer, and even public worship.[66] In 1794, he sailed to the West Indies and on to France in the following year.[67] In 1797, he moved to England where he took a position at an academy in Kensington, near London.[68] During the next two years, Blythe examined the tenets of a variety of religious groups, searching for a consistent and credible set of religious teachings and practices. His search was fruitless. He served on the Hospital Staff of the Army until 1801 when he was commissioned to travel to the West Indies. Blythe's first-born son died during that passage. Overwhelmed with grief, he sought comfort in religious reading and prayer. Blythe worked in hospitals in the West Indies and established a "Charitable Institution" in Martinico (Martinique) for the care of destitute children.

Poor health prompted his return to Boston in 1805. There he resolved questions concerning the Roman Catholic Church which had preoccupied him for several years. The Reverend Mr. John Cheverus, who

---

[66]Ibid., p. 6.

[67]The Montreal edition contains a few more details about his life during those years abroad. Blythe served as an officer in the French army. He was assigned to hospital work in Brest and later lived in Paris. In 1796, he was sent to the United States to deliver dispatches; he visited with relatives in Massachusetts and returned to France.

[68]The Montreal edition mentions his marriage to Miss Kingsley of East Middlesex in 1799.

149

later became Bishop of Boston, and the Reverend Dr. Francis Anthony
Matignon assisted Blythe in his study of Roman Catholicism.[69] After
Blythe returned to Salem, he continued to correspond with Mr. Cheverus
for four years. Blythe converted to Roman Catholicism in 1809, ending
more than a decade-long search for religious truth. Shortly thereafter,
Blythe and his family moved to Canada where he established a medical
practice. The move to Canada reflects his desire to live in an environment that would "fortify" the influence of the faith.[70]

The biographical framework serves as the structure of organization in the narrative, providing the background against which Blythe
discloses his religious history. There are two levels on which the
disclosure takes place. The first is expository: Blythe recounts
the events and experiences which he judges to have been significant
in his religious development and which culminated in his conversion.
The second level is interpretative: Blythe reveals his understanding
of what occurred in his religious life. He communicates his understanding through his selection and ordering of events and experiences
which he considers essential to his story.

Blythe refers to his early religious experiences very briefly.
He was baptized an Episcopalian. However, since the local Episcopal
Church was closed during the Revolutionary War, as were most Episcopal
churches, his family worshipped with the Congregationalists until their

---

[69]John Cheverus (1768-1836), French-born priest, was named
Boston's first bishop in 1808. Francis Anthony Matignon (1753-1818),
also a French-born missionary assigned to Boston by Bishop Carroll,
served as an aide to Bishop Cheverus.

[70]Blythe, p. 19.

church was reopened in 1783. Early in his life, Blythe came into contact with the longstanding Calvinist heritage of New England. His first
reading was the Westminster Catechism, the "compendium of Calvinistic
doctrines then generally adhered to in New-England [sic]."[71] He
recited it along with the other children in the congregation. Blythe
records no reaction to that early exposure to Calvinism, except to
mention that while he was in Charleston, he lost sight of "those
solid maxims of piety and prudence" that he "brought with him from
New-England [sic]."[72] He "lost all relish for serious reading and
prayer -- and in a short time neglected public worship."[73]

Blythe reports an awakening of religious sensibility during
adolescence. While at St. Phillip's, he read Bunyan's Pilgrim's
Progress and Harvey's Meditations. The former inflamed his imagination,
the latter "charmed" him with "the glitter of their stile [sic], and
their useful moral."[74] Young's Night Thoughts, recommended to him
by his Grandmother, impressed him profoundly: "It presented me with
new and more exalted views of the government of God, and the final
destination of Man."[75]

At the age of nineteen, he moved to Charleston and re-read
Young. But he failed to escape the "snares" of the world; he lost

---

[71] Ibid., p. 4.

[72] Ibid., p. 6.

[73] Ibid.

[74] Ibid.

[75] Ibid., p. 5.

sight of the pious practices of his youth.[76] Reading Thomas Paine's

Age of Reason caused him to break with his past by overturning "the

whole fabric" of his religious belief with "a single blow."[77]

Blythe became a convert to Deism.[78] The spirit of rationalism that

informed France reinforced Blythe's deism. Nevertheless, Blythe's

"infidelity" was short-lived.

During his late twenties and early thirties, Blythe engaged in

a religious quest that led him to examine a variety of religious

groups: Moravian Brethren, Universalists, Society of the New Jerusalem,

Quakers, and Unitarians or Socinians. He explored each in turn and

found each unsatisfactory. The "notions of faith" espoused by the

Moravian Brethren seemed "wild and incoherent" to Blythe.[79] The

doctrines of the Universalists, he judged to be "untenable by any who

adhered to the plain text of scripture -- it was solely supported by

some detatched passages, obscure and equivocal."[80] Swedenborg's New

Jerusalem fared no better with Blythe: there was no authority with

which to support Swedenborg's pretensions."[81] The "nudity of Quaker

worship displeased him, and the doctrine of the "Divine Light within"

---

[76]Ibid., pp. 5-6.

[77]Ibid., p. 6.

[78]In the Montreal edition, he reflects on that conversion: "The Religion of Nature, in my estimation, afforded sufficient sanctions for every purpose of moral government; and I considered all supernatural Revelation superfluous, devised by priestcraft, and addressed to the fears of man" (p. 9).

[79]Blythe, p. 8.

[80]Ibid.

[81]Ibid., p. 9.

Blythe deemed to be merely a rephrasing of the belief in conscience as "our soul [sic] interior guide."[82] The Socinians maintain that reason is the only guide and yet deny and affirm doctrines without consistency, denying the virginity of Mary and the incarnation and divinity of Christ and affirming the miracles recorded in Scripture.[83]

These explorations seem to have been motivated by intellectual curiosity. But the experience which followed awakened Blythe's religious sentiment. It was the reading of Doddridge's Rise and Progress of Religion in the Soul during a confinement due to illness. The work, he says, was "of a high Calvinistic cast" and "written with much pathos."[84] This book aroused fear and trembling within him and he resolved to dedicate himself to God if he re-covered from his illness. The attitudinal shift is striking: religion is no longer presented primarily in intellectual terms but is now clearly a matter of feeling as well. His quest had ended in disappointment: "I saw on every side clusters of sects which claimed divine truth as exclusively their own, while the Bible served them all as a vast armoury [sic], from which they supplied themselves with weapons, and waged an interminable war against each other."[85] Another shift is evident: the disappointment is expressed in logical terms: all the sects claim the one Truth, yet all give different renderings of that Truth.

---

[82]Ibid., pp. 9-10.

[83]The mention of Mary suggests that Blythe is re-examining Socinian teaching from his perspective as a Roman Catholic convert.

[84]Blythe, p. 11.

[85]Ibid., p. 11

153

Blythe explicitly states that he never considered the "Catholic Faith" during this time. He had heard Rev. John Thayer preach in Salem but was unmoved.[86] While in London he had attended a Catholic chapel, "attracted by the music, and not by the doctrine."[87] Anti-Catholic prejudices, acquired during his youth, prevented him from conceiving that any truth could be found in that "sink of idolatry and corruption."[88]

Frustrated by his fruitless search among the Christian sects, he began to study Islam, or "Mahometanism," as he called it. This was a brief curiosity, for when Blythe wrote to the Turkish Ambassador concerning his desire to take instruction, he received an "unmeaningful" reply, grew ashamed of this project, and abandoned it."[89] Deism again appeared to be the only alternative available to him.

The turning point in Blythe's religious search came with the death of his first-born son. In his grief, he found himself without hope, without the comfort of belief in the afterlife. So Blythe resolved again to re-examine the evidence of Revelation and to perform "without faith, the works of faith" and he began a program of religious reading and prayer.[90] Two years later, in 1803, Blythe experienced what

---

[86] In the Montreal edition, he writes that he admired Thayer's "eloquence, but was indifferent to his theme" (p. 16).

[87] Blythe, p. 12.

[88] Ibid.

[89] It is curious that Blythe's brief encounter with "Mahometanism," the account of which occupies but a paragraph of the text, was the aspect of Blythe's quest that drew the attention of nineteenth and early twentieth-century Catholic historians.

[90] Blythe, p. 13.

might be called a first conversion. He dedicated himself to God
formally; he read his "Covenant," signed and sealed it. Blythe does
not describe the content of that Covenant. It is clear, however, that
it was a personal act of faith in God and that it occurred outside
the auspices of any denomination or sect. Blythe worshipped within
the Church of England at this time, but he had already begun to make
serious inquiries concerning Roman Catholicism. As a result of his
reading of Massilon's Sermons, Blythe began to question the validity
of his long-standing negative impressions of Catholicism.

When he returned to Boston in 1805, Blythe was ready to make
formal inquiry into the teaching of the Roman Catholic Church. For
the next four years, he read and studied. He also corresponded with
the Reverend Mr. Cheverus. Blythe maintains that he scrupulously
examined every article of Catholic doctrine. Teachings, concerning
transubstantiation, purgatory, Mary and the saints, relics and images,
and above all the Trinity, caused him difficulty.[91]

Blythe describes his conversion to Roman Catholicism as an
act of submission:

> ...after an obstinate contest I began to give way, and in a
> short time afterward announced my surrender, and proposed to
> enter directly into fellowship with the Catholic Church....
> At every step in this important enquiry, more and more light
> was shed upon my path; and I at length perceived that to resist
> any longer, were [sic] wilful and unpardonable obstinacy.[92]

---

[91] In the Montreal edition, Blythe recalls that he also found
it difficult to abandon some "anti-Catholic" tenets: the "Fate" of
Seneca, the "Predestination" of Jonathan Edwards and the Calvinists,
and the law of "Philosophical Necessity" proposed by Dr. Priestley
and the Socinians (p. 22).

[92] Ibid., pp. 18-19.

His conversion occurred when there was simply nothing else for him to
do. He had explored the teachings of diverse religious groups. None
satisfied him. He had deliberately pondered the articles of the
Roman Catholic faith until he could no longer resist. Then he surrendered. Blythe represents his conversion in negative rather than
positive terms: it is not fulfillment but submission.[93]

Though Blythe carefully recounts the chronology of events, he
fails to reveal the inner dynamics of his conversion. He catalogues
his religious adventures instead of subjecting them to careful scrutiny.
The reader hears only that Blythe converted to Roman Catholicism because he found in it the consistency that he sought and because he
felt that he had no other option.

Blythe's Apology is a narrative of conversion. The fact of his
conversion is indeed the focus of his narrative. His conversion functions
as the principle of selection. All that is included in the narrative
bears upon the process by which he came to be a member of the Roman
Catholic Church. Even the apologetic section, which is appended to
the autobiographical account, is part of the convert's statement and
evidence that he wishes to present the Roman Catholic teaching and
practice which he has adopted in a favorable light. The purpose of
Blythe's narrative is what the title of the New York edition suggests --
apology, defense of his submission to the Roman Catholic Church and
defense of its truth.

---

[93]This is not the experience of some of the other convert authors,
notably the Episcopalians who converted at mid-century. Walworth, Hewit,
and their colleagues argued that they became converts because they found
the fullness of Christianity in the Roman Catholic Church.

Blythe's narrative is, for the most part, similar in form and tone to that of John Thayer. The only notable difference between the two is Blythe's extensive discussion of Roman Catholic issues. In other ways, the two narratives are alike; they even share the same flaw. Neither Thayer nor Blythe probes nor analyzes his life story; neither has learned the art of self-scrutiny. The result is narrative which falls short of spiritual autobiography at its best. These narratives focus on the outer frame of events in the authors' lives. They merely hint at the dynamics of the inner life.

Neither Thayer nor Blythe assumed important positions in the American Catholic Church. Thayer never achieved the success which he sought as a Roman Catholic priest. He is well-known as a result of his narrative, but he is known because of the fact of his conversion rather than because of his contribution to the Roman Catholic Church. And, for all practical purposes, Blythe never lived as a Catholic in America. He sought refuge in the Catholic milieu of Montreal. But even in such a predominantly Catholic environment, his convictions were shaken and he eventually left the Church.

The value of the narratives lies in what they disclose about the passage from New England Congregationalism to Roman Catholicism. Thayer and Blythe grew up in similar religious environments, created by the "standing order" of New England. Both travelled abroad where childhood prejudices against Roman Catholicism were called into question and interest in Catholicism was aroused. Both converted after lengthy periods of study and reflection. Thayer and Blythe found intellectual satisfaction in Roman Catholicism. In that, they represent the experience of other converts to Roman Catholicism in the late eighteenth and early nineteenth centuries: "far from being regarded as the result of an emotional reaction, the conversion was seen to be the <u>intellectual</u> acceptance of a creedal statement."[94]

<u>Catholic Worship and Piety,</u>
<u>Explained and Recommended</u>

The text of <u>Catholic Worship and Piety</u> consists of an introduction which summarizes the reasons why Daniel Barber acknowledged that the Roman Catholic Church is the true church, a narrative of his conversion to Episcopalianism and to Roman Catholicism, assorted letters, his farewell address to his Episcopal congregation, and a "Paper of the late Dutchess of York," describing her conversion to Roman Catholicism.[95] Such a compilation of materials has resulted in a loosely structured text. What structure there is comes from the conversion focus. The varied inclusions are unified by this common concern: Barber's desire to explain why he changed his religion and why others ought to follow his example by carefully examining the Roman Catholic religion. As the title suggests, he sought to explain and recommend Catholic worship and piety. <u>Catholic Worship and Piety</u> is, in part, a conversion narrative.

Daniel Barber focuses entirely upon his later religious history in the narrative. He provides his readers with additional biographical

---

[94]Gibson, p. 221. Gibson maintains that in the period prior to 1829, most converts to Roman Catholicism came from the New England and Middle Atlantic States, where the largest number of immigrants had settled. "Contact with these immigrants and with Catholic principles led to their investigation" (p. 221).

[95]<u>Catholic Piety and Worship, Explained and Recommended, in Sundry Letters, to a Very Near Friend, and Others.</u> By Daniel Barber, A. M. and not long since a Minister of the Protestant Episcopal Church in Claremont, State of New Hampshire (Washington City: E. De Krafft, 1821).

details in The History of My Own Times, a popular history of life

in New England, filled with personal reminiscences.[96] Daniel Barber

was born in Simsbury, Connecticut on October 21, 1756 to a prominent

New England family. The Barbers were Congregational Dissenters.[97]

Religious discussions were commonplace in the Barber home and Daniel's

parents were well versed in defending their beliefs with appropriate

Biblical texts. Religious observance was strict, as required by the

Standing Order. Laws governing the observance of the Sabbath, were

especially rigid. Even the activities of children were severely

restricted on the Sabbath:

> ...small children were not allowed either to walk abroad in
> fields or gardens, or to gather grapes or any kind of fruit,
> excepting such things as were necessary for the kitchen. If,
> in case of necessity, they were sent to the field, they were
> charged to walk softly and make no noise. Children, of course,
> took but very little pleasure in being told it was Saturday
> night, and that they must stop their play and go to bed early.
> Sunday morning drew a darkening veil over every countenance,
> changing and distorting the natural cheerfulness of the face
> of man to an appearance in itself sullen, morose, and forbid-
> ding; which indeed, was a comfortless addition to the relent-
> less confinement and thraldom of the day. It was the wish
> and design of parents, by this mode of sanctifying the Sabbath,
> to bring children to the love of religion and the Bible; and,
> also, to prepare their minds to receive the outpourings of the
> Spirit, which, as was commonly supposed, had its periodical
> influence or visitation among them.[98]

No doubt, this environment had its influence upon young Daniel, as did

---

[96]Daniel Barber, The History of My Own Times (Washington City:
S. C. Ustick, 1827). For additional information on Daniel Barber and
the Barber family, see the Dictionary of Catholic Biography, the
Catholic Encyclopedia, and the New Catholic Encyclopedia. For a detailed
account of the conversion of the Barber family, see Gibson, pp. 195-219.
Also see Clarke, pp. 114-116; J. G. Shea, pp. 517-518.

[97]Barber, Catholic Worship and Piety, p. 28; The History of
My Own Times, p. 6.

[98]Barber, The History of My Own Times, p. 6.

another early experience. His father was taken into custody and
prosecuted for attempting to attend the meeting of a religious sect;
he was found guilty of "a breach of the Sabbath" and was fined.[99]
Barber also came into contact with strong anti-Catholic sentiment,
which prevailed in New England; Popery was feared and Catholics were
despised.[100] But none of these experiences find a place in the
conversion narrative.

Little is known of Barber's early adult life, except that
he served as a soldier in the Continental Army. At the age of
twenty-seven, he became an Episcopalian and three years later, he
was ordained a minister. He held appointments at Scanticook, New York;
Manchester, New Hampshire; and Claremont, New Hampshire.[101] Some thirty
years later, he was again troubled by questions regarding the true
religion, questions he thought he had resolved when he became an
Episcopalian. After much reading, reflection, and discussion, he
resigned his position in the Episcopal Church and followed other members
of his family into the Roman Catholic Church. Two years later, in
1821, he published Catholic Worship and Piety. He died in 1834,
a resident of the House of the Society of Jesus at St. Inigoes,
Maryland.

Daniel Barber experienced two conversions during his lifetime. The dynamics of the two experiences were quite similar. In
the explicitly narrative section of Catholic Worship and Piety, Barber

[99]Ibid., p. 10.

[100]Ibid., pp. 17-18.

[101]Gibson, p. 198.

outlines the process of thought that brought him first to
the Episcopal Church and then to the Roman Catholic Church. It
was the issue of the true priestly authority that caused him to
question his religious position as a Congregational Dissenter.
An Episcopalian neighbor, whom he identified as D.P., questioned
the "true sacerdotal authority" of Barber's minister and gave
Barber a book which argued for apostolic succession of the priesthood.[102] Barber was unable to rebut D.P.'s contention. And Barber
found his minster unwilling to even discuss the issue with him.
A public debate on the question of congregational succession between
the same D.P. and a Dissenter brought the issue to a head for
Barber; the Dissenter was unable to defend his position and the
Episcopal minister did not even participate in the debate. That
was the turning point for Barber: he felt "compelled to quit a
society, whose ecclesiastical authority or Priesthood was of such
a nature" that neither he nor his fellow churchmen were able to
defend it.[103] Despite his strong intellectual conviction, he
hesitated. Separating himself from the Dissenters meant breaking
with family and friends: "To separate from them and form a religious
connection with strangers, was such a trial as excited me and awakened
many tender feelings, which I have not forgotten to this day."[104]
After a year's reflection, he joined the Church of England and later was
ordained a minister. It was not an easy course to follow. The Episcopal

---

[102] Barber, Catholic Worship and Piety, p. 28.

[103] Ibid, p. 30.

[104] Ibid.

Church was unpopular in New England during Barber's time: "To be
a church-man there was at least a sort of disfranchisement in the public
esteem."[105]

Twenty years passed before Barber was again troubled. Once
again, the issue concerned valid ordination. Barber read a book
which questioned the validity of Episcopal ordination. The case under
discussion was the ordination of Archbishop Parker. The author
alledged that when Queen Elizabeth was unable to find a Catholic
bishop who would consecrate Matthew Parker, she herself empowered
William Barlow to perform the consecration. This "unlikely passage"
forced Barber to reconsider the validity of his own ordination.[106]
He wrote to a fellow clergyman concerning the issue but received
no reply.

So Barber addressed his questions to a Catholic priest, the
first he had ever seen.[107] The priest, the Rev. Dr. Cheverus, later
Bishop of Boston, answered Barber's questions satisfactorily and
lent him books explaining the Catholic religion. Barber says
nothing about the internal dynamics of his conversion. Nor does
he mention the earlier conversion of his son, his wife, or other
members of his family.[108] He merely says that he bid farewell to
his congregation with pain and a sense of loss. His last address

---

[105] Ibid., p. 31.

[106] Ibid., p. 32.

[107] Ibid.

[108] Barber, The History of My Own Times, Part II, pp. 19-20.

to the congregation reveals the cost of his decision.[109] He left

behind a circle of friends, people whom he knew well and cared for

deeply.

Which came first -- Protestantism or Catholicism? That was the

critical question for Barber. If Protestantism, then how could one

account for the apparent innovations in Catholic doctrine and practice?

Barber posed the question this way:

> Now, if Protestancy, which allows of but two sacraments, was
> the religion taught by the Apostles, and the established reli-
> gion, I ask any man to judge by what means five new sacraments,
> never heard of in the time of the Apostles, could afterward
> have been imposed upon the church, and rendered articles of
> faith, with greatest difficulty, without clamor, noise, and
> the most stubborn opposition? The thing is almost incredible.[110]

The Catholic religion, he concluded, was the most ancient. Its practices,

the sacraments, the mass, auricular confession, clearly prove that it

was the Church as "made and constituted by Jesus Christ."[111] And when

he was convinced that the Roman Catholic Church was the true Church,

he had to become a Catholic for his eternal salvation required it:

"Nothing could have tempted me to change my religion, but a full

conviction of the danger and risk I must run of losing my future life,

and that world to come, in which dwells righteousness."[112] The

Catholic faith is the most ancient religion, "the only one sanctioned

by Jesus Christ, its divine founder, and the only one, too, to which he

---

[109]See Barber, Catholic Worship and Piety, pp. 35-37.

[110]Ibid., p. 6.

[111]Ibid., p. 5.

[112]Ibid., p. 10. Barber identifies this motive for his conversion in the first letter included in the text.

has promised the Holy Ghost, and a permanent continuance to the end of the world."[113]

The letters which comprise a substantial part of <u>Catholic Worship and Piety</u> reveal other aspects of Catholicism which Barber found attractive: its unity and the stability and comfort which it offered. The first three letters deal explicitly with doctrinal aspects of the Roman Catholic religion; these are apologetic in tone and intent. The letters identify issues that Barber considered to be particularly important for himself and for other potential converts. The Roman Catholic Church is the true Church; the Church is one. Unlike Protestants who are divided by their practice of individual interpretation of Scripture, Catholics are unified in their understanding of the faith. The Catholic Church will endure despite persecution. In fact, those who suffer persecution for the sake of the Church will be rewarded for all eternity as the example of the martyrs shows. Despite the trials it endures, the Church offers its members a secure haven.

Roman Catholic teaching was also a source of personal comfort for Barber. The Church's firm belief in the promise of Resurrection was especially meaningful to him because he had experienced bereavement at the death of his youngest child, a son not yet three and a half years old. His letters of condolence reveal his sensitivity to persons who have experienced similar losses. Roman Catholicism afforded comfort and hope to the bereaved. The dead will rise again as Jesus Christ did. The bonds between the living and the dead are not severed.

---

[113]Ibid., p. 14.

Barber assures a father that his deceased daughter has not forgotten
him: "according to Scripture and the Primitive church, there, still
inspired by that charity which never fails, she is praying for her
parents, her nearest friends and relatives on earth, perhaps for me!"[114]
What is more, the living are not powerless either. They are urged to
pray for the dead, as pious people have done even before the time of
Jesus Christ. That these letters of condolence are included in the
text of Catholic Worship and Piety is revealing: the piety of the Church
is a source of strength and solace. What drew Barber to the Church
was not simply a set of carefully reasoned arguments but also the
appeal of a faith that provides support in the face of life's crises.

But the promise of life after death does not erase death's
terror not its threat. The moment of death is the moment of reckoning,
the time of judgment. The thought of death reminds a person of his
responsibilities. In the final letter, Barber advises Miss A. to take
account of death:

> Reflect often on death; it may be near, and on that world to
> which we are hastening. Give only small portions to amuse-
> ments, and be careful to bring back with you an innocent mind.
> Never go abroad without first repeating the Apostle's [sic]
> creed and Lord's prayer. Be thoughtful in the midst of your
> pleasures, and from those things which are short and fleeting,
> collect something which may be durable. When you dance, forget
> not the last dance, the dance of death; as also sickness, old
> age, and the last groans on a dying pillow. When dancing,
> reflect how many have danced before you, and who are now
> mouldering in the dust, or perhaps in their last agonies.
> Never forget to pray, "Lord Jesus have mercy on departing
> souls."[115]

No one can escape death; no one knows the hour of its coming.

---

[114] Ibid., p. 28.

[115] Ibid.

Therefore, the pious man and woman are always prepared; the salvation
of their eternal souls requires it.

The appended letters show that piety is a strong motive for
conversion. Barber emphasizes the comfort to be derived from the
Church's teaching on the immortality of the soul. The Church encourages prayers for the dead and in this way offers meaningful and
effective solace to the bereaved. Thoughts of death ought to bring
anyone contemplating conversion into the Church for who can afford
to risk the damnation of his eternal soul? The Roman Catholic Church
is a source of strength and stability: the Church is one and the
convert can rely on the truth of its teaching.

In light of the content of the letters, purposefully appended to
the narrative, it is significant that the narrative per se focuses on
the truth of Roman Catholic claims, emphasizing that the Roman
Catholic Church is the Church of Christ. Once Barber established that
to his satisfaction, he had no choice but to convert. Conversion
became a matter of intellectual integrity and, more important still, the
way to eternal salvation. To knowingly refuse to join the Church,
once a person has perceived its truth, is to risk damnation.

An examination of the early narratives, written by Thayer,
Blythe, and Barber, shows that the experiences of these converts
were similar in several respects. For all, conversion to Roman
Catholicism was a gradual process set in motion by dissatisfaction with
the teachings and practices of the convert's former religious community,
intellectual curiosity about the Roman Catholic Church, and the desire
to affiliate with the true Church of Christ. Although the personal
and social costs of conversion were high, becoming a Roman Catholic

was the way to salvation. The narratives serve two purposes: they provide the authors with a forum for self-explanation and they furnish a vehicle for defending the truth of Roman Catholicism. The narratives blend together personal testimony and apologetic.

The Narratives of Brownson and Hecker

During the 1850's, three converts published accounts of their conversions to Roman Catholicism: Orestes A. Brownson, Isaac T. Hecker, and Levi Silliman Ives. Ives' account, The Trials of a Mind in its Progress to Catholicism appeared in 1854. A year later, Hecker's Questions of the Soul was published and, in 1857, Brownson published The Convert; or, Leaves From My Experience. It seems appropriate to postpone the discussion of Ives' narrative in order to consider him along with other Episcopalians who made their way to the Church during the forties and fifties and to turn to the works of Hecker and Brownson.

Isaac T. Hecker and Orestes A. Brownson stand out among the convert authors. They are linked together not only by their deep friendship but also by a striking parallel in experience. Both were original thinkers who grappled with religious questions as though each was the first to ask the question. Both sought a religion consonant with human nature. In the course of his search, each covered some of the same ground. And each, in turn, concluded that Roman Catholicism was the religion he had sought; Hecker decided that Roman Catholicism met man's deepest human needs and Brownson discovered that being a Roman Catholic did not diminish a person's exercise of reason in even the slightest way. But each was a unique individual, who approached the Roman Catholic Church in his own way; this their narratives show.

Questions of the Soul

Isaac T. Hecker did not write a typical narrative of conversion -- replete with reminiscences of early religious history and details of experiences that led to his becoming a Roman Catholic. He recorded the story of his religious development in his diaries and in correspondence with friends and family. His first biographer, Walter Elliott, notes that Hecker once thought of writing the history of his conversion and even set down some thoughts on the subject and collected letters and other memoranda for the purpose.[116] But Hecker never wrote such a history. What he did write was Questions of the Soul. Questions of the Soul is not a first person account. The few passages in which Hecker explicitly speaks of the change he underwent in becoming a Catholic are phrased in the first person plural, "we."[117] The contrast between the restraint that marks his public writings and the impassioned tone of his private papers is striking. Nevertheless, a study of personal narratives on conversion by nineteenth-century American converts would be incomplete without a discussion of Hecker's Questions. In that book, Hecker does what he said Brownson did in The Convert: Hecker leads us "step by step, through the very processes of his own actual experience."[118] The book is autobiographical:

---

[116]Walter Elliott bases his biography of Hecker on information contained in those private papers. See The Life of Father Hecker (New York: The Columbia Press, 1891; reprint ed., New York: Arno Press, 1972).

[117]In a diary entry made on the day on which he was baptized by Bishop McCloskey, August 1, 1844, Hecker uses the pronoun "we": "We know not why it is we feel an internal necessity of using the plural pronoun instead of the singular." Cited by Elliott, p. 176.

[118]Isaac T. Hecker, "Dr. Brownson's Road to the Church,"

it traces the process of thought and feeling by which Hecker became
a Roman Catholic.[119] Even though Hecker cites the thoughts of numerous
literateurs and philosophers, ancient, modern, and contemporary, it is
his own story that he recounts. The questions which he poses are the
questions of his own soul; the answers he sets forth are the answers
which ultimately satisfied him. The text is at once a personal
confession and public apologetic. Insofar as the focus of Questions
of the Soul is the result of the process of thought by which Hecker
became a Roman Catholic, there is good reason to view the work as a
type of conversion narrative.

Isaac Thomas Hecker was born in New York City in 1819, the
third son of John and Caroline Hecker.[120] For some years, his father
operated a brass foundry. When that business venture failed, financial
difficulties forced Isaac to interrupt his education and seek employment.
During the early years of his adolescence, he prepared mailings for the
Methodist Book Concern, worked at a type foundry, and finally joined
his brothers in a bakery business. Even as a young boy, Isaac was
conscious "of having been sent into the world for some special purpose."[121] At the age of fourteen, he met Orestes Brownson, who was then

---

The Catholic World 46 (1887):3.

[119]Vincent F. Holden observes that the first part of Questions
of the Soul is "almost autobiographical, with each chapter revealing
different periods in the author's life." I maintain that the autobiographical cast marks the whole book. The Yankee Paul: Isaac
Thomas Hecker (Milwaukee: The Bruce Publishing Co., 1958), p. 188.

[120]For brief biographical sketches, see the New Catholic
Encyclopedia and the Dictionary of Catholic Biography.

[121]Elliott, p. 8.

lecturing in support of the Working-Men's Party.[122] Hecker's involvement in politics had begun a few years before when he actively
participated in meetings and worked at polling booths.[123] He continued
to be active in politics for the next few years. Political action
was for him a natural outgrowth of his social concern. But in
June, 1842, Hecker came to a turning point in his life: he shifted
his attention from politics and social reform to the pressing question
of the destiny of man and more particularly his own destiny.[124]

> A new life, a new world had suddenly burst upon his conscious-
> ness. It mystified him, it distressed him. He could not un-
> derstand it nor explain it to himself, much less to others....
> He had suddenly become aware, how or in what way he does not
> reveal, of the only True Reality, God. Aside from this, every-
> thing else was meaningless and empty for him.[125]

In effect, a "new self" was being born. The experience was unsettling,
even bewildering. Vincent F. Holden, one of Hecker's biographers, goes
so far as to describe the experience as "a violent and abrupt twist."[126]
Hecker's family did not understand what was happening to him. His
mother thought that he was experiencing a typical religious awakening
and that he would soon be all right.[127] But he became more distressed
and fell ill. In December, 1842, he turned to Orestes Brownson for

---

[122]For Hecker's recollections of those days, see "Dr. Brownson
and the Workingmen's Party Fifty Years Ago," The Catholic World 45
(1887):200-208.

[123]Elliott, pp. 12-22.

[124]Holden, p. 25.

[125]Ibid.

[126]Ibid., p. 26.

[127]Ibid., p. 29.

advice. Brownson urged him to go to Brook Farm and Hecker did so in
January, 1843. Brook Farm provided Hecker with the time and the atmosphere conducive to soul-searching. Oddly enough, it was at Brook
Farm that he began to consider the Church and what it had to offer
him. He asked himself whether the Church was able to satisfy his
deepest longings. Sometimes the answer was an overwhelming yes
as this passage from his diary shows:

> The Catholic Church alone seems to satisfy my wants, my faith,
> life, soul. These may be baseless fabrics, chimeras dire, or
> what you please. I may be laboring under a delusion. Yet my
> soul is Catholic, and that faith responds to my soul in its
> religious aspirations and its longings. I have not wished to
> make myself Catholic, but that answers on all sides to the
> wants of my soul. It is so real, so full. One is in harmony
> all over -- in unison with heaven, with the present, living
> in the material body, and the past, who have changed. [sic]
> There is a solidarity between them through the Church. I
> do not feel controversial. My soul is filled.[128]

At other times, he was tormented by doubt: "All is dark before me,
impenetrable darkness....Nothing seems to take hold of my soul,
or else it seeks nothing."[129] Whether or not to join the church --
Protestant or Catholic -- was not the issue. "For him, there was
a much more immediate and pressing problem: what was he going to
do with his life?"[130] One thing he knew: he must live in Christ.
Life at Brook Farm was not free of the financial exigencies of life
in the world. He could no longer afford being a boarder. As an
associate member, he would have to spend much of his time, more than he

---

[128]Hecker's diary entry, 24 April 1843, as cited by Elliott,
p. 63.

[129]Hecker's diary entry, 4 May 1843, as cited by Elliott, p. 65.

[130]Holden, p. 54.

wanted, working to support himself.[131]

Another Utopian experiment attracted Hecker's attention. In

July, 1843, Hecker moved to Fruitlands in pursuit of "a more ascetic

and interior life: than he could lead at Brook Farm.[132] But he stayed

less than two weeks before deciding to return to his family home

in New York. He arrived there in mid-August, 1843 after visiting at

Brook Farm for several weeks. It was not long before Hecker experienced

the shortcomings of life at home: "I feel this afternoon a deep

want in my soul unsatisfied by my circumstances here, the same as I

experienced last winter when I was led from this place."[133] While at

home, Hecker made several critical decisions. One was to dedicate

his time "to study for the field of the Church."[134] He had not as yet

resolved the question of which church he would join. He also decided

that he would prepare himself to study for the ministry.[135] In the

light of that decision, he called on Bishop John Hughes to inquire con-

cerning requirements for the Catholic priesthood. Holden observes that

it must have been an odd request coming as it did from a non-Catholic.

At any rate, Hecker was not impressed by the interview or by the Bishop

for that matter.

The R [oman] C [atholic] Church is not national with us, hence

---

[131]Ibid., pp. 54-55.

[132]Elliott, p. 76.

[133]Hecker's diary entry, 18 October 1843, as cited by Elliott,
p. 109.

[134]Hecker's diary entry, 10 March 1843, as cited by Holden,
p. 74.

[135]Holden, pp. 74-77.

it does not meet our wants, nor does it fully understand and sympathize with the experiences and disposition of our people. It is principally made up of adopted and foreign individuals.[136]

In March, 1844, he made his decision to withdraw from business and from the secular life and to continue his study of the Church. He settled in Concord, where he boarded with the Thoreau family.

Early that year he had begun an examination of Protestantism, a task that added to his dissatisfaction with the Protestant churches:

Not having had personal and experiential knowledge of the Protestant denominations, I investigated them all, going from one of them to another -- Episcopal, Congregational, Baptist, Methodist, and all -- conferring with their ministers, reading their books. It was a dreary business, but I did it.... the more you examine the Protestant sects in the light of first principles the more they are found to weaken human certitude, interfere with reason's native knowledge of God and his attributes, and perplex the free working of the laws of human thought. Protestantism is no religion for a philosopher, unless he is a pessimist -- if you can call such a being a philosopher -- and adopts Calvinism.[137]

There was nowhere else to turn; the only alternative left was the Roman Catholic Church. Again, Brownson played a critical role in counseling his friend. Hecker was troubled by his desire to give more of his time to contemplation. He laid his dilemma before Brownson: should he give up his studies and give himself entirely to the contemplative life? On June 6, 1844, Brownson wrote to Hecker,

---

[136]Brownson Papers, Isaac Hecker to Orestes Brownson, 28 March 1844, as cited by Holden, p. 80.

[137]Isaac T. Hecker, "Dr. Brownson and Catholicity (Conclusion)," The Catholic World 46 (1887):231. This statement suggests either that Hecker had no significant association with any Protestant church during his youth or that he failed to recall any particularly influential early experiences. The latter is more likely the case. Holden notes that Hecker attended church with his mother, who was a "fervent and devout" Methodist (p. 7). So he must have been at least moderately acquainted with Methodism. But in the statement quoted above, he makes no mention of these early years.

urging him to join the Roman Catholic Church if he believed in it
and to put himself under the direction of the Church:

> You are not to dream your life away. Your devotion must be
> regulated and directed by the discipline of the Church....
> Your cross is to resist this tendency to mysticism, to senti-
> mental luxury, which is really enfeebling your soul and pre-
> venting you from attaining to true spiritual blessedness....
> If you enter the Church at all, it must be the Catholic.
> There is nothing else.[138]

Hecker went to Boston the day after he received Brownson's letter to
meet with Bishop Fenwick and tell him of his desire to enter the
Church, just as Brownson had encouraged him to do. Hecker's decision
brought him peace:

> I feel very cheerful and at ease since I have consented to
> join the Catholic Church. Never have I felt the quietness,
> immovableness, and the permanent rest that I do now. It is
> inexpressible. I feel that essential and interior permanence
> which nothing exterior can disturb, and no act which it calls
> on me to perform will move in the least. It is with a perfect
> ease and gracefulness that I never dreamed of, that I shall
> unite with the Church. It will not change but fix my life.
> No external relations, events, or objects can disturb this
> unreachable quietness or break the deep repose in which I am.[139]

Hecker was conditionally baptized by Bishop McCloskey on August 2,
1844; he had been baptized in infancy by a Lutheran minister.

But his conversion did not satisfy his spiritual longing
completely. He found himself tormented by a sense of sinfulness and
scrupulosity. He resisted suggestions that he study for the secular
priesthood. The "intimate and careful spiritual guidance" which he
expected to find in a religious community attracted him to the

---

[138]Brownson to Hecker, 6 June 1844, as cited by Holden,
pp. 90-91.

[139]Hecker's diary entry, 13 June 1844, as cited by Elliott,
p. 154.

Redemptorists.[140] Clarence Walworth and James McMaster, also new

converts, sailed to Belgium with Hecker to begin their novitiate at

St. Trond. Hecker and Walworth took their vows on October 15, 1846.

McMaster had been advised to leave; his novice master suggested

that McMaster's vocation was to be an editor. Hecker was ordained

in October, 1849. After a year of study in England, he returned to

the United States to work as a missionary to the German immigrants.

Hecker conducted parish missions with Walworth, Augustine Hewit, and

Frances Baker. During this time, Hecker wrote Questions of the Soul

and Aspirations of Nature.[141] Both grew out of his concern for an

apostolate to non-Catholics. In 1857, Father Hecker was chosen by

his colleagues to go to Rome to plead their case for the establishment

of an English-speaking house for the American Redemptorists. That event

changed the course of his life. When Hecker arrived in Rome, he was

expelled by the Superior General for a breach of vows; Hecker had failed

to seek permission to make the trip.[142] Pope Pius IX intervened in

the case, dispensed the American Redemptorists from their vows, and

urged them to establish an American religious community. That marked

the beginning of the Paulists. Hecker served as the superior of the

order from 1858 until his death in 1888. His concern with the apostolate

to non-Catholics gave the work of the Paulists its distinctive stamp.

Hecker was convinced that the Church would prosper in America;

---

[140]Elliott, p. 196.

[141]Isaac T. Hecker, Aspirations of Nature (New York: J. B. Kirker, 1857).

[142]Elliott, p. 251.

he believed that the Roman Catholic Church was well suited to meet the needs of the American people. The press became his pulpit; in 1865 he founded The Catholic World and in 1866, he established the Catholic Publishing Society, later known as the Paulist Press. Four years later, he founded a magazine for youngsters called Young Catholic. A year before he died, he published his last book, The Church and the Age.[143] He died at the age of sixty-nine.

I have sketched Hecker's journey to the Roman Catholic Church at some length, quoting freely from his private papers, in order to show that the content of Questions of the Soul is indeed auto-biographical. In the Preface, Hecker writes: "One thing we can truly say of the following sheets; they are not idle speculations. Our heart is in them, and our life's results."[144] His purpose in writing Questions of the Soul was to teach and to inspire: he sought "to explain the Catholic religion in such a manner as to reach and attract the minds of the non-Catholics of the American people."[145] He wrote the book during the latter half of 1854, while he was actively working on the mission circuit. The book expresses his growing interest in an apostolate directed at non-Catholics.

---

[143]Isaac T. Hecker, The Church and the Age (New York: The Catholic Book Exchange, 1896).

[144]Hecker, Questions of the Soul, p. 6.

[145]From the statement prepared by Hecker while he was in Rome, as cited by Elliott, p. 246. Hecker remarks that he secretly re-garded these books "as the test whether God had really given to me the grace and vocation to labor in a special manner for the conversion of these people." Much to his satisfaction, Questions of the Soul, published in three editions, was "the means of many and signal conversions in the United States and England."

Questions of the Soul reflects Hecker's own experience: he
demonstrates that the Roman Catholic Church satisfies the deepest
longings of the human soul. The affective appeal of Roman Catholicism
was indeed a primary factor in Hecker's conversion. Reason alone was
not able to satisfy him.

The structure of Questions of the Soul derives from the nature
of the process by which Hecker committed himself to Roman Catholicism.
The fundamental questions of the soul are questions of identity, origin,
and purpose: who am I? where did I come from? why am I alive? Man
must answer these questions if he is to fulfill his destiny and so
achieve true happiness. Where ought he seek his destiny? Neither
nature nor the world can satisfy the deepest longings of the soul.
No created thing or being can ultimately satisfy man. "The end
and ground of all seeking is God, and the soul finds no rest till
it finds God...."[146] It is with God and in God that the destiny
of the soul is fulfilled. Each person has a special destiny, a definite
and "great" work to do -- "great in its purpose, important in its
accomplishment, divine in its results."[147] But some are marked in
a special way:

> there is a class of souls that cannot satisfy their natures
> with the common modes of life. A hidden principle leads them
> to seek a better and more spiritual life. The longing after
> the infinite predominates in these souls, and all other ties
> must be loosed and sacrificed, if need be, to its growth and
> full development.[148]

---

[146]Hecker, Questions of the Soul, p. 28.

[147]Ibid., p. 34.

[148]Ibid., p. 37.

These persons, and there have been some in every age, choose a
rigorous, disciplined communal style of life. The members of the
Institution of Pythagorus, the Essenian Community, the sect of
Therapeutae, and orders of Buddhist monks had in common this need
to live an ascetic existence. This desire to live a fuller spiritual
life was not limited to the ancient people. Hecker found that some
of his American contemporaries wanted to live such a life as much as
he did. In fact, he maintained that these persons were more numerous
in the United States than elsewhere because political and economic
circumstances were conducive to such a lifestyle. The geography of
the land, its wide, open spaces accomodated those seeking solitude
and silence. Hecker was intent on demonstrating that the lifestyle
which he pursued was a natural and rather common course. His preliminary
discussion of those who seek a fuller spiritual life serves as the
basis for his defense of religious life in the Roman Catholic Church.

The communities at Brook Farm and Fruitlands exemplified the
American search for spiritual fulfillment in the communal life. It
is appropriate that Hecker allowed those who were involved in the
movements to speak for themselves: Orestes Brownson, William H.
Channing, Nathaniel Hawthorne and other unnamed residents voice the
ideals of communal living. Hecker casts himself in the role of the
observer and legitimately so. Hecker's private papers reveal that
during his stay at Brook Farm he remained something of an outsider,
preoccupied with the struggles of his interior life. His thoughts
repeatedly returned to the Church. And though he relished conversations
with his friends, Hecker found that life there did not satisfy his
deepest needs. His time at Brook Farm and his contact with the thought

178

of the Transcendentalists was for Hecker but a time of passage.

The conviction that communal life nurtured interior life also encouraged the formation of the Brotherhood of the Holy Cross at Valle Crucis, North Carolina and a similar community at Nashota, Wisconsin. Hecker observes that these communities were inspired by the same tendencies as were Brook Farm and Fruitlands, "but in a more ecclesiastical aspect."[149] Though Hecker was not involved in the communities at Valle Crucis and Nashota, he was impressed by their ideals and by their style of life, which included vows of obedience, poverty, and chastity. The goal of the Brotherhood was twofold: to promote the individual's progress "in a more perfect life" and to serve others more effectively through a combined effort.[150] Hecker's discussion of these Anglican communities reveals his own growing conviction that religious life was most conducive to spiritual growth. Hecker's inclination toward the Roman Catholic Church and his disposition toward religious life sprang out of the same inner source: his desire to satisfy his deepest longings for communion.

A social structure which encouraged the nurturing of the spiritual life was vital. But more important still was the discovery of a model of the full spiritual life. Hecker found this model in Jesus Christ, who is "a perfect pattern of life, one who unites in his nature both God and man."[151] Jesus is God's response to man's deepest need:

---

149 Ibid., p. 86.

150 Ibid., p. 84.

151 Ibid., p. 94.

> ...man not only needs a God-man to be to him a model of a per-
> fect man, he also needs that this God-man should be to him
> a pattern in every relation of life. He must feel all the
> burdens of life, experience all its pains, suffer all its
> miseries, drink of all its woes, meet all its difficulties,
> and overcome them all in his own person.[152]

Jesus provided man with a model for fulfilling his responsibility to

God, to himself, and to mankind. Jesus acted in accordance with the

will of the Father; he taught that persons should seek the Kingdom

of God above all else; he lived for the whole world, for all of humanity.

He was humble, truthful, couragous, compassionate, and loving. His life

and his death exemplify the perfect life and death, Hecker concluded.

But how are persons of this generation to experience Christ?

> To send man back eighteen centuries, or tell him to read
> a book, however good, when he feels the pressing need of the
> love of the infinite God in his heart, is downright mockery.
> If Christ is to be to us a Savior, we must find him here, now,
> and where we are, in this age of ours also; otherwise, he is
> no Christ, no Savior, no Immanuel, no "God with us."[153]

This passage is significant: it reveals Hecker's passion for experience

in religion. Religion is not and indeed cannot be simply an affair of

the intellect. Religion arises out of painful and complex probing

of the very purpose of life, what Hecker calls the questions of the

soul. Hecker's awareness of the centrality of the experiential dimension

of religion reveals his sensitivity to the religious needs of the total

self. Of course, Hecker resolves the question of how Christ continues

to be present in this age by pointing to the Church. Hecker carefully

demonstrates that the Church answers the wants of man: his need for

divine guidance, his need to obey a divine authority, his need to be

---

[152]Ibid., p. 102.

[153]Ibid., pp. 110-111.

taught how to achieve his destiny.

The Church is necessary because it provides man with what he cannot provide for himself: knowledge of the destiny of man and the "shortest and most speedy way of realizing it."[154] The dogmas, the sacraments, rites, and ceremonies of the Church fulfill that two-fold function. More specifically, Hecker argues that the Church must meet the special needs that persons experience during a lifetime: the need of the child to be attracted to the spiritual life and nurtured as he grows in it, the need to unburden himself when he has sinned, the need to be fed the Bread of Life, and the need for support in the face of death. No aspect of man's experience falls outside the parameters of the Church's solicitude. Christ makes himself present to man through the Church.

Even when Hecker had progressed this far in his thinking, one critical question still had to be answered: "where and which is the church?" As might be expected Hecker first turned his attention to the Protestant church but he found it wanting. The Protestant church, and he makes no denominational distinctions, fails on three counts: "as insufficient to meet the wants of man's heart, as unable to satisfy the demands of man's intelligence, and as faithless in representing the authority of Christ."[155] The Protestant church answers "like a step mother -- 'Be your own guide.'"[156] The principle of private judgment or private interpretation cannot satisfy man's need

---

[154]Ibid., p. 144.

[155]Ibid., p. 130.

[156]Ibid., p. 134.

for divine guidance.

In the chapters that follow, Hecker argues that Protestantism fails to meet man's needs, needs which are indeed met by the Roman Catholic Church. Protestantism neglects the needs of the sinner; Roman Catholicism offers the sinner reconciliation through confession. Protestantism tells man that he can only "commune with God" in faith; Roman Catholicism recognizes that man is body and spirit, that he needs "divine food" to sustain life. Protestantism offers no consolation to the dying; Roman Catholicism comforts the dying and imparts to them "a new vigor" in the sacrament of Extreme Unction.[157] Furthermore, the Roman Catholic teaching on the communion of saints satisfies man's deepest longing for communion.

> Though the soul has reached heaven, the bond of sympathy between it and the Church is not broken; it still continues to be her child, --yea, more hers now than ever, for the triumphant Church in Heaven, the militant Church upon Earth, and the suffering Church in the place of Purification, are one, and united closely in sympathy as one body.[158]

Protestantism ignores "virtues which lead to Christian perfection."[159] Roman Catholicism encourages the practice of virginity, poverty, penance, and mortification.

Protestantism, Hecker argues, is unsatisfactory as a system of personal comfort and support: the individual is cast back on his own resources. It arouses man's religious wants but fails to satisfy them.

---

[157] Hecker wrote that it was the teaching on the communion of saints that ultimately brought him to the Church. Personal immortality satisfied the deepest longing of the soul. See Elliott, pp. 56, 151, 163-4.

[158] Hecker, Questions of the Soul, p. 217.

[159] Ibid., p. 163.

> We condemn Protestantism as not being the Church of Christ,
> because it fails to represent Christ; fails to give us a
> divine authority in her teachings, fails to produce Christian
> virtues in the hearts of men; fails to guide the soul in the
> way of a Christian life; fails in not claiming the power of
> pardoning sin; fails by not believing the real presence
> of Christ upon earth; fails by abandoning the soul at death
> and beyond the grave; and fails, finally, in not giving an ex-
> pression to the virtues which lead to Christian perfection.[160]

Roman Catholicism, on the other hand, responds to the whole spectrum

of man's needs, including his need for a divine guide. Roman

Catholicism satisfies the child's hunger for beauty, symbol, and

pageantry:

> The altar, the crucifix, the robed priests, the surpliced
> acolytes, the pictures and the statues of holy saints, the
> stained windows, the organ the bells, -- all combine together
> to give to the child's picturesque-loving mind, a better and
> more sublime idea of religion than years of reading and
> preaching can do.[161]

The atmosphere, the mythology, and the symbolism that are part of the

Catholic experience satisfy the adult as well as the child: both

need to experience the affective dimension of religion.

The experiences which brought Hecker to the Roman Catholic

Church also carried him into religious life. He was attracted to

a style of living which nurtured the interior life. His desire to

live the full spiritual life was already evident during his stay at

Brook Farm. Religious life most closely mirrored the life of the

primitive Christian community as it is described in the second chapter

of the Book of Acts. The life of poverty, chastity, and self-denial

re-centered the soul on God. The Roman Catholic Church had for centuries

---

[160]Ibid., pp. 162-163.

[161]Ibid., p. 175.

successfully accomplished what people at Brook Farm, Fruitlands, and

elsewhere were attempting to achieve in nineteenth-century America:

the social context which would free the person to nurture the interior

life. But the Transcendentalists failed to reach beyond the self;

they failed to see man in relation to God.

His conversion, as he describes it, consisted in recognizing

that his life was grounded in God. It is that insight which

separated him from the Transcendentalists. Hecker describes the

change that occurred to him in two paragraphs that comprise the

conclusion of Questions of the Soul

> Once we were their companion and bosom friend; -- but we
> are changed. Changed, not in our aspirations, not in our
> heart's affections, not in our purposes in life; -- no, these
> are not changed, but exalted, purified, and enlarged! Our
> change was this; to pass from a natural to a supernatural
> basis of life, thus giving our nature a new and extraordinary
> participation in the Divine Nature, and bringing up our being
> to the archetype of man, existing in the Divine Mind. For
> Jesus Christ did not come down from heaven to contradict or
> destroy man's nature, but to ratify and restore it, and to
> give to man a new, superior, divine mode of life and activity.
> Jesus Christ became man in order to enrich men with the gift
> of his own Divinity.
> This was our change, and it was one of the happiest moments
> of our life, when we discovered for the first time, that it
> was not required of us, either to abandon our reason, or drown
> it in false excitement of feeling, to be a religious man. That
> to become a Catholic, so far from being contrary to reason,
> was a supreme act of reason. It was a joy for us, to find
> that instead of being required to play the hypocrite, or the
> blind fanatic, and thus renounce our manhood in order to be-
> come a Christian, we were called upon to make an act which
> all the faculties of being spontaneously united in making.[162]

This was the conversion -- the answer to the questions which

Hecker had been asking. Man's destiny is in his relationship to God.

God makes himself known in Jesus -- who reveals the deepest

---

[162]Ibid., p. 286.

possibilities of the spiritual life. Because Jesus Christ became man, mankind is transformed. Conversion was, for Hecker, an affirmation of the potential of all humanity as well as his own humanity. Conversion satisfied the demands of reason and affections. Hecker recalls his pleasure in realizing that he did not have to drown reason "in a false excitement of feeling." It is likely that this is a reference to the sudden, tumultuous outbursts associated with the conversions occurring at Protestant revivals. But surely the phrase is not meant to exclude all feeling and sentiment. Throughout Questions of the Soul, Hecker consistently addresses the religious needs of the whole person -- paying attention to the needs of sense and sensibility.

Once Hecker had experienced this interior transformation, becoming Roman Catholic was a natural consequence. "For what else is the Church," he writes, "but God made manifest to the hearts and minds of men; -- his Body."[163] Hecker's conversion was an inner transformation; affiliating with the Roman Catholic Church signified that the conversion had already occurred.

Questions of the Soul may be viewed as a type of conversion narrative -- despite its apparently impersonal tone and its apologetic thrust. The parallel between Hecker's experiences (as recorded in his diaries and letters) and the issues discussed in Questions of the Soul is obvious. What is most important is that the issues and the experiences intersect in Hecker's life. His presentation of dogmatic points lacks the abrasive tone of the zealous apologist

---

[163]Ibid., p. 289.

who musters arguments to proselytize. Hecker testifies to his own
conversion: he reveals the process by which he became a Catholic
in the hope that others might be moved by what moved him: the
Roman Catholic Church satisfies the deepest cravings of the heart.

The Convert; Or, Leaves From My Experience

As preacher, author, social critic, editor, philosopher,
and apologist, Orestes Augustus Brownson left his mark on nineteenth-
century America. He was an ingenious and prolific writer who
chronicled many of the intellectual, social, and religious movements
which attracted the attention of Americans during the first part of
the century. He wrote about what he knew firsthand: currents of
thought which he had pursued and investigated.[164] A Presbyterian
at the age of nineteen, a Universalist minister at twenty-two and
a Unitarian at twenty-nine, Brownson became a Roman Catholic at
forty-one to the amazement of many familiar with his liberal thought.
Prior to conversion, Brownson had advocated social reform; the programs
of Robert Owen and Fanny Wright stimulated his thinking on that topic.
The ideas of Benjamin Constant, Pierre Leroux, and St. Simon excited
his imagination, leading him to speculate on man's need for social
organization and so laying foundation for his doctrine of life in
communion. Moving through a wide spectrum of religious perspectives

[164]The Works of Orestes A. Brownson, collected and arranged
by Henry F. Brownson, 20 vols. (Detroit: H. F. Brownson, 1887-1907).
The multi-volume Works comprise (about a third of his total output."
Charles Carroll Hollis, "The Literary Criticism of Orestes Brownson"
(Ph.D. dissertation, University of Michigan, 1954), p. vi, quoted
in Thomas R. Ryan, Orestes A. Brownson: A Definitive Biography
(Huntington, Ind.: Our Sunday Visitor, 1976), p. 851.

and social concerns, he shaped his own distinctive system of thought --
one which eventually led him to the Roman Catholic Church.

The Convert; Or, Leaves From My Experience is, in some ways,
a typical conversion narrative and, in other ways, an atypical one.[165]
The Convert is "a simple narrative" which records Brownson's story,
as it pertains to his "religious convictions" and, particularly, to
his conversion to Roman Catholicism.[166] Conversion is the dominant
motif of the work; Brownson reviews his life prior to conversion and
the experience of conversion itself from the standpoint of "the convert,"
who has been a member of the Church for more than ten years. The
conversion focus is conventional in narratives written by nineteenth-
century converts. What is distinctive about this work comes from the
singular combination of experience and ability that sets Brownson
apart from his fellow converts. The Convert is informative,
comprehensive, and tightly structured. Brownson's story affords
glimpses of American life and thought during the first half of the
century, as he himself points out.[167] His own intellectual and
religious life intersects with the movements he describes. Brownson
writes a personal apology -- which sets forth the system or method
of thought which brought him to the threshold of the Roman Catholic
Church. In so doing, Brownson surpasses the rough attempts of the
earlier converts at self-justification and at defense of Roman

---

[165]Orestes A. Brownson, The Convert; Or, Leaves From My Experience
(New York: D. & J. Sadlier, 1857; reprint ed., Detroit: H. F. Brownson,
1902), 5:1-205. All citations refer to the later edition.

[166]Brownson, The Convert, pp. 2, 1.

[167]Ibid., p. 190.

Catholicism. The Convert is sophisticated and persuasive. Brownson

is intent on presenting his experience of conversion as a paradigm for

intelligent, reflective persons involved in the religious quest. His

experience was singular and his narrative is such as well. As his

friend and fellow-convert, Isaac Hecker, put it: "He was routine

in nothing."[168]

Orestes Augustus Brownson was born in Stockbridge, Vermont

in 1803.[169] His father, Sylvester Augustus Brownson, died shortly

after Orestes and his twin sister, Daphne Augusta, were born. His

mother, Relief Metcalf, was unable to support the family and sent

Orestes to live with guardians at the age of six. From them, he

learned the valued New England virtues of honesty, frugality, industry,

and faithful observance of the Sabbath.[170] His family re-united in

1817 and moved to Ballston Spa where Orestes attended the local

---

[168]Isaac T. Hecker, "Dr. Brownson in Boston, "The Catholic
World 45 (1887):466.

[169]Sources of biographical information are numerous and
accessible. Thomas R. Ryan's definitive biography is invaluable.
The oldest but nevertheless indispensable resource is the three
volume biography edited by Henry F. Brownson, Orestes A. Brownson's
Early Life: From 1803-1844; Orestes A. Brownson's Middle Life;
From 1845-1855; Orestes A. Brownson's Later Life: From 1855-1876
(Detroit: H. F. Brownson, 1898-1900). Other book length biographies
include: Arthur M. Schlesinger, Jr., Orestes A. Brownson: A Pilgrim's
Progress (Boston: Little, Brown and Co., 1939); Theodore Maynard,
Orestes Brownson: Yankee, Radical, Catholic (New York: The Macmillan
Co., 1943); and Per Sveino, Orestes A. Brownson's Road to Catholicism
(Oslo: Universitetsforlaget, 1970; New York: Humanities Press, 1970).
The latter work focuses on Brownson's conversion, as the title
indicates. Brief biographical sketches appear in the Catholic
Encyclopedia, the New Catholic Encyclopedia, the Dictionary of
American Biography, and the Dictionary of Catholic Biography.

[170]Brownson, The Convert, p. 4.

academy and became a printer's apprentice. At the age of nineteen,
he became a member of the Presbyterian Church. Dissatisfied, he
left the Presbyterians and joined the Universalists, who ordained
him to the ministry. He married Sally Healy in 1827. In 1829,
he became the editor of the Gospel Advocate and Impartial Investigator,
published in Auburn, New York.

As Brownson's theological ideas grew more liberal, he found
himself increasingly uncomfortable with Universalism and with his
inability to reconcile the use of reason and the authority of Scripture.
Before long, he severed his connection with the Universalists. At
twenty-eight, he began a career as an "independent preacher," expounding
his thoughts on the religion of humanity. After leaving the
Universalists, Brownson had turned his attention to the betterment
of this world. He studied the ideas of Robert Dale Owen and Frances
Wright and worked for the Working-Men's Party, editing its
journal.[171] In 1832, Brownson was accepted as a Unitarian minister.
Four years later, he founded his own church, calling it the Society
for Christian Union and Progress; he explained his views in his first
book, New Views of Christianity, Society, and the Church, in which
he described the church of the future, a church which would be neither

---

[171]Both were radical social reformers; both were born in
Scotland. Robert Dale Owen (1801-1877) founded the community of
New Harmony at Posey, Indiana in 1826. Owen believed that given the
proper environment (one in which the evils of religion, marriage,
and private property were eliminated), men could create the perfect
society. Frances Wright (1795-1852) shared Owen's belief in the
possibility of creating a perfect society. She founded an experimental
community in Nashabo, Tennessee in 1825.

Protestant nor Catholic.[172] That year he became a member of the
Transcendentalist Club, as this select group of American liberals
came to be called, and exchanged ideas with Ralph Waldo Emerson,
George Ripley, and Bronson Alcott. Both his son, Orestes, Jr.
and his friend, Isaac Hecker, lived at Brook Farm for a time and
Brownson visited them there. It was Brownson who encouraged Hecker
to go to Brook Farm.

In 1838, Brownson founded the Boston Quarterly Review and in
1840, he published Charles Elwood; or, The Infidel Converted, a
fictional account in which the adventures and concerns of the title
character closely resemble those of Brownson himself.[173] Brownson
wrote for the Democratic Review after it merged with the Boston
Quarterly. During this period, he reflected on the nature of
government and called for the union of the spiritual and the material
in a new organization. In 1844, he established Brownson's Quarterly
Review. He converted to Roman Catholicism in October of that year.

His conversion forced Brownson to take stock of this future.
How was he to support his family? Should he continue to write? He
had always written about philosophical and religious topics but he
knew little about Roman Catholic theology. Bishop John Bernard
Fitzpatrick suggested that Brownson use the Quarterly as an organ for
the explanation and defense of Roman Catholic doctrine and instructed

---

[172] Orestes A. Brownson, New Views of Christianity, Society,
and the Church (Boston: C. C. Little and J. Brown, 1836).

[173] Orestes A. Brownson, Charles Elwood; or, The Infidel
Converted (Boston: C. C. Little and J. B. Brown, 1840; reprint
ed., Works, vol. 4). This work is discussed at some length below.

him in Roman Catholic theology to prepare him for the task.

Under the cautious and sometimes censoring eye of the Bishop,

Brownson became one of the century's foremost apologists.[174]

In 1854, Brownson published The Spirit-Rapper, misleadingly

sub-titled an autobiography.[175] The preface states that the book

is intended to establish the "connection of spirit-rapping, or

the spirit manifestations, with modern philanthropy, visionary

reforms, socialism, and revolutionism."[176] The Convert; Or, Leaves

From My Experience was published in 1857, thirteen years after

Brownson became a Roman Catholic.

Brownwon wrote voluminously, even during the period, 1864-1873,

when he suspended publication of his Quarterly. His countless

articles and essays appeared in the New York Tablet, The Ave Maria,

The Catholic World, and the American Catholic Quarterly Review and

he published two book-length works: The American Republic: Its

Constitution, Tendencies, and Destiny and Conversations on Liberalism

---

[174]See Ryan, pp. 313-330 for a discussion of Brownson's role
as apologist. John Bernard Fitzpatrick (1812-1866), co-adjutor of Boston
during the tenure of Bishop Benedict J. Fenwick, succeeded Fenwick to
the see of Boston in 1846. When Brownson told Fenwick of his intention
to become a Roman Catholic, the Bishop introduced him to Fitzpatrick
from whom Brownson took instruction in the Catholic faith.

[175]Orestes A. Brownson, The Spirit-Rapper; An Autobiography
(Boston: Little, Brown & Co., 1854; reprint ed., Detroit: Thorndike
Nourse, 1884). Brownson writes: "It is not a novel; it is not a romance;
it is not a biography of a real individual; it is not a dissertation,
an essay, or a regular treatise; and yet it perhaps has some elements
of them all, thrown together in just a way as best suited my convenience,
or my purpose" (p. 1).

[176]Ibid.

and the Church.[177] Brownson resumed publication of the Quarterly Review
in January, 1873. The last number was published in late 1875. He died
in 1876.

Throughout his life, both before and after his conversion,
Brownson found himself in the thick of controversy. He was a man
of conviction, outspoken and obstinate, always ready to take on
his opponents and, just as often, the subject of their criticism and
censure. That is hardly surprising given the subjects he dealt with
during the course of his life: social reform, politics, government,
slavery, and the assorted philosophical and religious topics that
were his favorite fare. Brownson was "a man completely absorbed by
the issues which for the time occupied his mind. Indeed, neutrality,
disengagement, cool objectivity were not his characteristics."[178]
He stands out among nineteenth-century converts; his life and work
are still of interest in America today.[179]

In his preface to The Convert, Brownson sets forth his purpose:

> ...to render to all who may take an interest in the matter, an
> account of my conversion to Catholicity, and to enable the
> curious in such matters to discover the connecting link between
> my past and my present life, in order to enable them to dis-
> cover the connecting link between nature and grace, the natural
> and the supernatural, and to perceive that, in becoming a
> Catholic, a man has no occasion to divest himself of his nature,

---

[177]Orestes A. Brownson, The American Republic: Its Constitution,
Tendencies, and Destiny (New York: P. O'Shea, 1866); Conversations
on Liberalism and the Church (New York: D. & J. Sadlier, 1870). A
bibliography of Brownson's writings appears in Ryan, beginning on p. 851.

[178]Sveino, p. 13.

[179]Ryan documents the revival of interest in Brownson and his
work. See pp. 723-733.

or to forego the exercise of his reason.[180]

In this statement, he calls attention to the fact that many regarded

his conversion "as a sudden caprice, or rash act taken from a momentary

impulse or in a fit of intellectual despair."[181] Those who were

acquainted with his thought were unable "to perceive any logical

or intellectual connection" between what he said before his conversion

and what he said afterward.[182] They were astounded to hear him

defending his conversion in traditional Catholic terms. Thus the

narrative was meant to establish that connection between his past and

present and to show that his conversion was a natural outgrowth of

his religious quest and theological reflection. Conversion, Brownson

argued, is compatible with reason even though it cannot be explained

solely in natural terms. It was Brownson's experience that God's

grace acts upon the convert, but it is reason that brings him to

the threshold of the Church. At no point is the work of grace in

conflict with the ways of nature. Conversion does not require that

a person abandon reason; on the contrary, it is a most reasonable act.

Self-justification was a motive for Brownson's writing his

conversion narrative in a distinctive sense: he was not simply

justifying his Catholicity; he was defending the credibility of

the process by which he came to the Church. Brownson wrote The Convert

after he had achieved some independence in theological perspective.

Shortly after his conversion, Bishop Fitzpatrick began to instruct

---

[180]Brownson, The Convert, p. 1.

[181]Ibid., pp. 173-174.

[182]Ibid., p. 173.

him in Catholic theology and continued for some time to exercise

considerable influence over Brownson's theological writings, most

especially by insisting that Brownson adhere to traditional

apologetics. Brownson acceded but the cost was high; Brownson set

aside the doctrine of life by communion which he claimed had brought

him to the Church. But in The Convert, Brownson reaffirms his belief in

the orthodoxy and the practicality of his method, arguing that motives

of credibility "should be adapted to the peculiar character and wants

of the age, or class of persons addressed."[183] In the eyes of some,

Brownson's reaffirmation came too late: "Had he held to the way inside

the Church which he had pursued outside the Church in finding her,

he would have carried with him some, and might perhaps have carried many,

non-Catholic minds of a leading character."[184] Nevertheless, in

The Convert, Brownson sets the record straight: he describes his

route to the Church and proclaims the exemplary value of his experiences.

The Convert is addressed to all -- Catholic and non-Catholic

alike and appropriately so since Brownson explains the process of his

conversion to non-Catholics and argues the hidden agenda of the validity

of his method for the sake of his Catholic readers. In a sense,

The Convert was also addressed to God; writing the narrative became

the occasion for thanking God "for having conducted me, after so many

wonderings, from the abyss of doubt and infidelity to the light and

truth of his Gospel, in the bosom of his church, where I found peace

---

[183]Ibid., p. 175.

[184]Isaac T. Hecker, "Dr. Brownson and Bishop Fitzpatrick,"
The Catholic World 45 (1887):5.

and repose so long denied me."[185]

The structure of the narrative is dictated by Brownson's
purpose in writing: to demonstrate that his process of spiritual
search and growth was evolutionary and that conversion to Roman
Catholicism was the natural outcome of that process. Again and
again, he reminds his readers that he was moving toward Christianity
even when he appeared to be far away; he asserts that the principles
of William Godwin have "a certain reflection of Christian truth,"
that his involvement with the Working-Men's Party moved him closer
in the direction of Christian truth, that reading the work of Pierre
Leroux headed him "in the direction of real Christian beliefs."[186]
The Convert is not simply a chronological narration of events.
Chronology provides the framework for demonstrating organic development
in the religious life: Brownson finds himself dissatisfied with
Protestantism in both its orthodox and liberal forms. He passes
through a period of unbelief during which he discovers and celebrates
the importance and value of this world and finds himself returning to
Christianity and finally moving toward Rome.

"Properly speaking, I had no childhood, and have more of
the child in my feelings now then at eight or ten years of age."[187]
Brownson's father died shortly after his birth; his mother, unable
to care for the children, placed Orestes with an aged couple in
Royalton. Brownson recalls that they "had been brought up in New

---

[185]Brownson, The Convert, p. 3.

[186]Ibid., pp. 55, 67, 133.

[187]Ibid., p. 4.

England Congregationalism, were honest, upright, strictly moral, and far more ready to suffer wrong then to do wrong, but had no particular religion, and seldom went to meeting."[188] Brownson learned the basic virtues, the Shorter Catechism, Apostles' Creed, the Lord's Prayer, and the rhyme, "Now I lay me down to sleep...." They were kind but Brownson looked back on those early years with regret. Deprived of the company of other children, Brownson says he developed "the manners, the tone, and the tastes of an old man" before he was a boy.[189] He became an avid reader and claims to have read through the Scriptures before he was eight and to have committed much of the Bible to memory by the time he was fourteen. His reading fostered his interest in religion and prepared him to take an active part in conversations regarding religion. At the age of nine, he argued against Jonathan Edwards' position on free will in a conversation with two other men. Brownson recalls taking delight in the goodness of the Lord who submitted to "the most cruel death" in order to save mankind and he admits to holding a spiritual conversation with Mary and the Angel Gabriel.[190]

Those recollections of early childhood experiences are revealing. Brownson's interest in religion and his preoccupation with spiritual matters appears to be related to the isolation he experienced as a child. Denied the ordinary pursuits of childhood, he turned inward. Given the fact that he grew up under the influence of the "Standing

---

[188]Ibid.

[189]Ibid., p. 4.

[190]Ibid.

Order" of New England, it seems likely that his conversations with
the Blessed Mother and the Angel Gabriel are a later interpolation.
But there is no doubt that his interest in religion was already
well-established in childhood: he recalls that his earliest ambition
was to be a minister.[191] Per Sveino suggests another way in which
early experiences affected Brownson's religious sentiment:

> ...his way to traditional Christianity and, more particularly,
> to Catholicism was his fervent search for a FATHER. The
> tragic loss of his father in childhood seemed to motivate
> to a great extent his desire of believing in a heavenly father.[192]

Deprivation and loss as well as kindness and virtue made a deep and
lasting impression upon the young Brownson.

During adolescence, Brownson came into contact with evangelical
Christianity; he attended Methodist meetings and gatherings of the
Christians, a sect founded in 1800 by Elias Smith and Abner Jones.
Although Brownson was "well disposed to believe," he failed to "get
religion."[193] The sought after change of heart never came about.
No one told him what to do; they simply insisted that he be born
again or else he would be damned. His fears grew and his love of God
diminished: "I became constantly afraid that the devil would come and
carry me off bodily."[194]

When Brownson was twelve, an elderly woman warned him to
"beware of sects and New Lights: they will make you fair promises,

---

191 Ibid., p. 6.

192 Sveino, p. 307.

193 Brownson, The Convert, p. 7.

194 Ibid., p. 8.

but in the end will deceive you to your own destruction."[195]   Although

not a Catholic herself, she advanced what Brownson later recognized was

a Catholic argument: join the church that began with Christ.

But Brownson's road to Rome was not destined to be so direct.

At fourteen, he fell into unbelief amidst the sectarians, universalists,

deists, atheists, and nothingarians.[196]   At nineteen, he sought relief

from confusion and uncertainty by joining the Presbyterian Church

and, in 1822, became a Presbyterian minister.   His tenure with the

Presbyterians was brief and left him disillusioned.   Though he tried

to submit to "Calvinistic discipline," he was unable to do so.[197]

Brownson is harsh in his condemnation of the Church, describing its

members as bigoted, uncharitable people who were encouraged "to spy

on each other" in the name of "fraternal affection."[198]   And though

the Church exercised "most rigid authority" over him, it "disclaimed

all authority to teach" him.[199]   He was simply told to get a Bible,

read it, and judge its meaning for himself.   He sought an authoritarian

teacher and father but did not find either.[200]   He concluded that the

Presbyterian Church, founded as it was in Scotland, some three hundred

years ago, could not be the Church of Christ; it had not maintained

unbroken succession with the apostles.   The Roman Catholic Church had

----

[195]Ibid.

[196]Ibid., p. 9.

[197]Ibid., p. 13.

[198]Ibid., p. 12.

[199]Ibid., p. 13.

[200]Ibid., p. 20.

but joining it was out of the question. In 1824, anti-Catholic
sentiment was strong and pervasive; Brownson did not escape its
influence. Since he could not become a Catholic, he must become
"a no-church man, and deny all churches."[201] With that thought,
Brownson had come full circle; he had sought "the rule of faith"
and failing to find it, he was forced "to fall back on the Scriptures
interpreted by...private judgment."[202]

In retrospect, Brownson termed his Presbyterian experience a
"mistake," a "capital blunder," and "an irrational, an unmanly act."[203]

> Not that I was insincere, or governed by bad motives, but be-
> cause, feeling the insufficiency of my own reason to guide me,
> I turned my back upon reason, and took up with what I supposed
> to be authority without a rational motive for believing it
> divinely commissioned. As far as I could, I abnegated my own
> rational nature, denied reason to make way for revelation,
> rational conviction to make way for authority.[204]

Calvinism, he argued, could not reconcile grace and nature or revelation
and reason as long as it insisted on man's depravity. Brownson found
the abnegation of reason untenable. Relinquishing reason meant
surrendering his "essential character as a man"; reason "must at
least be the preamble to faith, and nature must precede and be pre-
supposed by grace."[205]

Not quite ready to proclaim hinself a "no-church man," Brownson

---

[201]Ibid., p. 16.

[202]Ibid.

[203]Ibid., pp. 16, 18.

[204]Ibid., p. 18.

[205]Ibid., p. 18.

joined the Universalists. He had read some Universalist writings during adolescence, Hosea Ballou's <u>Treatise on the Atonement</u> being among them. For a time, Brownson was comfortable with the Universalist rejection of endless punishment.

> Taking reason for my guide and authority, I supposed that the Scriptures were to be explained in accordance with reason, so as to teach a rational doctrine; and certainly, I said, Universalism is a far more rational doctrine than its opposite. It may be that it is not proved by the strict letter of Scripture, but the letter killeth, it is the spirit that giveth life; and we must not be held to a strictly literal interpretation.[206]

Becoming a Universalist meant rejecting "all the mysteries of faith" and reducing Christianity "to a system of natural religion, or of moral and intellectual philosophy."[207]

In 1826, Brownson was ordained a Universalist minister. He returned to New York State, where Universalism was attracting a substantial following. By 1845, Universalists almost equalled Epsicopalians in number of congregations and counted twice as many members as the Catholic Church in the Burned-over District.[208] It was with good reason that evangelical leaders viewed this liberal Universalist Church as a threat and that revivalist preachers launched a zealous offensive against it.

> New converts in revivals regularly found themselves advertised as former Universalists, made wicked by the evil doctrine, and now regretting their former wallowing in sin....Debates held between Universalist and orthodox preachers were of course boasted as orthodox triumphs....The religious press constantly labeled criminals prominent in the news as Universalists, suggesting that without the fear of eternal punishment one could

---

[206]Ibid., p. 29.

[207]Ibid.

[208]Cross, p. 18.

not remain moral. School houses, court houses, and other public
places were usually closed to Universalist and Unitarian meetings
alike, and in some places the appropriateness of allowing
Universalist testimony in court was debated.[209]

Despite revivalists' efforts to discredit them, Universalists made

their mark on the religious environment of New York State. And

Brownson made his contribution to the growth of the Church in New

York State as a preacher and as editor of the Gospel Advocate and

Impartial Observer, published in Auburn under Universalist auspices.

Brownson's theological difficulties surfaced again. He was

unable to reconcile the authority of Scripture with reason. If the

Bible is the divinely inspired word, then it is authoritative. But

on what basis was he to affirm the Bible as God's Word? Where was

the infallible authority to be found? "The Bible...without an

infallible authority to assert it and deduce its sense, can never

be authority sufficient for believing a doctrine to be reasonable,

when that reasonableness is not apparent to the understanding."[210]

On what ground was he to reject eternal punishment? If there is no

punishment for sin, how is it possible to speak of Jesus as Savior?

Who can say what Jesus actually taught? Was Jesus a Universalist who

proclaimed "that vice has no punishment, virtue no reward"?[211]

Universalism, Brownson concluded, undermined the basis of moral

responsibility: "God inflicts pain only for the sake of reformation...

---

[209] Ibid., p. 44.

[210] Ibid., p. 35.

[211] Ibid., p. 36.

he never punishes sin or rewards virtue."[212]   In the end, the

principle of immediate satisfaction defines morality: virtue brings

happiness, vice misery.[213]

Unable to preach what he did not believe, Brownson left the

Universalists: "The moment I broke off my connection with the Univer-

salists, and took my position openly and above-board, not as a dis-

believer, but as an unbeliever, I felt restored to my manhood, I

felt like a new man."[214]   As a Presbyterian, Brownson had realized

the primacy of reason; as a Universalist, he had come to see that

the claims of revelation had to be consistent with the evidence of

reason.   He had recognized that he was unable to sacrifice reason, but

he had not yet discovered an authority to which he could submit with

reason intact.   Universalism had made him "doubt the utility of all

labors for another world: and so he turned to this world.[215]   But

he could not lay his religious concerns to rest entirely.   Between

1829 when he left the Universalists and 1844 when he joined the

Roman Catholic Church, he continued to grapple with the critical

relations between nature and grace, reason and revelation.

An "independent preacher" -- that is how Brownson described

himself in 1831.[216]   His message was the religion of humanity; he

---

[212]Ibid., p. 38.

[213]Ibid.

[214]Ibid., p. 40.

[215]Ibid., p. 41.

[216]Ibid., p. 67.

"put humanity in the place of God."[217] Religion, he maintained at
this time, was an effective vehicle for promoting social reform:
what was needed was "religion of some sort as the agent to induce man
to make sacrifices required in the adoption of my plans for working
out the reform of society, and securing to man his earthly felicity."[218]
Brownson formulated this argument for the necessity of religion while
he was thinking about and reacting to the ideas of several nineteenth-
century reformers.

Man is passive in the formation of his character; "his character
is formed...for him, by education, or the circumstances in which he
is born, grows up, and lives."[219] In short, man is a product of
his socialization. Therefore, as Robert Owen proposed, world-reform
could be effected by the restructuring of man's environment, the
creation of model communities. New Harmony, Indiana was such an
experiment in forming a community in which all persons were equal and
all property was held in common. Though the experiment failed,
Brownson acknowledged that Owen's ideas and work drew his attention
"to the social evils which exist in every land, to the inequalities which
obtain even in our own country, where political equality is secured
by law, and to the question of reorganizing society and creating a paradise on earth."[220]

Owen's ideas became the foundation for Brownson's socialism.

---

[217]Ibid., p. 69.

[218]Ibid., p. 67.

[219]Ibid., p. 42.

[220]Ibid., p. 43.

By 1829, Brownson held that earthly happiness is man's goal and belief in progress is his creed.[221] Honesty and justice are the primary virtues. If God is to be found, he is to be found in man. Brownson had fixed his attention on this world; he had abandoned both hope for and fear of the afterlife.

In retrospect, Brownson maintained that even the socialist glimpses certain aspects of Christian truth.[222] And though the radical individualism of William Godwin's Enquiry Concerning the Principles of Political Justice was unacceptable, Brownson recognized "a certain reflection of Christian truth" in Godwin's principles.[223] Insisting that the liberal views he was exploring at this time contributed to his eventual conversion to Roman Catholicism was Brownson's way of asserting the developmental character of his religious life.

Frances Wright's program for social reform was the most radical that Brownson encountered. Wright called for secularization, that is, deliverance from tutelage to the supernatural, and devised a plan by which reform of the American people might be accomplished.

The first step to be taken was to arouse the American mind

---

[221]For Brownson's "Creed" of 1829, see The Convert, p. 49.

[222]Ibid., p. 51.

[223]Ibid., p. 55. William Godwin (1756-1836), English philosopher, maintained that government is the cause of all social evils. In An Enquiry Concerning Political Justice, and Its Influence on General Virtue and Happiness (1793), he argues that government, as we know it, cannot escape corruption. Brownson observes: "Even the absurdest and most mischievous of Godwin's principles have a certain reflection of Christian truth. His doctrine, that we should love the most worthy, irrespective of their personal relation to us, is true in the abstract; and hence we are to forsake father and mother, wife and children, houses and lands, and even give up our own life for our Lord, our God, the infintely worthy."

to a sense of its rights and dignity, to emancipate it from superstition, from its subjection to the clergy, and its fear of unseen powers, to withdraw it from the contemplation of the stars or an imaginary heaven after death, and fix it on the great and glorious work of promoting man's earthly well-being. The second step was, by political action, to get adopted, at the earliest possible moment, a system of state schools, in which all the children from two years old and upward should be fed, clothed, in a word, maintained, instructed, and educated at the public expense.[224]

Wright intended to overcome three enemies to worldly progress: religion, marriage and family, and private property. In their stead, she proposed a science of the world of the senses, a community of men and women free to cohabit at will, and a community of goods. Brownson's interest in Wright's proposals led him into the Working-Men's Party. He served as editor of the party's journal for a few months. The Party was working to gain political clout in order to establish a system of state school as proposed by Fanny Wright but Brownson disassociated himself from that goal, stating that he "never really approved" of such an educational system and that he did not "relish the idea of breaking up the family."[225] He claimed that he became active in the party in order to benefit the workingman.

Unlike Owen and Wright, Brownson concluded that religion was useful as a lever for social reform and was therefore desirable. He had found that his own religious sense was too deeply engrained to be easily eradicated: "I found in me certain religious sentiments that I could not efface; certain religious beliefs or tendencies of which

---

[224] Brownson, The Convert, p. 58.

[225] Ibid., pp. 65, 66.

I could not divest myself."[226]   His religious sentiment was Christian

in a very limited sense. Jesus Christ is a model man, a reformer, and

insofar as Brownson followed the example of this great man, he considered

himself a Christian. This was his stand as a preacher on his "own

hook."[227]

The Unitarian Church next claimed Brownson's loyalty. Dr.

William Ellery Channing's sermon on the "Dignity of Human Nature" drew

him to the Unitarians and he became a minister of that church in 1832.

Brownson fully expected to feel at home with the Unitarians because they

were liberal: they "allowed the unrestrained exercise of reason, and

left their ministers each to stand on his own private convictions, and

to arrange matters each as best he could with his own congregation."[228]

As a Unitarian, Brownson became acquainted with the thought

of two philosophers, Benjamin Constant and Pierre Leroux. Their

work helped Brownson to sharpen his own ideas regarding religion

and so brought him closer to Rome. Constant's Religion, considered

in its Origin, its Forms, and its Developments, set forth the thesis

that "religion has its origin in a sentiment natural to man, which may

be termed a law of nature."[229] This universal sentiment finds its

expression in forms of worship which evolve during the course of history

as do man's ideas of the holy. Constant stressed that the development

of religicus forms is progressive: each religious form is a "stepping-

---

[226]Ibid., p. 69.

[227]Ibid., p. 67.

[228]Ibid., p. 71.

[229]Ibid., p. 72.

stone to newer and still greater progress."[230]   At critical points
in history, old forms are destroyed and new institutions arise. What
impressed Brownson most was Constant's observation that "man naturally
seeks to embody his religious ideas and sentiments in institutions,
and that these institutions, serve as instruments of progress."[231]
Brownson decided that what the world needed was a new religious institution. The old forms had outgrown their usefulness. Catholicity,
once a boon to civilization, had ceased to be of benefit to mankind.
Protestantism was the instrument of its destruction, a destruction at
once deserved and justified. But "Protestantism is no-churchism, is
no positive religion; and while it serves the purpose of criticism and
destruction, it cannot meet the wants of the soul, or erect the temple
in which the human race may assemble to worship in concord and peace."[232]
Unitarianism, Brownson added, "satisfies nobody"; it is "negative,
cold, lifeless."[233]   The only hope lay in "The Church of the Future."
In July, 1836, Brownson organized "The Society for Christian Union
and Progress" and shortly thereafter, he published his first book,
New Views of Christianity, Society, and the Church, in which he set
forth the reasons why a new church was necessary and the principles
upon which it was to be established. The new church would be neither
Protestant nor Catholic; it would avoid the exclusive spiritualism of
Catholicism and the exclusive materialism of Protestantism. Catholicism

---

[230]Ibid., p. 73.

[231]Ibid., p. 74.

[232]Ibid., p. 76.

[233]Ibid.

has neglected the natural order: it "fitted men to die, but not

to live; for heaven, but not for earth, -- promising a heaven hereafter,

but creating none here."[234] Protestantism denies the spiritual: it

"takes care of this life, but neglects that which is to come; amasses

material goods, but lays up no treasures in heaven; rehabilitates

the flesh, but depresses the spirit; elevates humanity, but obscures

the Divinity."[235] Each is right in what it offers but wrong in what

it excludes. The new church which Brownson envisioned would bring

together the best of both.

Charles Elwood; or The Infidel Converted was published in

1840 but was written for the most part in 1834.[236] In The Convert,

Brownson simply describes it as "a philosophico-religious work,

strung together on a slight thread of fiction."[237] He says nothing

more regarding Charles Elwood, perhaps because he retraces the

history of his thought during the same period in the explicitly

autobiographical mode of The Convert. Charles Elwood is semi-auto-

biographical:

> The characters introduced are of course fictitious, yet I
> may say that I have myself had an intellectual experience
> similar to that which Mr. Elwood records, and what he has said
> of himself would perhaps apply in some degree to me. I am
> willing the public should take the book as an account which
> I have thought proper to give of my own former unbelief and
> present belief. So far as it can be of any use, I am willing
> that what is here recorded should have the authority of my own

---

[234]Ibid., p. 87.

[235]Ibid., pp. 87-88.

[236]Orestes A. Brownson, "Charles Elwood Reviewed," Boston
Quarterly Review 5 (1842); reprint ed., Works 4:316.

[237]Brownson, The Convert, p. 90.

experience.[238]

Elwood's "purely spiritual experience" parallels Brownson's; the rest is fancy.[239] The purpose of the work is didactic:

...to state with a little more than ordinary clearness and philosophic precision, the leading questions between believers and unbelievers; to show the unsatisfactory character of the answers usually given to those questions; and to indicate with some distinctness a better method of treating them.[240]

Charles Elwood is an infidel, engaged to Elizabeth, a young woman who experiences a conversion during a religious revival. Despite the efforts of her pastor, Mr. Wilson, Elwood is unmoved and remains unconverted. Pressured by her clergyman and her newly converted brother, Elizabeth breaks her engagement with the unbeliever. Elwood suffers yet another loss, the death of his mother and becomes more deeply depressed: "I had no future....All for whom I could have lived, labored, and died, were gone, or worse than gone. I had no end, no aim."[241] Gradually, moved by what he observes around him -- social injustice, inequality, and oppression, he dedicates himself to the task of reforming society. For a time, world-reform becomes his religion, "a faith and a culture, of which I was the apostle and felt I could be the martyr."[242] But before long, Elwood becomes a champion of rational religion, an exponent of reason's compatibility with Christianity. Mr. Morton, a persuasive preacher, introduces Elwood to

---

[238]Brownson, Charles Elwood, p. 173.

[239]Brownson, "Charles Elwood Reviewed," p. 317.

[240]Ibid., p. 316.

[241]Brownson, Charles Elwood, p. 223.

[242]Ibid., p. 225.

the ecclectic school of thought associated with French philosophers
such as M. Victor Cousin.[243] Before the story ends, the infidel is
converted to "a new Christianity" which is nothing but "the old
Christianity which all the world has believed, under a new aspect,
perhaps, and an aspect more peculiarly adapted to the wants of the
present age."[244]

Charles Elwood is patently autobiographical. Elwood's
resolution of his religious inquiry is indeed Brownson's in the
late 1830's. The themes which reoccur in The Convert with frequency
appear in Charles Elwood as well: the religious sentiment is natural;
reason is compatible with Christianity; the time is ripe for a new
Christianity. Elwood's experiences mirror Brownson's: both rejected
orthodox Christianity; both were self-proclaimed infidels; both were
attracted to the work of world-reform; both became advocates of
reason in religion.

Charles Elwood makes its primary contribution as a chronicle
of Brownson's earlier religious experiences: his childhood impressions
and his adolescent encounter with revivalism. Charles Elwood both
corroborates and elaborates upon Brownson's report of his early years
as set forth in The Convert. This passage, detailing Elwood's early
fascination with religion and his terror in the face of unbelief,
actually describes Brownson's experiences as a lonely child and identifies
the needs that brought him to the Presbyterian Church:

Religion I had loved from my infancy. In my loneliness, in

---

[243]See the Preface to Charles Elwood, p. 174.

[244]Ibid., p. 315.

my solitary wonderings, it had been my companion and my support.
It had been my pleasure to feel that wherever I went the eye
of my Father watched over me, and his infinite love embraced
me. I was never in reality alone. A glorious presence went
always with me. When I was thrown upon the world at a tender
age without a friend, and left to buffet my way unaided,
unencouraged, and felt myself cut off from all communication
with my God, I could hold sweet and mysterious communion
with this Father of men; and when I smarted under a sense
of wrong done me, I could find relief in believing that
He sympathized with me, and made my cause his own. God had
been to me a reality, and though I had been nurtured in
the tenets of the gloomiest and most chilling of Christian
creeds, I had always seen him as a father, and as a father whose
face ever beamed with paternal love. I could not then lose
my faith, and see all my religious hopes and consolations
escape in the darkness of unbelief, without feeling that I
was giving up all that had hitherto sustained me, all that was
pleasant to remember, that could soothe in sorrow, strengthen
under trial, inspire love, and give the wish or courage to
live.[245]

And though both Elwood and Brownson were subjected to the persuasive

preaching of evangelicals calling for conversion, neither "got

religion" in that sense. Brownson describes his adolescent encounter

with the revivalists only briefly in The Convert. In Charles Elwood,

he describes what he observed in the "sinners apartment" of an inquiry

meeting: persons "of both sexes, all ages, and all conditions," some

brought there by their longing for forgiveness and salvation, others

by their desire for more immediate gratification.[246] Among the latter

were the village trader and the village lawyer, "trying in vain to

look sad and penitent"; one was there "because he wanted more customers

and better bargains, the other because he wanted more fees and more

votes."[247] Brownson is critical of the clergyman who tries to convert

---

[245]Ibid., pp. 197-198.

[246]Ibid., p. 192.

[247]Ibid., p. 193.

Elwood, accusing him of "weak and sluggish" moral sentiments.[248]

But on the whole, Brownson is sympathetic to the goals of revivalism

even though he questions its methods. Revivals have "succeeded

in shaking dry bones, in reviving a good work, in preparing

...a more advanced state of the church and of society."[249] The

benefits of revivalism outweigh its evils: "They undoubtedly en-

gendered much fanaticims, much bigotry and sectarian animosity; but

these, after all, disastrous as they may be, are less to be

deprecated, then the selfishness and indifference they aimed to

remove."[250]

Charles Elwood charts the course of Brownson's religious thought

during a particularly exciting time, a time when Brownson is examining

and evaluating a variety of philosophical and religious perspectives

and honing his own. But it is by no means a last word; judging from

the very brief mention of the book in The Convert, after his conversion

to Roman Catholicism, Brownson saw Elwood's resolution as little more

than a step in the right direction.

Conspicuous by its absence is explicit reference to Brownson's

participation in the meetings of the Transcendentalists. Sveino observes

that Brownson "seems to have underrated the impact of Transcendentalism

on his mind."[251] Brownson had been present at the first meeting of

what came to be known as the Transcendental Club in September,

---

[248]Ibid.

[249]Ibid., p. 193.

[250]Ibid., p. 192.

[251]Sveino, p. 17.

1836.[252] He attended four of the thirty meetings of the Club, held

between 1836 and 1840. He shared their dissatisfaction with

Unitarianism, which, in Brownson's words, had "demolished Calvinism"

and "made an end in all thinking minds of every thing like dogmatic

Protestantism."[253] The Transcendentalists experienced "a hunger of

the spirit for the values which Unitarianism had concluded were no

longer estimable."[254] Brownson shared in their search for "new forms

of expression instead of new formulations of doctrine," their openness

to European thought, their view of religion as a natural human sentiment,

and their conviction that man is capable of "knowing truth intuitive-

ly."[255] But he parted company with them when the term "Transcendental-

ism" was understood to place

> ...feeling above reason, dreaming above reflection, and
> instinctive intimation above scientific exposition; in a word,
> when it means the substitution of lawless fancy for an en-
> lightened understanding, as we apprehend it is understood in
> this neighborhood, by the majority who use it as a term of
> reproach, we disown it, and deny we are Transcendentalists.[256]

Brownson differed from Transcendentalists in two important ways:

"he did not share their dislike of churches and institutions" and he

---

[252]Also present were Amos B. Alcott, James F. Clarke, Ralph
W. Emerson, Frederic Hedge, and George Ripley. Other "more or less
regular" members of the Club were Theodore Parker, Christopher Pearse
Cranch, John Sullivan Dwight, W. H. Channing, Cyrus Bartol, Caleb
Steton, Margaret Fuller, Sophia Ripley, and Elizabeth Peabody. The
Transcendentalists, ed. Perry Miller (Cambridge: Harvard University
Press, 1967), p. 106.

[253]Brownson, The Convert, p. 76.

[254]The Transcendentalists, p. 8.

[255]Ibid., p. 9; Sveino, p. 129.

[256]Orestes A. Brownson, "Two Articles for the Princeton Review,"
Brownson Quarterly Review 3 (1840):322-323, cited by Ryan, p. 151.

was more skeptical toward Protestanism than were the others.[257]
On the latter point, Sveino observes that most Transcendentalists
were opposed to "Calvinist orthodoxy, not to the Protestant emphasis
on individual reason and conscience"; they did not share "Brownson's
positive appraisal of medieval Catholicism."[258] Finally, the
Transcendentalists did not share Brownson's desire "to expand
Transcendentalism into a wide application to the more practical affairs
of life, the social question, government and politics."[259]

History has assigned Brownson a place among the Transcendentalists. Why did Brownson make so little of this association in The
Convert? He readily acknowledges the influence of numerous individuals
on his thought, among them Owen, Wright, Constant, Cousins, and Leroux.
He associates himself with various religious groups to which he belonged
and admits his sympathy with certain political groups. Perhaps it
was Brownson's independence of thought in religious matters (at
least until he became a member of the Roman Catholic Church) that kept
him from stressing his company with the Transcendentalists. Perhaps,
Brownson was reluctant to associate himself with a movement that was
characterized by such a vast variety of opinions, especially given
his substantive disagreement with a number of their loosely held tenets.
Or perhaps Brownson was reacting to their reluctance to count him as
one of their own. Dr. Hedge is said to have remarked that "Brownson
met with us once or twice, but became unbearable, and was not afterward

---

[257]Sveino, p. 131.

[258]Ibid.

[259]Ryan, p. 153.

invited."[260] Brownson's "militant" nature, his conversion to Roman

Catholicism, and his habit of "administering ferocious chastisement" to

Protestantism and Transcendentalism in his Quarterly did little to

endear him to the Transcendentalists.

Brownson's reaction to some lectures given by Theodore Parker,

a member of the Transcendentalist Club, marks a critical shift in

Brownson's thinking. In the autumn of 1841, Parker delivered several

lectures which were later published as part of A Discourse of Matters

Pertaining to Religion.[261] Although Parker's views on religion were

essentially in agreement with Brownson's ideas regarding the religion

of humanity, Brownson reacted negatively to the doctrine as Parker

stated it. Listening to the lectures, Brownson discovered a "radical

difference" between them:

> We had both, it is true, placed the origin and ground of reli-
> gion in a religious sentiment natural to man; but while I made
> that sentiment the point of departure for proving that reli-
> gion is in accordance with nature and reason, and therefore
> of removing what had been my chief difficulty in the way of
> accepting supernatural revelation, he made it his starting-
> point for reducing all religion to mere naturalism....He held
> and applied it nakedly, in an unbelieving spirit; I held it
> in connection with many elements of my early traditional
> faith, and applied it in a believing spirit....he seized upon
> it as an instrument for demolishing the Christian temple,
> overthrowing the altar of Christ, and of sweeping away the Bible,
> and all creeds, dogmas, forms, rites, and institutions of
> religion.[262]

Brownson was moving closer and closer to Christianity, indeed to

---

[260]Quoted by Harold Clarke Goddard, Studies in New England Transcendentalism (New York: Columbia University Press, 1908; reprint ed., New York: Humanities Press, 1969), p. 36.

[261]Theodore Parker, A Discourse of Matters Pertaining to Religion (Boston, 1842; reprint ed., New York: Arno Press, 1972).

[262]Brownson, The Convert, pp. 156-157.

Catholicism. His ideas regarding religion were becoming ever more

orthodox. He readily admits to his "horror of unbelief" and to his

readiness to become a believer as soon as he could believe "without

violence" to his nature, without denying his reason.[263]

During the four years prior to his conversion to Roman

Catholicism in 1844, Brownson formulated several major ideas which

successively brought him to the threshold of the Church. In 1840,

he published an essay on "The Laboring Classes," which met "with

one universal sense of horror," Brownson recalls.[264] He presented

a three-pronged program: demolish the visible church, annihilate

the priesthood, and resuscitate the Christianity of Christ.[265] "The

Christianity of the church has done its work."[266] It can do no more

good but it does much harm. The Christianity of the church

> ...now unmans us and hinders the growth of God's kingdom. The
> moral energy which is awakened it misdirects, and makes its
> deluded disciples believe that they have done their duty to
> God when they joined the church, offered a prayer, sung a psalm,
> and contributed of their means to send out a missionary to
> preach unintelligible dogmas to the poor heathen, who, God
> knows, have unintelligible dogmas enough already, and more than
> enough.[267]

The Christianity of the church has failed to bring about the social

reform which the Gospel demands. Organized religion perpetuates

social injustice; justice will be realized only when the community

---

[263]Ibid., p. 157.

[264]Ibid., p. 105.

[265]Ibid., p. 108.

[266]Ibid.

[267]Ibid.

216

is christianized. Brownson called for the reorganization of the state
on Christian principles, a departure from his earlier call for a new
church.[268] Restructuring the state required the redistribution of
property, that is, the abolishment of the hereditary right to property,
and the abrogation of the wage system. The political and economic
implications of Brownson's proposal caused concern among his readers.
But Brownson's gradual recognition of the importance of order, government, and authority had more serious consequences in the development of
his views on the church. After he had expounded his "so-called
'horrible doctrines,'" he advanced rapidly toward religious conservatism.[269] In short, Brownson realized that it is impossible to effect
the progress of man without a new organization, a new church.

But how would that new organization, that new church, come
into existence? Ideas do not actualize themselves, Brownson concluded;
even "true ideas" may never be translated into action. Man is not a
church-builder.

> My new church, then, if it is to elevate the race and be the
> means of their progress, must embody a power above that which
> they now have. Whence is that power to come? How am I to
> obtain it, and obtain it I must, without my new church, and
> obtain it as the condition of organizing it?[270]

That power is derived from man's natural communion with God. Building
on the philosophy of Pierre Leroux, Brownson formulated the doctrine
of life by communion, the doctrine which led to his conversion.

Leroux proposed that man lives "by communion with that which

---

[268]Ibid., p. 111.

[269]Ibid., p. 123.

[270]Ibid., p. 124.

is not himself."[271] This is true at every level: at the vegetative

level, by assimilating food and drink; at the sensory level, by

sensing an object which is outside himself; at the intellectual

level, by thinking of an object outside himself.[272] Love too is

'a synthesis of subject and object."[273] Man lives in communion

with that which is outside himself. The relation, the communion, that

occurs between subject and object is life-giving; man's "elevation,

his progress as well as his very existence, depend on the object.

He cannot lift himself, but must be lifted, by placing him in communion

with a higher and elevating object."[274] Leroux maintained that man

"'communes with nature through property, with his fellow-men through

family and the state and with God through humanity.'"[275] Brownson

accepted the first two assertions and rejected the third. Communion

with humanity is not really communion with God. And communion with

humanity does not explain progress. If man can only make progress

by communion with an object higher than himself, he cannot make

progress by communion with God through humanity, which is "nothing

---

[271]Ibid., p. 131. Pierre Leroux (1797-1871), French philosopher
and economist, was a member of the sect of Saint-Simonian Socialists
until 1832. He founded several reviews and journals: the Revue
encyclopédique, Encyclopédia nouvelle, the Revue indepéndante, and
the Revue sociale. His major work, De l' Humanité, was published
in 1840.

[272]Malone, p. 63. For a detailed discussion of Brownson's
apologetic argument from the doctrine of life, see pp. 60-79.

[273]Ibid., p. 63.

[274]Brownson, The Convert, p. 131.

[275]Ibid., p. 132.

but communion with the race."[276] Brownson concluded that

...man is not and cannot be in himself progressive, and that
his progress depends on the objective element of his life, or,
in other words, on his living in communion with God, and not
only in a natural communion as held by Leroux, but also in
a supernatural communion.[277]

How is supernatural communion to be achieved? Brownson again

took his lead from Leroux, who argued that the race would be elevated

by the aid of the "Providential Men."[278] These men, providentially

elevated by God "to an extraordinary or supernatural communion with

himself," would themselves live "a divine life" and "we by communion

with them would also be elevated, and live a higher or more advanced

life."[279] Throughout history, these men had lifted mankind to new

levels of consciousness; these men were the vehicles of God's revelation.

Sveino observes that

Brownson's idea of Providential messengers reflected the Romantic
and Transcendentalist belief in particularly gifted individuals
like poets and prophets: veritable depositories of divine
inspiration. More especially, apart from the direct influence
from Leroux, Brownson's Providential men had parallels to
Cousin's "le vrai representant," Emerson's "Représentative
Men" and Carlyle's "Heroes." But far more markedly than the
others, Brownson considered these "individual messengers"
primarily religious leaders and not poets, artists, and
philosophers.[280]

In retrospect, Brownson saw that the idea of the Providential

Men bridged the gap between the natural and the supernatural: God was

---

[276]Malone, p. 68.

[277]Brownson, The Convert, p. 133.

[278]Ibid., pp. 134-135.

[279]Ibid., p. 134.

[280]Sveino, pp. 247-248.

able "to afford us supernatural aid without violence to our natures."[281]

In other words, God was free to intervene in creation. In recognizing

God's freedom, Brownson realized his own. Brownson's God was not the

disinterested architect of the Deists; God was his Father and he was

"no longer fatherless."[282] One by one, the obstacles to faith were

removed and Brownson stood nearer the Catholic Church than ever before:

> I found that I could reasonably accept the ideas of providence,
> special as well as general, supernatural inspiration, super-
> natural revelation, and Christianity an authoritarian reli-
> gion, and must do so, or be false alike to history and my hopes
> of progress. I felt, as I had felt from my boyhood, that I
> had need of an authoritative religion; and that a religion
> which does not and cannot speak with divine authority, is
> simply no religion at all.[283]

This is the fundamental assertion of the doctrine of life

by communion. God effects the progress of man and society through

supernatural aid rendered by Providential Men. The next step was

to affirm that Jesus Christ is the epitome of the Providential Man.

Brownson argued that

> The Son, by his supernatural or miraculous communion with the
> Father, lives a divine-human life; so the apostles and disciples,
> by communion with the Son, lived the same life, and through
> him become one in life with the Father and with one another,
> and were elevated above their actual life, and set forward in
> the career of progress.[284]

Through communion with the Lord, man communes with the Father; Jesus

Christ is the mediator between God and man. Because we cannot communi-

cate directly with Christ, we rely on communion with the apostles,

---

[281] Brownson, The Convert, p. 135.

[282] Ibid., p. 144.

[283] Ibid., p. 138.

[284] Ibid., p. 150.

transmitted from generation to generation. The church is the
community of all who share in the life of Christ. Christ's body
is an organic body, "one because its life is one, and catholic
because it includes all who live the life, of whatever age or nation,
and because all men in every age and nation may by communion live
it."[285] The church is the highest authority, "the highest manifestation
of both the divine and the human."[286] Therefore, it is reasonable to
submit to its authority. By tradition, each generation communes with its
predecessors, and derives its life from that relation. In this way,
Brownson demonstrated both the necessity and the fact of apostolic succession.

Determined to proclaim this doctrine of life by communion,
Brownson agreed to become one of the editors of The Christian World,
a new Unitarian weekly, published by George G. Channing, brother
of William Ellery Channing. In this new journal, he published "The
Mission of Jesus," a series of essays designed to apply the doctrine
of life to Christianity. He "hoped to draw attention to the church
as a living organism, and the medium through which the Son of God
practically redeems, saves, or blesses mankind."[287] Seven essays
were published, pleasing Unitarians, Puritans, Tractarians, and
Catholics, in turn. The eighth was not published; the publisher of
The Christian World refused to let it appear. That last essay was to

---

[285]Ibid., p. 151.

[286]Ibid., p. 152.

[287]Ibid., p. 160.

answer the question: "Which is the true church or body of Christ?"[288]

In the process of writing the series, Brownson realized that logic required him to accept the Roman Catholic Church. But he hesitated for a year before he finally submitted. What accounted for his hesitation?

"The work of conversion is, of course, the work of grace, and without grace no man can come into the church any more than he can enter heaven."[289] Though Brownson insisted that his doctrine of communion had brought him to the threshold of the Roman Catholic Church, he always affirmed the indispensible role of grace in conversion. Reason is not a substitute for grace but the workings of grace are never contrary to reason or to free will. A rational subject must make a free choice. In The Convert, Brownson was determined to make it clear that the process by which he came to the Church was critical but not in itself sufficient to account for his conversion.

That conversion is the work of grace does not in itself account for Brownson's delay. How does Brownson himself account for it? In a number of ways. Brownson enumerates some personal difficulties which kept him from submitting to the Church. It was one thing to see the logic of the Church's claims, another to make up his mind to accept them. He was reluctant "to condemn the whole Protestant world, so large a portion of mankind" and as he had always believed "the more moral,

---

[288]Ibid., p. 160.

[289]Ibid., p. 167.

enlightened, and energetic portion."[290] His "poor opinion of Catholics"

made him unwilling to become one of them; he had been accustomed "to

regard the Catholic nations of Europe, since the time of Leo X., as

unprogressive, and the mass of their population as ignorant, degraded,

enslaved, cowardly, and imbecile."[291] He attributed the "supposed

inferiority" of Catholics to a failure of leadership. Catholic clergy

"must have lost the deeper sense of their religion, become men of

routine, and incapable of comprehending or meeting the wants of the

age."[292] They were a defensive lot, fearful of progress and determined

"to keep masses in ignorance and slavery, that they might keep them

in the faith."[293]

> Nor was this all. To pass from one Protestant sect to
> another is a small affair, and is little more than going from
> one apartment to another in the same house. We remain still
> in the same world, in the same general order of thought, and
> in the midst of the same friends and associates. We do not
> go from the known to the unknown; we are still within soundings,
> and may either return, if we choose, to the sect we have left
> or press on to another, without serious loss of reputation,
> or any gross disturbance of our domestic and social relations.
> But to pass from Protestantism to Catholicity is a very dif-
> ferent thing. We break with the whole world in which we
> have hitherto lived; we enter into what is to us a new and
> untried region, and we fear the discoveries we may make there,
> when it is too late to draw back. To the Protestant mind this
> old Catholic Church is veiled in mystery, and leaves ample room
> to the imagination to people it with all manner of monsters,
> chimeras, and hydras dire. We enter it, and leave no bridge
> over which we may return. It is a committal for life, for
> eternity. To enter it seemed to me, at first, like taking
> a leap in the dark; and it is not strange that I recoiled,

---

[290]Ibid., p. 161.

[291]Ibid., p. 162.

[292]Ibid., p. 163.

[293]Ibid.

and set my wits to work to find out, if possible, some com-
promise, some middle ground on which I could be faithful to
Catholic tendencies without uniting myself with the present
Catholic Church.[294]

The personal cost of conversion was reason enough to proceed
with the utmost caution. Conversion to Roman Catholicism meant
losing one's place in society and assuming a new personal identity.
Aware as he was of the price, it is little wonder that Brownson
drew back, taking refuge in the fact that he had not established
the infallibility of the Roman Church. That the Roman Church was
the largest fragment of the true body of Christ was undeniable
but why should we not "labor, from the point where Providence has
placed us, to effect in the surest and speediest manner possible
the reunion of all the fragments, and thus restore the body of
Christ to its original unity and integrity."[295]

Joining the Anglican communion was not a viable option for
Brownson: "It was far better to go at once to Rome than to Oxford."[296]
But Brownson acknowledged that the Tractarian movement was "a promising
sign of the times" which indicated "a tendency on the part of a large
portion of the Protestant world to return to church principles."[297]
He hoped that this tendency, evident in the sects as well as in the
Catholic Church, heralded the reunion of Christianity. To contribute
to that cause, Brownson founded the quarterly which bore his name.

---

[294] Ibid.

[295] Ibid., p. 165.

[296] Ibid.

[297] Ibid.

Brownson's hesitation at the threshold of the Church may
be attributed to his awareness of the personal and social price of
conversion and his inherited antipathy toward Roman Catholicism,
as well as to the fact that conversion was more than a simple
conclusion to a syllogism. What was required was that he submit
himself to the Church and "Take her explanation of herself and of her
dogmas."[298] But there was no other alternative. To do otherwise
was to risk eternal punishment. So Brownson resolved to act:

> As the Catholic Church is clearly the church of history, the
> only church that can have the slightest historical claim to
> be regarded as the body of Christ, it is to her that I must
> go, and her teachings, as given through her pastors, that I
> must accept as authoritative for natural reason.[299]

In this frame of mind, Brownson approached Bishop Benedict Joseph
Fenwick in May, 1844, announced his desire to become a Catholic,
and asked to be introduced to someone who could instruct him and
prepare him for reception. Bishop Fenwick sent Brownson to John
Bernard Fitzpatrick, the man who would succeed Fenwick as bishop
of Boston in 1846. Brownson recalls that Fitzpatrick received him
"with civility, but with a certain degree of mistrust."[300]
Fitzpatrick was prejudiced against him and suspicious of his motives.
The initial uneasiness between them continued for two or three months;
Brownson was hesitant to explain the process by which he had come to the
church, namely his doctrine of life by communion, and Fitzpatrick

---

[298]Ibid., p. 167.

[299]Ibid., p. 168.

[300]Ibid., p. 170.

225

sensed his reserve and "want of entire frankness."[301] Though Brownson

denied any special attachment to the doctrine as such and was willing

to give it up, without it he had no reason for accepting the authority

of the Church. He resolved that difficulty by accepting the traditional

Catholic argument for the credibility of the Church. Brownson accepted

the "motives of credibility" and so entered the Church. But he is

quick to point out that it was not the method by which he moved from

unbelief to the threshold of the Church. Indeed, he suspects that

"it would never have brought me to the church, -- not because it is

not logical, not because it is not objectively complete and conclusive,

but because I wanted the eternal and subjective disposition to understand

and receive it."[302] At the time of his conversion, Brownson "suppressed"

his philosophical theory. At the time, it had seemed appropriate, even

desirable to do so out of modesty and humility befitting a convert:

"Was it likely I had discovered anything of value that had escaped

the great theologians and doctors of the Church."[303] That move caused

many to question his credibility -- more so than would have been the

case if he had simply converted to Roman Catholicism; the lack of

connection between what he said before his conversion and what he said

afterward led many to conclude that his conversion was "a sudden

caprice, or rash act taken from a momentary impulse or in a fit of

intellectual despair."[304]

---

[301] Ibid.

[302] Ibid., p. 171.

[303] Ibid., p. 173.

[304] Ibid., pp. 173-174.

Twelve years later, when he was writing The Convert,
Brownson was ready to reaffirm the validity of his method. He
engaged in a lengthy discussion of the value of his way and the inadequacy of traditional methods of proof. Standard apologetic arguments
do not address real objections, do not meet non-Catholics where they
are: the motives of credibility "start from principles which they
[non-Catholics] do not accept, or accept with so much vagueness
and uncertainty, that they do not serve to warrant assent even to
strictly logical conclusions drawn from them."[305] Effective methods
of demonstration must be adapted to the needs of those to whom they
are addressed. The doctrine of life by communion is an effective
method of bringing unbelievers to the Church because it answers
their primary question: how can faith and reason be reconciled?
Brownson maintains that his argument demonstrates that the order of
nature and the order of grace are not "mutually antagonistic," that
"they correspond one to the other, and really constitute but two
parts of one comprehensive whole, and are equally embraced in the
original plan and purpose of God in creating."[306] He sums up his
argument in this way:

> The doctrine that all dependent life is life by communion of
> the subject with the object...shows the common principle
> of the two orders, and thus prepares the mind to receive and
> yield to the arguments drawn from the wants of nature, the
> insufficiency of reason, miracles, and historical monuments;
> for it shows these to be in accordance with the original in-
> tent of the Creator, and that these wants and this insufficiency
> are wants and insufficiency, not in relation to the purely
> natural order, but in relation to the supernatural. Natural

---

[305]Ibid., p. 176.

[306]Ibid., p. 179.

reason is sufficient for natural reason, but it is not sufficient for man, for man was intended from the beginning to live
simultaneously in two orders, the one natural and the other [307]
supernatural.

Not only was Brownson determined to defend the process of thought by

which he made his way to the Church; he was, at the time of writing

The Convert, resolute in proposing his experience as a paradigm for

other non-Catholics. He was convinced that his method was an effective

way of removing the obstacles to faith that keep non-Catholics from

the Church and that his experience was indeed exemplary. The Convert

is unique among the conversion narratives because no other convert

author shares Brownson's purpose. Brownson wrote to tell his story

and to present his conversion as a reasonable act but he also sought

to demonstrate the validity and the value of the way by which he came

into the Church.

How did Brownson view his conversion? As a reasonable act

of submission to the authority of the Church, which means submission

to highest reason. Brownson saw his conversion to the Roman Catholic

Church as "an act of reason, though indeed of reason assisted by

grace."[308] As such, it was radically different from his earlier

conversion to the Presbyterian Church, a conversion which required

him to abandon reason.

The act of submitting to Presbyterianism was a rash act, an
irrational act, an act of folly; because no man either can
or should divest himself of reason, the essential and characteristic element of his nature; and because I neither had nor
asked any proof that the Presbyterian Church had been instituted

---

[307] Ibid.

[308] Ibid., p. 180.

by our Lord, and commissioned by him to teach me.[309]
When Brownson became a Roman Catholic, he had proved to his own
satisfaction that the Catholic Church was instituted by God "as
the medium of communion between him and men."[310] Conversion to
Roman Catholicism meant submission to the authority of the Church,
which derives from the Church's communion with God incarnate,
from the action of the Holy Spirit present in those who exercise the
Church's authority. Submission to the Church is "an act of reason herself in the full possession and free exercise of her highest powers."[311]
Never had he discovered any doctrine of the Church to be inconsistent
with reason.

Roman Catholicism is the way to eternal salvation. Brownson
ends his narrative by explaining that he is a Catholic "because he
believes the Catholic Church is the church of God, because he believes
her the medium through which God dispenses his grace to man, and through
which alone we can hope for heaven."[312] He proposes that "the real
reason why we should become Catholics and remain such, is, because she
is the new creation, regenerated humanity, and without communion
with her, we can never see God as he is, or become united to him as
our supreme good in the supernatural order."[313] Earlier in the text,

---

[309]Ibid.

[310]Ibid., p. 181.

[311]Ibid., p. 187.

[312]Ibid., p. 205.

[313]Ibid.

Brownson pointed to his fear of being damned if he continued
living the life he was living outside the Church.[314] It was unpleasant
to submit himself to the pastors of the Church and seek their counsel,
"but to be eternally damned would, after all, be a great deal
unpleasanter."[315]

Why did Orestes A. Brownson become a convert to Roman
Catholicism? What were the motives which led this complex and often
controversial American from childhood Congregationalism and exposure
to Methodist revivalism, through Presbyterianism, Universalism, Socialism,
Unitarianism, and Transcendentalism to Roman Catholicism? In The Convert,
Brownson states some motives explicitly; others lie between the lines
of his narrative. As noted above, his desire for salvation contributed
to his eventual submission to Rome. Once he had overcome the numerous
obstacles to belief, the fear of being damned for all eternity moved
him to seek instruction. Roman Catholicism satisfied his intellect;
it is, as he never tired of saying, consistent with reason. Becoming
a Roman Catholic did not require sacrificing reason or acting in a
manner contrary to his nature. His desire to maintain intellectual
integrity, to act in a manner consistent with his theory accounted for
his frequent alternations and finally contributed to his conversion to
Roman Catholicism.

Roman Catholicism appealed to Brownson's longing for unity
and authority. Per Sveino observes that "a never failing quest for

---

[314]Ibid., p. 168.
[315]Ibid.

230

unity or synthesis" dominated Brownson's thinking.[316] Brownson

worked hard to overcome the dichotomy of the secular and the sacred:

reason and revelation, nature and grace, materialism and spiritualism.

Brownson's

> ...idea of a "catholic" Unitarianism, his ecumenical vision of
> a higher Christian unity in an all-comprising really universal
> church, his espousal of Eclecticism, his synthetic philosophy,
> and, finally, his doctrine of life and communion, there was
> all the way an intense, consistent striving for unity, for the
> reconciliation of different principles in a real synthesis.[317]

The Roman Catholic Church represented the fullness of Christian truth.

In its unity, its catholicity, its apostolicity -- the Roman Catholic

Church symbolizes its union with God incarnate.

"I am incapable of directing myself. I must have a guide."[318]

This thought led Brownson to the Presbyterian Church at the age of

nineteen. He abnegated reason and submitted to the Church. He sought

an authoritarian teacher and a rule of faith. He found neither and

left the Presbyterian Church to become a Universalist, because

Universalist doctrine was more rational, even though it was unsupported

by Scripture. But Brownson never abandoned his search for an authority

to which he could submit -- reasonably, of course. In the Roman

Catholic Church, he found his guide. Though he constantly affirms that

his conversion was consistent with reason, he nevertheless makes it

clear that conversion involves submission -- submission to the Church,

its pastors, and its view of itself. He writes that his own thinking

---

[316]Sveino, p. 306.

[317]Ibid.

[318]Brownson, The Convert, p. 10.

had brought him to the point where he either had to renounce reason "or go further and accept the church and her doctrine, in her own sense."[319] That was the most difficult step, but Brownson did submit, even to the point of laying aside the theory that had brought him to the Church. In his relationship with Bishop Fitzpatrick, Brownson acted out the submission which conversion demanded: Fitzpatrick became his instructor, confessor, spiritual director, and friend.[320] Under his tutelage, Brownson became versed in traditional Catholic theology and apologetics.[321] Brownson became the leading American apologist of the nineteenth century. Thomas R. Ryan, author of the definitive biography of Brownson, suggests that Brownson's personal appreciation of authority served him well in his role as apologist:

> He had at long last found an authority that could give him security against error. He had had much sad experience with error in its multiple forms as he had painstakingly picked his way through various systems of thought both of the ancient and modern world until he was finally led, humanly speaking, along the road of philosophy to the threshold of the Catholic Church. Search as he would, he had long been the sport and the victim of many an ignis fatuus. A few weeks after his conversion, in an oration in Old Broadway Tabernacle in New York City, he compared himself for the last twenty years to one stepping on cakes of ice, each one of which was barely enough to support his weight until he could reach the next, until at last he had come to solid ground.[322]

He had come to his father's house.

Several key passages in The Convert suggest that from the

---

[319]Ibid., p. 161.

[320]Ibid., p. 169.

[321]More than ten years passed before Brownson put forth a strong argument for the superiority of his own method of bringing unbelievers to the Church.

[322]Ryan, p. 329.

time of his fatherless childhood Brownson was searching for a

father. Per Sveino has traced this motif in Brownson's life, as

has Donald Capps.[323] Brownson's account of his early childhood

leaves no doubt that he felt abandoned and isolated and consequently

turned inward, becoming preoccupied with religion to a degree unusual

for a child his age. His inner life made up for the dissatisfaction

and excitement lacking in his social life, but there is no doubt that

he felt his deprivation keenly. Brownson had a strong desire to see

God as Father, to believe in God as his father. One incident,

recounted in The Convert, reveals the Fatherhood of God as a central

metaphor for Brownson. When he realized that God could freely

intervene in behalf of his creation, he was overcome with relief and

joy:

> This threw a heavy burden from my shoulders, and in freezing
> God from his assumed bondage to nature, unshackled my own
> limbs, and made me feel that in God's freedom I had sure pledge
> of my own. God could, if he chose, be gracious to me; he
> could hear my prayers, respond to my entreaties, interpose
> to protect me, to assist me, to teach me, and to bless me. He
> was free to love me as his child, and to do me all the good
> his infinite love should prompt. I was no longer chained,
> like Prometheus to the Caucasion rock, with my vulture passions
> devouring my heart; I was no longer fatherless, an orphan left
> to the tender mercies of inexorable general laws, and my heart
> bounded with joy, and I leaped to embrace the neck of my Father,
> and to rest my head on his bosom. I shall never forget the
> ecstasy of that moment, when I first realized to myself that
> God is free.[324]

No longer was he an orphan. He could commune with his God. This

passage serves another purpose: it reveals the depth of the affective

---

[323]Sveino, especially pp. 307-310. Donald Capps, "Orestes
Brownson: The Psychology of Religious Affiliation," Journal for
the Scientific Study of Religion 7 (1968):197-209.

[324]Brownson, The Convert, p. 144.

dimension of Brownson's spirituality; his was, by no means, merely
a cerebral religiousity.

Becoming a Roman Catholic marked the end of Brownson's search
for a religious system that was consistent with reason, one that
offered guidance and the assurance of salvation, satisfied his desire
for unity and synthesis, met his need to belong and to achieve communion
with men and with God.

The Convert is singular in this: it recounts the experience
of a man who was clearly in a class by himself. Brownson's experience
was atypical; the route by which he made his way to the Church was
distinctively his own. Few have given themselves so whole-heartedly
to the religious quest and fewer still have paved their own roads
to the Church. Of this road, his friend, Isaac Hecker writes:
"It was a new path he struck; he followed it faithfully to his
reception into the church, and gave us The Convert what, to my
knowledge, no one else has ever done before or since -- the philosopher's
road to the church."[325] It is significant that Brownson saw the process
of thought by which he had come to the Church as paradigmatic. In this,
he is also unique among the convert authors; Brownson clearly intended
that his experience be a model for others to imitate. He maintained
that his doctrine of life communion could bring others to the Church
as it had brought him there. The Convert is a narrative of Brownson's
experience but it is also an argument for the superiority of his method
of approaching the Roman Catholic Church.

---

[325]Isaac Hecker, "Dr. Brownson's Road to the Church," The
Catholic World 46 (1887):3.

Gropings After Truth:
A Life Journey from New England Congregationalism
to the One Catholic and Apostolic Church

Joshua Huntington's Gropings After Truth is the account of a

convert from "popular Protestantism" and so serves as a paradigm.[326]

The "history of such a mind is not purely individual, but also

representative" inasmuch as the narrative points to the experience

of "a large class, completely disappointed by New England theology,

and yearning for a doctrine more satisfactory to the demands of

reason, the dictates of conscience, and the events of the soul."[327]

Such was the assessment of Augustine Hewit, a fellow convert. But

more significant to the present reader is the informative character

of the narrative. Huntington wrote a detailed account of the process

of his conversion as well of his early religious history. That is

to be expected given the sub-title of the narrative which attests

to the significance of his Congregationalist past as the starting

point for his religious journey. What is unexpected is his careful

description of those early experiences and his extensive post-conversion

critique of his previous religious experiences. Although apologetic

concerns occupy Huntington's attention, his treatment of matters of

doctrine and practice does not detract from the essential focus

of the text which is conversion. As Huntington recounts the change

---

[326] Joshua Huntington, Gropings After Truth: A Life Journey
from New England Congregationalism to the One Catholic and Apostolic
Church (New York: The Catholic Publication Society, 1868). In the
Preface to Gropings After Truth, Augustine Hewit points out that the
narrative makes it clear that the Roman Catholic Church attracted more
than High-Church Episcopalians (p. iii).

[327] Ibid.

in his thinking regarding the Church, he frequently explains Catholic

doctrines and rituals, but he does so in the informal, conversational

tone of a layman intent on explaining how he came to be as he is.

The narrative is the primary source of information regarding

the life of Joshua Huntington. His name does not appear in the standard

reference works which contain biographical sketches of most of the

other convert authors.[328] Brother David attributes Gropings After

Truth to Jedediah Vincent Huntington (1815-1862), also a convert to

Roman Catholicism.[329] But David is mistaken. Gropings After Truth

was written by Joshua Huntington, born Joseph Eckley Huntington,

in Boston on February 11, 1812, the first-born son of Joshua

Huntington and Susan Mansfield.[330] After the death of his only

brother, Joshua (1819-1821), Joseph's name was changed to Joshua.

The entry which appears in the geneology of the Huntington Family is

brief but sufficent for a positive identification of this Joshua

Huntington as the author of Gropings After Truth. Joshua graduated

---

[328]These works include the Dictionary of American Biography, Dictionary of Catholic Biography, the Catholic Encyclopedia, and the New Catholic Encyclopedia.

[329]David, pp. 115-117. See the Dictionary of American Biography, the Dictionary of Catholic Biography, the Catholic Encyclopedia, and the New Catholic Encyclopedia for brief biographical sketches of Jedediah V. Huntington. An account of his conversion and a discussion of his work as a novelist appear in the two part essay by James J. Walsh, "Doctor Jedediah Vincent Huntington and the Oxford Movement in America, I. To the Time of His Conversion; II. After His Conversion," Records of the American Catholic Historical Society of Philadelphia 16 (1905):241-267, 416-442. It is likely that Joshua Huntington's allusion to the conversion of "J____ and M____" refers to the conversion of Jedediah and Mary Huntington (Huntington, Gropings After Truth, pp. 9-10).

[330]The Huntington Family in America: A Geneological Memoir

from Yale in 1832.

> He has pursued a professional course of study, both in medicine
> and theology. He graduated in medicine at Yale College,
> in 1837, and from 1838 to 1845 he was in the United States
> naval service as assistant surgeon. He was for several years
> engaged in teaching in a private school for boys in the city
> of Brooklyn, N.Y. From 1864 to 1876 he was a clerk in the
> U.S. Treasury Department, Washington, D.C. He was at first
> a member of St. John's Episcopal Church in Washington, but in
> his later years was a Roman Catholic. He died March 23, 1900.[331]

Joshua Huntington spent much of his leisure time researching the

geneology of the Huntington family; the material which he gathered

"was of very great value in the construction of the geneology of the

family, published in 1863.[332]

The information which appears in the family geneology completes

some of Huntington's fragmentary references: the school he founded

in "B____" was in Brooklyn and "St J____'s Episcopal Church" is

St. John's in "W____," that is, Washington, D.C.[333] In his narrative,

Huntington concentrates on his religious history; he neglects to mention

his career in medicine but that is not surprising given that he intended

to write a narrative of his conversion.

The narrative yields a number of biographical details per-

tinent to Huntington's religious life. The Huntingtons were Con-

---

of the Known Descendents of Simon Huntington from 1633 to 1915
(Hartford, Conn.: Huntington Family Association, 1915), pp. 460-462.

[331] Ibid., p. 462.

[332] Ibid.

[333] Huntington, p. 74. Another corroborating fact: in his
narrative, Huntington mentions that his mother died when he was
eleven years of age. Susan Mansfield Huntington died in 1823; Joshua
was born in 1812. (Huntington, p. 15; The Huntington Family, p. 460).

gregationalists and though Joshua experienced the strict and somber
ethos of Calvinism as a young boy, he did not become a professing
Christian until he was nineteen and a student at Yale. He had passed
through two other revival seasons, one at Andover Academy and the other
at Amherst, without experiencing the sought after change of heart.
But at Yale he experienced conversion. After his graduation, he
began theological studies at Princeton. Before completing them, he
lost his faith in the Christian religion. For the next ten years,
Huntington says that he wondered around the world in a state of
unbelief. Actually, his wondering was not as purposeless as the
narrative suggests; he was serving as a surgeon in the U.S. Navy at
the time. Thirteen years after renouncing his faith in Christianity,
he reaffirmed his membership in the Congregational Church and began
theological studies at Andover. He became a minister but abandoned
the pulpit after a year, having decided that he could not preach what
he did not believe. Huntington established a school in Brooklyn, where
for the next twelve years, he continued to attend the "P____ church."[334]
When he moved to Washington, he began attending the Episcopal Church.
Less than three years later, Huntington converted to Roman Catholicism;
he was in his mid-fifties at the time of his conversion. He wrote
Gropings After Truth shortly after becoming a convert. Joshua
Huntington was a prominent convert, coming as he did from an established
New England family. His name appears among those of some seven hundred

---

[334]Most likely the reference is to the Protestant Church in
light of his subsequent discussion of the Episcopal Church
(Huntington, p. 74).

converts published by Clarke.[335] He came to be known as "The Groper,"
a nickname inspired by the title of his narrative.[336]

The structure of Huntington's account of conversion reflects
the external framework of his religious history: his experience
of revival religion during childhood and adolescence, his becoming
a professing Christian while at Yale, his interlude of infidelity,
his renewed connection with Christianity, his attendance at an
Episcopal Church, and finally his conversion to Roman Catholicism
after a period of apparent religious contentment.[337] Huntington
does more than describe events; he communicates his understanding
of their significance to his reader. The result is a series of
reflections on the nature of revivals, the problem of religious
education, and the nature of conversion.

The narrative is framed as a letter addressed to a friend,
who shared Huntington's earlier distaste for the superstition and
idolatry of Roman Catholicism.[338] Huntington wrote the narrative
to justify his conversion, to present it as a reasonable course
of action which he arrived at after a year and a half of consideration,
study, reflection, and prayer. Huntington proposes to give "a detailed
account" of his religious experiences. His friend knew only the
externals of Huntington's religious history. He knew nothing of the

---

[335]Clarke, "Our Converts," p. 548.

[336]J. Haven Richards, A Loyal Life: A Biography of Henry
Livingston Richards with Selections from His Letters and A Sketch
of the Catholic Movement in America (St. Louis: B. Herder, 1913), p. 278.

[337]Huntington, p. 8.

[338]The friend is not identified by name.

inner turmoil which Huntington resolved through his conversion:

> ...I have been wandering in a fog all my life...my religious
> opinions have been undergoing one change after another, year
> after year, and...never, until I was led by God's grace into
> the Catholic Church, have I felt sure that I was not standing
> upon a treacherous sand-bank, that would be washed away and
> leave me to be swallowed up in the flood.[339]

It is Huntington's inner life, his thought and sentiment, that constitutes

the core of the narrative.

Conversion is the pivotal motif of the narrative, as it was the

central theme in Huntington's religious life. He experienced a series

of conversions: as a Congregationalist, he became a professed Christian;

later, he became an Episcopalian; finally, he became a Roman Catholic.

Each of these conversions resolved a crisis; each of the first two

brought him closer to the Roman Catholic Church -- despite his initial

antagonism toward Romanism.[340]

The ethos of popular Calvinism dominated Huntington's early

years. The severity of Calvinism, as he experienced it, led him to

conclude that religion was "disagreeable" at best:

> ...whenever religion came forward, it was always with a stern,
> repulsive face, to do something which I disliked. It inter-
> fered with my sports, checked all my gayety, took away my play-
> things and picture-books, made me sit still and learn verses
> and hymns as a task, forbidding me to do what would have given
> me pleasure, and compelling me to do what I hated.[341]

Sabbath observance was especially harsh, monotonous, and generally

oppressive. But Huntington observed a significant difference between

his response to religion and the response of others: while he found

---

[339] Huntington, p. 8.

[340] Ibid., pp. 9-11.

[341] Ibid., pp. 12-13.

religion "a very disagreeable thing," he noticed that "pious people enjoyed it, because they often said it was the source of all their happiness."[342] He explained his dissatisfaction with religious practice by pointing toward what he considered to be his personal deficiency. So he concluded that he found religion repulsive because he was not a Christian and that only the experience of conversion would enable him to enjoy religion as others did. The expectations of the community, no doubt, inspired his explanation. His first experience of a revival, "one of those periods of religious awakening upon which New England Calvinists chiefly depend for the conversion of sinners," ended in disappointment.[343] He was ten at the time and a student at Andover Academy. His friends suggested that Huntington's use of the "means of grace" was fruitless because he had persisted in sin and so "grieved away the Holy Spirit."[344] Huntington claims that he was not the least disturbed by their analysis since he knew that he had really sought a conversion and that he had done all he could to experience one. Was Huntington that certain of his position at the tender age of ten? Perhaps, though it would certainly be unusual for a youngster of that age to consider and reject the judgment of his peers and elders.

Four years later, Huntington found himself in the midst of another revival, this time at Amherst Academy. He was "very anxious to become a Christian": he read the Bible, prayed, attended prayer

---

[342]Ibid., p. 13.

[343]Ibid., p. 14.

[344]Ibid.

meetings -- again to no avail.[345] He felt nothing which would have

signaled an experience of conversion. His teacher finally advised

Huntington to resume his studies since he "seemed resolved not to

yield to the influence of the Holy Spirit."[346] Again, he denied

feeling guilty; he had done everything within his power to experience

a conversion.

At nineteen, Joshua was or at least imagined himself to be

converted. The setting was a revival at Yale. The religious excitement

again aroused his desire to experience a conversion:

> ...I could do nothing but have recourse to my old prayers and
> holy books and pious conversations. How long I had continued
> in this way, seeing others daily "rejoicing in hope" around
> me and myself still passed by, I do not remember. But one
> day, after having wearied myself out with praying and weeping
> and dejection, my vital excitement suddenly gave way, and a
> sort of apathy came over me, so that I felt indifferent to
> everything about me. It was a purely physical phenomenon,
> resulting from nothing but exhaustion, such as I have expe-
> rienced many times since; but it was sufficient for necessi-
> ties; it aroused a hope that I was converted, and the hope
> gave me joy and a sense of complacency toward God and my
> fellow creatures, which emotions increased the hope and were
> increased by it, each mutually adding to the other until all
> my anxiety vanished. My confidence was also sustained by my
> pious friends, to whom I gave an account of my feelings, and
> who regarded my sudden change from despondency to rejoicing
> as in the highest degree satisfactory.[347]

But the effects were short-lived: the "happy sensations" soon

vanished. Huntington feared he had deceived himself, but one of his

professors quieted his doubts. Convinced that he was converted,

---

[345]Ibid., p. 16.

[346]Ibid., p. 17.

[347]Ibid., pp. 24-25.

Huntington resolved "to serve God and keep his commandments."[348]

Looking back on the experience, Huntington saw his resolution as the
essential happening, the critical conversion. He was converted when
he determined to do God's will, not when he felt the transient excitement
of conversion. The emotional experience was important insofar as it
prompted him to make the more fundamental decision. Had he not had
the "experience" of conversion, it would never have occurred to him to
publicly profess his faith in Christ. As it was, he joined the college
church, confessing his belief in the articles of faith proposed to him.

New England Congregationalists expected the experience of
conversion to be sudden, intensely emotional, and therefore unforgettable.
Conversion was expected to occur during periods of religious awakening.
Conversion consisted in "an overwhelming sense of the goodness of God"
or of personal wickedness, a "strange ecstatic feeling, different from
anything ever felt before" which produced "a vivid assurance" that
the convert was "born again."[349] The change was memorable; the time
and place at which it occurred were forever engraved on the convert's
memory.

Instructions given to the would-be-converts were simple. Those
"under conviction" were expected to prepare themselves; they were
"exhorted to pray, to read the Bible and religious books, to fix their
thoughts upon God and holy things, to attend prayer-meetings, and con-
verse with pious people on the subject of the salvation of their

---

[348]Ibid., p. 26.

[349]Ibid., p. 18.

souls."[350]   In addition, the would-be-convert was advised to yield
to the Spirit, to give his heart to God, to submit to the will of God.
Huntington found these instructions too vague to be helpful. The simple
directive, decide to do God's will and "strive after holiness, and...avoid
all that is sinful," would have sufficed.[351]   But such was contrary to the
Congregational belief that decision could only follow conversion. The
sinner could do no more than make preliminary preparations and await
God's action. Prior to the experience of conversion, a person was
believed incapable of any good act. Human nature was corrupt and man
was impotent in the face of his corruption. And the "convicted," who
passed through a revival without experiencing conversion, were sure to
slide even deeper into the mire of sin.

Huntington's conversion reveals the importance of social
expectation in determining the acceptable mode of conversion. A
person experienced an authentic conversion if the members of his
community concluded that he had been converted. The criteria were
simple: an experience of intense excitement, occurring during a period
of religious awakening. Such a conversion was a pre-requisite to full
status in the church; without it, a person was powerless, condemned
to the ranks of sinners. If a person "felt" converted and members of
the religious community agreed, his conversion was genuine.

During the course of theological study in preparation for the
ministry, Huntington re-examined his conversion. He realized that he
had actually not changed at all: "In a word, I was the same man, or

---

[350]Ibid.

[351]Ibid., p. 14.

boy more properly, that I had always been."[352] He concluded that

he had interpreted "a giddiness of the head" to be a change of heart;

his supposed "new birth" was a product of his fancy.[353] His fellow

students were no more changed then he was; neither were the "pious

people" he had known. Conversion, he concluded, was "wholly a

delusion."[354] And since Huntington understood conversion to be the

"very cornerstone" of the Christian experience, he lost "all faith in

the Christian religion" when the teachings on conversion lost their

credibility.[355]

In retrospect, Huntington realized that his problem of faith

resulted from his inability to distinguish between Calvinism and

Christianity. To him, they were one and the same. Since he no longer

found Calvinism tenable, he concluded that he was no longer a Christian.

He did not doubt the goodness and holiness of God nor his obligation

to "please" God and address him in prayer; he rejected "only the

religion revealed in the Scripture" which he identified with Calvinism.

During the next ten years Huntington kept his lack of faith to himself.

He led a moral life even though he was not a member of any church.

Toward the end of that period, he became increasingly dissatisfied and

began to doubt the safety of his position: He feared that he had

rejected truth and that he might die in his unbelief.

---

[352]Ibid., p. 31.

[353]Ibid.

[354]Ibid., p. 32.

[355]Ibid., p. 33.

Gradually, Huntington resolved his doubts in favor of the Christian religion, convinced that this religion was what it claimed to be: a religion established at the time of the apostles by men who had first hand experience of the person of Jesus. The rites of "the religion of the cross" were handed down since those first days; people would simply have rejected subsequent innovations. The succession of believers establishes continuity with the first community and its practice. The apostles testified'to the authenticity of the miracles which demonstrated the divine character of Jesus' mission. Huntington believed himself to be a Christian, but he did not view church membership as essential:

> I regarded all churches as merely associations of believers, holding the fundamental doctrines of the New Testament, indeed, but interpreting them each according to its own fancy, and requiring that their members, as a condition of membership, should subscribe beforehand to views prepared for them by men who had no authority whatever to prescribe to others what they should believe and profess.[356]

But Huntington's refusal to join a church deprived him of the opportunity for a public profession of faith and of partaking the Lord's Supper. The church controlled access to the Lord's table, by dictating what its members must believe. Huntington did not feel the deprivation keenly: he regarded the sacrament "as having no virtue in itself; as being nothing more than a ceremony designed to keep in memory the death of our Lord, and affording a means by which Christians may periodically make a public profession of their faith in him."[357] The inconsistency of his position slowly became apparent to Huntington

---

[356]Ibid., p. 36.

[357]Ibid.

and he resolved to make a public profession of faith, reasoning that
such proclamation was "a safeguard against the temptations to sin."[358]

Although Huntington had been attending an Episcopal Church,
he decided to reaffirm his membership in the Congregational Church after
reading of the persecution inflicted on Puritans by the Church of England.
He presented himself to the local Congregational Church, was received
into communion, and again professed the Articles of Faith, which he had
publicly accepted at Yale. But his profession was marked by considerable
reservation:

> I considered it necessary to unite myself to a Christian
> church, and in order to do so I was compelled to acquiesce in
> the "articles of Faith" agreed upon by its members and minis-
> ter; but in assenting to them I did not consider myself bound
> by them for one moment longer than I was myself satisfied of
> their truth.[359]

Huntington's reluctance to commit himself to unquestioning obedience
stemmed from his views on authority. The Bible was, for him as for
countless others, the sole rule of faith. He could not reconcile
the obligation of private judgment with the church's claim that it had
the right to define the content of faith. No one had the right to
impose his interpretation upon another -- even if he be a Martin Luther
or a participant of the Synod of Dort or the Westminster Assembly. The
teachings of the church were contradictory because they were based on
opinion. Huntington argued "that very different views were held and
taught by different theologians; that the creed of a church is generally
that of its minister, and his that of the school at which he was

---

[358]Ibid., p. 37.

[359]Ibid., pp. 39-40.

educated...."[360] How else was a person to choose among the various purported truths except by taking refuge in the Bible?

Huntington resumed theological studies in this frame of mind, resolving to listen critically to his professors at Andover and to reserve judgment until the reasonableness of a given doctrine became apparent. But he found himself unable to affirm any doctrine with certitude: his creed "came to be nothing but a collection of opinions held with various degrees of confidence, but containing almost no articles" which he could believe without reservation.[361] When he had completed his studies and received his license to preach, he was "totally unqualified to assume the spiritual charge of a congregation of men and women who might reasonably expect me to instruct them as to what they should receive as religious truth."[362] Given the uncertainty of his own convictions, he was hardly in a position to form the convictions of others. His creed was reducible to the fundamentals: the Bible is God's word; it was divinely inspired (though Huntington was uncertain as to how that was accomplished); the Bible is the sole rule of faith; each person must interpret its teachings for himself. The principle of individual interpretation was a direct consequence of the sufficiency of Scripture. Dependence on the opinions of others contradicted the sufficiency of the Bible as the rule of faith.

Fundamental as it was, Huntington's creed was nevertheless

---

[360]Ibid., p. 40. .

[361]Ibid., p. 42.

[362]Ibid.

frought with difficulty. He was unable to reconcile the justice

of God, which required that knowledge of God's law be available to all

who sought to fulfill his will, with the multiple, conflicting inter-

pretations of that law. How could God demand obedience if his will was

not clear? Given the multiple interpretations of God's law, put forth

by men of good will, how was a person to decide which was true? What

is the basis of intelligent choice? In the face of this quandry,

Huntington concluded that one of two courses of thought was inevitable:

> On the one hand, God has given his creatures a law so vaguely
> expressed that, with a sincere desire to understand it, many
> of them fail to do so, at the same time threatening with the
> most fearful penalties every transgression of that law; or,
> on the other, the matters with regard to which there is such
> a conflict of opinions are unessential, and no evil will re-
> sult from leaving them undecided.[363]

The former position was "too monstrous for belief;" so he was "compelled"

to settle on the latter.[364] Huntington was unable to distinguish

between the essentials and the non-essentials. Unitarians rejected

beliefs that appeared essential to Huntington. Was not belief in the

divinity of Jesus Christ peripheral to Christian belief? On the basis

of their reading of the Bible, Unitarians failed to conclude that

Jesus Christ was God. Their sincerity and "perfect confidence in the

correctness of their belief" was beyond question; many studied the Bible

carefully.[365] Even this teaching, apparently a fundamental tenet of

Christian faith, did not warrant the universal agreement of Christians.

Was this then "one of the doctrines which may be safely left undecided;

---

[363]Ibid., pp. 48-49.

[364]Ibid., p. 49.

[365]Ibid., p. 50.

does it, or does it not, belong to the class of non-essentials?"[366]

Huntington did not know and that disturbed him. Was there no firm,

common ground of belief? Salvation depends upon belief, yet man is

unable to discern what he is required to believe. A dilemma to be sure:

> What one learned and pious professor reveres as divine truth,
> another ridicules as sheer nonsense, and a third repels with
> holy horror as rank heresy. In deciding among these various
> opinions, I had no guide but the Bible; and whatever point of
> doctrine might be accepted by me as true, I would be sure to
> find other men battling against as false, and just as ready
> as myself to prove from the Bible the correctness of their
> opinion....I wanted knowledge of the truth, not a mere balance
> of probabilities, and I saw no possible means of ever acquiring
> it.[367]

Huntington parted ways with his fellow-churchmen on a number

of doctrinal issues: universal guilt for the sin of Adam, punishment

for sin, and the depraved nature of man. He did not share their con-

viction that man was incapable of any good until he was converted.

Huntington believed that man could resolve to renounce sin -- with

God's assistance but without waiting for extraordinary circumstances

or experiences. He objected to the common Protestant practice of

requiring allegiance to "confessions of faith" which prescribed belief

in disputable doctrines. The practice "compels many persons to profess

to believe what they do not."[368] Huntington regarded ministers with

suspicion; they did not seem to have "any special calling or any special

fitness for the position which they occupied."[369] But the most critical

---

[366] Ibid., p. 51.

[367] Ibid., p. 57.

[368] Ibid., p. 69.

[369] Ibid.

point of difference concerned conversion. When was a person converted?

When did he become a Christian "in the New England sense of the

phrase"?[370] Huntington could not identify the time of his own conversion.

Nevertheless, he was certain that he was a Christian; though he knew

himself to be a sinner, he also knew that he earnestly tried to avoid sin

and that he repented when he had the misfortune of falling into sin.

Huntington describes his "conversion" to Christianity as a gradual, calm,

and deliberate process. He did not experience "anything like a state

of religious excitement" nor did he undergo the "violent change" which

New England Congregationalists termed conversion.[371]

Huntington's tenor in the Congregational Church, as layman and

as minister, brought him little satisfaction, as his movement in and out

of its fold indicates. His discontent contributed to his decision to

join the Episcopal Church. In part, that decision was based on the fact

that he was no longer able to "conscientiously profess" the Articles of

Faith.[372] And the style of its service appealed to Huntington. Three

years beforehand, he had begun to attend an Episcopal Church. He approv-

ed of the congregation's active participation in the service and the

minister's use of a prescribed form of prayer pleased him. He was also

impressed by the example of the Episcopalians. Their young people

were "truthful, reliable, amiable, and under the control of right moral

feelings."[373] Their virtues reflected the expectations of their parents

---

[370]Ibid., p. 72.

[371]Ibid., pp. 71-72, 78.

[372]Ibid., p. 75.

[373]Ibid., p. 77.

who saw them as "lambs of Christ's flock," rather than as naturally sinful, corrupt, and depraved.[374] Even though the members of the Episcopal Church had not experienced "the prescribed course of conviction and conversion," they were pious and faithful Christians.[375] The experience of the Episcopalians countered the singular model of conversion prescribed by New England Congregationalists. It appeared likely that the intensity of change wrought by conversion was consistent with a person's character. Those whose lives were characterized by "persistent rebellion" against duty were likely to experience a "deep and violent" change; persons "who seem always to have been under the influence of right moral feelings, and who have never been happy with the consciousness of having done wrong until they have confessed their fault and been forgiven" were unlikely to experience more than a slight change.[376] Children of the church "might be expected to grow up into mature Christians as naturally as the kernel of wheat that grows into a wheat-stalk and not into a thistle."[377]

New England Congregationalists failed to recognize the importance of baptism of water in their enthusiasm for promoting the baptism of the spirit. They refused baptism to those who had not already experienced regeneration through conversion. Thus, Huntington observed, they rejected the clear imperative contained in Christ's reply to Nicodemus: "Except a man be born of water and of the Spirit, he cannot enter into

---

[374] Ibid., p. 76.
[375] Ibid., p. 77.
[376] Ibid., pp. 80-81.
[377] Ibid., p. 81.

the kingdom of God." Contrary to the biblical teaching, Calvinists
attributed no real significance to the rite; it "means nothing and
effects nothing."[378] Huntington believed that he had been born again
in baptism. Calvinism, he resolved, was "nothing more than a turning
of the affections from the world to God" and as such could occur more than
once: "Indeed, every act of penitence is a partial conversion toward
God, as every sinful act is a partial retroversion from him."[379] This
statement indicates how far Huntington had moved from the view of
conversion which he learned during youth. It is the statement of the
convert to Roman Catholicism who sees the sacrament of penance as the
context for conversion.

As an Episcopalian, Huntington still maintained that the
Bible was his sole rule of faith. The Thirty-nine Articles expressed
human opinion as had the Confession of Faith of the Congregationalists.
Huntington did accept the Apostles' and the Nicene Creeds as valid
and binding. His reason for doing so was somewhat vague -- a general
belief that the creeds were "sustained by the word of God."[380] Gradually,
he realized that the authority of the creeds rests in their antiquity.
While the Articles were of recent origin, the creeds expressed the faith
of the early church. At this time, Huntington began to revise his
opinion of the Roman Catholic Church. Reading The Catholic World forced
him to do so. He could not reconcile what he had always believed to be
true about the church: that it persecuted heretics, that it practiced

---

[378]Ibid., p. 83.

[379]Ibid.

[380]Ibid., p. 87.

a type of religious pragmatism in which the end justifies the means, that priests sold pardons for sins committed and permissions to sin, that Catholicism substituted ritual and ceremony for piety. Gradually, Huntington pared away the misconceptions that characterized the popular nineteenth-century Protestant view of the Roman Catholic Church.

Joshua Huntington became a Roman Catholic because the Roman Church provided what he had always needed: "a reliable interpretation of the word of God."[381] Authority was a primary issue for Huntington. Once he was convinced that the Church's claim to speak with divine authority was valid, conversion was imperative. Huntington's conversion was the last step in a lengthy process that began in his youth and came to term in mid-life after a year of careful analysis of the claims of Roman Catholicism. During that year, Huntington resolved his difficulties: "At length I began to think her claims might be well founded, and by a gradual process of change my admission of the possibility of this was converted, through the aspirations of my own mind, into a conviction of its possibility, and finally into a full belief in its truth."[382] Huntington claims to have purposefully avoided any contact with Catholic persons, clerical and lay, and he denies having read any Catholic books. By keeping his interest in Roman Catholicism private, he hoped to deflect what he anticipated would be the reactions of his friends to his conversion (if he did become a convert): that he had succumbed to "the craft and deceit of

---

[381]Ibid., p. 92.

[382]Ibid., pp. 92-93.

of the Jesuits."[383] Only after he was convinced that the Roman Church was the true Church of Christ did he consult a priest, who gave him a copy of Milner's End of Controversy. That book helped Huntington to resolve what doubts remained.

This is all that Huntington says about his conversion; his emphasis is on the process of thought through which he advanced toward the Catholic Church. Conversion is a change in thinking that culminates in affiliation with the Roman Catholic Church. The central issue was that of authority. Huntington's dissatisfaction with the lack of teaching authority in the Congregational Church accounted for his defection from the church. The realization that the teachings of the Episcopal Church had their origin during the reigns of Edward VI and Elizabeth forced Huntington to search beyond the Episcopal Church. The appeal of the Roman Catholic Church lay in its firm and certain guidance; the Roman Catholic Church demanded obedience and fidelity because it spoke with divine authority and because it could trace its origin to the apostles.

Having recounted his religious history, Huntington alters his focus and his tone. He centers on the doctrinal issues that played a major role in his decision to become a Catholic. His purpose is clearly apologetic. Huntington is intent on persuading his reader to acknowledge the logic of his thinking and then act accordingly. With that purpose in mind, he warns his reader

...that it is illogical and irrational to deny the conclusion, while you are unable to show where the reasoning which leads to it is false, unless you have such evidence of its falsity

_____

[383]Ibid., p. 93.

as ought to be satisfactory to every one who means to believe [384]
what God has said, whether it is sustained by argument or not.

The remainder of the text, some seventy pages, is apologetic rather

than narrative. In a brief aside, Huntington remarks that he will

employ outline form "for the sake of distinctness" even at "the

risk of giving my narrative the appearance of a doctrinal treatise."[385]

But it is the content of these pages and not simply the style in which

they are written that determine their character. Huntington shows

a predilection for defense of his own position and for exposition of

Roman Catholic thought; that is typical among the convert authors.

Huntington's major contribution lies in his detailed account

of his experience prior to his conversion to Roman Catholicism: an

experience of successive conversions. Although the conversion to

Roman Catholicism is the central one for Huntington, as the very

existence of the narrative demonstrates, he neglects to say anything

about the experience itself. He contents himself with tracing the

changes in thought that led up to the conversion to Roman Catholicism.

Perhaps his reserve is an outgrowth of his rejection of Congregational

understandings of conversion, which emphasized a sudden change, marked

by intense religious excitement. Huntington was very aware of the

degree to which his own view -- even prior to his joining the Episcopal

Church -- conflicted with the prevelant New England understanding of

conversion. Describing the "conversion" which resulted in his final

break with Congregationalism, he stresses the progressive nature of his

---

[384]Ibid., p. 94.

[385]Ibid., p. 95.

experience:

> The last revolution in my views and feelings was so gradual,
> that I was not myself conscious of the changes going on in
> them unless I compared them at long intervals; and at no time,
> so far I recollect, was I aroused into anything like a state
> of religious excitement, I was as calm and deliberate in my
> reasonings and conclusions as if I had been studying some
> purely scientific subject, and admitted one truth after
> another only as I became convinced that it could no longer
> be doubted.[386]

Such was the nature of his conversion to Roman Catholicism --

deliberate and reasonable.

Huntington's apologetic begins with the identification of two

conclusions which led to his conversion. First, Huntington explains how

he became convinced that the Bible was not in itself a sufficient rule

of faith. The basis of his argument is his own experience: the Bible

was insufficient for him, as is well-documented in the narrative.[387]

Further evidence of insufficiency is found in the Bible itself. The

truths of the Bible are not self-evident; these truths are not stated

with the clarity and distinctness that assures that all will understand

them. The sacred writers did not suspect nor therefore, intend, that

their writings would "be regarded as containing the whole code of the

Christian religion."[388] Peter himself warned that some of what is con-

tained in the Pauline Epistles is difficult to understand and that mis-

understanding might lead to perdition. Prior instruction or some

guidance in interpretation is essential lest the ignorant misunderstand.

Huntington further notes that even Protestants do not hold the

---

[386]Ibid., pp. 71-72.

[387]Ibid., p. 95.

[388]Ibid., p. 96.

doctrine of the sufficiency of Scripture. Long before children
can read the Bible they are taught what their parents believe to
be the truth. Should they later abandon their parents' faith, they
are regarded as apostates and condemned. Parents allow the child
to regard the Bible as his rule of faith only as long as his interpretation coincides with theirs. Indeed, the Bible ought not to
constitute a person's first introduction to truth: "Protestants admit
that it is hazardous for a man to enter upon the study of the Bible
with the assumption that he knows nothing already of Scripture doctrine,
and that everything is to be learned from the written word."[389]
Furthermore, Protestants themselves "hold as revealed truth what is not
taught at all in the Bible," as evidenced by their celebrating the
Sabbath on the first day rather than the seventh, their practicing infant baptism, and their baptizing validly by sprinkling.[390] But
Protestants also reject doctrines and practices which are taught in
the Bible, such as the doctrine of regeneration by baptism (a doctrine
rejected by the non-Episcopal sects) and the practice of fasting.

The belief in the Bible as the sole rule of faith has contributed to the emergence of "hundreds of sects" and will give rise
to more since there is no authority to settle disagreements. The
doctrine of the sole sufficiency of the Bible has undermined the very
importance of belief. Since nothing is certain, what is believed is
insignificant. Only sincerity matters. Huntington maintains that the
doctrine of the sufficiency of the Bible is absurd: its truth cannot

---

[389]Ibid., p. 99.

[390]Ibid., p. 101.

be verified in the Bible. Furthermore, one cannot even establish what writings existed as discrete texts. The Church declared what constituted the Bible and what did not. The process of handing down the Bible, copied over again and again, made the texts vulnerable to corruption. The very process by which the Bible was handed down makes it impossible to establish with certainty that a particular epistle was indeed written by Paul for one example.

> It would certainly have been far easier to introduce corruptions into these manuscripts, which were almost exclusively in the hands of the clergy, than into the faith which was the common profession of the whole body of the people, Yet the church is accused of having done the most difficult of the two things, and is not suspected of having attempted the easiest.[391]

Such is the shape of Huntington's argument against the sole sufficiency of Scripture.

Huntington admits that he withheld his assent to his conclusion until he was convinced that Jesus Christ had established a body of teachers. The first conclusion would have left him "like a ship in a fog, without chart or compass -- unable to decide in what direction lay the rocks" or what course to steer around them.[392] The second conclusion provided him with the certainty he sought and did not find in the Bible alone. Huntington gained new insight into the meaning of the directive which Jesus gave to the apostles (Mt. 28: 19-20). He had always understood the text of "Go, tell all nations..." to refer to the commission to take Christ's teaching to "the farthest limits of the

---

[391]Ibid., p. 113.

[392]Ibid., pp. 114-115.

earth."[393] But it occurred to him that the reference had a temporal meaning and, on consulting the Greek text, he found that the words meant
"'until the completion or termination of time'" and could signify nothing
else.[394] In employing the preposition "into" rather than "until,"
translations of the English Bible obscured the meaning of the text.

The necessity for "living teachers" contributed to Huntington's
belief in the existence of such a body of teachers. Individual Christians
require teachers to instruct them in belief and correct practice since
the Bible itself is unable to do so. The Church also needs teachers in
order to maintain the unity appropriate to the Church of Christ. The
dissension in the church conflicted with what Christ had intended: Christ

> ...never intended that those calling themselves his disciples
> should be divided and subdivided as they now are into numberless
> factions, holding different faiths, practicing different bap-
> tisms, each party excluding all others from the Lord's table,
> and all contending quite zealously against one another as
> against the wickedness which exists in the world. Parents
> and children, husbands and wives, brothers and sisters, all
> professing to be children of the same Heavenly Father, yet
> refusing to kneel before him at the same altar, to worship him
> from the same temple, to receive his sacraments from the same
> ministers. These things are shocking....[395]

Unity, however, is essential to the Church of Christ, as the Bible
testifies. The metaphors are numerous: one fold and one shepherd,
the oneness that exists between Father and Son, one body, one Spirit,
one Lord, one faith, and one baptism. Huntington rejected the Bible
as the sole rule of faith but that did not keep him from citing Biblical
evidence alongside other sources which supported his argument. That

---

[393]Ibid., p. 116.

[394]Ibid.

[395]Ibid., p. 119.

the church believed that there was a body of teachers who spoke with
authority until the Reformation provides Huntington with an argument
from antiquity. Those sects which insist on the sole sufficiency of
the Bible simultaneously maintain the unique interpretation of
Christianity, expressed by founders such as Martin Luther and John
Calvin or by the authoritative formulation of a governing body such
as the Westminster Assembly, or by the teaching of a theologian or
minister. In practice, Protestants have recognized the central role
of living teachers. Oral teaching, Huntington argues, is consistent
with human need. It is unreasonable to expect that the common, uneducated people will learn the truth, when they cannot read the Bible,
much less discern the meaning "which cannot be agreed upon by the wise
and the learned."[396]

Having established to his satisfaction that Christ founded a
Church and empowered that church to teach in his name, Huntington had
only to "find" this church.[397] Episcopalians, or at least High-church
Episcopalians, claim that the Episcopal Church speaks with authority.
But Huntington concluded that "neither the compilers of the English
Book of Common Prayer, nor the American bishops who revised it for use
in this country, ever thought of claiming for their church a right to
teach religious truth with divine authority."[398] The Episcopal Church did
not bear the marks of the Church which are identified in the Nicene Creed:
it was neither one nor catholic; it could not claim to be apostolic

[396]Ibid., p. 124.

[397]Ibid.

[398]Ibid., p. 128.

unless it affirmed that it was one with the Roman Church. Only the

Roman Church had the "authority to teach the religion of Jesus Christ."[399]

In the final section of Gropings After Truth, Joshua Huntington

parries the objections levelled against Roman belief and practice. His

defense completes his apologetic: no other church bears the marks of

the true Church; no aspect of Roman teaching and practice is inconsistent

with its claim to be the true Church. Huntington rebuffs those who charge

that the Roman Church teaches what is contrary to the Bible, challenging

them to prove the allegation, but he admits that the Church teaches more

than is explicitly contained in the Bible. For example, the Catholic

Church teaches that Sunday is a day of rest, a day of sacred observance,

and that infants ought to be baptized. However, many Protestants do

the same. The crux of Huntington's defense is that the Bible was

never intended to exclude or to be a substitute for oral teaching.

Teachings, transmitted orally by successive generations of teachers,

are also valid and binding.

Protestants accuse Roman Catholics of doctrinal innovation.

But the charges are unsubstantiated. Indeed, it is absurd to believe

that churchmen could have successfully introduced a new teaching and

convinced others, both clergy and laity, that the teaching in question

was not a novelty at all, that it had always been taught by the Church.

Huntington argues that even the idea of such a conspiracy is ludicrous.

A community that valued its fidelity to the teachings of the apostles

was not likely to engage in such fraud.

Huntington addresses a number of charges: the Church's alledged

---

[399]Ibid., p. 131.

suppression of the second commandment and its worship of idols, the granting of pardon to persons confessing their sins whether or not they are truly penitent, the prohibition against reading the Bible, the deification of Mary, and the belief that all opinions and pronouncements of the Pope are infallible. Huntington defends Roman Catholicism against each of these charges in turn. Finally, he discusses the dilemma of a holy priesthood sometimes exercised by unworthy men. The example of Judas, the traitor who was nevertheless empowered to heal and cast out devils, illustrates that even among the chosen we might expect to find wicked men.

The last few pages of the narrative consist of Huntington's confession of beliefs -- some of which he claims to hold in common with his Episcopal brethren:

> I hold as true everything which you consider essential to
> salvation. I believe with you the doctrine of the Trinity,
> of the Incarnation, of the Divinity of Jesus Christ; I believe
> that "there is no other name given under heaven by which we
> may be saved;" sic that I can of myself do nothing to merit
> eternal life; that it is the free gift of God through Jesus
> Christ, and my daily prayer to him is, "God be merciful to me,
> a sinner."[400]

Huntington parts company with the Episcopalians because he does not believe that the Protestant Episcopal Church of America is the One, Catholic, and Apostolic Church. Huntington characterizes the distinctively Catholic beliefs and practices which he has embraced as essentially harmless. It is an unusual course of defense, reducible to this: if I am mistaken, what of it? Where is the harm in believing that Christ is present in the Host, in saying prayers before a crucifix, in

---

[400] Ibid., pp. 153-154.

believing that Mary, the angels, and the saints intercede for man before

God or in believing in the existence of purgatory? Huntington rests his

case on the fact that what he believes and practices as a Catholic is

consistent with the Christian faith. In becoming a Catholic, he has not

ceased to be a Christian.

In a subtle but effective manner, Huntington makes it clear

that piety is a motive for conversion to Roman Catholicism. "When

I bow down before the sacrifice of the Mass, I am worshipping the

Lord Jesus"; the gesture of prostration is a meaningful act of worship.[401]

Praying before the image of the crucified Lord brings to mind the event

of the crucifixion: "Catholics pray with their eyes wide open, and

place some object before them which may aid in the direction of their

thoughts, making their senses minister to their devotions."[402] The use

of images does not provoke idolatry; Catholics, even the ignorant ones,

do not confuse the image with what it represents. The use of images

encourages fervent devotion. Persons who believe that Mary, the angels,

and the saints heed the prayers of men and offer them together with their

own before the throne of God feel a special bond with heaven. This teach-

ing is therefore useful even if it is false.

> There is a natural longing in the human heart to bring earth
> into closer communion with heaven than the almost infinite
> doctrine at which Protestant theology separates them. If you
> could yourself believe it to be true that glorified saints
> and blessed angels are ever watching over you to guard you
> against sin, and even praying to God for you night and day,
> you know that such a belief would so encourage you in your
> resolves to resist temptation, would so strengthen you in every

---

[401]Ibid., p. 154.

[402]Ibid., pp. 155-156.

holy purpose, that your life afterward would be very different from what it was before.[403]

This "intimate communion with heaven" is a force for good. What harm is there in maintaining such a belief -- even if it is groundless? So too with the belief in purgatory: Catholics hold that few persons are worthy to enjoy God's presence at the time of death. In purgatory, those who are not yet ready to undergo a period of suffering in order that "they may be freed from all the consequences of the sins which have been pardoned by the grace of God."[404]

In the course of his defense of these beliefs, Huntington reveals the importance of piety in Roman Catholic life. Although he portrays his movement to Roman Catholicism as an intellectual quest, he acknowledges the importance of the affective element in religion. Images provide the believer with a visible focus of faith. Devotion to Mary, the angels, and the saints provides the believer with a bridge to heaven, a point of contact. The belief in purgatory simultaneously affirms man's unworthiness and God's mercy. Huntington found these beliefs attractive and comforting and expected that his readers would do likewise.

His argument is incontrovertible: these beliefs are harmless and indeed positively beneficial. Certainly, it is "injurious" to believe what is false and to act on that belief.[405] But who is to decide which beliefs are true and which are false? Huntington says that the Church, instituted by Jesus Christ "to remain through all ages as the authorized

---

[404]Ibid., p. 160.

[405]Ibid.,

265

expounder of his truth" ought to decide.[406]   His former colleagues

in the Protestant and Episcopal churches disagree. The choice is

clearcut: one either accepts the authority of the Roman Church or

one does not. Authority is the fundamental issue.

Huntington's conversion to Roman Catholicism was inevitable,

or so he leads his reader to believe. Step by step, he was led to

the Roman Church. He overcame his prejudice, clarified his miscon-

ceptions, and perceived the logic and truth of the Church's position.

After that, he could not repudiate its claims upon him; that would be

mortal sin. So he became a convert, risking alienating his friends

and injuring his "worldly prospects."[407]

The narrative ends with a prayer that God will make the truth

known to Huntington's readers. Huntington pleads that his readers

be open, that they give ear to their suspicions (which may indeed be

the proddings of the Holy Spirit). He wrote in order to arouse "a

suspicion that there must be something worthy of examination" in

arguments which convinced him.[408]   In that, he is like other convert

authors who hope that their stories will help to convert non-Catholic

readers.

From Canterbury to Rome

During the late 1830's and 1840's, the opposition between

High and Low Church Episcopalians in America grew more intense. What

---

[406]Ibid., p. 161.

[407]Ibid., p. 162.

[408]Ibid., p. 166.

accounted for the widening gap was the enthusiasm with which some American churchmen greeted the Oxford Tracts and the horror with which others denounced their content and the religious sentiment which they expressed. The Oxford writers deplored the extent to which the Anglican Church had renounced its ancient, authentic, Catholic past. With the publication of Newman's Tract Ninety in 1841, the lines of battle were drawn. Newman argued that the Catholic doctrines which he and the other Tractarians espoused could be reconciled with the Articles of Faith. In America, Tract Ninety heightened the controvery in Episcopal circles; most Episcopalians equated Tractarianism with Romanism and a few confirmed the worst suspicions of the majority by defecting to Rome.

The General Theological Seminary was the center of theological disputes engendered by the Tracts. Students and faculty heatedly debated topics like apostolic succession, auricular confession, celibacy, use of the crucifix, and veneration of the saints. Before the crisis at the Seminary was resolved, some students were examined to determine their orthodoxy and faculty members were subjected to an inquisition conducted by a committee appointed by the General Convention in 1844. Some students converted to the Roman Catholic Church; Clarence E. Walworth was among them.

The authors of the narratives which follow were influenced by the Oxford Movement. They were Episcopalians who grew increasingly dissatisfied with the Episcopal Church and eventually converted to Rome: Levi Silliman Ives, Augustine Hewit, Clarence Walworth, William Richards, and B. W. Whitcher. They shared common concerns and their reasons for becoming Roman Catholics were in many ways similar, but the narratives show that each experienced his conversion in a deeply personal and singular way.

The Trials of a Mind in its Progress to Catholicism: A Letter to His Old Friends

Levi Silliman Ives, former bishop of the Episcopal Church, wrote his conversion narrative in the form of a letter addressed to his brethren and friends.[409] His purpose was to explain his reasons for becoming a Roman Catholic. His method was to trace the development of his thought regarding the Roman Catholic Church. The product was "a consideration of the history of my mind in its progress to Catholicism."[410] The narrative is an apology in two senses: first, it is an attempt to justify his personal course of action, namely his conversion; second, it is a deliberate defense of the Roman Catholic Church as the one, catholic, and apostolic Church, the Church which is in continuity with the primitive community founded by Jesus Christ. Ives sets forth the historical and doctrinal evidence for the Roman Catholic position in order to show why he decided to become a Roman Catholic. In brief, he did so because he judged that the evidence in favor of Roman Catholicism was incontrovertible.

Levi Silliman Ives was born in Meriden, Connecticut on

---

[409]Levi Silliman Ives, The Trials of a Mind in its Progress to Catholicism: A Letter to His Old Friends (Boston: Patrick Donahoe, 1854). Note the text of the dedication: "To His Late Brethren of the Protestant Epsicopate and Clergy, To Those Amongst Whom He So Long Ministered, and To All Who Pray To Be 'led into the Way of Truth,' The following pages are humbly and affectionately transcribed, in the earnest hope that they may one day find both truth and peace in the bosom of the One Catholic and Apostolic Church" (p. 3).

[410]Ibid., p. 12.

September 16, 1797.[411] He grew up in West Turin, New York where

his family had settled in the hope of finding more fertile farmland.

Levi attended school until the age of fifteen, then enlisted in the

military during the War of 1812. After the War, he enrolled at

Hamilton College, Clinton, New York, but left before graduation due

to illness. His first position was that of instructor at an academy

in Potsdam, New York where he also led the Sunday service since there

was no Presbyterian pastor in residence. It is said that he employed

"revival measures" with notable success.[412] But his association with

the Presbyterians was brief. His growing distaste for Calvinist

teaching and for revival tactics may have contributed to that break.

What is certain is that years later, he still "regarded both with

abhorence."[413]

In 1820, Ives was confirmed in the Episcopal Church. In a letter

to John Henry Hobart, bishop of the diocese of New York, Ives stated

his reasons for becoming an Episcopalian and declared his intention

to study for the ministry.

---

[411]Biographical sketches of Ives appear in the Catholic
Encyclopedia, the New Catholic Encyclopedia, and the Dictionary
of Catholic Biography. For a detailed history of Ives see Michael
Taylor Malone, "Levi Silliman Ives: Priest, Tractarian, and Roman
Catholic Convert" (Ph.D. dissertation, Duke University, 1970). Malone
analyzes Ives' conversion to Roman Catholicism from within the perspective of the history of the Episcopal Church in America. He concludes
that the Episcopal Church contributed to Ives' conversion by its rigid,
inflexible response to his proposals. For a biography of Ives written
by a Catholic, see John O'Grady, Levi Silliman Ives: Pioneer Leader
in Catholic Charities (New York: P. J. Kenedy & Sons, 1933).

[412]M. T. Malone, p. 5.

[413]Ibid., p. 15.

> My opinions are founded on the nature of the church's commis-
> sion and the perpetuity of the same. That this commission
> was derived to the church in the Episcopal order is evident
> from the practice of the Apostles and that of the primitive
> church. And that the present Ep. Ch. [sic] is the true
> church I think is evident from the uninterrupted succession
> of her ministry & [sic] the primitive form of her worship.[414]

The concern with apostolic succession and fidelity to the primitive

model which drew Ives to the Episcopal Church later played a major role

in his conversion to Roman Catholicism. His letter to Hobart marked the

beginning of a relationship which influenced both his professional and

his personal life. Hobart became his mentor. Bishop Hobart was an

articulate supporter of the High party; his theological position was

clearcut: he stood among those

> ...who laid heavy emphasis upon the sacramental system, apos-
> tolic succession, rejection of rationalism and emotionalism,
> insistence upon historical continuity with the church of the
> past, relative distinctions between laity and clergy, the pre-
> eminence of the office of bishop in the church's government
> and life, and strict adherence to the requirements of the
> Prayer book (as opposed to minimizing its distinctness in the
> interests of ecumenical fraternity).[415]

Ives' studies under Bishop Hobart grounded him firmly in the thought

of High Churchmen. Ives completed his studies for the ministry at

the General Theological Seminary and was ordained in 1823. In 1825,

he married Bishop Hobart's daughter, Rebecca.[416]

Ives moved quickly and successfully through the ranks of the

---

[414] L. S. Ives to J. H. Hobart, 7 October 1820, Hobart Papers, Church Historical Society, Austin, Texas, as cited by M. T. Malone, p. 6.

[415] M. T. Malone, pp. 6-7.

[416] According to the Dictionary of Catholic Biography, the Catholic Encyclopedia, and the New Catholic Encyclopedia, the marriage took place in 1822. Malone and O'Grady record 1825 as the year of the marriage.

Episcopal Church. After holding several rectorships in the northeast, he was consecrated bishop of North Carolina. He was only thirty-four years of age at the time. One of the critical problems which Ives faced during the early years of his episcopate was that of attracting and retaining clergy. He established an Episcopal school in the hope that education would alleviate the problem but the school was a financial failure. In 1845, Ives founded the Brotherhood of the Holy Cross at Valle Crucis. He intended Valle Crucis to be a center for the training of candidates for the ministry. Instead, it became a haven for those who sought to live an ascetic, monastic life. The apparently "Catholic" practices of its members, such as auricular confession, belief in the Real Presence, and monastic vows, attracted the attention and the condemnation of many within the diocesan community.

By this time, the spirit and thought of the Oxford movement had affected Ives' ideas of the church. He believed that it was possible to enjoy the benefits of Catholic practice without becoming a Roman Catholic. His appeal for the reintroduction of auricular confession was a case in point. Ives did not call for the restoration of confession as practiced by the Roman Catholic Church. But his statements on the practice of auricular confession were "sufficiently ambiguous for High Churchmen to give them somewhat serious endorsement and for Low Churchmen to consider their general drift 'Popish.'"[417] Because they were vague, they were subject to misinterpretation. Michael Taylor Malone's summary of Ives' statement on confession is enlightening:

...what had Ives said and not said? He had urged the reintro-

_____

[417]M. T. Malone, pp. 204-205.

duction of auricular confession at least as an occasional rite
for the hardened heart, and had intimated that the better
churchman might profit from it as well. He had said that the
priest possesses a fallible but authorized duty to pronounce,
an invitation to do so, on the adequacy of repentence prior
to the penitent's receiving absolution, but he had not ruled
out the possibility that forgiveness might be received apart
from priestly mediated absolution. He had proposed a general
need of some parishioners to confess privately, because it
was in this way that a parishioner could obtain a more accurate
assessment of himself, but Bishop Ives had said nothing about
whether absolution was to be given in the context of that
private confession or whether it was to be pronounced only in
the course of the Sunday morning services.[418]

Ives' position was neither Roman Catholic nor High Church Episcopalian.

But his ideas about confession coupled with the fact that he was held

responsible for the aberrations at Valle Crucis aroused the ire of

his fellow churchmen. After several years of public debate and public

criticism, he was arraigned by the Episcopal convention. That experience

made Ives realize that he could not be "a true Catholic" while remaining

a Protestant -- an arrangement he had formerly believed to be viable.[419]

Ives recanted and reaffirmed his fidelity to the Episcopal Church. But

his doubts continued; Ives found himself unable to live with his

recantation. His letter of resignation revealed that he had struggled

to remain an Episcopalian but without success:

...in spite of my resolutions to abandon the reading &
the use of Catholic Books -- in spite of earnest prayers &
entreaties that God would protect my mind against the disturbing influence of Catholic truth & in spite of public and
private professions & declarations, which in times of suspended
doubt, I sincerely made, to shield myself from suspicion and
...restore the confidence of my diocese, which had been well-
nigh lost. In spite of all this...[420]

---

[418]Ibid., p. 204.

[419]Ibid., p. 294.

[420]Letter to the Convention of the Episcopal Church, Diocese

the doubts continued. On December 22, 1852, he submitted to Roman Catholicism.

While Roman Catholics applauded, Ives' fellow Episcopalians accused him of mental instability and even insanity. Those charges gained the credence of the Episcopal community, eager to explain the defection of a Bishop.[421] The "series of misstatements, misunderstandings, insinuations, and honest errors combined to give him a reputation of being a changeable, unpredictable, devious, ambiguous man, who either in sickness or with wicked deliberation designed to mislead the public."[422] The damage to his reputation was irreversible. The hostility of the Episcopal community surfaced again after the publication of The Trials of a Mind in 1854. The press denounced the book, proclaiming it "weak," its arguments, "beyond contempt," and its author, "a man of unsound mind."[423]

And so the Episcopal Bishop became the Roman Catholic layman, losing both status and sole source of support. Rome had directed the American bishops to offer him financial assistance until he was able to re-establish himself.[424] Archbishop John Hughes arranged several

---

of North Carolina, 22 December 1852, as cited by Malone, p. 311.

[421] In his study of the life of Ives, M. T. Malone calls these charges into question. Although Malone admits that Ives may have suffered bouts of instability and "severe emotional insecurity" in the three or four years preceding his conversion, he maintains that Ives was by no means insane (pp. 344-347).

[422] Ibid., p. 344.

[423] Ibid., pp. 338-340.

[424] O'Grady describes the arrangements made by the American bishops for Ives' support (pp. 45-51).

positions for Ives: as professor of rhetoric at St. Joseph's Seminary, which had been founded in 1840 and was at the time located at Fordham, New York, and as a lecturer at the convents of the Sacred Heart and the Sisters of Charity.[425] He made his major contribution to the Catholic community through his work in Catholic charities. He enthusiastically promoted the work of the St. Vincent de Paul Society, which he viewed as an ideal form of lay apostolate. His primary interest was the care of destitute and dependent children; he established the New York Protectory, designed to provide care for Catholic children. His views on childcare were revolutionary: Ives took issue with the prevalent practice of placing dependent, neglected children on farms in the west and proposed that children ought to be kept near their former homes and that family members ought to be encouraged to maintain contact with the children.[426] Ives said that he found the Roman Catholic Church attractive because it was concerned with the poor.[427] It is not surprising, therefore, that he found his ministry in helping the Church meet its responsibilities to the poor in a changing society.

The Trials of a Mind in its Progress to Catholicism differs from the other narratives in its form. Although the convert authors generally shunned biographical details, most used a chronological framework to provide structure for their narratives. Ives did not. The structure of his narrative springs from the course of his inquiry:

---

[425]See O'Grady, pp. 50-51 and Dictionary of Catholic Biography.

[426]For an informative discussion of Ives' philosophy of childcare, see O'Grady, pp. 80-90.

[427]Ives, p. 20.

it is a record of ideas rather than events. The plan of the narrative grows out of a careful process of clarifying issues of history, doctrine, and practice in order to identify the true church. Ives begins with the fact of his conversion rather than ending his narrative with the conversion event. His desire to justify the conversion determines the tone of the narrative. Given his former position and the lengthy period of public controversy which preceded his conversion, it is reasonable to assume that Ives felt a greater compulsion to explain and justify his actions than did most of the other converts and that he was able to presume that his readers knew something of his life history.

The Trials of a Mind is a curious blend of apologia and apologetic: justification of the conversion and defense of Roman Catholicism. Though the entire text is written in the first-person, there are two distinct sections: the apologia, consisting of explicitly autobiographical statements, and the apologetic, detailing Ives' progress through the articles of faith with which he struggled prior to his conversion. The former is confined to the introduction and a few pages of the conclusion.[428] The latter comprises the bulk of the text. But apologia and apologetic are integrated by the constant focus on conversion.

Conversion to Roman Catholicism was a "serious" and "trying" step, involving the loss of both clerical status and social position.[429] Ives, a bishop in the Episcopal Church for more than twenty years, became

---

[428]Ibid., pp. 11-28; 229-233.

[429]Ibid., p. 11.

"a mere layman" in the Roman Catholic Church.[430] His conversion ended

many years of doubt and uncertainty about his position as a Protestant.

He confesses that he may not have always acted wisely or "with perfect

consistency," but he attributes his "seeming inconsistencies" to too

great an effort "to remain a Protestant."[431] However, he insists that

"self-apology" is not his primary purpose; he writes to reveal the

history of his mind.[432] In fact, Ives apologizes for the personal nature

of his text:

> And if, in giving it, I should seem to any to make too much re-
> ference to myself, my plea will be found in the nature of the
> undertaking; vix., to present the train of thoughts and reasonings
> through which my own mind had passed in its progress to a
> certain faith.[433]

His statement reveals the attitude of reserve and hesitancy regarding

self-revelation that generally characterized these authors. It is as

though the converts feared that by personalizing their accounts they

would detract from their defense of Roman Catholicism.

What prompted Ives to investigate the Roman Catholic faith?

First, for some years, he had sensed "a mysterious influence" which

filled him with "yearnings for something in religion more real" than

what he had already experienced.[434] Second, Ives began to question

the truth of what he had learned as "the facts of Protestantism -- or

the real history of the Catholic Faith" when he attempted to apply the

---

[430]Ibid.

[431]Ibid., p. 12.

[432]Ibid.

[433]Ibid., pp. 12-13.

[434]Ibid., p. 13.

principles which govern historical study to the English Reformation.[435]
Both the affective impulse and the cognitive search led him to the early
Fathers. He read their writings as well as Moehler's Symbolism.[436]
His progress Romeward was interrupted by illness and by what he describes
as a succession of "distracting and embarrassing oppositions" to his
Catholic tendencies.[437]

Opposition, paradoxically, was a "stimulus" to further inquiry
because it increased Ives' distrust of the Episcopal Church and his discontent with its "unreasonableness."[438] Ives recalled that "every
attempt to understand and rightly appreciate Catholic truth" met with
jealousy, harshness, and alarm.[439] The Catholic Faith was considered
dangerous. Ives began to think that "'the danger' apprehended from
a thorough knowledge of Catholic teaching was not so much danger to
the truth of God, as to the system of Protestantism."[440] As Ives
saw it, questions and doubts aroused disapproval but produced no answers.
The prevailing Protestant opinion was that the Roman Church was corrupt
and unworthy of anyone's serious consideration. Protestants were unable
to deal reasonably with the claims of the Catholic Church. Ironically,

---

[435] Ibid., note, p. 13.

[436] John Adam Moehler, Symbolism, Or Expositions of the Doctrinal
Differences between Catholics and Protestants, as Evidenced by Their
Symbolical Writings, 5th ed., trans. James Burton Robinson (New York:
Benzinger Brothers, 1906).

[437] Ives, p. 14.

[438] Ibid., pp. 18, 14.

[439] Ibid., p. 14.

[440] Ibid., p. 15.

negative Protestant response to his so-called Catholic tendencies
encouraged Ives to continue his investigation of Catholicism. Ives
was particularly annoyed by the charge of dishonesty which Protestants
levelled against converts to Roman Catholicism; these were the same men
who merited the respect and esteem of their Protestant brethren prior
to their defections. Protestantism encouraged inequities: "I could
see nothing which marked it as the hope and the home of the wretched;
nothing which proclaimed its peculiar fellowship with 'the poor.'"[441]
The pew system, for example, closed houses of worship to the poor
or at least relegated them to the least desirable places.

What disturbed Ives most was the absence of "any instituted
method among Protestants for the remission of post-baptismal sin."[442]
As a minister and later as bishop, he was unable to offer people the
relief which they needed and which the early Church had provided in the
sacrament of penance. The issue of auricular confession was a critical
factor in effecting Ives' eventual break with the Episcopal Church.

These assorted reactions to Protestantism and the comparisons
to Catholicism, which they invited, drew Ives closer to the Roman
Catholic Church, as did his firm conviction that from the moment of
his baptism, the church had a claim to his faith, love, and obedience.[443]
By baptism, a person becomes a true member of the one, catholic, and
apostolic church.

Convinced, therefore, that I was originally placed by bap-

---

[441]Ibid., p. 20.

[442]Ibid.

[443]Ibid., note, pp. 21-22.

tism within the pale and under the authority of "the One Catholic and Apsotolic Church," and that I should be guilty of an
act of deadly schism in resisting the Catholic authority (the
only authority under heaven entitled to my submission) by
longer siding with a national and uncatholic communion, I felt
bound on every principle of duty and safety to return with a
broken and contrite heart to the arms of my true mother, from
whom I departed; the moment I consented, as an adult, to be
considered a member of the protestant body [sic]. Instead,
therefore, of unfaithfulness to the Anglican or American
communion, which is sometimes pleaded, I was convinced, that
in my return, I did nothing more than throw off an unlawful
allegiance imposed upon me without my consent, and take steps
for my restoration to that Catholic fellowship -- that "Communion
of Saints," of which I was made a member at my baptism. I felt
as one may be supposed to feel who in his unconscious childhood
had been borne off asleep from his native shore on some wreck
to a desert Island, and then, in his manhood, after long subjection to want and hardship, becomes convinced of the disaster
and returns to the father that begot him, and the mother who
cherished his infancy.[444]

Ives reveals two dimensions of his understanding of conversion in this

statement: cognitive and affective. Ives asserts that the conversion to

Roman Catholicism is not the adoption of a new faith or of a faith new

to him. His conversion does consist acknowledging that he is and has

always been a member of the Roman Catholic communion; at baptism, he

had become a member of the Church. Conversion to Roman Catholicism

requires that he publically proclaim what is already true. The images

which Ives uses to make his point reveal the affective aspect of his

understanding of conversion. Conversion is the return to one's true

mother, the Church. Conversion involves the rediscovery of the old self,

the true self. In contrast to the image of rebirth which so many converts

use to describe their experience, Ives chooses metaphors of recovery and

return. Ives views the church as mother, protecting and nurturing her

child. His return might be described as a symbolic return to the womb,

---

[444]Ibid., note, p. 22.

the place of origin and primal safety. But Ives' experience is also like
that of the prodigal son: he merely needs to return repentent to claim
the rights and benefits of sonship. God, the forgiving father, welcomes
his son with joy and offers him the comfort and security of his home.
Ives does not mention the parable himself but it aptly expresses his
view of conversion.

A sense of ambivalence characterized Ives' response to the
prospect of conversion. Although he looked at conversion as a return
home, he was fully aware of the personal and social cost of conversion
which was, in a word, prohibitive. He viewed the possibility with
"horror"; conversion required that he sacrifice everything: position,
family, friends, and the safety of the familiar. He shrank back from
giving up his

> ...claims as a bishop, a minister, a Christian in any safe
> sense; and...being compelled as an honest man to give up my
> position. A horror enhanced by the self-humiliation with which I
> saw such a step must cover me, the absolute deprivation of all
> mere temporal support which it must occasion, not only to
> myself but to one whom I was bound "to love and cherish until
> death." The heartrending distress and mortification which it
> must involve, without their consent, a large circle of the
> dearest friends, the utter annihilation of all that confidence
> and hope which under common struggles and common sufferings, for
> what we deemed the truth, had been reposed in me as a sincere and
> trustworthy bishop.[445]

Ives was certainly not a man given to understatement. He went on to
tell that the prospect made him consider whether he ought simply to
stay and to risk the salvation of his soul.

But the example and the instruction of Paul sustained him:
those who lose all and suffer for Christ will gain all. Ives submitted

---

[445] Ibid., pp. 22-23.

himself to Christ vowing to "<u>follow Him</u> whethersoever He would lead."[446]
Although Ives wrote that he would not attempt to tell his readers what
his surrender cost, he actually left little to the reader's imagination.
But Ives reassures his readers that he has been "<u>repaid ten thousand fold</u>
in the blessings of present peace, and in the certain hopes of eternal
life."[447]

Ives advises those of his friends who have experienced any
"doubt or suspicion of their safety as Protestants" to "commit themselves to the guidance of God's Spirit."[448] Conversion requires submission to the Spirit. Ives' insistence on the necessity of submission
constitutes a counterpoint to the careful, deliberate discussion of dogma
that follows. Ives came to the Church as a result of a process of
intellectual inquiry. But his conversion was not simply or solely a
matter of the mind. The "mysterious influence," divine guidance, and
submission to the Spirit -- all were essential to his experience of
conversion.

Conversion is a matter of salvation. The investigation of
religious truth presupposes two conditions: a firm conviction that
the salvation of one's soul for all eternity is the ultimate concern
(a concern which may require total sacrifice) and the belief that God's
will is the "only sure guide" in the salvation of one's soul.[449] Eternal
salvation is the fundamental motive for conversion.

---

[446]Ibid., p. 25.

[447]Ibid., p. 26.

[448]Ibid.

[449]Ibid., p. 27.

In the last few pages of The Trials of a Mind, Ives describes
the last year and a half of his episcopacy as "the most painful period"
of his life, "although one of apparent quietness, official success, and
restored confidence."[450] His recantation did not quiet his doubts
concerning Protestantism; indeed, it caused him additional pain: "I
felt I had shrunk publicly from the consequences of that truth which God
had taught me -- felt that I had denied that blessed Master who had
generously revealed Himself to me."[451] Ives blamed himself for the
suffering: he had resisted his convictions; he ought to have known
himself better; he "ought to have known the way of God's grace and truth
better."[452] He draws his autobiographical account to an end with a
prayer that others will come to believe in the Roman Catholic Church.

Apologetic comprises the major portion of The Trials of a Mind.
But the apologetic stems from the process of Ives' inquiry. In this
respect, it differs from the standard nineteenth-century apologetic
treatises. The substance of Ives' apologetic appears in a concise
summary of the stages through which his mind passed.[453] The summary
offers easy access to the questions and issues with which Ives
wrestled before his conversion. The first three steps consisted in
these conclusions:

> 1. I have seen, with a clearness which I cannot well express,
> that "the friendship of the world is at enmity with God."
> That "we cannot serve two masters" -- cannot secure the favor

---

[450]Ibid., p. 230.

[451]Ibid., p. 231.

[452]Ibid., pp. 231-232.

[453]Ibid., pp. 227-229. Ives identified ten steps in the

of two utterly and mutually opposed worlds. 2. That every
dictate of reason echoes the voice of God -- "what can it
profit a man to gain the whole world and lose his own soul?"
3. That, to save the soul, self-will must be renounced, and
God's will be submissively followed.[454]

The dualistic world view, the paradox of loss and gain, and the need
for total submission are motifs which describe Ives' preconversion
experience. But it is not at all clear that these insights constitute
the initial steps which Ives took toward Rome, as the summary listing
suggests. Rather, it seems plausible that Ives depended on these themes
in resolving his ambivalence concerning conversion.

The primary religious question for Ives was this: "What must
I do to be saved?"[455] The answer was to follow the way of man's
salvation, revealed by God. Man can achieve a certain knowledge of
God's will. This insight constituted the fourth step in Ives'
movement toward the Church:

...the fact that God has revealed His will -- that he commands
us to know His will -- that he promises to "lead us to all
truth" in respect to it -- all concur with the yearnings of
our hearts to justify the expectation of certainty in faith.[456]

How is certainty to be achieved? Man must submit to God's revelation
without reservation. Scripture is the written mode of that revelation.
But God alone can help man to know his will as contained in Scripture.
How does he guide us? Protestants suggest "that through prayer, God
would enlighten each man's mind to understand, after diligent study,

---

process of inquiry that led him to the Roman Catholic Church.

[454]Ibid., p. 227.

[455]Ibid., p. 29.

[456]Ibid., p. 227.

the true sense of the Bible."[457] But Ives concluded that private

judgment is insufficient, God's help ought to be universal, but only

some are able to possess, critically read and interpret Scripture.

Christ is our teacher:

> ...Christ leads us out of ourselves and away from mere human
> aid and invites us to "take His yoke and learn of Him;" [sic]
> to look through His commissioned priesthood, to Himself, as
> our ever-present, ever-unfailing teacher and guide.[458]

This was the fifth stage of the progress of his mind and it led

directly to Christ's Church, which interpreted God's will for men.

Ives gathered numerous citations from the Fathers and from councils

which support the authority of the Church and suggest that the word

spoken by the Church is the word of God.[459] The Church does not

interpret God's will in any partial sense. The authority of the Church

must be accepted without reserve. Ives' experience in the Episcopal

Church was inconsistent with what he believed he had a right to expect --

guidance from those who shared in the priesthood of Christ. His personal

experience as an Episcopalian contributed to his progress toward Roman

Catholicism. He summarizes the next steps this way:

> ...while professedly having a part in that priesthood, and so
> appearing as Christ's representative in teaching His infallible
> will, I felt in my conscience wholly unable to tell with certainty,
> and in many vital particulars, what that will is....when I
> turned for relief to my brethren associated with me in the
> Episcopate, (and here let me affectionately and earnestly
> appeal to them for the truth of my convictions,) I found that
> the uncertainty had increased almost in a direct ratio with
> the increase of numbers, till confusion, and discord, and
> national strife were the only answers that met the anxious

---

[457] Ibid., p. 38.

[458] Ibid., p. 227.

[459] Ibid., pp. 45-55.

sinner as he came to inquire, "What must I do to be saved?"
...such a state of things so unfriendly to truth -- so utterly
repugnant to the declared purposes of Christ's priesthood --
so absolutely submissive of the unity and Catholicity of His
Church -- so derogatory to His honor, and so fatal to His
promise, could not possibly proceed from His own institution.
And hence...the cause of this doubt and misery, attendant upon
the working of the Anglican Communion and her American daughter,
must be sought in that fatal act which separated her from a
divinely constituted spiritual head, the representative of
Christ, and placed him professedly under the supreme guidance
of a temporal sovereign, but, in reality, under the direction
of each individual judgment.[460]

Ives' reasoning proceeded in what he ascertained to be a reasonable

direction. If one could expect to know God's will with certainty,

if the knowledge of God's will cannot be gained through individual

judgment -- then the Church, authorized by Christ himself to speak

His word, ought to offer guidance. Relying on the Church means

submitting to "the wisdom of her divine Head."[461]

The disunity of Christians conflicts with the unity of the

Church proclaimed by the Church Fathers:

...I began to realize, with awful clearness, that I had little
safety where I stood. For, when I asked for certain knowledge
of God's will, I heard around me only "confusion of tongues."
When I asked for authority, I found only individual opinion;
-- for infallibility, a confession of doubt; for unity in
fundamental faith, division and mutual crimination; -- no
claim to universality, and no agreement even in the narrowest
sectarianism! But when I turned my ear, and listened to the
voice of the Fathers, echoing the voice of God, I heard
clearness and positiveness of speech, -- heard the assertion
in the Church of divine authority, Catholicity, infallibility,
and necessary abiding unity! What should I do?[462]

The exclamatory tone and the numerous underscored words and phrases

---

[460] Ibid., p. 228.

[461] Ibid., p. 68.

[462] Ibid., p. 83.

reveal the intensity of Ives' involvement in these issues. This
was for Ives a profound personal struggle. At this point, Ives reminds
his readers, he had not yet had any intercourse with Catholics; his study
of the Fathers and their Protestant interpreters had been a private one.

The Church of Christ is Catholic, that is, "not restricted
either in her privileges or prerogatives to any one nation, but made up
of believers fathered out of all nations."[463] How then did the Church
of England come to be? Ives argues that the Catholic Church was the
teaching authority in England for at least eight hundred years before
the Reformation.[464] Until 1543, Christians believed there were seven
sacraments. If this teaching was true in 1543, how could it be false
later? The Church of England failed to take tradition into account.
Tradition, that is, the teaching and practice of the Apostles, preceeded
Scripture.

> It is tradition which made the faith plain to the unlettered,
> and forced it round, and protected it against the inroads of
> private judgment and royal dictation; which supplied saving
> knowledge in the absence of the Holy Scriptures and of the
> proliferations to read them, and vindicated the providence of
> Almighty God for delaying what seemed to be an essential means
> for their general distribution till fourteen long centuries
> had passed away.[465]

It is this tradition that is "a part of God's Word, the unwritten
part, given before the written part," that the Church of England
disregards.[466]

---

[463]Ibid., p. 87.

[464]Ibid., p. 101.

[465]Ibid., p. 116.

[466]Ibid., p. 117.

Ives concludes that "the sole cause which led to the rupture

between England and Rome was a personal one -- was no other than the

righteous refusal of Pope Clement VII. to divorce Henry VIII. from

his lawful wife, and to countenance his adulterous connection with

his mistress."[467] The Protestant Episcopal Church in the United States

shares the defects of its mother church. Apostolic succession has been

broken; the source of authority in the Anglican episcopacy is merely

that of Elizabeth and the English Parliament.

The final stage of Ives' progress to the Roman Catholic Church

consisted in these conclusions:

> ...that the Church, which is the body of Christ, and which,
> as such, we are all commanded by him to "hear," is manifestly
> that "one Catholic and apostolic Church" which, at first
> founded by Him on the "rock," St. Peter, has ever since enjoyed
> His own presence, as the centre of unity and source of apostolic
> power in the See of that prince of the apostles. And that this
> Church, made manifest by her divine foundation and her no less
> divine preservation, yea, by her obvious principle of divine
> life and cohesion and assimilation, rewards every sincere
> effort to investigate her claims by new proofs of her
> divinity -- by making it more clear, the more closely
> her history is examined, that she has always, every where,
> and by all her sons, held and taught the "one faith, once for
> all delivered to the saints." That what has been charged
> upon her as an addition to that faith is resolvable either
> into necessary and lawful changes in her discipline and
> ceremonial, into the unauthorized extravagances of overwrought
> individual minds, or the misconceptions, exaggerations, and
> misstatements of interested opponents. That, in short, the
> Fathers of the first five centuries taught as distinctly,
> though not as formally as did the Fathers of the Council of
> Trent, the various dogmas set forth by that Council as
> necessary to the faith and practice of the Christian man.
> And hence, that the Gospel standard of faith and the Gospel
> rule of obedience, are to be found only within her pale;
> particularly as she alone professes to have, through the
> presence of Christ, that infallibility which is essential to
> such a standard, and in her members that childlike submission
> without which such a rule would be useless -- "Except ye be

---

[467]Ibid., p. 126.

converted, and become as little children, ye cannot enter into the kingdom of heaven."[468]

The primacy of the Holy See was crucial for Ives. The Church is a visible body as well as a spiritual one and as such ought to have a single leader "to secure unity of purpose and action."[469] The fact of the existence of the primacy of St. Peter is an argument for its existence. Basing his understanding of the papacy on two scriptural passages (John 1:35-42 and Matthew 16:18-19), Ives concluded that the change of Peter's name was the foundation for Christ's promises that the Church shall be built upon him and that the foundation of the Church would withstand its adversaries. Peter was made "Christ's visible representative, invested with a primacy or supremacy of jurisdiction."[470] The Fathers confirm the "natural sense" of these scriptural passages: Peter is the rock.[471] Ives interprets Christ's directive, "feed my lambs, feed my sheep" (John 21:15-17) as the conferral of "chief pastorship" upon Peter: Peter was to feed the lambs and the sheep, the ministers and the people, the entire flock.[472] The Pope is the infallible guide to truth. The primacy of Peter was taken for granted in the early Church, establishing a pattern that required no explanation or defense; Peter was and is the "visible centre of unity."[473]

---

[468]Ibid., p. 229.

[469]Ibid., p. 161.

[470]Ibid., pp. 166-167.

[471]Ibid., pp. 168, 172.

[472]Ibid., p. 176.

[473]Ibid., p. 182.

Fellowship with the Apostolic See is essential to the possession

of the true faith:

> ...to have vital evangelical union with Christ, certainly [sic]
> in the faithfulness of charity and good hope of salvation, it
> is by God's institution made essential that each and every
> member of Christ's body be in visible and real fellowship
> with the See.[474]

At the end of his careful inquiry, Ives discovered that he stood with

Rome; his position as an Episcopalian was no longer tenable for him.

Ives published his narrative in 1854, two years after becoming

a Roman Catholic. His particular circumstances, most especially his

prominence within the Episcopal Church, motivated him to give a prompt

accounting of his conversion. The time which elapsed between conversion

and the publication of a narrative was generally longer for most convert

authors.[475] But however long the time lapse, this is certain: the

accounts reflect the converts' current status as Roman Catholics and

are shaped by their motives for writing. In the case of Ives, it is

especially clear that "the Catholic convert" is the author. Ives

remembers and records the progress of his mind in its trek to Rome

from the standpoint of a Roman Catholic convert. Ives' progress

Romeward was not as direct as his summary of the steps or stages

suggests. It was the convert who selected and ordered his recollections

and fashioned an account of the process, an account which presented his

action positively and persuasively. The "stages" appear as such in

---

[474] Ibid., p. 225.

[475] The time span between conversion and publication varied
widely as these examples show: Thayer published his account the same
year; Walworth published his account fifty years after he became a
Roman Catholic.

retrospect.

Ives' conversion ended a demanding course of study and reflection and a lengthy personal struggle. The process involved a gradual revision of his theological position and a consequent shift of affiliation. His conversion did not come "in a flash of heat and light."[476] The Trials of a Mind testifies to the significance of intellectual inquiry in the process of conversion. But is also emphasizes the less tangible dimension of conversion -- the affective experience which Ives describes as a return to the place of his birth.

"How I Became a Catholic"

Augustine F. Hewit's essay, "How I Became a Catholic," is a concise narrative of conversion, tracing Hewit's progress from New England Congregationalism to the Episcopal Church and on to the Roman Catholic Church.[477] Hewit's narrative differs from other narratives in two respects: it is brief and pointed and it appeared in a periodical. The narrative is sharply focused. Unlike some convert authors, Hewit was not distracted from his primary purpose of describing the process of his conversion by lengthy and labyrinthian apologetic. He tells his story with simplicity and discipline. Certainly the journal format accounts, at least in part, for the brevity and clarity of the narrative. Hewit was a competent writer; his narrative exemplifies the narrative

---

[476]Ives developed these themes in a sermon which he preached in 1844. L. S. Ives, The Apostles' Doctrine and Fellowship: Five Sermons Preached in the Principal Churches of His Diocese, during His Spring Visitation, 1844 (New York: D. Appleton, 1844), pp. 15-28 as cited by M. T. Malone, p. 154.

[477]Augustine F. Hewit, "How I Became a Catholic," The Catholic World 46 (1887):pp. 32-43.

of conversion in its purest form.

Nathaniel Hewit was born in 1820 in Fairfield, Connecticut.[478]
His father, for whom he was named, was a Congregationalist minister; his
mother, Rebecca Hillhouse, was the daughter of a United States senator.
Nathaniel attended Philips Academy, Amherst College, and the
Theological Institute of Connectict at East Windsor. He was licensed
to preach by the Congregationalists in 1842. In March, 1843, Hewit
joined the Episcopal Church and in October, he became a deacon. Three
years later, Hewit converted to Roman Catholicism. He was ordained
a priest in 1847, taking the name of Augustine Francis. Hewit taught
at the diocesan seminary of Charleston, South Carolina, where he also
served as vice-principal. During this time, he helped to edit the
works of Bishop John England for publication. In 1849, Hewit joined
the Congregation of the Most Holy Redeemer in order to satisfy his
yearning for "a stricter religious life."[479] The Redemptorists, as
members of that community were commonly called, attracted other
prominent converts: Isaac Hecker, Clarence Walworth, George Deshon,
and Francis A. Baker. The American Fathers, as they came to be known,
conducted numberous, successful parish missions. In the course of
the controversy regarding the establishment of an American house that
led to Hecker's expulsion from the order, Hewit and the other American

---

[478]Brief biographical sketches of Hewit appear in the
Dictionary of Catholic Biography and the New Catholic Encyclopedia.
A more personal, if somewhat less objective, profile is that written
by Henry E. O'Keeffe, "Very Rev. Augustine F. Hewit, C. S. P.,"
American Catholic Quarterly Review 28 (1903):535-542. Hewit's
conversion narrative is a good source of information concerning his
life.

[479]O'Keeffe, p. 541.

Fathers were released from their vows and joined Hecker in founding the Paulists.

Hewit's work as a Paulist took many forms. He taught at the Paulist Seminary; he served as managing editor of The Catholic World and the American Catholic Quarterly Review; he became an accomplished apologist. He wrote the biography of one of his colleagues, the Memoir of the Life of the Rev. Francis A. Baker.[480] Hewit died in 1897.

"How I Became a Catholic" contains all of the essential elements of a conversion narrative. Hewit discusses his religious roots and identifies the attitudes which his early experiences engendered. He describes the critical turning points in his religious development and lists the influences which contributed to his conversion. In brief, Hewit portrays "the process" of his religious development. This was his express purpose in writing: to describe the process "without formally giving the reasons" for his conversion, "except in short and simple statements by way of explanation."[481] He accomplished his objective satisfactorily. He wrote a personal document which is both candid and insightful.

Hewit was raised in the Congregationalist Church, "in the strictest Calvinistic doctrine."[482] The cultural and the religious milieu of New England affected Hewit deeply, leaving him a "New-

---

[480]Augustine F. Hewit, Memoir of the Life of the Rev. Francis A. Baker (New York, 1859; 7th ed., New York: The Catholic Publication Society, 1887).

[481]Hewit, "How I Became a Catholic," p. 32.

[482]Ibid.

Englander in heart as by birth and descent."[483] He gained respect

for the civil, social, and religious virtues of his people. In

particular, he acknowledges their religious bequests to him: belief

in the Bible and in the divinity of Christ and a "sound morality."[484]

His initiation satisfactorily grounded him in Christianity, even though

the tradition of his countrymen was a "defective one."[485] Hewit argues

that a person owes no special allegiance to his ancestral religion;

a person's first loyalty must be to divine authority. Hewit's

insistence on this point reflects his conflict with his father who

disapproved of his son's change of religion.[486]

Respect and gratitude notwithstanding, Hewit conceded that

he "never felt any sympathy with Puritanism," which was quite an

understatement as this quotation shows: "A spontaneous repugnance

of mind and heart to this narrow, harsh, and dreary system of religion

sprang up in me as soon as I began to have thoughts and sentiments of

my own."[487] His aversion toward Calvinism was as strong as his attraction

to Episcopalianism. His conversation with Episcopal relatives and friends,

his reading of English history, literature and controversial works, and

his attendance at Episcopal services fostered his attraction to the

Episcopal Church. He believed he would have fared better in his

---

[483]Ibid.

[484]Ibid.

[485]Ibid.

[486]Letter to his father, 19 February 1846, as cited by O'Keeffe, pp. 539-540.

[487]Hewit, "How I Became a Catholic," p. 33.

early religious development if he had been free to choose his religious

affiliation. "As it was, I only made occasional and fitful efforts

in that direction, under the influence of the emotional excitement

to which young people in the evangelical sects are at times liable,

especially during what they call 'revivals.'"[488] He recalls that he

never even made his "profession of religion" until some months after

his graduation from Amherst College.

That profession took the form of a "conversion":

My thoughts and aspirations were irresistibly turned from this
earthly vision, which vanished like "a castle in the air,"
toward God and eternity. It was my most intense desire to be
completely freed from sin, to be reconciled with God, to seek
for him as the supreme good, to devote myself to his service,
and to attain the true end of my being in the future life by
an everlasting and perfect vision united with God. I believed
firmly that this could only be accomplished through the grace
of the Divine Redeemer and Mediator, Jesus Christ. It never
occurred to me to imagine or to wish that there was any way
of entering into or persevering in the state of grace except
the one way of obedience to the law of God -- obedience to
the law which commands us to believe what he has revealed,
to avoid what he has forbidden, and to do the good works which
he has prescribed through the natural conscience and the precepts
of the Gospel. I determined firmly to follow the light of
truth in my mind, and to obey all the dictates of conscience
with the most perfect fidelity possible, recognizing also the
veracity of God as the absolute standard of truth, and the
will of God as the absolute rule of right. I have never since
that time retracted this resolution. In virtue of it I became
and remain a Catholic. It produced a great and decisive change
in my moral state and attitude toward God and the world which
has not been succeeded by any similar change, and therefore
I call it emphatically a "conversion."[489]

Hewit's conversion involved profound personal transformation. The

conversion did not involve any overt communal action or relation nor

did it effect a shift in affiliation although it did contribute to

---

[488]Ibid.

[489]Ibid., p. 34.

Hewit's subsequent decision to join the Episcopal Church and later

the Roman Catholic Church. However, Hewit's conversion did involve

a radical change, the birth of a new self, a new beginning. Hewit's

conversion was two-fold: moral and religious.[490] His moral

conversion consisted in perceiving the supreme value of faithful

obedience to God's law, as revealed through conscience and the Gospel.

Hewit also experienced a religious conversion: he was "grasped by

ultimate concern"; he experienced "total and permanent self-surrender

without conditions, qualifications, reservations."[491]

Hewit came to view this experience as authentic and fundamental

conversion. But at the time, he feared that this experience would fade

just as other periods of religious excitement had waned. A chance

statement made by his father helped Hewit to resolve his difficulty.

The elder Hewit argued that according to John Calvin "a baptized

person might claim all the privileges of a child of God which are

signified by baptism, if he were willing to acknowledge and ratify his

own part in that covenant of adoption of which the sacrament is the

sign and seal."[492] Upon hearing this, Hewit recognized that there was

indeed a path of action open to him: he could trust that he was a child

of God and begin to live as God's child. Hewit maintains that this

experience made him become a Catholic:

> I think that probably I did receive at that time the grace
> which I had received in baptism, and that from this time for-

---

[490] I use these terms as defined by Bernard Lonergan, Method
in Theology (New York: Herder and Herder, 1972), pp. 237-244.

[491] Ibid., p. 240.

[492] Hewit, "How I Became a Catholic," pp. 34-35.

ward I was united to the soul of the Catholic Church, by faith, hope, and charity, several years before I was received into her outward communion and formally absolved from all censures and sins which I had incurred since my baptism in infancy.[493]

This is a critical point in Hewit's understanding of the meaning of conversion. The affiliational shift is clearly of secondary importance. The inner transformation, the operation of grace in his soul -- that is what truly matters. Hewit carefully distinguishes between the process of conversion which effects an inner transformation and the outcome of conversion which is the public change of religion.

Hewit's fundamental conversion occurred while he was still in the Congregational communion. During the course of his seminary studies, he realized that Calvinism was no longer credible to him; he "rejected the Calvinistic doctrines as merely human and spurious additions to the faith, or travesties of genuine Christian doctrines."[494] Furthermore, he recognized that only the episcopal order of church polity was consistent with the apostolic church. This led him to the critical issue of apostolic succession. Only a church which could point to uninterrupted succession could claim divine teaching authority. The debate engendered by the Oxford movement and High-Church support of "primitive and Catholic doctrines" drew Hewit to the Episcopal Church.[495] But it is important to note that intellectual satisfaction was not the sole reason for Hewit's conversion. The piety of the Episcopal Church had appealed to him in childhood; it had been "the

---

[493]Ibid., p. 35.

[494]Ibid.

[495]Ibid., p. 36.

church of my boyish reverence and love."[496] At any rate, it was "not so

far a cry from Geneva to Canterbury."[497]

At the time of his conversion, Hewit believed that

> ..."the Anglican Communion" was a true branch of the One, Holy,
> Catholic, Apostolic Church, of which the Roman Catholic Church
> and the Greek Church were also branches; that it had been justly
> and lawfully reformed in some respects, and was the real con-
> tinuation of the old Catholic Church of England, although
> unfortunately estranged and separated, in respect to external
> communion, from its sister-churches and the somewhat haughty
> and unkind mother-church of Rome.[498]

But his conviction about the status of the Episcopal Church was short-

lived. He "travelled rapidly Romeward" without suspecting the direction

of his progress. Protestant, rather than Catholic influences, encouraged

his movement toward Rome. He had read few books written by Catholics

and had few Catholic acquaintances. But he recalls some "certain

distinctively Catholic impressions" -- few and rare -- which he deemed

worthy of mention.[499] New Testament texts pertaining to the Eucharist

and St. Peter laid the foundation for Hewit's acceptance of the doctrines

of Real Presence and apostolic succession. Dr. Hughes reference to

Catholicism as "a holy but calumnated religion" in the course of The

Controversy between Dr. Hughes and Dr. Breckenridge helped Hewit decide

that his ideas of the evils of the Roman Church were probably calumnies.

Other readings corrected his views of Roman Catholicism; among them were

Ranke's History of the Popes and Guizot's History of European Civiliza-

---

[496]Ibid.

[497]Ibid.

[498]Ibid., pp. 36-37.

[499]Ibid., p. 35.

<u>tion</u>. Hewit also recalls that he was deeply moved by the Roman

Catholic mass -- "the most august and suitable form of worship of

Almighty God."[500] He heard Dr. Hughes preach and thereafter, the

prayer service at the General Theological Seminary seemed "flat and

tame."[501]

Why did Hewit not move directly to the Roman Catholic Church?

Because his understanding of the Church did not demand it. The Anglican

Church was not separated from the Catholic Church, any more than the

Roman or Greek Churches were. Hewit uses an apt metaphor to make his

point:

> I looked on the Roman Catholic Church as the choir and nave,
> the Greek Church as a great transept, and the Anglican Church
> as a side-chapel with its porch opening on another street. As
> I was born, bred, and then dwelling on that street it was more
> natural and easy to go in by the side-porch to the chapel
> than to go all the way around to the grand front entrance.
> If the chapel was served by priests, and one could have the
> sacraments and other privileges of the church in it, he would
> not need to pass through into the nave or to distress himself
> because the passage was barred.[502]

Such a universal ecclesiology did not force a decision for Rome.

In fact, Hewit observes that one can be near to Rome in doctrine

and discipline without seeking membership as long as he believes

that "intellectual, moral, and spiritual community in ideas, sentiments,

sympathies, together with the reception of the sacraments of baptism

and the Eucharist, in what he conceives to be a valid and lawful manner,

---

[500]Ibid., p. 38.

[501]Ibid.

[502]Ibid., p. 39.

make up the essential bonds of Catholic unity."[503]   In this instance,

that which binds is invisible. But if the structure of the Roman Church,

its unity under Peter and its practice of apostolic succession, is

recognized as an essential aspect of the true church, then the Church

of England is unsatisfactory.

It took Hewit three years to decide that the Roman Catholic

Church demanded his allegiance. He passed through several levels of

argumentation before he reached that decision. First, he regarded the

Anglican branch as "nearest to the primitive standard," then the Greek

Church, and finally the Roman Church.[504]   Later, he believed the

Greek Church as the "nearest to the model of ancient Christianity"

and considered the Roman Catholic Church to be next in line. Finally,

Hewit joined those who maintained that

> ...certain Christian communities separated from the communion
> of the Roman Church are in an irregular and anomalous condition,
> a state of secession and revolt which is wrong and unjustifiable,
> but not destructive of the essential Catholic unity, the organic
> identity of what they call the universal church in all its
> parts and members, which, though severely wounded, are not
> severed.[505]

In line with that current of thought, working for reunion from within

appeared to be an acceptable course of action. Such was the thinking

of Hewit's American High-Church colleagues. But Hewit realized that

the view of the Episcopal Church which he and his colleagues shared

was just that: an understanding based on their interpretation. But

it was not the Church of England as it existed: "our Catholicism was

---

[503]Ibid.

[504]Ibid., p. 40.

[505]Ibid., p. 41.

an affair of books, of the imagination, of a certain set of individuals."[506]

In the last paragraph of the text, Hewit outlines the theses that might be appropriately included in an apologetic treatise if he were writing one. The theses reflect the issues which he judged essential to a justification of the Roman position:

> First. Every rational and instructed man ought to believe in God.
> Second. One who believes in God ought to believe in Christ and his revelation.
> Third. Whoever believes in Christ and Christianity ought to believe in the Catholic Church, whose centre of unity and seat of sovereignty is the Roman See of Peter.[507]

This is a simple summary of the ideas that brought Hewit to the threshold of the Roman Catholic Church.

The example of Newman further encouraged Hewit. Hewit made his decision to convert during a stay on a North Carolina plantation, where he had been confined due to serious illness. His intellectual inquiry had set the stage for a "finish leap across the Rock."[508] That leap was made possible through God's grace. Nevertheless, Hewit insists that his going over to Rome was "a perfectly reasonable act, and one which can be justified on the most satisfactory rational grounds."[509] It is impossible to assess to what extent the life-threatening nature of his illness influenced Hewit's decision to convert.

Augustine Hewit describes his narrative as a "piece of

---

[506] Ibid., p. 42.

[507] Ibid.

[508] Ibid.

[509] Ibid.

psychological history."[510] What he has written indeed comes closer
to being such a history than any of the other narratives. The merits
of Hewit's work are evident: clarity, conciseness, and detailed
description of the process by which Hewit became a Roman Catholic.
Hewit gives more attention to the inner experience of religious life
than do the others. He does not reduce conversion to a series of
external events, which culminate in a change in affiliation. Hewit's
first and fundamental conversion was an interior experience. It
occurred long before he became an Episcopalian or a Roman Catholic.
That Hewit was able to recognize the qualitative difference between
the two types of religious change reveals his awareness of the complex
nature of religious growth. The experience of conversion, in its most
basic meaning, shapes Hewit's view of the whole of his life. He does
not simply tell about his conversion; he discloses the meaning which
conversion had for him.

Hewit differed from the other convert authors in this as well:
he confined the narrative to an account of his personal experience.
Though he indeed may have intended to attract others to Roman
Catholicism through his essay, he did not use the narrative as a
starting point for the writing of apologetics. This is an asset; there
is nothing to distract the reader from the primary focus of the work,
conversion. That Hewit chooses to limit himself to the personal account
may well reflect a conviction that the experience of conversion speaks
for itself.

---

[510]Ibid., p. 143.

The Oxford Movement in America; or,
Glimpses of Life in an Anglican Seminary

Clarence E. Walworth's Oxford Movement in America, aptly

sub-titled Glimpses of Life in an Anglican Seminary, is broader in

scope than the other narratives.[511] Walworth affords his readers

a view of conversion as experienced by himself and others associated

with the American Oxford movement. He characterizes his work as

"reminiscences."[512] It is indeed a memoir, most accurately described

by its sub-title; it is not a typical conversion narrative. Walworth's

concerns extend beyond the conventional parameters of a conversion

narrative -- an account of the author's own spiritual life which

culminates in conversion to Roman Catholicism and a justification of

the reasonableness of his conversion. Walworth tells the story of a

group of seminarians who journey Romeward together. While other

converts told personal stories, Walworth recounted a communal

experience.

Life at this Anglican Seminary was for Walworth and for a

significant number of his classmates an exercise in conversion.

Walworth describes the setting in which the groundwork for conversion

was laid and identifies the characteristics of Roman Catholicism which

attracted himself and his comrades to the Church. He charts the course

of his spiritual development as he records his recollections of life

at the General Seminary.

---

[511] Clarence E. Walworth, The Oxford Movement in America; or,
Glimpses of Life in an Anglican Seminary (New York: The Catholic Book
Exchange, 1895; reprint ed., New York: United States Catholic
Historical Society, 1974). References pertain to the 1895 edition.

[512] Walworth, pp. 1-2.

Clarence Augustus Walworth was born in Plattsburg, New York in 1820.[513] His father, Reuben Hyde Walworth, was a staunch Presbyterian. After Clarence graduated from Union College in Schenectady, New York, he studied law, gaining admission to the bar in 1841. He practiced law for a year before beginning studies at General Theological Seminary in New York City. Walworth spent three years at the Seminary during a time when it was the scene of heated controversy over Tractarianism. He joined Edgar P. Wadhams for a brief monastic interlude in the Adirondack Mountains; their experiment in communal living was modelled after the Nashotah community in Wisconsin.[514] He converted to Roman Catholicism in 1845 and joined the Redemptorists along with Isaac Hecker and James McMaster, who were also new converts. He studied in Belgium, where he made his vows in 1846. After further studies at Witten, Holland, Walworth was ordained a priest in 1848. His first assignment took him to England. In 1851, Walworth returned to the United States to begin a seven year stint preaching missions with Hecker, Hewit, and Francis A. Baker. The four were dispensed from their vows, as was another of the American Fathers, George Deshon. Walworth continued his mission work as a member of the Paulist Fathers, the religious community founded by Hecker and his fellow converts and former Redemptorists.

----

[513]Brief biographical sketches of his life appear in the Dictionary of Catholic Biography, the Dictionary of American Biography, the New Catholic Encyclopedia, and in David, pp. 214-215. Additional information appears in E. H. Walworth, Life Sketches of Father Walworth (Albany, J. B. Lyon Co., 1907); W. Elliott, "Father Walworth: A Character Sketch," The Catholic World 73 (1901):320-337.

[514]Walworth, pp. 114-118.

Walworth was best known for his notable accomplishments as
a preacher; he was an eloquent evangelist who spoke with the fervor
and enthusiasm that were common among the best of his Protestant
counterparts. Ellen Walworth describes Father Walworth's effect on
the congregation of St. Joseph's Church, Albany where he preached
a mission in 1852; the response of that congregation was typical.

> The crowds that came day after day seeking admission to that
> small parish church, as it was then, extended far out into the
> streets, especially when Father Walworth preached, as his
> well-modulated voice was clear and had great carrying power
> even in a whisper. But only those within, of course, could
> see his gestures, which were always graceful and telling,
> whilst at times his action was startingly dramatic. It seems
> that at this place, he not only pointed over to the tall
> black cross but he even clung to it, till it swayed back and
> forth with the weight of his body, whilst the people conscience-
> stricken and pale with emotion watched and listened in almost
> breathless silence.[515]

Father Walworth was an extraordinary preacher. Walter Elliott praised
his unique powers of persuasion: "many a time, they who came to scoff
remained to pray, aye, and what is infinitely more, remained to
confess their sins with sobs of grief."[516]

> His voice was marvellous [sic]. It was of medium pitch, clear,
> musical, but it had a great quality of its own; it was wonderfully
> winged as if with a preternatural magnetism. His sermons cut
> to the division of the soul and the spirit. His manner, though
> unaffected, was yet full of dignity. Seldom was a preacher
> so eloquent by his looks and bearing as was Father Walworth;
> and his action on the platform was a perfect match for his
> great themes, his ringing voice and his well-chosen matter.
> If one can make the distinction, he was dramatic without
> being theatrical.[517]

---

[515] Walworth, p. 129.

[516] Elliott, "Father Walworth: A Character Sketch," p. 331.
Portions of Elliott's remarks also appear in E. Walworth's text
(pp. 132-134).

[517] Ibid.

Certainly Walworth stands among the great Catholic revivalists.[518]

Why? He was gifted with eloquence but more important, he was positively

disposed toward revivalism as a method for evangelization. His childhood

experience of revivalistic Protestantism was both favorable and signifi-

cant, as he explains in a public letter written in response to a

college classmate who asked how Walworth viewed his evangelical conversion

now that he had become a Roman Catholic. Was that early conversion a

"delusion"? No, Walworth answered, it was not.

> I look back to it with pleasure, and hail it as a happy reality.
> That many delusions existed in my mind at that time is certain
> enough. But equally certain am I that a real, substantial, and
> lasting impression was made upon me which changed the whole
> current of my life. You ask whether I "secured my salvation"
> at that time. I consider no man's salvation secured except by
> perseverence until the end -- finis coronat opus....This much,
> however, I may say -- had death come then, I know of no good
> reason why I should not have met with such hope of mercy as
> becomes a Christian penitent.[519]

Walworth's attitude toward the conversion he experienced during youth

was more than tolerant. He argues that that conversion was the "turning

point" in his life: "Not that my faith began then, but that then I

began to prize and cultivate what I had."[520] Walworth never abandoned

his early religious convictions.

> This may seem strange to you, remembering that, having been
> reared by Presbyterianism, I afterwards became an Episcopalian,
> and am now a Catholic. But I declare to you that I have never
> abandoned a single point of religious belief which I ever had.
> (I say of religious belief, by which I mean positive doctrine,
> for a negative doctrine is not the matter of belief: it is
> merely protesting against some positive tenet of faith --

---

[518]Jay P. Dolan calls him "one of the most forceful preachers
to step into a pulpit" (Catholic Revivalism, p. 69).

[519]Cited by E. Walworth, p. 41.

[520]Ibid.

merely a refusal to believe.) I have cast away many prejudices
of former days; I have accepted many things which I once did not
believe; and thus the horizon of my faith has been enlarged.
This transition of mind is never painful, for it is only
following the natural law of growth. But I have never yet
felt the shock of a lost faith.[521]

Not only did Walworth view his youthful conversion as a valid and

valuable experience, he saw it as the foundation for future spiritual

growth which brought him into the Episcopal and then the Roman Catholic

Churches. Walworth describes his religious life as a process of

development, an evolutionary process in which each new experience

builds on the old.

Walworth's positive reading of his early religious experiences

points to an intriguing paradox. As a Tractarian, he was an adversary

of Low Church, Evangelical Episcopalianism, which favored revivalistic

methods. Nevertheless, he neither dismissed nor rejected his experience

of revivalism as irrelevant or meaningless.

The pace of his ministry took a toll on Walworth's health.
He left the Paulists and joined the Albany diocese, serving as a
pastor there until his death in 1900. Walworth championed a number of
social causes including political and industrial reforms and temperance.
He was a prolific writer. His major publications include The Gentle
Skeptic (1863), The Doctrine of Hell (1873), Andiatorocte and Other
Poems (1888), Reminiscences of Edgar P. Wadhams (1892), The Walworths
of America (1897), and The Oxford Movement in America.[522] He also

---

[521]Ibid., p. 42.

[522]The 3rd edition of Reminiscences of Edgar P. Wadhams was
published under the title, Early Ritualism in America: Reminiscences of
Edgar P. Wadhams (New York: Christian Press Association Publishing
Company, 1911). The first four chapters of the book parallel and

wrote numerous pamphlets, articles, and tracts.

The Oxford Movement in America begins with an account of the
first crucial phase of Walworth's spiritual development: becoming
an Episcopalian. During the summer of 1842, while practicing law in
Rochester, New York, Walworth found himself more concerned with
religion than ever before: "I felt growing up within me a strong
desire to devote myself entirely to the church."[523] With the encouragement of his rector, he decided to enter the General Theological Seminary
and became a candidate for orders. At this time, he described himself
as an Evangelical Anglican, neither High nor Low Church. He had become
a member of the Episcopal Church somewhat by chance. While Walworth
was studying law, a fellow lodger in Canandaigua, who was organist at
the Episcopal Church, invited Walworth to join the choir. He did and
continued to attend services "by mere habit" until 1839 when he was
confirmed.[524] Though he had "some very strong religious convictions,"
he writes that he could as easily have become a Presbyterian or a
Methodist.[525]

Before entering the Seminary, he attended an annual meeting
of the American Board of Foreign Missions with his father, a Presbyterian. Discussion at the meeting focused on a proposal calling for
celibate missionaries. The reason given in support of the proposal
was a pragmatic one: large families of married missionaries represent

---

complement the content of The Oxford Movement in America.

[523] C. Walworth, The Oxford Movement, p. 1.

[524] Ibid., p. 13.

[525] Ibid.

a drain in time and revenue. The proposal met with objections that were peripheral, not substantive. The church would be unable to attract missionaries if celibacy was required and though the mission effort achieves only limited success, the "thought of foreign missions helps keep religion alive at home."[526] The Presbyterians, Walworth concluded, were maintaining "a great humbug."[527] He decided that if celibacy was "practically necessary" to missionary work, it was also an advantage for all Christian ministers.[528] Already, Walworth was gravitating toward Roman practice.

The "peculiar atmosphere" of the Seminary encouraged him in this way:

> Some called it Catholic; some called it Romish and superstitious; some called it a spirit of reform, and return to true doctrine and genuine piety; and others regarded it as a release into religious darkness and barbarism. Whatever it might be, however the seminary was recognized by all as the focus of a new religious life in the Episcopalian body. It was not low-churchism, neither was it "high-and-dry."[529]

Doctrinal debates were commomplace. No teaching was exempt from scrutiny, as an early discussion regarding baptismal regeneration illustrates. On that occasion, James McMaster and Arthur Carey argued that regeneration occurs at baptism and Walworth recalls that he gradually accepted the power of the sacramanet to "convey"

---

[526]Walworth attributes this statement to his father (The Oxford Movement, p. 4).

[527]Ibid., p. 5.

[528]Ibid.

[529]Ibid., p. 8.

grace.[530] Walworth recalls that change in thinking as "the entering
wedge of a new faith."[531] The vigorous theological debates, regular
fare at Chelsea, found Walworth unprepared. He was hardly a staunch
churchman of one party or another and he was "a greenhorn in theology"
to boot.[532] But it was impossible to remain at the Seminary without
becoming well-versed in theological controversy. And before long,
Walworth became a critical observer and an active participant.

Changing a theological position was an imperative to action
as this incident reveals. Learning that a baptism performed by a
dissenting minister, who was considered to have the status of a layman,
was invalid, Walworth was rebaptized by an Episcopalian minister in
1843.

Chapters III and IV focus on the major controversy occasioned
by the trial and ordination of a fellow student, Arthur Carey. Though
this section constitutes a departure from Walworth's initial personal
focus, it is consistent with the aim of personal narrative. As he
recounts the history of the Carey affair, Walworth continues to tell
the larger story -- the tale of traveling "a crooked course towards
Rome."[533]

Arthur Carey was subjected to a special examination to
determine "whether he was a genuine Episcopalian or a candidate

---

[530]Ibid., p. 9.

[531]Ibid.

[532]Ibid., p. 17.

[533]Ibid., p. 61.

with Romanizing tendencies."[534] The examination was "a veritable

persecution," though not intended to be such, and Carey was an

innocent victim, "faithful and true to that communion to which he

clung."[535] Carey's case, Walworth argues, must be viewed in the

context of the essential compromise which marked the Anglican Church

from its earliest days. Elizabeth had sought to satisfy both Protestants

and Catholics. As a result, the Anglican Church was set on a course

that is most appropriately described as via media. The Book of Common

Prayer is itself a compromise: the "Articles and Liturgy are so

skillfully hammered out that all parties, both Catholics and

Protestants, by using the large latitude always practically allowed

them, may arrange their consciences comfortably upon the same liturgies

and formulas."[536] Carey followed the example of his fellow churchmen;

he took advantage of the leeway granted him. "Carey was sincerely

Catholic, and believed that under the original compromise he had a

right to be, and that, without any necessity of attacking the Roman

Catholic Church or any of its members, he could honestly remain where

he was and advocate Catholic principles."[537] His examiners were of

different minds; two were "square Protestants," deeply suspicious of

any sign of Catholicity and the rest were "via media men."[538]

The decision declaring Carey fit for the Episcopal ministry, reflected

---

[534] Ibid., p. 36.

[535] Ibid., p. 37.

[536] Ibid., p. 38.

[537] Ibid., pp. 41-42.

[538] Ibid., p. 42.

the majority view, the via media. The "square Protestants," Drs. Henry
Anthon and Hugh Smith, stood firm in their opposition to Carey. They
voiced their objections on the occasion of Carey's ordination, accusing
him of holding doctrines contrary to the teachings of the Episcopal
Church, doctrines "too nearly bordering on popery."[539] Bishop
Benjamin T. Onderdonk maintained that there was no reason to deny
Carey orders since he had carefully examined him and judged him to be
a worthy candidate for the ministry. Carey was ordained in July, 1843.
On April 1, 1844, he died while on route to Havana with his father; he
died two months before his twenty-second birthday.

Though his life was brief, Arthur Carey unwittingly played
a central part in the history of American Episcopal Church. The
trial and ordination of Carey brought the conflict among churchmen
of different parties to the public forum. Each member of the
examining committee put forth a public statement defending his position.
A new periodical came into being; the Protestant Churchman was intended
to be a voice opposing the ideas presented in the more liberal
Churchman. Sermons and lectures against Tractarianism filled the
first issues of the Protestant Churchman.

The account of Carey's trial and ordination appears in
Walworth's essay for two reasons. Obviously, Walworth intends to
give his readers a "glimpse" of life in the Seminary and the Carey
affair was a critical event at the Seminary during Walworth's time
there. But the controversy which centered around Carey was also
personally significant for Walworth. Carey's trial brought the

---

[539]Ibid., p. 52.

intensity of the conflict between Low and High churchmen to light.
Walworth recalls that although in many respects he was unchanged
by the beginning of his second year at the Seminary, one thing was
certain: he could no longer call himself an Evangelical, though
he was "still Protestant."[540]

Walworth and his colleagues found two aspects of the Roman
Catholic experience particularly appealing: its missionary effort
and its monastic tradition. Indeed, they were attracted by the
combination of the two: Walworth and several other members of
the Missionary Society looked forward to a missionary life, sustained by the opportunities for prayer and retreat that the monastic
tradition made possible. But their hope was neither inspired not
encouraged by the Episcopal Church. "All the life that existed in
Episcopalianism was concentrated in a struggle to keep itself alive,"
Walworth cynically observed. However, the appearance of William
George Ward's Ideal of a Christian Church provided the perspective
they were searching for -- an understanding of priesthood that joined
contemplation with action.[541] Ward contrasted the preparation given to
candidates for orders in the Anglican and Roman Churches and he found
the Anglican Church lacking, particularly in its program for the
preparation and nurture of its priests. The Anglican Church lacked
"the spiritual weapons" which the Church of Rome wielded in priestly
formation:

---

[540]Ibid., p. 67.

[541]William George Ward, Ideal of a Christian Church, 2nd ed.,
(London: J. Tonney, 1844).

Meditation, to make the truths of religion more vivid; constant examination of conscience, that sin may not be passed over or forgotten; occasional retreats, as a fresh start after neglect; the literature of ascetic theology and hagiology to stimulate in the service of God by example and precept; the confessional for pardon and direction; moral theology to save priests from caprice, and give them the benefit in advising their penitents of the experience of the Corporate Church....[542]

Walworth and his fellow seminarians lighted upon the first "weapon," meditation. It was the practice least well understood by Protestants, who, Walworth points out, lack a systematic mode of prayer of the type exemplified by the spiritual "Exercises" of St. Ignatius.[543] Meditation was a distinctive feature of Roman Catholic piety and one which supported the missionary endeavor. Roman Catholic priests, nourished by a life of prayer and meditation, were well-prepared to awaken the laity to a life of fervent piety. "Giving missions" was a most effective way of arousing the faithful.[544] Missions, given by deeply spiritual preachers, contributed to the vitality of the Roman Catholic Church.

Ward's Ideal satisfied the deep longings of the seminarians at Chelsea for a "practical piety."[545] His account of the Rule of Life, practiced at a French Ecclesiastical Seminary, excited young men who were already attracted to monastic life.[546] Romanism offered

---

[542]C. Walworth, The Oxford Movement, p. 88. Walworth cites Wilfred Ward, William George Ward and the Oxford Movement (London and New York: Macmillan, 1889), pp. 279, 289 as his source.

[543]C. Walworth, The Oxford Movement, pp. 91-93.

[544]Ibid., p. 93.

[545]Ibid., p. 88.

[546]See C. Walworth, The Oxford Movement, pp. 88-93 for a discussion of the provisions of the Rule.

the pattern of ritual, common and private prayer, and discipline

which they sought.

The movement Romeward was slow and deliberate. The very

character of the Protestant mind searching for truth accounts for

this gradual pace; the Protestant mind is not contented with short-cuts

or doctrinal reduction as the heathen mind might be.

> When the Christian revelation is fairly presented to the heathen
> mind, their ignorance has so little to show in opposition that
> they are more ready to embrace it trustfully and in its entirety.
> The obex, or obstacle, to truth presented by their simple
> superstitions is a comparatively small one. The Protestant
> mind, on the contrary, however cultivated, is by no means simple,
> nor in the same sense ignorant. It is nearer the truth to
> say that they know too much. They are oftentimes, to quote
> St. Paul, "more wise than it behoveth to be wise." Their minds
> are too much possessed with things that are not so. The obex
> which they present to Catholic truth is something multitudinous,
> complex, over-refined. It is so engrafted, so closely webbed
> and interwoven with all their past thoughts and memories, that
> they mistake prejudice for a rational conviction. True doctrine
> "in a nutshell" is not truth presented in a form in which they
> can receive it.[547]

Walworth speaks for the Protestant mind in a general way but he also

speaks his own mind. Popular controversial works proclaiming the

simplicity of Catholic truth and blatancy of Protestant error failed

to satisfy Walworth and his friends: "So far as I know of, no convert

of the Chelsea Seminary was brought to the door of the Catholic Church

either by Milner's End of Controversy or Bossuet's Variations, strong

though they be."[548] Moehler's Symbolism was another matter. Walworth

claims that Moehler's work did more than any other book to help him

---

[547] Ibid., p. 97.

[548] Ibid., p. 101

take "the final step of entering the Catholic fold."[549] Moehler's
careful exposition of the articles of Catholic doctrine provided
Walworth and his colleagues with the evidence they needed in order
to make a decision regarding the truth and validity of the Roman
Catholic position. The deliberateness with which converts approach
Catholicism is an asset according to Walworth. In the first chapter
of an examination of the impact of the Oxford Movement in England,
Walworth suggests that the slow process of conversion leaves
converts "well acquainted with all the ground over which they have
fought their way."[550] Indeed, converts have a certain advantage
over hereditary Catholics: "If Catholicity is with them something
more studied and less instinctive, it is also, for that very reason,
something more thoroughly investigated."[551]

"Doctrinal vitality" or "the eagerness to know the real
truth" characterized the seminarians at Chelsea.[552] But hunger
for truth was coupled with the desire to lead a holy life. The
Lives of the Early English Saints, a series written by Anglicans
in the Oxford Movement, encouraged this desire by providing models
of piety consonant with Roman Catholic truth and life. Piety, as
Walworth's remarks reveal, is indeed a motive for conversion. Piety,
that is practical piety, is synomymous with the religious life as

---

[549] Ibid.

[550] Clarence A. Walworth, "Reminiscences of a Catholic
Crisis in England Fifty Years Ago," The Catholic World 69
(1889):398.

[551] Ibid.

[552] C. Walworth, The Oxford Movement, p. 102.

lived.[553] It involves the visible structures of worship, sacrament, and devotions as well as membership in a community of faith. That community includes the living as well as the dead, particularly those who witnessed to the faith during their lives, i.e. the saints. And for converts-to-be at Chelsea, piety meant the experience of life in community, the monastic life.

Walworth tells of two experiments in monasticism inspired by Tractarianism. The first was the community founded in Nashotah, Wisconsin by James Lloyd Breck, a Chelsea graduate of 1841. The community at Nashotah was founded to promote colonization, missionary labor, and the monastic life. Successful in achieving the first two goals, the community failed in the third. The monastic experiment was at best merely tolerated by the American Anglican Church and toleration did little to inspire loyalty and commitment. Some early members left to marry; six converted to Roman Catholicism. Walworth observes that the absence of a community practice of contemplative prayer accounted for the failure of the community. The religious practices at Nashotah differed little from those at seminaries and colleges.

The second experiment was smaller in scale; it involved but two members: Edgar P. Wadhams and Clarence Walworth. They occupied the upper story of a house at Wadham's Mills, where they tried "to practice, in such ways as actual circumstances would permit, a religious life, the truest type of which we even then believed to be found in the

---

[553]Ibid., p. 88.

Catholic Church, though our knowledge of it was very significant."[554]

They dreamed of moving to a tract of land in the Adirondacks: "a noble

monastic pile giving shelter and seclusion to a cowled community of

contemplatives, missionaries, scholars."[555] But the experiment was

short-lived; the community never grew beyond its initial membership of

two.[556]

What finally precipitated the conversion of Walworth and his

friends? The break-up of Tractarianism, which Walworth attributed to

the trial of Arthur Carey and to the scandalous trial and suspension

of Dr. Onderdonk, president of the Seminary and Bishop of New York,

set the scene for their conversions. Onderdonk had angered the

opposing faction by ordaining Carey. Unable to prove charges of

doctrinal unorthodoxy, the prosecuting bishops charged Onderdonk with

immorality and impurity. He was found guilty and suspended. The

humiliating attack on Onderdonk demoralized his supporters and inflamed

his opponents. Seminary students with Tractarian tendencies found

themselves without shelter and under direct attack. Students who,

in jest, rumored that Jesuits were residing at the Seminary in disguise

were dismissed. Suspicions regarding the existence of a popish

conspiracy flourished. Walworth was one of the students named in

that conspiracy. This atmosphere of mistrust "forced so many enthusi-

astic young Tractarians either to climb back unto the Protestant ship

and stay quiet, or else take to the water and swim for their

---

[554] C. Walworth, Early Ritualism in America, p. 23.

[555] C. Walworth, The Oxford Movement, p. 116.

[556] Walworth notes that the religious sisterhoods fared better

lives."[557]

Clarence Walworth's conversion was the first conversion
"following the great scare at Chelsea in January, 1845."[558] At the
time of the "great scare," Walworth was in the midst of his monastic
experiment in the Adirondacks but he nevertheless was suspected of
conspiracy at Chelsea. When the monastic venture failed, Walworth
would not return to Chelsea nor to his father's house in Saratoga,
where "the atmosphere was more stifling even that the sheer pretense
to Catholicity so rife in Episcopalian Protestantism."[559] His family
and friends were unsympathetic to his Tractarian ways. He made plans
to work at a lath-mill until he was ready to convert to Roman
Catholicism and become a priest. James McMaster upset his plan by
recommending that Walworth see a Redemptorist priest in New York and
makes plans to join that order of missionary priests. Walworth followed
McMaster's advice: "My determination to become a Catholic was fixed
and resolute. To unite with the Catholic Church all I needed was an
introduction to it. The opportunity was now offered and I embraced it
immediately."[560] Father Gabriel Rumpler examined Clarence Walworth
and judged him ready for admission into the Roman Catholic Church.
Walworth made his profession of faith on May 16, 1845 and received
First Communion a week later. He was confirmed shortly thereafter

---

in the Episcopal Church (The Oxford Movement, pp. 117-118).

[557]Ibid., p. 141.

[558]Ibid., p. 142.

[559]Ibid.

[560]Ibid., p. 143.

and in August, he sailed to Belgium with McMaster and Hecker to begin their novitiate.

The brevity of Walworth's account of his conversion reflects the nature of his conversion. It was for him, as it was for the other convert authors, a process. Affiliation with the Church formalized gradual movement toward Rome in thought and sentiment and a growing acceptance of its teachings and its style of piety. The moment of public profession was less significant than the religious development which preceded it. But it was a momentous occasion. Walworth recalls being filled with a sense of awe and unworthiness as the day of profession approached:

> It seems as if I were about to separate from everything I love, and my poor heart, faithless and unconscientious, wants to be left behind among the Protestants. I am not manly enough to make a stout Catholic; but it is a great privilege to be a weak one.[561]

The last pages of The Oxford Movement in America concern the impact of Tractarianism on the Episcopal and the Roman Churches. Tractarianism sowed the seeds of dissent within the Episcopal Church; Tractarianism accented the differences between High and Low churchmen.[562] And the Roman Catholic Church gained converts, modest in their number but impressive in their contribution to the American Church as David O'Brien points out:

---

[561]C. Walworth to E. Wadhams, 5 May 1845, as cited in Early Ritualism, p. 76.

[562]See James Thayer Addison, The Episcopal Church in the United States 1789-1931 (New York: Charles Scribner's Sons, 1951; reprint ed., New York: Archon Books, 1969), pp. 161-163. Addison points out that the Tractarian movement caused divisiveness within the Episcopal Church but it also "imparted increased vitality to many groups and to many phases of Church life, emphasizing principles and practices

These men meant much to American Catholicism. At a time when the fledgling Church was overwhelmed by massive numbers of immigrants and beset by nativist, anti-Catholic movements, the converts from Episcopalianism, together with those other convert-intellectuals, Hecker and Orestes Brownson, gave the Church respectability in the eyes of non-Catholic Americans. The charges of supersition and idolatry and the fear of Catholicism as foreign and alien to America were at least partly offset by its attraction to men of such impeccable native credentials. The early, upper-class, English-speaking Catholic leadership was sorely tested by the immigrant surge. Recruits like Hecker, Bayley and Walworth reinforced their effort to keep open the lines of communication between the Church and American society. Their theological sophistication and cultural concern helped to preserve a Catholic intellectual core which could engage outsiders and influence the developing self-consciousness of the American Catholic community itself.[563]

Walworth's collection of reminiscences is useful in two ways. It records the history of Walworth's passage to Roman Catholicism (which is, in part, the history of experiences shared with friends who were also moving Romeward) and it provides an insider's description of the atmosphere created by the ideas generated by the Oxford Movement. Walworth's religious history intersects with that of the General Theological Seminary from 1842 to 1845. Critical happenings at the Seminary -- Carey's trial, Onderdonk's suspension, the interrogation of Seminary faculty on order of the General Convention, and other attempts to purge the Seminary of unorthodoxy -- constituted turning points in Walworth's religious life and in the lives of his colleagues. The Oxford Movement in America might well be called a communal narrative of conversion.

---

in normative Anglicanism that need to be restated and restored" (pp. 162-163).

[563]David O'Brien, Introduction to the reprint of The Oxford Movement in America, p. xv.

The Story of a Convert,
as Told to His Former Parishioners
after He Became a Catholic

Unlike his classmates at General Theological Seminary, with

whom he shared an interest in and an attraction to Roman Catholicism,

Benjamin W. Whitcher delayed his conversion to the Roman Catholic

Church for some ten years. And unlike some of his classmates who

are still remembered for their contributions to the American Church,

Whitcher appears as a somewhat obscure figure in the histories of

both the Episcopal and the Roman Catholic Churches.[564] His wife,

Frances Miriam Berry, was well known for her humorous verse and

witty sketches.[565] Hers was hardly the appropriate career for the

wife of an Episcopal minister. Frances' caricatures and satires

---

[564]Benjamin W. Whitcher's name does not appear in standard
Catholic reference works such as the Catholic Encyclopedia, the
New Catholic Encyclopedia, and the Dictionary of Catholic Biography.
Nor is it to be found in the Dictionary of American Biography.
Clarke mentions a Rev. Mr. Whitcher in his listing of prominent
converts (p. 546). Clarence Walworth identifies Whitcher as a
student at the General Theological Seminary during the Tractarian con-
troversy (p. 14).
     Whitcher's name sometimes appears as Whicher. George E.
DeMille, author of The Catholic Movement in the American Episcopal
Church (Philadelphia: Church Historical Society, 1941; reprint ed.,
New Brunswick: Vogt Printing Co., 1950) uses both spellings.
DeMille indexes the name as Whicher; he names a Benjamin W. Whicher
among those who seceded to Rome between 1817 and 1858 (p. 106); and
he mentions Whitcher's wife, Frances Miriam Berry (noting that she
was more famous than her husband and that he did not secede until
after her death [p. 107]). The single index entry suggests that
Whitcher and Whicher are the same person. Records at General
Theological Seminary show Benjamin Whicher to have been a member of
the graduating class of 1844. Anne-Marie Salgat, Librarian of
St. Mark's Library, General Theological Seminary, to Christine M.
Bochen, 6 September 1979.

[565]Frances Miriam Berry Whitcher (1814-1852) was born in
Whitesboro (also called Whitestown), New York. She studied at the
local academy and in Utica, New York, developing her artistic and
teaching skills. She was known for her caricatures as well as her

antagonized her husband's parishioners, most especially those who

saw themselves as victims of her pen. Perhaps this, in part, explains

Walworth's caustic reproach: Whitcher's "first backward step was when

he took orders in the Episcopalian communion. The second was when he

took a Presbyterian wife. Still later, on becoming a widower, he took

a second wife, and became surrounded by a family of children."[566]

---

prose and verse. She published her first humorous sketches,
"The Widow Spriggins" in a newspaper in Rome, New York. The first
installments of The Widow Bedott's Table Talk" appeared in the
Saturday Gazette and Lady's Literary Museum in 1846, under the
pseudonym of "Frank." She continued to write the Widow Bedott
series until 1850; the sketches were collected and published as
The Widow Bedott Papers, with an Introduction by Alice B. Neal
(New York: J. C. Derby, 1856). Her illustrated sketches appeared
in Godey's Lady's Book. A second collection of her work was
published after her death under the title, Widow Spriggins, Mary
Elmer, and Other Sketches (New York: G. W. Carleton, 1867).
      Frances married the Rev. B. W. Whitcher on January 6, 1847.
The following year she accompanied him to his parish in Elmira,
New York. Mrs. Whitcher's work and reputation caused some difficulty
for her husband: "Her fame as a humorist did not endear her to
her husband's parishioners. Her always strong sense of the
ludicrous and the absurd tempted her to satirize much that she
found in small-town society. She dealt sharply with the sewing
circle, the donation party, and with the pretentiousness of the
self-satisfied. As she was good at portraiture, some of her sketches
gave offense to persons who fancied that they recognized the originals"
(Dictionary of American Biography). The antipathy of the parishioners
forced Rev. Whitcher to leave the parish (The National Cyclopedia of
American Biography, 1896 ed.). He and his wife returned to Whitesboro
in 1850. Frances' health declined after she gave birth to a daughter
in 1849. Rev. Whitcher took a parish in Oswego, but his wife stayed
there only briefly, returning home to Whitesboro where she died in 1852.
      Brief biographical sketches of Frances Miriam Berry Whitcher
appear in Who Was Who in America: Historical Volume 1607-1896, 1963
ed.,; B. F. Fullerton, Selective Bibliography of American Literature
1775-1900 (New York: William Farquhar Payson, 1932), pp. 294-295;
Stanley J. Kunitz and Howard Haycraft, American Authors 1600-1900:
A Biographical Dictionary of American Literature (New York: The
H. W. Wilson Co., 1938), p. 803; David, pp. 218-219. Fullerton
notes that The Widow Bedott Papers ran through twenty-three editions
in two years (p. 295).

[566]C. Walworth, The Oxford Movement, p. 149.

Benjamin Whitcher's narrative, The Story of a Convert, as Told to His Former Parishioners after He Became a Catholic, is the best source of information regarding his life.[567] But it is hardly complete. Whitcher was less concerned with providing his readers with the facts, such as the time and place of his birth, than he was with describing the religious changes he experienced during his lifetime. Consequently, the narrative lacks basic biographical details. Unfortunately, these details are not to be found elsewhere. The date of Whitcher's birth is uncertain but it is known that he was a student at the General Theological Seminary and a member of the graduating class of 1844.[568] It is likely that he was the same age as his classmates at the Seminary, one of whom was Charles Platt, a cousin of Clarence C. Walworth. Walworth mentions that Whitcher and Platt were a year ahead of him in the Seminary.[569] That would suggest that Whitcher was born circa 1820.

Unlike a number of his fellow students at the Seminary, Whitcher remained an Episcopalian and was ordained to the deaconate on July 18, 1844 by Bishop William H. DeLancey, Bishop of the Episcopal Diocese of Western New York.[570] His first assignment as deacon was as a missionary

---

[567] Benjamin W. Whitcher, The Story of a Convert, as Told to His Former Parishioners after He Became a Catholic (New York: P. O'Shea, 1875).

[568] Records at the General Theological Seminary verify these facts but yield no further biographical information (Salgat to Bochen, 6 September 1979).

[569] C. Walworth, The Oxford Movement, pp. 13-14. Walworth was born in 1820.

[570] George Burgess, List of Persons Admitted to the Order of Deacons in the Protestant Episcopal Church in the United States of

to Oreskany, Remsen, and adjacent parts of Oneida County.[571] The list

of clergy appended to the Proceedings of the General Convention of the

Protestant Episcopal Church, held in 1847, names Rev. Benjamin W.

Whitcher as the rector of Trinity Church, Elmira, New York in Chemung

County.[572] It was customary for deacons to be ordained to the priest-

hood at least one year after ordination to the deaconate.[573] Lists

of clergy appended to the Proceedings of the General Convention and the

Convention of the Diocese of Western New York show that Whitcher resided

at Whitestown in Oneida County in 1849 and 1850,[574] served as a

missionary at Theresa and Redwood in Jefferson County in 1852 and

---

American, From A. D. 1785, to A. D. 1857, both inclusive (Boston: A.
Williams & Co., 1875), p. 31.

[571]Journal of the Proceedings of the Bishops, Clergy, and
Laity of the Protestant Episcopal Church in the United States of
American Assembled in a General Convention, Held in St. Andrew's
Church in the City of Philadelphia From October 2d, to October
22d, inclusive, in the Year of Our Lord 1844. With an Appendix
Containing the Constitution and Canons, A List of Clergy, &c
(New York: James A. Sparks, 1845), p. 262.

[572]Journal of the Proceedings of the Bishops, Clergy, and
Laity of the Protestant Episcopal Church in the United States of
America Assembled in a General Convention, Held in St. John's Chapel,
in the City of New York, From October 6th, to October 28th, inclusive,
in the year of Our Lord 1847. With an Appendix Containing the
Constitution and Canons, A List of Clergy, &c (New York: Daniel
Dana, Jr., 1847), p. 252. Also see the Journal of the Proceedings
of the Eleventh Annual Convention of the Protestant Episcopal Church
in the Diocese of Western New York, Held in Trinity Church, Geneva, on
Wednesday, August 16th, and Thursday, August 17th, A. D. 1848. To
Which is Prefixed a List of the Clergy of the Diocese (Utica: H. H.
Curtiss, 1848), p. 8.

[573]Canonical Forms and Requisites for Persons Seeking Holy
Orders in the Protestant Episcopal Church. Prepared by the Standing
Committee of the Diocese of Ohio (Cincinatti: Robert Clarke & Co., 1872).

[574]Journal of the Proceedings of the Twelfth Annual Convention
of the Protestant Episcopal Church in the Diocese of Western New York,

and 1853,[575] and returned to Whitestown in 1854.[576] Whitcher converted

to Roman Catholicism in 1855 and was deposed from the priesthood of the

Episcopal Church on April 24, 1855.[577] After his conversion, Whitcher

delivered public lectures, explaining his reasons for becoming a Roman

Catholic. These served as the basis for The Story of a Convert, pub-

lished in 1875, some twenty years after his conversion. In the course

of his narrative, Walworth mentions that Whitcher "died recently a

Catholic layman," that is, prior to 1895.[578]

Held in Trinity Church, Geneva, on Wednesday, August 15th and Thursday, August 16th, A. D. 1849. To Which is Prefixed A List of Clergy of the Diocese (Utica: H. H. Curtiss, 1849), p. 6. Whitcher did not attend the convention (p. 7). Also see the Journal of the Proceedings of the Bishops, Clergy, and Laity of the Protestant Episcopal Church in the United States of America Assembled in General Convention, Held in Christ Church, in the City of Cincinatti, From October 2d to October 16th, inclusive, in the Years of Our Lord, 1850. With an Appendix Containing the Constitution and Canons, A List of Clergy, &c (Philadelphia: King & Baird, Printers, 1851), p. 244.

[575]Journal of the Proceedings of the Fifteenth Annual Convention of the Protestant Episcopal Church in the Diocese of Western New York, Held in St. Paul's Church, Syracuse, on Wednesday, August 18th, and Thursday, August, 19th, A. D. 1852. To Which is Prefixed a List of the Clergy of the Diocese (Utica: Curtiss & White, 1852), p. 6; Journal of the Proceedings of the Sixteenth Annual Convention ...Held in St. Paul's Church, Buffalo, on Wednesday, August 17th and Thursday, August 18th, A. D. 1853 (Utica: Curtiss & White, 1853), p. 6; Journal of the Proceedings of the Bishops, Clergy, and Laity of the Protestant Episcopal Church in the United States of America Assembled in a General Convention, Held in Trinity Church and St. John's Chapel, in the City of New York, From October 5th to October 26th, Inclusive. In the Year of Our Lord 1853 (Philadelphia: King and Baird, Printers, 1854), p. 420.

[576]Journal of the Proceedings of the Seventeenth Annual Convention...Held in Trinity Church, Utica on Wednesday, August 16th and Thursday, August 17th, A. D. 1854 (Utica: Curtiss & White, 1854), p. 6.

[577]Burgess, p. 31.

[578]C. Walworth, The Oxford Movement, p. 14.

The Story of a Convert began as a series of lectures, given

...first to former parishioners and others, who felt an interest
in hearing the reasons why a man would encounter certain
pecuniary loss and worldly advantages for the sake of a
religion which was held in contempt by most of his neighbors.
Afterwards, at the request of friends, they were given in some
of the eastern and western cities of the country.[579]

A newspaper report of a lecture which Whitcher gave in 1871 in Rochester,

New York tells something of the content and format of his presentations.

Mr. Witcher's [sic] Lecture. -- There was a good audience
at Corinthian Hall last night to listen to the lecture of B.
W. Whitcher, who had announced his subject to be "Reasons why
I became a Catholic." The lecturer was an Episcopalian
clergyman, and went over to the Roman Catholic Church. He
gave the history of his conversion. He began when a student
to doubt the truthfulness of the statement that the Catholic
Church had shown a bloody and persecuting spirit. He also
denied the charge of idolatry, and entered into an examination
of the charges, and gave what we deemed to be convincing proof
that both charges were erroneous. The forms of worship were
considered at length, and those of the Protestant and Catholic
Churches compared. The lecture was well-written, and delivered
with good effect. The speaker endeavored to satisfy his
audience, which was large, considering the state of the
weather.[580]

Because his lectures were generally well received, he put them in

a more permanent written form, "thinking that they might fill a place

in the Catholic literature of the time."[581] Whitcher preserved the

original lecture format. The text consists of a preface and three

lectures which deal with his early religious history as a Congregation-

alist, his experience as an Episcopalian, and his progress toward Rome.

In the midst of the widespread disintegration of religious beliefs and

principles that characterized the Protestantism of his day, Whitcher

---

[579]Whitcher, p. 5.

[580]Union & Advertiser, Rochester, New York, 13 Feburary 1871.

[581]Whitcher, p. 5.

appealed to "the common sense" of all Americans with the example of his conversion to Roman Catholicism.[582]

Whitcher began formulating his account two years after his conversion, when he began to deliver lectures, but the narrative was published some twenty years after he became a Catholic. He spoke and wrote to explain why he became a Catholic and why he had not done so sooner.

The Whitchers were Congregationalists. As a child, Benjamin memorized the catechism long before he knew what the words meant.[583] He also learned the Lord's Prayer and what was more important, in his estimation, he developed confidence in the power of prayer: "Indeed my faith in prayer was so strong that no childish sorrow afflicted my heart, no pain or discomfort my body but was removed or supplied by prayer."[584] As he entered adolescence, he began to doubt the truth of Calvinist teaching, questioning church teachings regarding foreordination and free will. Even in this "dark and gloomy region of doubt," his link with the faith of his childhood was not entirely broken: "there was one golden and blessed link which bound me to a vague and indefinite faith. I believed something, I know not what, because my mother believed."[585]

His anti-Catholic feeling was strong. He heard the Roman Church described as "the mother of abominations" and believed what

---

[582]Ibid., p. 8.

[583]Ibid., p. 25.

[584]Ibid., p. 24.

[585]Ibid., pp. 29, 30.

he heard repeated by teachers and preachers alike.

During Whitcher's adolescence, his family moved to western
New York State, to the area designated as the Burned-over District,
where the fires of religious fervor were carefully stoked by enthusiastic
revivalist preachers. Methodists and Baptists dominated the religious
scene; they were divided by numerous religious disputes but united by
a common desire to convert the masses. Religious controversy was
commonplace.

> Disputes soon ran high. The corners of the streets, the
> taverns, the steps, and the fireside of almost every house,
> echoed these wranglings. Scripture was hurled against Scripture,
> text against text; -- the passions of men were aroused; neighbor
> became alienated from neighbor, and even families were divided,
> in the fruitless attempt to settle the difficulties of doctrine
> by the rule of private judgment.[586]

Witnessing such dissension increased Whitcher's own doubts regarding
religious truth. All claimed to speak the truth but each faction
delivered its own reading of that truth and derided the views of
its opponents. Denominations even stooped to name-calling.

Both the content and the style of revivalist teaching were
distasteful to Whitcher. He took issue with the Calvinists and
Baptists who discounted the role of good works in the plan of salvation.
They "were saved by the decrees of God, while the Methodists were
saved by the voluntary act of 'getting religion.'"[587] In either case,
good works seemed insignificant. Indeed, Whitcher observed, "the
profane, the intemperate and otherwise immoral characters were far more
likely to submit to the terms of the Gospel, and 'get religion' then

---

[386]Ibid., p. 36.

[387]Ibid., p. 37.

the sturdy upright men."[588]

Methodists dominated the area and "protracted meetings" became
the place to "get religion." Whitcher found these meetings "fearful
to behold. The midnights were made hideous by the groans and screams,
and sometimes the fearful howls of the multitudes of those who flocked
around the 'anxious benches.'"[589] Whitcher was not converted; he resisted the efforts of a delegation sent to urge him to attend the meetings.
He justified his refusal by denying their authority to preach the Gospel;
he argued that they could not be God's messengers. But rejecting the
dominant religious perspective meant inviting social isolation. The
school debating club focused on religious questions; so he withdrew
from it. Evangelicals shunned him: "at one of their church meetings it
was resolved to hold no intercourse, except on business, with the
unconverted. Thus I was placed under a social ban, which was
rigorously enforced for several months."[590] It is noteworthy that
Whitcher interpreted this formulation of policy as an act directed
against him personally.

His early doubts regarding Calvinist teaching and his antipathy
toward evangelical Protestantism led him to reject Christianity in
favor of natural religion. He modelled himself after Benjamin
Franklin, a fellow infidel, and constructed a table of virtues against
which he could evaluate his behavior. He had hoped this list would
function as a creed, but found it deficient as such. This guide to moral

[588]Ibid., pp. 37-38.
[589]Ibid., p. 39.
[590]Ibid., p. 53.

conduct failed to satisfy his deepest needs. "It related only to personal conduct, but settled no question of truth, satisfied none of those longings of the heart -- those questionings of the soul, about which I was so much bewildered and lost in vain thought."[591] In choosing a "natural religion," Whitcher had not rejected revealed religion as such; what he rejected was a particular image of God -- that portrayed by the evangelicals: "I longed for God and knew not who or what I longed for. I did not believe in the God I heard preached."[592]

This was a time of emotional turmoil for Whitcher; he was beset by doubts and questions. He could not return to the Congregationalists; he found their teachings unacceptable. So he turned to the Methodists and attended their meetings for a year or so, despite his dislike for their ways. The hysteria manifested during the course of these meetings offended him, as did the theological ignorance of the minister. Whitcher criticized the self-righteousness of the evangelicals in the school paper. He notes that perhaps his essays were responsible for terminating the practice of non-intercourse with the uncoverted. Given his apparent aversion to the evangelicals, it is difficult to understand why Whitcher persisted in attending the meetings. Was his presence a concession to peer pressure or an expression of his deep hunger for religious meaning? Was his distate for revivalism as strong as he suggests that it was during his adolescence. Or did the antipathy grow later when he became an Episcopalian?

Whitcher's friendship with an Episcopalian minister was

---

[591]Ibid., pp. 55-56.

[592]Ibid., p. 56.

a turning point in his religious development. The difference between
the Episcopal minister and the Methodist ministers he had known was
striking.

> Here then to me was a new and most marvellous thing -- a
> clergyman evidently learned, who can talk commonsense -- does
> not believe in the total depravity of the human race, and does
> not think it is a sin to visit with a friend on a Sunday, and
> that, too, with one who is not regenerate.[593]

Episcopal and Methodist views of the church also differed. Methodists,
Whitcher concluded, saw the church as little more than "an aggregation
of men and women, called together by a town crier, and organized by a
vote of the majority."[594] But to the Episcopalians, the Christian
Church was "an entity, a real thing that had a beginning and a continuity of existence."[595] He became an Episcopalian and entered Geneva
College to begin studies for the ministry.[596]

The next section of the narrative, Lecture II, begins with an
account of Whitcher's discovery of the divisions within the Episcopal
Church. While a student at Geneva College, Whitcher first learned
about the different theological perspectives in evidence in the American
Episcopal Church. The president of the College as a man of the via
media but the rector of the local church was a Low churchman. Whitcher
recalls that when he first heard the rector speak of "vital piety" and

---

[593]Ibid., pp. 66-67.

[594]Ibid., p. 67.

[595]Ibid.

[596]Geneva College was chartered in 1822 as a theological
seminary. In 1826, the seminary was discontinued but the College
continued in existence and, in 1852, assumed the name of the man
who had been instrumental in its founding, Bishop John Hobart. See
William Wilson Manross, A History of the American Episcopal Church
(New York: Morehouse-Gorham Co., 1959), p. 244.

"evangelical views," he thought that he had come to the wrong church.[597]

And when the rector presented him with Low Church readings, he was struck

by the similarity between what he was reading and what he had found

so distasteful in revivalism: "I took the papers home and carefully

read over those articles, and found they differed in no respect

from the teachings which had so much disgusted me in the sermons, or

rather the rantings of my old Congregational and Methodist friends."[598]

Low Churchmen emphasized justification by faith alone, as did the

Congregationalists and Methodists.

Whitcher's friend, the Episcopal minister, explained that

there was a "great latitude of sentiment and opinion" to be found in

the Episcopal Church.[599] This explanation was consonant with the

motto of the Episcopal Church as expressed by the president of Geneva

College: "In all essential things agreed; in all things not essential,

freedom to differ."[600] For a time, Whitcher was satisfied with this

explanation. He saw the Episcopal Church as "that true Via Media, that

true and safe middle ground between popery on the one hand, and ultra-

Protestantism on the other."[601]

Although he is describing his experience as an Episcopalian,

---

[597]Whitcher, p. 77.

[598]Ibid., pp. 77-78.

[599]Ibid., p. 81.

[600]Ibid., p. 83. Benjamin Hale was president of Geneva College
during Whitcher's time there. Hale became president in 1836 and served
until 1858. Milton Haight Turk, Hobart: The Story of a Hundred Years,
1822-1922 (Geneva: W. F. Humphrey, 1921), p. 39.

[601]Whitcher, p. 90.

Whitcher concludes the second lecture by making several points about the
Roman Catholic Church. He recalls trying to convert "a papist" by citing
the persecutions for which the Roman Catholic Church had been responsible.
But his attempt was unsuccessful; he failed to convince the student of
the error of his faith and lost the debate. Whitcher departs from the
narrative form in order to refute the Protestant charge that invocation
of the saints is idolatrous.[602] By the time he had entered the General
Theological Seminary, Whitcher "saw clearly that the Catholic Church, in
point of fact, was not that church of persecution and blood" which he
had supposed it to be, and that "prayers offered to saints were not
idolatrous."[603]

As a student at General Theological Seminary, Whitcher shared
with many of his fellow students an interest in early church history.
And like the others, he also was suspected of being a Puseyite and
interrogated regarding his Roman ways. When he denied reading Romish
books and attending Romish worship, he escaped with the warning to
be cautious. While at the Seminary, Whitcher decided to read the Fathers
of the Church and to study church history prior to the Reformation. His
proposed course of reading met with the approval of his bishop and
faculty. But his stated intent reveals his growing interest in Roman
Catholicism: he was reading for the "express purpose of finding out the
exact origin of all the errors, superstitions, and corruptions of the

---

[602] It is likely that the Rochester lecture cited above (p. 168)
was essentially similar to the second lecture as it appears in the
text of the narrative.

[603] Whitcher, p. 118.

Church of Rome."[604]

The third section of the text, that is, the third lecture,
includes accounts of Whitcher's discoveries regarding the true Church
of Christ, his decision to remain an Episcopalian and seek ordination
in that church, and finally, his conversion to Roman Catholicism.
Whitcher's reading of the Fathers of the Church made him recognize
that the essential difference between the claims of the Fathers and those
of the "heretics" was the authority with which they were made. The
Fathers "summoned witnesses, to testify as to what was, and what was not,
the teaching of the Saviour and His Apostles."[605] The heretics relied on
their own interpretations of the Bible: "they heaped up text upon text,
and made exegetical analysis of these texts, and claimed that they had
the illuminating power of the Holy Spirit to enable them to put the
true interpretation upon the texts of the Bible."[606] The sects which
emerged after the Reformation resorted to this "heretical" method of
argument. Each, though differing from all the others in its interpretations, claims the Bible as proof of its truth. "In short,they
[the heretics] treat God's holy word as though they thought it some
old fiddle, which they could tune up, loosening a string here and
tightening a string there, turning one peg up and another peg down, then
twang off 'any tune you like, sir.'"[607] Though they differed in their
reading of Scripture, the heretics were united in charging the Roman

---

[604] Ibid., p. 123.

[605] Ibid., p. 135.

[606] Ibid., pp. 135-136.

[607] Ibid., p. 137.

Catholic Church with the "most outrageous crimes."[608]

The Fathers, Whitcher discovered, emphasized the visible
and infallible nature of the church with Peter as its head. Being
united with Christ required fellowship with his church: "That internal
union and communion with that visible body, of which, after the
ascension of Christ, St. Peter was the head."[609] The Fathers regarded
any schism which destroyed the unity of the Church as "a crime before
whose heinousness their bosoms trembled and their souls recoiled."[610]

Although the testimony of the Fathers led him to the threshold
of the Roman Church, Whitcher did not cross over. He so interpreted
their thought as to minimize their claim on him:

> ...if I had never read a book of controversy, or been entangled
> in their sophistries, I should have at once gone forward and
> sought admission into the Catholic Church, for that is the only
> one which dates back to the birth of Christ. He in Himself
> was the true Church, the true voice, and the only door. But
> my mind had been confused, and I was entangled by what seemed
> to me specious theories, especially in regard to the English
> or Episcopal Church. I think I can best explain my then
> condition of mind by a syllogism. It is the whole Church, and
> not a part of it, which is infallible. The Church of Rome is
> not the whole Church since the Greek and Anglican form parts
> of it; therefore, the Church of Rome is not the infallible
> Church.[611]

Though the Roman Church was "the organic continuation of the old
Apostolic Church, it had been "deformed" by heresy.[612]

A sense of duty kept Whitcher in the Episcopal Church; he

---

[608]Ibid., p. 138.

[609]Ibid., p. 142.

[610]Ibid., p. 143.

[611]Ibid., pp. 149-150.

[612]Ibid., p. 150.

felt that he must work to redeem "this branch of Christ's Church ...from

her errors and from her chains."[613] And though he discovered that

Protestants "consciously or unconsciously, had invariably, in some way,

misrepresented the teachings of the Catholic Church," he stood his ground

as Episcopalian.[614]

Ordination became his test and guarantee:

If then, I am ordained, with the full knowledge, on the part
of the constituted authorities, of my position, it will be
another proof, that with patience and toil, Catholic truth
will prevail over Protestant error. But if they refuse to
ordain me; I shall receive the refusal as proof that the
Episcopal Church is Protestant, and I will take my journey
into a strange land.[615]

Whitcher effectively dodged responsibility for his choice by allowing

others to make the decision for him. This experience, in part, explains

his delay in entering "a strange land."

But ordination did not resolve Whitcher's religious difficulties.

A few years in the ministry were enough to show him that he "might as

well write history upon the sands of the seashore as to permanently

teach Catholic doctrines in an organized Protestant body."[616] Still,

he was torn. How could he leave behind all who had been kind to him?

How could he impose the social and economic trials that his conversion

would bring upon his family?

If I break all these ties, spurn all these endearments, throw
away all these advantages, turn my back upon all your charities,
and bring scandal upon my whole body -- to you, and to them --

[613]Ibid., p. 163.

[614]Ibid., p. 160.

[615]Ibid., pp. 170-171.

[616]Ibid., p. 177.

I must appear as the most ungrateful of human beings.
Then again, those ten thousand family ties that are linked
-- around the heart, and around the life [sic]. To bring grief to
a large circle of relations and friends; to deprive my wife
of a peaceful and happy love; to drive her forth like a second
Eve from that little garden of flowers, which had been watered
by our mutual tears of joy or of sorrow; to destroy all prospects
of giving my children a proper education, if not depriving them
and myself headlong into poverty, followed, it might be, by a
tempest of indignation, if not vituperation and scorn.[617]

Whitcher's ambivalence kept him from becoming a Roman Catholic for some

ten years. He was attracted by Roman Catholicism, particularly by the

unity of its teaching but he was put off by the high personal and

social cost of conversion, a cost which he meticulously details in the

preceeding passage. In light of the high price of conversion, it is all

the more amazing that he ever became a Roman Catholic. Certainly,

Whitcher sees his disclosures of personal anguish as an asset to his

apology.

It took a three year examination of the history of the

Reformation to help Whitcher to resolve his doubts. The English

Reformation, he concluded, made "a new church, with new doctrines, and

new officers" by "an act of parliament."[618] The Church of England was

the work of the state. Only the Roman Catholic Church "maintained a

continuous existence, from the days of the Apostles down to our

own."[619] Even then, Whitcher was ambivalent, again citing his regret

that he would have to leave family and friends behind as the reason for

his hesitation: "I felt it like taking my life's blood to leave so

_____

[617]Ibid., pp. 178-179.

[618]Ibid., pp. 181-182.

[619]Ibid., p. 155.

many and such dear friends."[620]   The strain of anticipating the rejection

of others took its toll on mind and body alike.

> I saw the indignent scorn of my superiors in the Protestant
> Church, the frowns of my brother preachers, and more than
> all this the sad eyes of many, in whose hearts I knew it
> would cause the most profound anguish. All my relatives,
> strong in Protestantism of every shade -- High Churchmen,
> down through all forms of unbelief to naked infidelity --
> seemed to be looking at me and saying, Will you disgrace us,
> and all your Protestant ancestry, who only obtained a
> recognition of worth, in connection with the Protestant
> Bible? Can you not keep silent and save your soul where you
> are?[621]

The last question reveals Whitcher's reasons for becoming a Roman

Catholic -- salvation. Only the salvation of his eternal soul was

worth the pain of incurring the wrath and rejection of his colleagues.

That Whitcher was less decisive than his colleagues at

General Theological Seminary appears certain. He hesitated for ten

years before becoming a Roman Catholic. Intellectual satisfaction

was not sufficient reason for becoming a Roman Catholic. Even after

Whitcher had established that the Roman Church was the true Church of

Christ, which had maintained its unbroken link with the Apostles and

its unity under the headship of Peter, Whitcher hesitated. His

conversion was not simply the resolution of a period of theological

inquiry. Whitcher's account reveals his concern about the opinion

of others and his need for their support.

Clarence Walworth helped Whitcher to take the last step to

Rome.[622]   Whitcher and Walworth met in 1855 while Walworth was giving

---

[620]Ibid.

[621]Ibid., pp. 189-190.

[622]Ibid., pp. 191-192; C. Walworth, The Oxford Movement,

a mission at St. Patrick's Church in Utica, New York. Whitcher visited

him there. Walworth's approach was direct: "Why are you not a Catholic

long before this?"[623] Walworth urged him to see a priest and Whitcher

did so several weeks later. He became a convert that year and was depos-

ed from the Episcopal priesthood.

Why did he finally convert?

> I went...because everywhere outside of that Ark there was the
> darkness of desolation and death. The forked lightenings of
> sharp contention were in the gloomy sky of Anglicanism.
> Indifference like a heavy pall was settling down on all the
> other sects. The blackness of approaching infidelity was
> without; light and safety were within and while I was yet a
> great way off, I took up my journey and followed on, and, my
> friends, I have found, by the grace of God, not only a place
> of safety, but of refreshment and rest.[624]

The Roman Catholic Church was a haven for Whitcher; it offered him

security and refuge from religious dissension, indifference and

infidelity. The Roman Church provided immediate safety and the

assurance of eternal salvation. That Whitcher chose to explain why

he converted in metaphorical language is itself significant. His

language reveals that becoming a Roman Catholic satisifed strong

affective needs. Though theological issues and historical arguments

attracted his attention for years, the Roman Catholic Church satisfied

his deeply personal need for "a place of safety."

The Story of a Convert traces Whitcher's lengthy and circuitous

journey from Calvinism to Methodism to natural religion to Episcopalian-

ism and finally, to Roman Catholicism. The contribution of this

---

pp. 150-151.

[623]C. Walworth, The Oxford Movement, p. 150.

[624]Whitcher, p. 21.

narrative lies in its exposition of the ambivalence and hesitation
that could characterize a convert's journey because conversion to
Roman Catholicism signified a radical break with one's past during much
of the nineteenth century.

On the Road to Rome,
and How Two Brothers Got There

William Richards came to the Roman Catholic Church by way of
the Episcopal Church, as did his brother, Henry Livingston Richards.[625]
William's narrative, On the Road to Rome, and How Two Brothers Got
There, recounts the story of both their conversions.[626] William
records the changes in thought and sentiment that drew Henry
to the Roman Church and shows how Henry's conversion contributed to
his own.

Richards' narrative conforms to the pattern of conversion
narratives in structure and in content. Its structure is determined
by the chronology of Richards' religious history. And conversion to
Roman Catholicism serves as the principle of content selection. All
that Richards includes in the narrative concerns his own conversion or
that of his brother: early religious experiences, the change in atti-

---

[625]Henry Livinston Richards also did some autobiographical
writing. His son, J. Haven Richards, based his biography of his
father on a "manuscript autobiographical sketch" which his father
began at the request of his family. But he used the sketch with
discretion: "It is of a very intimate personal character, intended
chiefly to give to his children the interior history of his
conversion and to illustrate the goodness of God to one who, in
his loneliness of self-appreciation, considered himself one of the
greatest of sinners." A Loyal Life (St. Louis: B. Herder, 1913),
p. vii. The statement is reminiscent of conventional descriptions
of purpose, written by Puritan spiritual autobiographers.

[626]William Richards, On the Road to Rome, and How Two Brothers

tude toward Roman Catholicism, sources of dissatisfaction with
Protestantism, descriptions of currents of thought which shaped their
thinking, and the changes of mind which finally made conversion
inevitable. He is particularly attentive to the task of setting forth
his early negative impressions of Roman Catholicism and to describing
the way in which those early views were gradually revised.

On the Road to Rome grew out of two talks which William Richards
was invited to give in 1887: the first was delivered for the Carroll
Institute in Washington, D.C. on January 6; the second on March 20 as
part of an effort to raise funds for a monument in honor of Orestes
Brownson.[627] Richards remarks that the address appears "substantially
in the form" in which it was last delivered, with some additions by
way of notes."[628] The written text takes up one hundred and seventeen
pages -- a lengthy address to be sure. That the text was intended to
be delivered orally enhanced its narrative quality: Richards "tells"
his story well. The narrative flows freely and only occasionally does
Richards allow himself to engage in philosophical debate or religious
polemic. And then he does so with restraint. The lecture format of
the text precluded extensive apologetics.

It is worth noting that Richards had been invited to speak on
his "Reminiscences of the Catholic Church in Ohio." But by necessity,
his talk took on a personal rather than a local perspective; he had not

---

Got There (New York: Benzinger Brothers, 1895).

[627]The first talk was brief; it ends on p. 64 of the written
text. Richards includes the text of the first conclusion in a note
on that page.

[628]Richards, p. 4.

lived in Ohio as a Catholic. He suggests that the title, "How and Why

I Became a Catholic" more accurately reflects the purpose of his

address.[629]

William Richards was born in Granville, Ohio in 1819.[630]

Granville was a small village, settled some fourteen years before

William's birth by devout descendents of New England Puritans.

William's family was Congregationalist until 1827 when his father,

Dr. William Samuel Richards, took issue with the congregational mode

of church polity; he was particularly dissatisfied with the principle

of individual judgment and the church's inability to speak authoritative-

ly. Dr. Richards led the movement to establish an Episcopal Church

in Granville.[631] William's older brother, Henry, later strengthened

the family's ties to the Episcopal Church by beginning studies for

the Episcopal ministry at Kenyon College, Gambier, Ohio, where William

joined him. Following their graduations in 1838, Henry was ordained

---

[629]W. Richards, pp. 5-6. Richards writes: "it had so happened
that I had never entered a Catholic church but once before I accepted
the faith, and soon thereafter had emigrated to Koekuk, Iowa...."

[630]References to William Richards and his brother Henry
Livingston Richards are few. William Richards does not appear in
standard Catholic biographical works, such as the Dictionary of
Catholic Biography, the Catholic Encyclopedia, and the New Catholic
Encyclopedia. David mentions only the barest facts relating to
William Richards: the dates of his birth, death, and conversion;
his birthplace; and his having attended Kenyon College. David
cites On the Road to Rome as the source of his data. Some corro-
borating information appears in two books written by Henry
Livingston Richards: Forty Years in the Church (St. Paul, Minn.:
The Catholic Truth Society of America, 1892) and Fifty Years in
the Church (St. Paul, Minn.: The Catholic Truth Society of America,
1902). Also see J. H. Richards for a biography of Henry Livingston
Richards and a sketch of the Oxford movement in America.

[631]Dr. Richards practiced medicine in Granville (J. H.
Richards, p. 13).

and William continued his study of philosophy and political thought
under Dr. William Sparrow. William was at Kenyon while a revival was
in progress but he resisted the religious excitement. Perennial
philosophical and religious questions concerning the truth of religion,
the nature of man and society, and the question of religious authority,
occupied his attention at that time.

William Richards reveals few facts about his later life. In
1842, he studied law at Yale. By 1844, he was practicing law in
Newark, Ohio. That year, he was invited to give the commencement
address at Kenyon. In that address, he set forth "the prevailing
tendencies of the age in its social, political, and religious aspects,"
decrying the abuses of individualism, utilitarianism, unrestrained
competition, and private judgment.[632] Then he asked what for him
was the crucial question: "What is truth?"

> Is that necessarily truth which one may believe with ever so
> much heartfelt sincerity? If so, then is not the sincere
> Perfectionist, walking with the Bible in his hand, right?
> Is not the Transcendentalist who, with awful sincerity,
> finds the Most High God in the pure reason, right? Is not
> every sectarian right who holds his particular view or
> opinion with sincerity? Are, then, truth and duty dependent
> upon the transitory feelings and perceptions of each finite
> individual? Or is it not most certain that truth is eternal,
> at one with itself, and possessing a harmonious diversity in
> unity?...Is it not becoming the earnest, passionate cry of the
> times: Where is the version of truth that we can depend on?[633]

Richard's statement reveals his concern with what was a pressing issue
for some Christians, particularly Episcopalians, in the 40's. William
converted to Roman Catholicism in 1853, a year after his brother, Henry,

---

632W. Richards, p. 40.

633Ibid., pp. 61-62.

became a Catholic. Shortly after his conversion, William emigrated to

Keokuk, Iowa, where he pursued his career as a lawyer and journalist.[634]

These few facts comprise the body of biographical data contained

in the narrative. The paucity of detail is deliberate. Richards deemed

such detail insignificant to his purposes: "It is not necessary, and I

do not intend, to inflict upon you my biography."[635] Those facts or

events which he does mention serve "as a peg on which to hang a sign

indicating my progress to Rome."[636] The conversion is the primary

focus of the narrative.

Several motifs emerge as central in Richards' narrative,

precisely because he judged them critical to his eventual conversion

to Roman Catholicism: a strong anti-Catholic influence which he

experienced in his early years, his dissatisfaction with evangelical

Protestantism, his gradual revision of views regarding the Roman

Catholic Church, and his final break with Episcopal teaching over the

issue of religious authority. Each of these motifs is, of course,

presented in light of his conversion to Rome; or to put it another

way, the conversion sheds light on that which Richards remembers.

The anti-Catholic attitudes and sentiment which Richards

learned and absorbed early in his life were a staple in Calvinist

---

[634]W. Richards mentions his departure from Ohio in the
opening paragraph of his narrative (p. 5). J. H. Richards notes
that William abandoned his work as lawyer and journalist in Iowa
to take a post in the Internal Revenue Department during the Lincoln
administration. J. H. Richards describes William's role as advocate
of "the entire Northern position" (p. 300). William died in 1899
(David, p. 172).

[635]W. Richards, p. 19.

[636]Ibid., p. 20.

communities. The people of Granville were pious descendents of
New England Puritans. The majority were "Honest, sober, industrious,
and thirfty, their religion being deeply pervaded by the sourness
of Calvinism."[637] Richards learned some basic tenets of Calvinism
as soon as he began reading the "Little Primer." Along with the
ABC's, he learned such pedagogical couplets as: "In Adam's fall,
We sinned all."[638] Education was value-laden and attitudes were
effectively communicated to the young. The virtues of honesty, sobriety,
industry, and thrift were nurtured. But the counterpart to these solid
virtues instilled by Calvinists was a deep suspicion of all things
Catholic. As he looked back on his early years, from his perspective
as a convert, he recalled some incidents that shaped his negative
attitude toward Roman Catholicism. In the primer which first acquainted
him with the tenets of Calvinism, he saw a picture which contributed
to his "vague horror of Catholics and their religion."[639] It was a
representation of

> ...the so-called Protestant martyr, John Rogers, tied to a
> stake, standing in the midst of flames rising from a pile of
> blazing fagots, and gazed upon by his persecutors, and also
> by his weeping wife, who stood there, as the legend read,
> "with nine small children and one at the breast."[640]

This act of torture was attributed to "Bloody Mary," as this Catholic
queen of England was called. Richards also remembered hearing about
a Papist who, it was rumored, had sought permission from a Roman

---

[637]Ibid., p. 6.

[638]Ibid., p. 7.

[639]Ibid., p. 8.

[640]Ibid., p. 7.

Catholic priest to commit murder and received the priest's pardon in advance.[641]

Experiences such as these reinforced the view of the Roman Church as a corrupt, heinous institution. Their affect was far-reaching.

> I know from sad experience that a person brought up in the
> midst of such influences as I have indicated must inevitably
> be covered, as it were, with almost inexpugnable encasements,
> from which all the batteries of argument and logic rebound
> and roll off like water from the back of a duck in a rain-
> storm.[642]

In the light of such pervasive prejudice, Richards' eventual conversion to Rome appeared all the more amazing to him; indeed, it seemed to be "little less than a miracle."[643]

Richards' early experiences left him with a growing distaste for Protestantism and an increasing sense of dissatisfaction with its ways and teachings. In the narrative, he speaks of the "sourness" of Calvinism.[644] Certainly, the young bore the brunt of the hardship of demanding religious practice. Youngsters lacked the capacity for theological reasoning which might make sacrifice and deprivation, rigid discipline, strict observance of the Sabbath, and tedious lessons palatable.[645]

When Richards was eight years old, his father became an

---

[641]Ibid., pp. 8-9.

[642]Ibid., p. 12.

[643]Ibid., p. 17.

[644]Ibid., p. 6.

[645]J. H. Richards records the reminiscences of Henry Richards on this subject. Sabbath observance began at sundown on Saturday evening. "The joy with which, on the succeeding day, we young folks, who had been reined and restrained from every, even the least,

Episcopalian because he was dissatisfied with the "irresponsible individualism" that characterized the Congregational system.[646] Richards claims that the happenings which occasioned his father's action probably marked the first step which he and his brother took toward Rome. What happened was this: Rev. Ahab Jinks, the Congregational minister, permitted his workmen to labor on the Sabbath in order to finish building his house before winter came. Given the strictness of Sabbath observance in the community, the minister's action provoked controversy. Most demanded the minister's retirement, but some argued that his actions were necessary and even justifiable on scriptural grounds. Naturally, the issue at hand was the fight of the individual to interpret the meaning of Scripture. Richards' father was troubled by "the utter lack of authority" which the affair revealed.[647] And so Dr. Richards and a dozen or so other men, including Ahab Jinks, organized an Episcopal Church in Granville in 1827. William Richards recalls one practical consequence that his father's action had: he and the other youngsters exchanged the Westminster Smaller Catechism for the simpler catechism of the Episcopal Prayer Book -- an exchange

---

appearance of play, and kept diligently at work with our Bibles, Catechisms and religious duties, watched the decline of the king of day, was our indication that at that hour the sacred time had passed and we were free. Then the knitting work was resumed, the wash tubs were brought out and preparations commenced for the hebdomadal cleansing, and all things indicated that the 'Sabbath,' with its gloomy strictness, its prim propriety and its forced reserve, had passed. I have a distinct remembrance of having been chided for looking out of the window on the Sabbath, when a wagon was passing by" (p. 21).

[646]W. Richards, p. 15.

[647]Ibid., p. 14.

which brought "joy and relief."[648]   But there were long term effects

as well; primary among them was Henry's decision to study for the

Episcopal ministry. Both brothers were set on a course which led

to Rome.

William's distaste for evangelical Protestantism grew during

the course of the revival, which occured at Kenyon during the year he

was studying under William Sparrow. The idea of "getting religion" was

particularly abhorrent to Richards; he questioned the authenticity

and the permanence of the "change of heart" that occurred within a reviv-

al setting. He describes the experience of "getting religion" in this

way:

> "Seekers" were diligently impressed with the notion that they
> must expect, seek and pray for a "change of heart." And when,
> after a sharp struggle, sometimes lasting days or weeks, one
> could at last get up in meeting and say with tears of joy, or
> without, but with evident sincerity, that "at such an hour
> and such a place -- possibly behind a big log in the woods,
> or in the loft of the barn, or in the closet if he had one,
> or elsewhere -- while agonizing and praying to the Lord,
> suddenly he was convicted, light came in upon his soul,
> and he felt happy," then he was regarded and received as a
> convert. He had "experienced religion": he was no longer a
> mere worldling; he had come out from the world; the old Adam
> was put off; old things had passed away, and all things had
> become new.[649]

Richards observed that the feeling that accompanied this change was

not likely to persist and that many realized that they had not been

reborn at all. The "backsliders" were numerous. Real conversion,

Richards reasoned, did not require such an emotional upheaval: the

"calm" conversion of Rutherford B. Hayes. who later became president

---

[648]Ibid., p. 16.

[649]Ibid., pp. 21-22.

of the United States, showed that a tumultuous emotional upheaval was not essential.[650]

Richards gradually revised and clarified his views of Roman Catholicism. In the course of the narrative, he identifies several currents of thought that laid the foundation for a better understanding of Roman Catholic practice and teaching. During his studies with Sparrow, Richards came to an important conclusion about the nature of persons and society: both individual and society were "of divine origin."[651] Furthermore, society achieved its fullest expression in the State, which has an "organic life of its own" and is a reality in its own right.[652] Society is "a living organism, an organized body, having an organic life of its own, with a head, an office, a mission, as distinct as that of the individual."[653] This view of society made it possible for Richards to begin thinking about the Church as an organized body. Protestants, he says, saw their congregations as "simply meetings of individuals, each one asserting the unlimited right of private judgment, and their religious teachings being addressed to each one as if he had merely a spiritual nature."[654] But Catholics have an organic concept of church as "a continuous, ever-living, and teaching body."[655]

---

[650]Ibid., pp. 22-23.

[651]Ibid., pp. 27-32.

[652]Ibid., p. 31.

[653]Ibid., p. 34.

[654]Ibid., pp. 34-35.

[655]Ibid., p. 36.

By this time, Richards had become a "high churchman" as had his brother:

> ...we had begun to lay much stress upon the doctrines of
> apostolic succession, baptismal regeneration, the real
> presence, and that assertion in one of the Thirty-nine
> Articles "that the Church hath authority in controversies
> of faith." We had even come to admit that Luther's so-
> called Reformation was in fact no reformation, and that
> Protestantism was loaded down with sad and direful con-
> sequences. And yet we held that the Roman Church was
> overlaid with errors, while the Anglican Church -- founded
> as we fondly fancied by St. Paul himself -- was a pure
> reformed church![656]

The changes in thinking which the Richards brothers experienced reflected the concerns of a substantial number of American Episcopalians who were closely following the Tracts of John Henry Newman and his colleagues. As the address which Richards delivered at Kenyon College, in 1844, makes clear, he had become increasingly concerned with the issue of religious authority, namely, how truth is to be known and determined.

Richards mentions several other experiences which contributed to his progress to Rome. The first was a comment made by an acquaintance, a man "who did not profess any religious belief in particular," to the effect that "he could not see why any one who believed that God had become an infant in the womb of a virgin should have any difficulty in believing that He was present in the Host."[657] The statement made a lasting impression upon Richard and eased his difficulties with the Catholic teaching on transubstantiation. The second was his first visit to a Roman Catholic Church, during which he heard Bishop Purcell

---

[656] Ibid., p. 43.

[657] Ibid., pp. 68-69.

preach on the "completeness of Catholic doctrine" and the converts who
were drawn to the Church by its truth.[658] Richards was impressed with
the quality of the sermon and its content. The prevalence of "spirit-
rappings" and the growing number of persons who believed in the reality
of the spirit-world underscored the inadequacy of Protestant teaching
regarding spirits and most especially, good angels. As a result,
Richards was ready to receive the Catholic teaching regarding Guardian
Angels. And when Richards heard an Episcopal minister say that the
Mother of the Lord must have been "a woman of perfect purity" and
therefore was "entitled to the highest honor and veneration," he
dismissed the Protestant objections to Catholic teaching regarding Mary.
Richards recalls that he had no difficulty accepting the dogma of the
Immaculate Conception, which was defined in 1854. When Richards
realized that the Jewish people remained chosen despite "the errors
and crimes of its priests, and the dreadful backslidings of its stiff-
necked people," he concluded that the Roman Catholic Church could be
chosen despite its corruption in practice and "defection in doctrine."[659]
Finally, learning that the infallibility of the Pope did not imply
impeccability and that even the Pope confesses his sins relieved
Richards of yet another potential crux of misunderstanding of Roman
Catholic thought and practice.

There is a didactic purpose in setting forth such a list of
influences. It allows Richards to address some of the most frequently
misunderstood aspects of Roman Catholicism. Teachings on transub-

---

[658]Ibid., pp. 73-74.

[659]Ibid., pp. 79-80.

351

tantiation, guardian angels, the Virgin Mary, and papal infallibility
were most frequently a source of difficulty for Protestants. But
Richards also accomplishes another objective: he succeeds in showing
the ways in which his own thinking about Roman Catholicism was reshaped
and how he overcame his prejudices against Catholicism.

Despite these changes in his thinking, he stood his ground
as an Episcopalian by maintaining a "branch theory" of church; he saw
the Anglican Church (and so by derivation, the American Episcopal
Church) as a branch of the true church as were the Roman and the Greek
Churches.[660] Even in the face of his brother's announcement that he
was "a Roman Catholic in belief," William Richards was certain that he
could satisfactorily demonstrate that the Anglican Church was "the
true _via media_ and house of refuge, avoiding...the disintegrating individualism of Protestantism on the one hand, and...the liberty-killing
absolutism of the Papacy on the other hand."[661] Much to William's
surprise, Henry entered the Church.[662] William's failure to persuade
Henry that he did not have to become a Catholic made him question his
own position. William continued his inquiry, focusing his attention on
the issue of religious authority.

If the Bible is the sole rule of faith, how is it to be interpreted? Richards maintained that the "will or law of God is and must
be one and the same for all men in all times; and its interpreter must

---

[660]W. Richards, p. 81.

[661]Ibid., p. 82.

[662]Henry was received into the Roman Catholic Church on
January 25, 1852.

be some one having authority objective to each man, above each man, and
imperative upon all men."[663] Authority must be outside any one individual and yet accessible to all. Where is this authority? It is to be
found primarily in tradition rather than in Scripture. Jesus Christ
had vested his authority upon the apostles when he commissioned them to
teach. He gave them his word, not a book. Indeed, the last book of the
Bible was not even written until the end of the first century and
several centries passed before the canon of the Bible was fixed. Consequently, Christians could not rely on the written word for a knowledge
of God's law. The catechumens learned the essentials of the faith
by "word of mouth" or oral tradition. The precedent of oral transmission
of religious knowledge extended back some 2,000 years B.C.: the ancient
Vedic hymns had been transmitted orally.[664]

The doctrines of the Church gave formal expression to the
essentials of the faith. The Holy Spirit guided the Church in its
teaching: definitions of faith "prescribed what it was necessary
to believe and to do in order to be saved."[665] God "speaks to us
through these definitions, made and delivered to men authoritatively
in this way."[666] Therefore, the Church had authority over Scripture;
the Church was the protector of the "living interpretation" of
Scripture.[667] In arguing for the priority of the teaching authority

---

[663]W. Richards, p. 98.

[664]Ibid., pp. 101-102, note.

[665]Ibid., p. 103.

[666]Ibid., p. 104.

[667]Ibid., p. 106.

of the Church over that of Scripture, Richards in effect argued

against what he saw as the two critical points of the Protestant

position: the Bible as the sole rule of faith and individual inter-

pretation of the sense of Scripture.

In resolving the question of authority, he had in fact

experienced conversion. Richards refers to his conversion briefly:

> I found in the summer of 1853, a port of safety, a harbor of
> rest, and that sublime peace of soul which passes all understanding
> -- a peace which is based upon the believer's absolute conviction
> and certainty that the dogmas and points of faith of the Church
> flow logically from belief in God, thus verifying the famous
> saying of the French philosopher, Proudhon, who thought he was
> an atheist, but said: "Admit God, and the Roman Catholic Church,
> with its dogmas, is the logical consequence."[668]

Richards emphasized the effects of his conversion in the images he

chose: safety, security, rest, and peace. But his conversion was the

outcome of an intellectual struggle. Once reason was satisfied, he

converted. What his account lacks is any hint of emotional conflict.

Richards does not describe the sense of loss and alienation which

some of the other converts do. Maybe, he did not experience such

feelings. Or perhaps, the original format of the text kept Richards

from revealing his feelings more completely. Richards focused on the

process that led to conversion and neglected the interior dynamics of

the conversion experience. Conversion, he leads his reader, to believe,

was the last step of the journey and, as such, it was not nearly as

intriguing as the journey itself. But in the concluding pages of the

narrative, Richards hints at the interior experience when he discusses

aspects of Roman Catholic piety. He quotes the rhapsodic reflections of

---

[668]Ibid., pp. 108-109.

Father Faber on the Blessed Sacrament as symbol of the Incarnation; just as the Blessed Sacrament

> ...is the life of the Church, so is it the life of the individual, and becomes to every worthy communicant the seed of immortality whereby the lost image of the Word made flesh is restored to men, and the perfection of his nature is realized by participation in the divine life.[669]

In the sacrifice of the altar Jesus Christ maintains the organic unity of the Church. And the recipient reaffirms his membership in the visible Body of Christ. In the Roman Catholic Church, Richards found not only a "harbor of rest" but also a fount of consolation.

A Troubled Heart
and How It Was Comforted At Last

Charles Warren Stoddard is a convert author who stands apart from the others. His experience differs from that of Ives, Hewit, Walworth, Whitcher and Richards in that he was never a member of the Episcopal Church. In fact, his brief brush with Episcopalinaism left him with feelings of antipathy toward the Episcopalians. And unlike others who wrote conversion narratives during the nineteenth century, Stoddard was an author by profession. He published numerous books, among them several which chronicled his travels in the South Seas, including the well-known South-Sea Idyls.[670] He was a prolific poet whose early verse appeared alongside that of Samuel Langhorne Clemens

---

[669] Ibid., p. 117.

[670] Charles Warren Stoddard, South-Sea Idyls (Boston: J. R. Osgood, 1873). Among his better known works are The Lepers of Molokai (Notre Dame, Ind.: "Ave Maria" Press, 1885), In the Footprints of the Padres (San Francisco: A. M. Robertson, 1902); Hawaiian Life (Chicago: F. T. Neely, 1894); The Island of Tranquil Delights, a South Sea Idyl, and Others (Boston: H. B. Turner, 1904).

and Francis Brett Harte.[671] Despite his accomplishments as a writer,

Stoddard's narrative is similar to the other narratives, sharing their

common focus upon conversion and their conventional concern with

demonstrating the reasonableness of becoming a Roman Catholic.

What is distinctive about Stoddard's narrative is its dramatic flair.

Simply stated, Stoddard surpasses his fellow converts in the art of

story-telling.

Charles Warren Stoddard was born in Rochester, New York in 1843;

he was the son of Samuel Burr and Harriet Freeman Stoddard.[672] He was

a descendent of Rev. Solomon Stoddard, whose Northhampton, Connecticut

congregation experienced the religious resurgence that signalled the

beginning of the Great Awakening. The Stoddard family moved to San

Francisco in 1855 but Charles returned to western New York two years

later, where he lived with his maternal grandfather, a fervent evangeli-

cal Protestant. Charles returned to California in 1859, worked briefly

as a bookstore clerk, and then turned to his favorite pursuits: writing

and travel. He published his first poems in 1861. Poor health forced

him to interrupt his college education and in 1864, he made his first

journey to the Hawaiian Islands, where he met Father Damien of Molokai,

whose work among lepers Charles described in a later book. After

returning to San Francisco, Stoddard wrote for the Californian. In

---

[671]A collection of his poems was published by Ina Coolbrith
under the title, Poems of Charles Warren Stoddard (London: John
Lane, 1917).

[672]Biographical sketches of Stoddard appear in the Dictionary
of American Biography, the Catholic Encyclopedia, and the Dictionary
of Catholic Biography.

1867, at the age of twenty-four, he converted to Roman Catholicism. That same year, a collection of his poems, edited by Bret Harte, was published.

During the next five years, Stoddard travelled to Hawaii and Tahiti; his travels provided him with material for two books on the South-Sea Islands. In 1873, he became a foreign correspondent for the San Francisco Chronicle; that position took him to England, Italy, Egypt, and the Holy Land. While in London, he was secretary to Mark Twain. In 1879, Stoddard returned to San Francisco, then proceeded to Hawaii where he wrote the story of his conversion; A Troubled Heart and How It Was Comforted At Last was published in 1885, the year that Stoddard accepted an appointment as professor of English at the University of Notre Dame.[673] He resigned a year later due to ill health. In 1889, Stoddard was appointed lecturer of English Literature at The Catholic Universtiy of America; he resigned that position in 1902, again for reasons of health.[674] Stoddard lived for a time in Cambridge, Massachusetts before returning to California. He settled in Monterey, where he died in 1909.

A Troubled Heart and How It Was Comforted At Last was published

---

[673] Charles Warren Stoddard, A Troubled Heart and How It Was Comforted At Last (Notre Dame: "Ave Maria" Office, 1885).

[674] The biographical entries in the Catholic Encyclopedia and the Dictionary of Catholic Biography cite ill health as the reason for his resignation from both faculties. Carl G. Stroven, author of the sketch that appears in the Dictionary of American Biography writes that Stoddard "was ordered to resign his position" at The Catholic University. Stroven does not explain why; he merely notes that Stoddard tried to support himself by writing, that he fell ill, and that he left Washington to live with friends in Massachusetts.

in 1885, eighteen years after Stoddard converted to Roman Catholicism.
The narrative traces Stoddard's religious history from childhood to his
conversion to Roman Catholicism and describes his experiences as a convert. The last chapters explain and extol some central aspects of Roman
Catholic belief and practice. Stoddard risked revealing his heart to
"the possibly unsympathetic eye of the general reader" in order to
answer the questions of family and friends who remained Protestant.[675]
The narrative is informative and persuasive; Stoddard explains various
aspects of Roman Catholicism but he also tries to convince his readers
that his own decision to convert was reasonable. Stoddard's desire to
educate his audience prompts him to share those descriptions and
interpretations of his religious experiences that are likely to help
the reader to understand his choice and to follow his example.

"I was a lonely child." So begins Stoddard's recollection
of his early life. The loneliness of which he speaks was a restlessness
of the spirit, a deep longing of the heart. Surrounded by a loving
family and caring friends, he nevertheless was filled with fear. Strange
faces frightened him; darkness terrified him. Looking back he saw that
it was the fear of God that tormented him as a young boy, fear of a
jealous, wrathful God. This image of God, Stoddard observes, was the
legacy of his early religious training and practice. The Protestant
church which he attended as a child was stark, sterile, and dreary.
"There was nothing in all that dreary building for the eye to fall on
with a sense of rest; nothing to soothe or comfort the heart; nothing to
touch the soul, or to lift it even for a moment above the commonplaces

---

[675]Stoddard, A Troubled Heart, p. 7.

of life."[676] Neither music nor preaching relieved the somber setting.
Stoddard recalled that the preacher's "monotonous droning" met with
nodding heads. The two hour service seemed endless to Stoddard. His
only relief was the sight of a sunbeam's shadow, dancing on the ceiling,
or the occasional glimpse of an angel, which screened the organ-
blower.

The aesthetic privation of the Protestant meeting house and
service was a stark contrast to what little the young Stoddard saw and
to what more he imagined transpired in the Gothic-style Roman Catholic
Church that stood across the street from the Stoddard home. Crowds
flocked to the Catholic Church on Sunday, presumably with greater
enthusiasm than that demonstrated by their Protestant brethren. The
music thrilled Stoddard; the lit candles enchanted him. Only once
did he actually enter the Church; on that occasion, he was accompanied
by the family maid.

> I saw for the first time in my life a picturesque interior:
> tapering columns, pointed arches, rose-windows, pictures,
> statues, and frescos. I saw an altar that inspired me with
> curious awe; a throng of worshippers, who knelt humbly, and
> prayed incessantly, so that the quiet of the chapel was broken
> by the soft murmur of lisping lips. Some one in a long dark
> robe came from a hidden chamber and lighted the candles upon
> the altar. This figure seemed of an unnatural height, and more
> slender than any human being I had every known; the dark robe
> clung weirdly in long, straight folds; a strange covering was
> on the head; it was a beretta.[677]

That sight unleashed terrifying images of priests, gleaned from a book
on the Spanish inquisition. But it is fascination rather than terror
that colors Stoddard's recollection of that experience. Stoddard presents

---

[676]Ibid., p. 11.

[677]Ibid., p. 15.

a picture of a young child, excited by the aura of awe and mystery and enchanted by the array of extraordinary sights and sounds he beheld.

Shortly after the Stoddard family moved to California, Charles accompanied his older brother on a long sea voyage around Cape Horn. The journey was a trying one for young Charles. His mother had admonished him to read some chapters of the Bible each day. That he did, but what he read confused and mystified him. His confusion, coupled with his loneliness, produced an overwhelming sense of desolation and exaggerated the ordinary trials of adolescence. Stoddard's spiritual turmoil was only beginning. While his brother continued on to California alone, Charles settled in western New York, boarding at a school located near the home of his maternal grandparents. Though Charles' contact with his grandfather was confined to several visits at the school each month and an occasional weekend at his home, Charles did not escape Grandfather Freeman's influence in religious matters. While visiting at his grandfather's house, Charles attended his first revival.

Grandfather Freeman was among those lent enthusiastic support to the vigorous efforts of revivalist preachers in western New York, an area designated as the Burned-over District. Charles portrays his grandfather as "a thrifty New England farmer": "He was a very honest, practical, much respected man, of a pronounced Protestant type: relentless and even stubborn in his narrow religious views; he was one in whose veins the blood had flowed coldly from the dark days of the Plymouth Puritans."[678] After his death, a sketch of his exemplary life appeared

---

[678]Ibid., pp. 26, 27.

in the "Sabbath-School" libraries.[679] Grandfather Freeman's religious

affiliation was somewhat uncertain: "he was a Presbyterian, or a

Congregationalist, or a Baptist, or a Methodist, or something.

Whatever else he was, he was an "Evangelist."[680]

The arrival of a revivalist announced that the time was ripe

for Charles to experience a "change of heart."

> Presently my grandfather took me aside and asked me if I did not
> choose to love God. Most assuredly I did, but I had never yet
> learned how; for the only God I knew inspired fear rather than
> love....I began to feel my heart must be black indeed and greatly
> in need of being changed; and I the most hardened of sinners,
> because the very sight of the "Evangelist" repelled me and my
> soul sickened whenever he or his works were mentioned.[681]

Day after day, Freeman drove Charles to the church in the hope that

he would become a Christian.

The revival atmosphere was one of "unwholesome excitement"; the

room was over-heated, poorly ventilated and over-crowded.[682] Potential

converts, that is, those who acknowledged their sinfulness, were

assigned to the "anxious seat," a "rack of torture."[683]

> Some of them, embarassed and bewildered, wrung their hands
> and cried aloud. Once there, they were not permitted to retreat,
> but, surrounded by half-fanatic men and women, whose flushed
> faces and flashing eyes were fearful to behold, they were held
> forcibly upon the bench, where they suffered the torments of
> the damned, until the close of the session.[684]

---

[679]Ibid., p. 28.

[680]Ibid., p. 42.

[681]Ibid., p. 32.

[682]Ibid., p. 33.

[683]Ibid., p. 34.

[684]Ibid.

Charles found himself one of their number, driven forward by a crowd
determined to make him a Christian. Terrified, he lied when asked if
he wanted to be a Christian: he said yes. Though his answer allowed
him to leave the revival, he was not easily able to escape the inner
torment; he was convinced that he was wicked and even wished he had not
been born. An invitation to visit his paternal grandfather only added
to his upset. Would it not be "doubly sinful" to leave without having
experienced a "change of heart"?[685] So he hid the letter. But
Grandfather Freeman demanded to see the letter and sent him to visit
Grandfather Stoddard.

Charles' account of this period of his life is charged with
melodrama. But there is little doubt that the experience at the revival
disturbed him deeply. He had failed to achieve the sought after experience which the community equated with being saved. Worse yet,
he had lied to escape the pressure. He felt enormous relief in leaving
that "horrible atmosphere" and then guilt at feeling relief.[686]

Grandfather Stoddard was a Universalist. That meant several
things to Charles: Sunday was not called the Sabbath; he was free to
go to church or not; he attended his first circus; he could read what
he chose or even play on Sunday. In a word, Sunday was a holiday.[687]
The contrast between this community and the one he left behind was not
confined to Sunday liberties. A radically different view of man's nature
and destiny prevailed:

---

[685]Ibid., p. 39.

[686]Ibid., p. 41.

[687]Ibid., p. 43.

...all men are to be saved, whether they will or no;...it is a waste of time trying to be wicked; it is, moreover, ill-bred and disagreeable, and one must submit to salvation in the end, notwithstanding. In short...man's chief end was to be sociable and satisfied.[688]

Charles' exposure to Universalism brightened his spirit by making him realize that it mattered little what and even if he believed.[689] But Grandfather Freeman had yet another lesson to teach Charles. Just before Charles was to return to California, Grandfather Freeman escorted him to the funeral of a young boy about the same age as Charles. To Grandfather Freeman's way of thinking, there was no better lesson than this to teach Charles that "death is always with us."[690] Death comes without warning; one must always be prepared. But the death of the body is nothing compared to "the possible death of the soul -- of hope, of everything."[691]

That funeral did have a profound affect upon Charles but not in the manner that his grandfather had hoped. Charles was overwhelmed by the injustice of the death of one so young and distraught by the meaninglessness of the minister's message. What consolation could the minister offer other than to say that the young boy had "gone to his Maker"?[692] Charles wondered how the minister could know that and how God could take the life of the innocent. Why had he not been the one to die? He certainly "had often been miserable enough to

---

[688]Ibid., p. 44.

[689]Ibid., p. 47.

[690]Ibid., p. 50.

[691]Ibid., p. 51.

[692]Ibid., p. 53.

die."[693] What would this soul find? The same loneliness which he had

experienced in childhood likely awaited the young boy who had died.

Stoddard ends his account of his early childhood religious history as he

began it, describing himself as "a lonely child."[694]

The search for truth is the unifying theme of the next section

of the narrative; Stoddard describes the religious quest that eventually

brought him to the Roman Catholic Church. Stoddard was sixteen, "the

speculative age," when he returned to California and gave himself to the

task of self-analysis.[695]

> I knew God to be the source of all truth. I desired to worship
> Him; and as He was worshipped in one form or another in the
> many and various churches of the city, I wandered from house
> to house like a weary spirit, seeking that absolute rest which
> I had never known.[696]

Stoddard turned to the Unitarians. He found them intellectually

appealing but lacking in fervor: "the Unitarians offered me nothing

that I could take home with me, locked up in my heart of hearts, --

not even a grain of comfrot."[697] The Methodists also failed to satisfy

Stoddard. Their unrestrained emotionalism repelled him. None of the

remaining Protestant denominations satisfied Stoddard; he found "the

whole range of Protestantism...characterless, colorless, almost

formless, -- the poorest conceivable substitute for worship in the

---

[693]Ibid.

[694]Ibid.

[695]Ibid., p. 55.

[696]Ibid., p. 56.

[697]Ibid., p. 57.

true sense of the term."[698]   Ministers preached and their messages were criticized by members of the congregation who considered their opinions as valid as those of the preacher. The mere gathering of a congregation did not constitute worship; worship required some form, some symbols. Meeting places were sterile and somber; there was no beauty in Protestant worship.

As might be expected, Stoddard's desire for an atmosphere conducive to worship was satisfied in part by the Episcopal Church -- at least briefly. But his praise for the Episcopal Church was limited to acknowledging that it was the best of a poor lot. Dignity and reverence characterized its "somewhat meagre and meaningless" worship service.[699] The Episcopal Church had the form he sought: its prayers were beautiful; its music, elevating; its architecture, appropriate. But it was "a form without spirit or substance."[700] Stoddard concludes this brief recollection of his passing association with the Episcopal Church with a scathing remark: the Episcopal Church is "feebly and though expensively nourished by a severely, not to say frigidly, polite community, -- a community meagre in numbers, but of unquestionable taste."[701] Stoddard's antipathy for the Episcopal Church distinguishes him from the other convert authors, who concluded that the Episcopal Church was not the true Church of Christ but did not appear to harbor any hostility toward the Church.

---

[698]Ibid., p. 58.

[699]Ibid., p. 60.

[700]Ibid.

[701]Ibid., pp. 60-61.

Stoddard's search for a haven within Protestantism once led
him to a revival, conducted by the famous team of "Moody and Sankey."[702]
The meeting was held at noon for a group of businessmen. Stoddard says
he approached the meeting with an open mind, a claim that is tempered by
his clearly expressed antipathy toward revivalism. Predictably, the
"intense vulgarity of the proceedings, to say nothing of the blasphemy
that prevailed," disgusted Stoddard.[703] Moody and Sankey converted many,
but Stoddard was not a part of their harvest. In fact, his experience
at the revival alienated him from Protestantism.

Stoddard moved from the mainstream to the margins, from
Protestantism to Spiritualism. A friend, a woman whom he describes
as an "inspirational speaker," sparked Stoddard's interest in
spiritualism.[704] She entertained Stoddard with tales of the supernatural
until the spirits she claimed to see seemed real to him. Her accounts
fascinated him and soon he was drawn into the world of mediums and
seances; he began to see Spiritualism as "the salvation of the world."[705]
Stoddard did not explain how his faith in the supernatural was broken;
he merely makes a passing reference to "the grossest deception" to which
he fell victim.[706] The woman "proved to be a priestess among the modern

---

[702]Dwight Lyman Moody (1837-1899) and Ira David Sankey (1840-
1908) led successful campaigns across the country. Their message
was simple and their style, direct. Convert, be saved, and join a
church, any church. Ahlstrom, pp. 743-745.

[703]Stoddard, A Troubled Heart, p. 61.

[704]Ibid., p. 66.

[705]Ibid., p. 68.

[706]Ibid.

pagans, and an advocate of their unholy and lascivious rites."[707] So
ended Stoddard's spiritualist interlude.

Dissatisfied with the religious styles he experienced around
him, Stoddard retreated inward, imagining a temple in his heart, a temple
built to satisfy the longings that were not satisfied in any religious
body he had encountered. This space would be appropriate for prayer
and worship. There, he could be alone with God. But his retreat
was temporary; he was destined to find what he sought in community
rather than in isolation.

Music brought Stoddard to the Roman Catholic Church, via a
Roman Catholic cathedral. The music-master invited him to come to hear
the choir, but Stoddard did more than listen. The sight of the
Cathedral, candle-lit, filled with paintings and statues, enthralled
Stoddard. The congregation, he sensed, shared "a single sentiment,"
appearing to be "swayed by one emotion" even though each person was
absorbed in private prayer.[708] Although he did not understand the
meaning of the ritual, he was spellbound. The interior temple, which
he had imagined, did not exist. Stoddard quieted a momentary doubt, a
remnant of the anti-Catholic sentiment of his youth and resolved to
return to this church again.

The similarity between Stoddard's account of this experience
and his recollections of his glimpse into the neighboring Roman Catholic
Church during childhood is salient. In both instances, he describes
the atmosphere created by the music, art objects, candles, and the design

---

[707]Ibid., p. 69.

[708]Ibid., p. 75.

of the building itself. Both times, he comments on the prayerful
demeanor of the congregation.[709] Are both renderings faithful to
memory? Or was Stoddard constructing an effective literary parallel
intended to emphasize the lure of Roman Catholic worship? In both
accounts, it appears that the convert is speaking.

Stoddard began to attend Mass and Vespers regularly. And one
day, he found a copy of "The Poor Man's Catechism," a Catholic catechism,
in the family dining room. How it got there no one knew. Reading
that book was a turning point for him; he discovered that he could and
indeed did believe the tenets of Roman Catholic belief contained in the
pamphlet. He resolved to become a Roman Catholic. He assumed, as did
other non-Catholics, that joining the Church would be a simple matter.
It was not. He did not have any Catholic friends or acquaintances. The
family maid, the only Catholic he knew, advised him to see a priest but
he could not muster the courage to do that. So he did nothing for
months except attend Mass until the day when he brought home a
crucifix which he hid from from his family. By chance, Stoddard met
a Catholic woman who arranged for him to meet he confessor. Stoddard
was deeply moved by this young priest. In his company, he realized
how much he must "unlearn" -- namely, the errors and prejudice that
were the legacy of his upbringing. The young priest sent him off to
"read, mark, learn, and inwardly digest" several controversial
works.[710]

Shortly after they met, the priest was reassigned to a country

---

[709]Compare chapters I and XII of Stoddard's narrative.

[710]Stoddard, A Troubled Heart, p. 101.

parish. Their relationship had been brief but nevertheless signi-

ficant to Stoddard. He praised the young cleric generously; indeed,

he appeared to idolize him and with him the entire Catholic priesthood.

> What a world of care was his! it was a word of advice or
> encouragement to one; a little substantial aid to another; a
> willing promise to do this or that for a third -- enough, it
> seemed to me, to tax the strength of the stoutest and to keep
> a dozen busy for days.
> This was his daily life; rest he never knew; weariness
> he discountenanced; famine and pestilence he feared not;
> himself the servant of servants, worthy indeed of his hire,
> was unremunerated in a profession exacting to a degree, of
> increasing activity, and peculiarly circumscribed and exclusive.[711]

Stoddard had not known any ministers "worthy to be compared with this

modest young priest" who, like his fellow priests, led an abstemious

life that was markedly different from the comparatively luxurious life-

style of a young Protestant minister he had befriended.[712]

Stoddard continued his instruction under a Jesuit priest,

whom he refers to as Father A____.[713] The Jesuit counselled Stoddard

to read "what you will, so long as you read earnestly and honestly

the books I give you.[714] Stoddard read anti-Catholic and Catholic books

and claimed that doing go helped him to see the falseness and stupidity

of the anti-Catholic arguments. But he counselled others against

following his example: "A single page of plausible falsehood may

pervert an unprejudiced mind so that a whole volume of truth will

---

[711]Ibid., pp. 100-101.

[712]Ibid., pp. 101, 106-108. A few chapters later Stoddard
resumes his praise of the Roman Catholic clergy (pp. 144-149).

[713]Ibid., p. 104.

[714]Ibid.

hardly restore it; therefore leave them alone."[715]

Stoddard's parents were not pleased to hear of his decision
to become a Roman Catholic. His mother cautioned him against moving
too hastily and his father warned him to consider the matter thoroughly.
Though they were saddened by their son's choice, they did not speak
about the subject again.

Peter Burnett, himself a convert, served as Stoddard's god-
father at the request of Father A___; Stoddard did not know any
Catholic whom he could chose as his sponsor.[716] The baptism was an
extraordinary experience for Stoddard; he had never been baptized as
an infant nor had he experienced the "change of heart" required by the
evangelicals.[717] He recalls being filled with "an awe that dulled
rather than quickened" his senses and shedding "floods of tears."[718]

---

[715]Ibid., p. 105.

[716]Peter Burnett wrote a lengthy apologetic treatise, The
Path Which Led a Protestant Lawyer into the Catholic Church. Although
the text exceeds seven hundred pages, only the few pages that comprise
the preface tell of the process by which Burnett became a Roman Catholic.
This capsule account reveals that Burnett and Stoddard were attracted
to Roman Catholicism for the same reasons. Burnett recalls that when
he first attended Mass, as a spectator, he was overcome by the
"solemnity of the services -- the intense, yet calm fervor of the
worshippers -- the great and marked differences between the two forms
of worship -- and the instantaneous reflection, that this was the Church
claiming to be the only true Church, did make the deepest impression
upon my mind for the moment....I gazed into the faces of the worshippers,
and they appeared as if they were actually looking at the Lord Jesus,
and were hushed into perfect stillness, in His awful presence"
(pp. v-vi).

[717]Stoddard, A Troubled Heart, p. 111.

[718]Ibid., pp. 112-113.

He tells of surrendering his heart and experiencing "a great calm."[719]
Stoddard's conversion to Roman Catholicism was a deeply emotional
experience, differing from the typical evangelical conversion in
form but not in intensity. Protestants whom Stoddard for all practical
purposes equated with evangelicals, demanded an emotional experience
of conversion and designed a revival atmosphere most likely to stimulate
the desired response. Roman Catholics did not demand a particular
affective response; what Stoddard experienced was a spontaneous
outpouring of feeling.

His first confession filled him with awe and trepidation,
as well as with a sense of joy; he felt as if he were "literally
out of the world, and far beyond its reach."[720] He experienced the
absolution as a "fountain of healing and refreshment."[721] He
left the confessional filled with joy and gratitude. His first
communion filled him with "unspeakable peace."[722] The accounts of his
first confession and communion serve two purposes: narrative and
apologetic. Stoddard shares his personal experiences and so contributes
to the aura of mystery and awe surrounding these sacraments but he
also, paradoxically, demystifies them by giving his readers a firsthand account of a convert's reception of the sacraments.

Family members responded to Stoddard's conversion with disappointment but without rancor. His friends were less gracious; some

---

[719] Ibid., p. 113.

[720] Ibid., p. 116.

[721] Ibid., p. 118.

[722] Ibid., p. 122.

insulted and ridiculed him, others ignored him. The social cost of conversion was considerable; he was no longer held in esteem once the word of his conversion reached the public through journals and what Stoddard refers to as "the Protestant religious press."[723] Once, a group of his school-mates forced him to endure their mockery of Roman Catholic prayer and liturgy; they apologized later but did not explain the reasons for their cruel behavior. Some regarded Stoddard as foolish; others turned against him in anger. Clearly, Stoddard's friends and acquaintances did not regard his conversion as a private matter.

His father's financial reverses, the sudden deaths of two brothers, his own loneliness and poor health left him depressed. His confessor invited him to spend a few days at the seashore and there encouraged the disheartened new convert to make a pilgrimage to Rome. Stoddard did so. His travels took him to "primitive chapels in the Irish wilderness," to a small convent on the Nile, to Jerusalem, and finally to Rome. He visited wayside shrines throughout Europe. Wherever he went, Stoddard experienced " ongoing testimonials of the unity and universality of Holy Church."[724] The common faith overcame individual and cultural differences.

The last five chapters of A Troubled Heart extol the comforts afforded by Catholic beliefs regarding the Mass, the Virgin Mary, saints, miracles, guardian angels, and the afterlife.[725] Stoddard

---

[723]Ibid., p. 125.

[724]Ibid., p. 139.

[725]Ibid., pp. 155-178.

praises each aspect of Roman Catholicism as source of succor and joy. The Mass provides the opportunity to witness the drama of Christ's passion and death anew. Mary, the Queen of Heaven, comforts the afflict-ed.[726] The saints offer reassurance and hope as models of "human humility, and the purifying, sanctifying consuming love of God!"[727] Miracles are man's inheritance and guardian angels company and protect him. And at death's door, the Catholic finds comfort in the last sacraments, crucifix, blessed water, and the prayers whispered at his bedside. The Catholic is not abandoned at death. Prayers follow him beyond the grave to ease his suffering in purgatory until he finally finds eternal life in the gardens of Paradise. Such are the comforts that Roman Catholicism offers to the troubled soul; such is the appeal of Roman Catholic piety.

Piety is the primary motive for Stoddard's conversion. Stoddard did not engage in lengthy, intellectual inquiry to ascertain the truth of Roman Catholic teaching or to verify the Church's claim to be the authentic Church of Christ. Stoddard was dissatisifed with Protestantism, with its excessive emotionalism as well as with its lack of spiritual vigor. The Episcopal Church had form, but lacked substance. He moved from one religious body to another in the search for a compatible balance of structure and comfort. In Roman Catholic piety, he found both. The richness of Catholic devotional life appealed to him. The awe-inspiring atmosphere of worship, created

---

[726]Chapter XXVIII reads like a litany to the Blessed Virgin (pp. 160-163).

[727]Ibid., p. 164.

by music and art, the consolation of personal devotions to Mary, the saints, and guardian angels, the very "form" of structured liturgy and sacrament -- these drew Charles Warren Stoddard to the Roman Catholic Church and contributed to his conversion. Roman Catholicism satisfied Stoddard's deep longing for religious comfort.

Recurrent Themes

The dominant characteristic of personal narratives written by nineteenth-century American converts to Roman Catholicism is the focus on conversion. Analysis of the narratives reveals the converts' desire to present conversion to Roman Catholicism in a favorable light, thus meeting the needs of the authors as well as those of the Catholic community. By blending apologia with apologetic, the convert authors sought to justify their decisions to become Catholics while they also explicated and defended Roman Catholic teaching and practice. Although the narratives span more than a century, there are no differences between the earliest and the latest works that cannot be attributed to personal experience and literary talent. Even the oldest narratives, those of Thayer, Blythe, and Barber (published between 1783 and 1821) exhibit the concern with conversion that defines the form of the personal narrative as well as the twofold objective of self-justification and public apologetic. And though the situation of Roman Catholicism in America changed radically from the century's beginning to its end, the form and purpose of personal narratives remained the same.

The narratives of conversion generally included accounts of early religious experiences, identification of the reasons for the

author's dissatisfaction with Protestantism and often Anglicanism,
a description of the process of inquiry and search that led the convert
to the Roman Catholic Church, and an explanation of his reasons for
becoming a Roman Catholic. Explanation of Roman Catholic teaching
and piety frequently appeared in the course of the narrative and more
often than not comprised a substantial portion of the text.

Early Religious Experiences

Most authors of conversion narratives began with brief
accounts of their religious experiences during childhood and/or
adolescence. In so doing, they were able to identify early responses
to religious belief and practice. Generally, the authors disclose
their dissatisfaction with the spirit and ways of the religious
bodies of which they and/or their families were members. They
decry the abuses which they suffered at the hands of parents and
ministers in being forced to abandon pleasurable activities and to
substitute painful ones in their stead in order to satisfy the
requirements of demanding Sabbath observance,[728] in having to commit
catechism passages to memory,[729] in enduring the rigidity and harshness of a distasteful, even abhorrent, religious perspective,[730] or
in being frightened by stories of an angry and vengeful God.[731]
Without exception, these converts specify their exposure to New England

---

[728]Huntington, p. 12.

[729]Whitcher, p. 24.

[730]Hewit, p. 37.

[731]Stoddard, p. 13.

Calvinism of the Congregational variety.[732]

Most recalled some positive lesson learned during childhood.
Some remembered the efforts others made to instill virtue in their
childish hearts.[733] One convert was especially grateful that, as a
child, he learned to pray with confidence, another that early on he
had developed an interest in religious issues.[734]

Whether positive or negative, the converts' appraisals of
childhood experiences point to two significant facts: the converts
who recalled childhood experiences acknowledged that their religious
histories began during childhood and they saw these early experiences
as relevant to their subsequent conversions to Roman Catholicism.
Though the criticisms of childhood religion are voiced by adults, and
by converts to Roman Catholicism at that, the substance of the
criticism reveals the impressions made by early encounters with
religion at home and in church.

Anti-Catholic Sentiment

Of special importance to the conversion narrative was the
prevalent impression which these converts had had of the Roman Catholic
Church. Anti-Catholic feeling was pronounced in America during the
nineteenth century and the converts did not escape its influence.
Responses ranged from "a vague horror of Catholics and their religion"

---

[732]Hewit, p. 33; Stoddard, p. 33; Huntington (in the title
of his narrative); Whitcher, p. 24.

[733]Blythe, p. 6; Hewit, p. 32; Brownson, The Convert, p. 4.

[734]Whitcher, p. 24; Brownson, The Convert, p. 5.

to suspicion, hatred, and fear.[735] They saw the Roman Catholic Church portrayed as the "sink of idolatry and corruption,"[736] "the mother of abominations,"[737] the Antichrist which was to come in the latter days; as the embodiment of wickedness in its vilest form; wickedness concealing itself in the external garb of piety."[738] Catholic countries were barbaric and unenlightened.[739] In the pulpit and in the press, these converts-to-be encountered widespread denunciations of popery and Romanism that aroused their antipathy for all that was Catholic.

By attesting to their own anti-Catholic feeling during childhood, youth, and adulthood, the converts emphasize experiences which they had in common with most Protestants. They, who once shared the aversion toward Roman Catholicism, came to see the truth of the faith they despised and derided. Other Protestants ought to do the same.

Revival Experiences

Several converts came into direct contact with the fervent exercises of revivalistic Protestantism during the impressionable period of adolescence. They recalled their own inability to respond to such a religious style despite concerted efforts to promote their conversions to the Lord. The protracted meetings, "anxious benches,"

---

[735]Richards, p. 8. Also see Thayer, p. 6; Ives, p. 17; Stoddard, p. 18.

[736]Blythe, p. 16.

[737]Whitcher, p. 32.

[738]Huntington, p. 9.

[739]Whitcher, p. 34.

and enthusiastic preaching, intended to promote religious awakening, alienated these men. The meetings were "fearful to behold."[740] The atmosphere generated hysterical, emotional outbursts which the convert authors found repulsive and even frightening. Particularly disturbing was the pressure to conform to the expectations of the evangelicals: to experience a change of heart and the bodily effects which were part of the process of "getting religion."

Dissatisfaction with Protestantism

The religious histories of the convert authors prior to their entries into the Roman Catholic Church reveal their growing discontent with the Protestant denominations of which they were members or which they investigated in the search for religious truth. The source of their discontent was the disunity of Protestantism, a direct consequence of the lack of teaching authority within the Protestant denominations. It is clear that the converts shared a common need for guidance in religious beliefs and that they believed that the Roman Catholic Church provided such guidance. The teaching authority of the Roman Catholic Church insured the unity of faith which they sought.

The convert authors found Protestantism deficient in satisfying a variety of spiritual needs, what Hecker called "the wants of man's heart."[741] Brownson criticized Protestantism's lack of concern with the spiritual realm" Protestantism focused on material reality

---

[740]Ibid., p. 39.

[741]Hecker, Questions, p. 130.

to the exclusion of the spiritual.[742] The Protestant Church,

Hecker argued, failed to meet man's needs for reconciliation, for the

divine food which sustains life, for consolation in the face of death,

and for communion. Protestantism failed to provide man with a viable

piety. Attracted to Roman Catholicism because of its form of worship,

its sacraments, and its devotions, the convert authors were quick

to point out the formlessness of Protestant worship, its somber

meeting places, and its lack of an institutional method for the

remission of sin.[743] But the converts also emphasized the restraint

of Roman Catholic piety: Roman Catholicism avoided the pitfalls of

excessive emotionalism.

The converts offer additional reasons for their dissatisfaction

with Protestantism: the unreasonable attitude which Protestants

assumed toward Roman Catholicism, regarding any expression of interest

in the Church with suspicion and hostility;[744] the bigotry and

lack of charity exhibited by Protestants;[745] and the unwillingness

of Protestant ministers to discuss beliefs which they hold and to

explain why they do so.[746] Some took issue with particular Protestant

---

[742]Protestantism "takes care of life, but neglects that which is to come; amasses material goods, but lays up no treasure in heaven; rehabilitates the flesh, but depresses the spirit; elevates humanity, but obscures the Divinity." Brownson, The Convert, pp. 87-88.

[743]Stoddard, p. 58; Ives, p. 20.

[744]Ives, pp. 14, 18.

[745]Brownson, The Convert, p. 12; Whitcher, p. 36.

[746]Barber, p. 31.

teachings such as those regarding the role of good works in achieving salvation[747] and the significance of baptism.[748] But the greatest sources of dissatisfaction were disunity in teaching and lack of vital piety.

The following chapter explores the nature of conversion, as experienced by these authors, the reasons why they became Catholic, and their purpose in writing accounts of conversion.

---

[747]Whitcher, pp. 37-38.

[748]Huntington, p. 83.

CHAPTER V

CONVERSION TO ROMAN CATHOLICISM:

A MATTER OF MIND AND HEART

Personal narratives of conversion written by nineteenth-century converts to Roman Catholicism shed light on what it meant to become and to be a Roman Catholic in America during the previous century. The narrative authors reveal their understanding of conversion and identify the motives which brought them to the Church. It is clear that they chose to portray conversion as a process of religious growth rather than as the single, isolable event that typically defined conversion among evangelical Protestants. Moreover, the narratives offer compelling evidence that conversion was indeed a matter of mind and heart. Although their preoccupation with apologetics suggests that the authors understood and sought to portray their conversions as ends to rational, intellectual quests, the narratives disclose that the authors converted because Roman Catholicism was aesthetically appealing to them and satisfactorily met their affective needs. Lengthy though they are, their doctrinal discussions do not, in the end, obscure the fact that Roman Catholic piety drew the authors to the Church. Isaac Hecker aptly expressed the view of his fellow convert authors, when he wrote that Roman Catholicism best fulfills "the wants of man's heart."[1]

---

[1]Hecker, Questions of the Soul, p. 130.

Apologetics and Apologia

The convert authors wrote to defend the Church's teaching and to justify their own actions. Apologetics and apologia came together as the converts discovered that they could best justify their personal decisions to become Roman Catholics by explaining and supporting the Church's doctrine and practice. By their very existence, the narratives served the task of apologetics: they called attention to the fact that the Roman Catholic Church was attracting converts. Eminent converts were an asset to the Church and were recognized as such, as published lists of prominent converts indicate.[2] Even unknown converts were seen as credits to the Church as evidenced by the numerous brief accounts published in The Catholic World during the 1890's. Conversions mark the Church's "conquests," wrote Richard Clarke, and "converts are welcomed as heroic co-laborers in the great mission of the future."[3] Though the Roman Catholic Church welcomed the converts, members of their former religious communities denounced them. The narratives were an effective way of responding to the charges leveled against converts by their former fellow churchmen. Some converts wrote narratives of conversion shortly after they became Roman Catholics: Thayer, Blythe, Barber, Huntington, and Ives

---

[2] See Clarke, "Our Converts," pp. 542-550. See also Scannel O'Neill, Converts to Rome in America (Detroit, 1921) and collections of autogiographical accounts of conversion, such as, Georgina Pell Curtis, Some Roads to Rome in America (St. Louis, 1909) for examples of collected accounts and dictionaries that were popular in the early twentieth century. See Mannix, The American Convert Movement (pp. 138-139) for additional works.

[3] Clarke, p. 542.

published their narratives within six years of their conversions.[4]
Presuming that their non-Catholic readers were interested in learning
why they became Roman Catholics, the convert authors concentrated on
explaining the nature of their dissatisfaction with the Protestant
and Episcopal Churches and their attraction to Roman Catholicism.
Though more than a decade passed before some converts wrote accounts
of their conversions, their reasons for writing were similar to those
of converts who wrote within a few years of their conversions: all
wrote to justify their actions and to explain and defend Roman Catholic
belief and practice.[5]

By emphasizing the reasonableness of Roman Catholicism, its
intellectual appeal and its logic, the narratives represent conversion
to Roman Catholicism as the only sensible course of action and so
justify the converts' decisions to become Roman Catholics. The convert authors concentrated on the cognitive dimension of believing,
explaining the content of the faith and the nature of Roman Catholic
practice. The authors focused on those aspects of conversion which are

---

[4]Thayer published his account four years after his conversion;
Blythe and Barber published their accounts six years after they became Roman Catholics; Huntington's narrative appeared three years
after his conversion and Ives' narrative, two years after he became
a Catholic.

[5]Hecker's Questions of the Soul appeared eleven years after
his conversion; Brownson's Convert, thirteen years after he became
a Catholic; and Stoddard's Troubled Heart, sixteen years after conversion. The Episcopalians who converted to Roman Catholicism at
mid-century -- Hewit, Walworth, Richards, and Whitcher -- published
accounts twenty to fifty years after they became Catholics. Hewit's
account appeared forty-one years after his conversion; Walworth's,
fifty years; Whitcher's, twenty years; and Richards', forty-two
years.

accessible to an outsider, namely its effects: noticeable changes in what one believed and how one practiced his faith.

Intent on stressing the contrasts between Protestantism and Roman Catholicism, the converts denounced the deficiencies of Protestantism while extolling the benefits of Catholicism. In particular, the convert authors deplored Protestantism's lack of unity in teaching, its reliance on an insufficient rule of faith (the Bible alone), its failure to maintain communion with the apostles, and finally its inability to fully meet man's need for a vital piety. Roman Catholicism offered all that the converts had found to be lacking in Protestantism. The Roman Catholic Church was the authentic Church of Christ, bearing the marks of the true Church: one, holy, catholic, and apostolic. The converts emphasized the unity of the Roman Church; it was one in faith and one in its teaching. Because the Church traces its origin to the time of the apostles, it can legitimately claim divine teaching authority and so offer guidance to its members. Unlike Protestants, the converts claimed, Roman Catholics are not subjected to the contradictions of interpretation that result from the exercise of private judgment. While Protestantism is, in Hecker's words "faithless in representing the authority of Christ," the Roman Catholic Church teaches in the name of Christ, proclaiming his truth.[6] Unlike the Protestant denominations, the Roman Church insists on a unitive version of that truth.

---

[6]Hecker, Questions of the Soul, p. 130.

Event or Process:
Contrasting Views of Conversion

The convert authors rejected the spirit and tactics of evangelical Protestantism, especially its insistence that conversion was
to be a sudden, tumultuous, and memorable experience which determined
whether a person could consider himself a true Christian. Evangelical
conversion occurred in a controlled environment, designed to quicken
religious response and to encourage the emotional outbursts that
oftentimes accompanied the sought after change of heart. As a public
event, dramatic and observable, the authentic conversion was to conform to the community's expectations and to establish the believer's
place within the community. But the denominational affiliation that
followed conversion was less significant than the experience itself:
it mattered less to what denomination one belonged than that one had
undergone conversion, accepted Jesus Christ, and experienced the re-
quisite change of heart. Revivalists pared the Christian message to
bare essentials, viewing the intellectual inquiry and doctrinal debate that might accent denominational differences with suspicion.

The converts to Roman Catholicism emphasized the differences
between their experiences of conversion and the typical experience
of conversion endorsed by evangelical Protestants. The convert
authors portrayed conversion as a lengthy process of inquiry and
reflection, culminating in affiliation with the Church. The typical
convert author's journey to the Church was a private one, beginning
in dissatisfaction with his religious life and an express distaste for
the ways of evangelical revivalism and involving a gradual growth of
interest in and attraction to the Roman Catholic Church. The event

385

of conversion, the moment a convert realized that he had become a
Catholic, was less significant than the process by which he had done
so. Indeed, the converts suggest that one does not become a Roman
Catholic at any particular moment but rather one realizes that he already is a Catholic. The realization is an insight, a resoulution of
critical questions and issues, calling for surrender to God and submission to the authority of the Church. But it also involves feelings:
relief, peace, and a sense of becoming whole. The converts experienced
conversion as a process "by which a self hitherto divided, and consciously wrong [sic]inferior and unhappy, becomes unified and consciously right [sic] superior and happy, in consequence of its firmer
hold upon religious realities."[7] While the emphasis on the process
accents the intellectual dimension of conversion, the metaphors which
the converts used to describe conversion reveal that it was also a
deeply moving emotional experience. Huntington likens conversion to
coming out of "a fog"; the "still, small voice" of the Spirit of God
impelled him to consider forceful and conclusive answers which dis-
pelled his objections to the Catholic faith.[8] Divine grace, Brownson
insisted, "rolled back the darkness" before him and inclined his
heart to believe.[9] Ives described conversion as a return to "the
father that begot him, and the mother who cherished his infancy" after
having been "borne off asleep from his native shore on some wreck to

---

[7]James, p. 160.

[8]Huntington, pp. 6-8.

[9]Brownson, The Convert, p. 167.

a desert island" during childhood.[10] The converts described the Church
as a "port of safety" and "a harbor of rest."[11] Though a convert had to
submit to the authority of the Church, he understood his self-surrender
to be a return to wholeness.

Conversion involved a process of inquiry during which the convert-
to-be grappled with the truth of Church teaching and the legitimacy of
its practice as well as a personal struggle in the course of which he
dealt with the implications of his discoveries. He had to acknowledge
what he learned in action, often at great personal and social cost.
Conversion was a process of religious growth, which, when completed, could
be described in terms of its effects: feelings of relief, peace, security,
well-being, and the like. The feelings, accompanying the convert's
decision to act according to his newly found beliefs, represent the
outcome of the process that was conversion. Nevertheless, it is significant that the typical convert author, responding to the question "how
did I become a Catholic?" chose to begin with an account of early
religious experiences and to map out his long, sometimes circuitous,
journey to the Roman Catholic Church. Though he described how he felt
when he arrived at the end of his journey, it was the search, the process
of discovery, that he understood as essential and distinctive in the
experience of converting to Roman Catholicism.

Conversion: An Act of Faith

By retracing their religious development, the converts implied

---

[10]Ives, p. 22, note.

[11]Richards, p. 108.

that conversion to Roman Catholicism was a fulfillment of lifetime

religious aspirations rather than a repudiation of former convictions.

They had faith in God and in Christ long before they became Catholics.

Indeed, it was that faith which impelled them to undertake the search

that eventually led them to abandon their former religious communities

and join the Church, which, they believed, expressed that Christian faith

in its fullness.

Conversion to Roman Catholicism marked a shift in belief rather

than the birth of a new faith.

> Faith is deeper, richer, more personal than belief .
> It is engendered and sustained by a religious tradition, in
> some cases and to some degree by its doctrines; but it is a
> quality of the person, not the system. It is an orientation
> of the personality, to oneself, to one's neighbour, sic to
> the universe; a total response; a way of seeing whatever one
> sees and of handling whatever one handles; a capacity to live
> at a more mundane level; to see, to feel, to act, in terms
> of a transcendent dimension.[12]

Hewit and Huntington explicitly stated that their eventual conversions

to Roman Catholicism were natural outgrowths of earlier commitments

to God. Hewit experienced "a great and decisive change" in his "moral

state and attitude toward God and the world" which he considered to be

a fundamental conversion.[13] At that time, he surrendered himself to

God, promising his faithful obedience to God's law. Though he later

converted to the Episcopal Church and then to the Roman Church, he

never repudiated his first act of faith. Huntington had a similar

experience following his conversion during a revival. Though the

---

[12]Wilfred Cantwell Smith, Faith and Belief (Princeton:
Princeton University Press, 1979), p. 12.

[13]Hewit, p. 34.

effects of that conversion were short-lived, he resolved "to serve God and keep his commandments" as a result of it.[14] That resolution constituted an authentic conversion: a profession of faith in Jesus Christ. Both Hewit and Huntington saw their "first conversions" as decisive; faith in Christ was the foundation for eventual conversion to Roman Catholicism.

Faith gives rise to beliefs. "Faith is nourished and patterned by the tradition, is formed and in some sense sustained by it -- yet faith precedes and transcends the tradition, and in turn sustains it."[15] Faith is a fundamental human act. It has two dimensions, intellectual and affective: insight and response.[16] Faith involves both knowledge and commitment, the ability to recognize the truth and the courage to act on that recognition.

The narratives show that the convert authors were indeed men of faith, in the sense described here, prior to their becoming Roman Catholics. As Protestants and Anglicans, they had come to know the truth in Christ. Their decisions to become Catholic signalled their willingness to act on that knowledge. An intellectual process of inquiry brought them to the threshold of the Church; once there, they found it impossible to do anything other than to publically acknowledge their insight regarding the truth of Roman Catholic teaching. They were impelled by faith to affirm that membership in the Church was essential for their salvation. Their faith required that they profess beliefs, which, to their minds, better reflected their Christian faith.

---

[14]Huntington, p. 26.

[15]Smith, p. 5.

[16]Ibid., p. 12.

The convert authors call their readers' attention to those beliefs rather than to their faith; that is, they focused on the ideas which they held as Catholics and described the way in which they came to do so rather than exploring the inner life of faith which they experienced as Christians. However, some converts also recognize the bond of faith which draws persons and communities together despite their divergent beliefs. A Catholic theologian recently put the matter this way: "Beliefs do differ, but behind this difference there is a deeper unity."[17] That unity has as its basis in faith, "the eye of religious love, an eye that can describe God's self-disclosures."[18] Hewit realized that he was "united to the soul of the Catholic Church, by faith, hope, and charity," several years before he became a member.[19] Walworth refers to the bond that unites those searching for the truth, insisting that he never abandoned any religious belief he held when he became a Roman Catholic: "the horizon of my faith has been enlarged. But I have never yet felt the shock of a lost faith."[20] Stoddard speaks of wandering from church to church because he knew God to be "the source of all truth" and desired to worship him.[21] These men and their fellow convert authors were impelled by their faith to undertake the search that finally brought them to the Church. Though they learned that becoming Roman Catholic separated a person from all that was familiar,

---

[17]Lonergan, Method in Theology, p. 119.

[18]Ibid.

[19]Hewit, p. 35.

[20]Cited by E. Walworth, p. 42.

[21]Stoddard, p. 56.

though they realized that church teachings and practices could be a source of division among persons and congregations, they knew that faith in Christ bonded together those who believed in him. But in the face of the antipathy between Protestants and Catholics in nineteenth-century America, it is not surprising that the convert authors chose to accent the differences and to minimize the similarities between the two and to turn their attention to the task of setting forth and explaining specific points of contention.

The converts sought to defend the content of the beliefs (which they had affirmed in faith) by correcting the errors and dispelling the misunderstandings common among non-Catholics. It was far more important for them to describe the ways in which they had come to accept the conceptual and ritual components of their new religion than it was to explain the inner transformation they experienced, especially since they understood conversion to Roman Catholicism to mean accepting the Church's authority to articulate essential teaching and to determine correct practices. In emphasizing the intellectual aspect of their faith, they again expressed their distaste for conversion as it was defined by evangelical Christians, who viewed intellectual inquiry with suspicion and even hostility. The way in which converts tell their story is thus shaped by what they rejected as well as by what they accepted. But it remains a fact that, for them, conversion was both an intellectual and an affective experience.

The convert authors deliberately stressed the reasonableness of their decisions to become Catholic. While the evangelical Christians were unreflectively carried along by the heat of feeling, converts to Roman Catholicism acted coolly and unreflectively. At least, such is

the impression conveyed by the accounts of conversion and the carefully
honed apologetic briefs appended to them. But the texts reveal that
conversion to Roman Catholicism could hardly have been a dispassionate
action since the converts believed that they must become Catholics in
order to be saved: to do otherwise was to take the risk of being
damned for all eternity. The Roman Catholic Church was, for these men,
a haven of security and a means to eternal life.

Catholicism's Appeal to Mind and Heart

Although the converts stress Catholicism's appeal to intellect
in both the content and the structure of their narratives, they reveal
that Catholicism had a strong affective appeal. Neither their protracted
doctrinal discussions nor their portrayal of conversion as the resolution
to an intellectual quest for truth in teaching conceals the fact that
they found Roman Catholicism aesthetically satisfying. In fact, those
very qualities of Catholicism which the converts found intellectually
satisfying were also a source of affective gratification. The doctrine,
polity, and piety of the Roman Catholic Church appealed to mind and heart.

Roman Catholicism satisfied the converts' yearning for truth,
unity, and order. Roman Catholicism's uniformity in doctrine, its
authoritative teaching, as well as its spirituality met the converts'
need for "heart religion." Consequently, though the convert authors chose
to emphasize the logical appeal of their newly found faith, they sought
and found a faith which met a wide spectrum of human needs. Even those
aspects of Roman Catholicism which ostensibly brought the converts most
intellectual satisfaction fulfilled profound emotional needs.

The primary intellectual attraction of Roman Catholicism was the

uniformity of its teaching which in turn guaranteed the unity of faith.
In a word, Roman Catholicism was consistent in its interpretation of
the faith and thus differed from Protestantism with its diversity in
teaching and its multiplicity of interpretations. Having learned that
the Church Fathers insisted on the oneness of the Church, the convert
authors found themselves unable to tolerate the disunity exhibited by
the Protestant denominations and the Episcopal Church. Without unity of
teaching, there could be no certain knowledge, no authoritative statements,
no divine guidance. There could be no fixed rules of faith, as long as
each person was called to be his own exegete. In fact, it was theoretical-
ly possible to generate as many interpretations of the truth as there
were interpreters.[22]

Only an authoritative teaching body could ensure unity of faith
by insisting on a common rendering of the Bible. Only "living teachers"
could maintain the unity fitting for the teaching and practice of the
Church of Christ.[23] God's revelation of his will ought to be universally
available but not all persons are able to critically read and interpret
Scripture.[24] In order that Scripture be "perfectly intelligible to
everyone who sincerely wishes to know God's word," there must be a
teaching authority which is accessible to all.[25] That teaching

---

[22]Thayer, pp. 13-14. The insufficiency of private interpretation of Scripture is argued by Thayer (pp. 14-15), Ives (pp.
37-43), and Richards (pp. 98f.).

[23]Huntington, p. 119. Also see, pp. 49-53.

[24]Ives, pp. 37-40.

[25]Richards, p. 99.

authority is appropriately vested in the community, not in the individual, in the Church, not in the minister.[26] In its living tradition, the Roman Catholic Church exercises the teaching authority which Christ vested in his apostles. Christ did not give his apostles a book; he gave them his word.[27] He intended the Church to have authority over Scripture.[28]

The convert authors argued that the uniformity of teaching that ought to characterize the Church of Christ is found in the Roman Catholic Church and offers a compelling reason for conversion to Roman Catholicism. Uniformity of teaching is a source of intellectual and affective satisfaction: the convert was able to claim that he had established, to his satisfaction, that the Roman Catholic Church's claim that it is the true Church of Christ is legitimate. In so doing, the convert relieved himself of the personal responsibility to determine true doctrinal teaching and biblical interpretation. The Church offers guidance because it speaks with divine authority. The convert authors needed such guidance; they were constitutionally incapable of tolerating the multiple interpretations proferred by Protestant ministers. Doctrinal diversity caused them as much personal discomfort as had the emotionalism of revival religion.

Doctrinal uniformity presumes an appropriate form of church polity, a view of the Church as a visible body with visible leadership,

---

[26]Some convert authors had personally experienced the frustration of being unable to speak with authority on matters of faith, even while they were ministers in their churches.

[27]Richards, pp. 101-102.

[28]Ibid., p. 106.

and a visible head.[29] The Church is

> ...not only a <u>spiritual</u>, but a <u>visible</u> body. Knit together by
> visible ties -- governed by visible laws -- exercising visible
> functions -- contending with visible enemies -- maintaining a
> visible fellowship; and hence, so far as I could see, re-
> quiring a visible, ruling authority.[30]

The Church is a community with one flock and one shepherd.[31] As a

social organism, the Church requires a visible head as all associations

do in order to secure unity of purpose and action. The Papacy is the sign

of the Church's unity, a sign which effects the oneness which it

signifies. The converts insist that the hierarchical structure of

church government is essential to the maintenance of uniformity in

teaching and practice. The polity which makes authoritative teaching

possible contributed to the converts' sense of security. But it served

another purpose as well: the Church's structure expressed the inner

unity of the Church in a visible outer form. Thus, it appealed to the

converts' desire for order and pattern even as it satisfied their desire

for uniformity and truth.

The narratives reveal that the convert authors became Catholic

because the whole of Roman Catholicism appealed to them, and because it

appealed to them wholly. Conversion was an aesthetic response to the

structure and style of Roman Catholicism. Repelled by the disunity and

dissension that they perceived to be a by-product of the denominational

character of Protestantism, they were attracted to the oneness of Church

teaching, reflected in the centralized mode of church organization. They

[29]Whitcher, p. 142.

[30]Ives, p. 162.

[31]Hewit, p. 39.

believed that it was essential that Christ's Church reflect its

fundamental oneness in its structure for it was one body with one Lord.

And alienated by the excesses of evangelical Protestantism, the converts

found themselves drawn to the restrained yet moving style of Roman

Catholic piety.

Piety includes the complex of actions that comprise the spiritual

life and that are most likely to stimulate religious feeling or to occur

in response to such feeling: prayer, worship, reception of the sacraments,

and participation in devotions. But piety is not simply synonymous with

ritual; piety means the religious life as it is lived and so involves a

view of reality, a way of looking at self, at God, and at the world. Piety

is a religious sensibility, that is,

> ...the intellectual and affective perception which an indivi-
> dual and/or a community has of the relationship between religious
> experience and the various dimensions of life. As such, it is
> concerned with the underlying structure of the religious
> consciousness -- not just the externals of behavior but how
> and why people approach Christian existence in a certain
> way and interconnections which they make between their inner
> and outer lives.[32]

Roman Catholicism appealed to the convert authors because the Catholic

faith informed every aspect of life. From cradle to grave and beyond,

Roman Catholicism mediates man's relationship with God and with his

fellow believers, offering support and nourishment. The Church nurtures

the young and comforts the old. Through its sacraments, the Church

ministers to the needs of all persons. The converts welcomed the full

sacramental ministry of the Church which met their need for a vigorous

spiritual life, lived within community. To be a Catholic was to stand

---

[32]Joseph P. Chinnici, "Organization of the Spiritual Life:
American Catholic Doctrinal Works, 1791-1866," Theological Studies 40

before God as a member of the Roman Catholic community of faith; to be
a Protestant was to stand before God alone. The difference was a critical
one to the convert authors, who had rejected the individualism of evangelical Protestantism. They needed and wanted the support of a church which
could offer them guidance and assurance throughout their lives.

The form of Roman Catholic worship was a welcome contrast to the
"characterless, colorless, almost formless" Protestant services.[33] The
converts found the externals of Roman Catholic worship -- the "altar, the
crucifix, the robed priests, the surpliced acolytes, the pictures and
statues of holy saints, the stained windows, the organ, the bells"
especially appealing.[34] Observable differences in the atmosphere and
style of worship reflected more substantive differences: a prescribed
form for worship that left no room for clerical innovation, an attention
to aesthetic detail, and a respect for tradition. Roman Catholic ritual
reflected the same concern with unity that characterized Roman Catholic
teaching and structure and that the converts found so attractive.

Both Protestant and Anglican convert authors testify that
Roman Catholicism's initial appeal was aesthetic: hearing eloquent
preaching, attending an august ceremony, or beholding the vision of
a picturesque church, filled with colorful paintings and resounding
with majestic music were among the converts' first positive impressions
of the Church.[35] Deprived of aesthetic satisfaction in the stark and

---

(1979):235.

[33]Stoddard, pp. 59, 74-49.

[34]Hecker, Questions of the Soul, pp. 174-175.

[35]Blythe, p. 16. Blythe recalls that as a young boy he had

somber churches where they had formerly worshipped, the converts welcomed

the visual and sensual appeal of Roman Catholic ceremonies in much the

same way that Catholics of the sixteenth century welcomed the return to

simplicity and restraint of reformed worship services.

The quest for "a holy life" was as much a factor in fostering

conversion as was the search for truth.[36] In Mary and the saints, the

convert authors found models of the spiritual life, well-lived. Saints

were paradigms of Roman Catholic piety; they manifested the ways in

which belief might be translated into behavior and they testified

that such faith in action was indeed possible. Saints were "proofs of

human perfection achieved through the aid of special grace, absolute

humility, and the purifying, sanctifying, consuming love of God."[37]

The popularity of the Lives of the English Saints among Anglicans at

Chelsea who later converted to Roman Catholicism indicates the interest

which the converts generally took in the lives of those who had lived in

a way consistent with their beliefs. But the saints were more than

examples of life well-lived; they interceded between man and God.[38]

Careful to counter charges of idolatry directed at alledged Catholic

worship of Mary, the saints, and the guardian angels, the convert authors

insisted that angels and saints mediate the sacred and so grant access

---

heard the Rev. John Thayer preach and "admired his eloquence." Also see
Richards, pp. 72-74; Hewit, p. 38.

[36] C. Walworth, The Oxford Movement, p. 103.

[37] Stoddard, p. 164.

[38] See Blythe, pp. 55-56; Stoddard, pp. 160-165; Whitcher,
pp. 105-117; Thayer, pp. 22-24 on the Catholic understanding of the
role of the saints. See Richards, p. 75; Thayer, p. 16; Stoddard, pp.
167-171 for discussion of the role of guardian angels.

to the world beyond. The unity of the Church of Christ was reflected in the belief in the communion of saints, the belief that there were bonds uniting the church triumphant, the church suffering, and the church militant. This doctrine affirmed the effectiveness of praying for the dead.[39] The Roman Catholic Church was truly one; the solidarity of its members in time and in eternity was another way of proclaiming the oneness of the Church: Catholics are united in their life of faith and stand forever before God as one body.

Conversion was an aesthetic response, an affective response to form. What appealed to the convert authors was Roman Catholicism as a whole. Though they experienced difficulty in accepting certain teachings or practices, they were drawn to the Church, irresistably drawn. In its teaching, its polity, and its piety, the Roman Catholic Church satisfied their need for structure and form. In it, they discovered uniformity, order, and stability in the place of the diversity, disorder, and innovation which they had found so distasteful in the Protestant denominations and even in the Anglican Church.

There was no single motive for becoming a Catholic; each convert did so for reasons of his own. But all shared an inclination toward the Church and a predisposition to accept its modes of organization and worship. They became Catholics for the very reasons that they were unable to remain Protestants. In each case, they were responding to form -- rejecting one and embracing another. Form defines the manner in which a religious system embodies its perception of the transcendent -- in its organization, in its ritual, in its ministry,

---

[39]Barber, p. 28; Hecker, Questions of the Soul, p. 217.

and in its ethic -- the way in which it expresses faith. And an

aesthetic response is a response of the whole self; it involves

judgment and decision, operations of the intellect and will, but also

feeling, a perception of value that is, at root, a movement of the

heart. It is a total response of the person:

> The change we call "conversion," thus residing neither in the
> transfer of ecclesiastical relations to the church, nor in
> growth of ritualism into the external conduct, nor yet even
> in the adoption of Catholic doctrine as the individual's creed,
> must have its sphere of action in regions deeper and more
> fundamental than we have yet explored. The church of God looks
> with the eyes of God upon the souls of men. "Give me thine
> heart," is her, is his demand, confident that if this be given
> all else is also gained. The change she seeks in those whom
> God would make her children is a change, not of opinion, not
> of tastes, not of behavior, but of heart and will; a change which
> reaches to the citadel of life, and thoroughly and permanently
> converts the man. With nothing less than this can she be satisfied.
> On nothing less than this can she securely build.
> And this change is conversion.[40]

The language which the converts used to describe what it felt

like to become a Roman Catholic reveals the depth of the Church's appeal.

Conversion felt like a return to one's true mother,[41] an arrival at

a "place of safety...of refreshment and rest."[42] The converts spoke

of the "unreachable quietness," the "deep repose,"[43] the "great

calm,"[44] which came upon them when they decided to convert. As much

as they insisted that conversion was the result of a period of inquiry

---

[40]"The Philosophy of Conversion," p. 464.

[41]Ives, pp. 22, note.

[42]Whitcher, p. 21. Also see Richards, pp. 108-109.

[43]Hecker's diary entry, 13 June 1844, as cited by Elliott,
p. 54.

[44]Stoddard, p. 113.

and study, they made it clear that becoming Roman Catholic quieted
a deep restlessness within them and satisfied their need for a religious
tradition that appealed to the heart as well as to the mind.

Conversion Narratives:
Their Purpose and Contribution

Some authors express their motives for writing explicitly. Thayer
claimed that he wrote for the "edification of Christians" and the "greater
glory of God."[45] Blythe viewed the writing of his narrative as a matter
of personal responsibility; he sought to justify his actions and to
inspire others to follow his example.[46] Hecker wanted "to explain the
the Catholic religion in such a manner as to reach and attract the minds
of the non-Catholics of the American people."[47] Brownson wrote to
expose the links between his past and present life, between nature and
grace, between the natural and supernatural; he saw himself as a paradigm
for others to imitate. Ives intended to set forth the history of his
mind as he searched for religious truth.[48] Whether they said so
explicitly or not, the convert authors wrote to justify themselves,
to explain the tenets of their new faith, and to clarify the meaning
of their religious practices. They wrote to inspire as well as to
instruct, to edify as well as to persuade.

The convert authors addressed their narratives to two groups of

---

[45]Thayer, p. 16.

[46]Blythe, p. 3. In the revised edition, he stresses that the convert has an obligation to satisfy public curiosity by setting forth the
motives which impelled him to become a Catholic (Blyth, p. 5).

[47]Hecker's explanation is cited by Elliott, p. 246.

[48]Ives, pp. 12-13.

readers: members of their former religious communities and fellow
Roman Catholics. Most authors explicitly state that they were writing
for their former churchmen, whom they sought to educate regarding
Roman Catholic faith and practice and before whom they desired to
justify the decision to convert. The twofold concern with apologetic
and apologia reflects the convert author's sensitivity to the needs of
that audience and his willingness to comply with the demands to explain
his actions which he believed his former churchmen had imposed upon
him. But the situation in which he responded to what he perceived to be
the queries and objections of his former churchmen was hardly conducive to persuasion. The lines between Catholics and non-Catholics
were firm and apparently impenetrable. There is no reason to believe
that the conversion narratives were very effective proselytizing
mechanisms or that they prompted an open dialogue or promoted mutual
understanding. At best, they expressed the convert's zeal in writing
to persuade others to follow his example.

The converts were also writing for Catholic readers. The
conversion narratives served several important functions within the
Roman Catholic community. The convert authors inspired Catholic
readers with their example and their testimony. Their decision to
become Catholics, despite the high personal and social cost of
conversion, was a source of encouragement to the Catholic community.
Converts were a sign of triumph: the Church would survive and prosper
in America, despite strong anti-Catholic sentiment. New converts
strengthened the faith of born-Catholics. The narratives served the
Catholic community as an effective vehicle of instruction. Because
the converts intended that the narratives be read by Protestants and

Anglicans, they were careful to explain and defend those Catholic beliefs and practices that were most likely to be misunderstood, such as, teachings regarding purgatory, the power of a priest to grant absolution, and papal infallibility, and devotion to Mary, the saints, and the angels. What was intended to persuade non-Catholics informed Catholics, who were in need of instruction on such issues. The narratives provided them with brief courses in apologetics, preparing them to defend their faith against Protestant criticism.

In a sense, the convert was his own audience as well. Writing the narrative was a way of imposing order on experience and thereby affirming direction and pattern in one's religious history. The narrative met the convert's need for structure and organization, the same need which brought him to the Roman Catholic Church. By setting forth the details of his life history as they pertained to his conversion, the author was able to read his life experience in light of its critical turning point. The effects of conversion were disruptive: loss of status, destruction of social relationships, and disorganization of personal identity. Writing the narrative was a way in which the convert could counter that disruption and restore order to his life. In the course of the narrative, conversion appeared as a logical, reasonable, and necessary act. The Roman Catholic Church was the true Church of Christ; there was no alternative but to submit to its authority. Impelled by reason and supported by grace, the convert had to do what he did.

But the convert author's dialogue with himself was conducted in the public forum and the convert authors rarely rose above the self-conscious posturing that often characterized Roman Catholic polemics in the nineteenth century. The convert was defensive; his preoccupation with apologetics and self-apology precluded serious self-scrutiny. The narratives suffer from the authors' apparent inability to turn inward and explore the life of faith. But this seeming flaw reveals a central aspect of the converts' experiences: the life of faith was to be lived in the community, affiliation with the Roman Catholic Church was the decisive expression of faith. The public act mirrored the internal experience: a person became a Catholic in name after he had become a Catholic in belief and practice. For the convert to Roman Catholicism, the religious drama was inevitably brought to the public arena. Though the converts pursued private study and reflection, once they had decided to become Catholics, their religious lives became public -- by virtue of the necessity for public profession of faith as well as the nature of the Roman Catholic experience. Unlike the Puritans, whose spiritual autobiographies reflected a life-long interior struggle, the Roman Catholic convert authors experienced their entries into the Church as the resolution of their religious crises. Catholics were likely to restrict their self-examinations to issues of morality and to the subject of general progress in the spiritual life. The Church mediated man's relationship with God, offering guidance and the assurance of salvation. The Catholic lived his faith, supported by the community, by its teaching authority and in particular, by its sacramental ministry. The sacrament of Penance provided a way of resolving questions and doubts that precluded the need for intense introspection in journal or autobiography.

By focusing on conversion, the convert authors served their

own needs and those of their Church. But what is more significant to
the contemporary reader, the conversion narratives provide a glimpse
into the American Catholic experience that is unavailable elsewhere.
Personal documents illuminate a people's experience in a way which
studies focusing on religious bodies as institutions do not. Until
recently, studies of American Roman Catholicism have concentrated
on episcopal biographies, diocesan histories, and the histories of
religious orders. The experiences of the people remained unexplored.[49]
The conversion narratives offer new insight into the nineteenth-century
American Catholic experience, from the particular vantage point of the
convert. The narratives describe the converts' conversion experiences
but they also reveal the converts' perceptions of what the Roman
Catholic Church offered its members, namely, truth, the assurance
of salvation, and, what is most important, a religion of the heart.

The nineteenth century may aptly be described as the age
of conversion. "Heart religion," which had flowered during the Great
Awakening, established itself as a significant American religious style.
The popularity and pervasiveness of revival religion throughout the
nineteenth century made it clear that evangelical religion had become
a permanent aspect of American Christianity, more precisely, of
Protestantism. But evangelical religion was not confined to the Protestant denominations or to the Anglican Church. As Jay P. Dolan has shown,
"heart religion" became a central feature of American Catholicism in the
nineteenth century; the parish mission emerged as a Catholic counterpart

---

[49]The work of J. P. Dolan is an example of the growing
interest in the Catholic experience of the American people. But much
remains to be done in exploring the American Catholic experience.

to the Protestant revival.[50]

Upon first reading, the conversion narratives written by nineteenth-century converts to Roman Catholicism appear to reveal a vastly different picture of the American Catholic experience. Dissatisfied with Protestantism and most especially with its evangelical character, the converts looked to the Roman Catholic Church for satisfaction. They took issue with the evangelicals' demand for a sudden, tumultuous, dramatic conversion and they were quick to point out that the effects of such a conversion were short-lived. They denounced Protestantism for its lack of unity, for its inability to provide authoritative teaching, for its formless worship. And the converts proclaimed to have found all that they were searching for in the Roman Catholic Church -- after a careful, deliberate, reasonable study of Catholic doctrine and claims. Conversion was a logical conclusion to the study.

But this picture is one-sided. The converts became Roman Catholics because the Church satisfied the wants of reason and of the human heart. They chose to emphasize the Church's appeal to reason in order to defend themselves against the charges of non-Catholics, who viewed the decision to become a Catholic as the height of unreason. Emphasis on intellectual appeal was in part, a narrative convention, shaped in response to the controversy engendered by the converts' defections from their former religious communities. But conversion to Roman Catholicism did involve an experience of the heart. The converts were drawn to the Church by the beauty of its

---

[50]Dolan, Catholic Revivalism.

churches, by the awesome drama of its liturgy, and by its pious
devotional life. They were attracted by the style of Roman Catholic
life as surely as they were pleased by doctrinal uniformity and organi-
zational order. Conversion was not simply the consequence of compelling
arguments supporting the Church's claim to truth. The converts were
brought to the threshold of the Church by reason and by affections.
The testimony of nineteenth-century American converts who wrote
narratives of conversion confirms that "religion of the heart"
was indeed a central aspect of their experience even though they
chose to stress Catholicism's distinctive appeal to reason.

Conclusions

On the basis of my study, I conclude the following:

1. The personal narratives written by nineteenth-century
American converts to Roman Catholicism do constitute a distinctive
form of spiritual autobiography: conversion is clearly their focus
and it determines what elements of the life story the authors include
and what elements they exclude.

2. Although the narratives were written over the course
of a century, there are no substantial differences between the earlier
and the later works. The narrative authors reflect common concerns:
like early religious background; anti-Catholic sentiment; dissatisfaction
with Protestantism; attraction to the Roman Catholic Church; the process
of inquiry that led to conversion; and an explication of doctrines and
practices most likely to be misunderstood by non-Catholics.

3. The convert authors wrote to justify their decisions to
convert and to defend the teaching and practice of the Roman Catholic

Church. This twofold purpose of apologia and apologetics determined
the content and the tone of the accounts. The converts emphasize the
reasonableness of their decisions to become Catholic, stressing that
they came to the Church after a lengthy period of careful, critical
inquiry.

4. Their concern with apologia and apologetic shows that
the converts intended that their narratives be read by Protestants
who might, by their reading, be drawn to the threshold of the Church.
But the narratives served to edify and educate Roman Catholic readers
as well, both by example and by deliberate instruction on matters
of faith.

5. The converts were Christians whose faith impelled them
to join the Roman Catholic Church. Although they emphasize their
dissatisfaction with Protestantism, their conversions point to a
continuity between their early religious experiences as Protestants
and Anglicans and their conversions to the Roman Catholic Church.
Although they focus on the new beliefs which they adopted as
Catholics, they are united to their Protestant and Anglican brethren
in faith.

6. The converts deliberately accent the differences between
conversions as experienced by evangelical Protestants and conversion to
Roman Catholicism. Thus, they emphasize that the latter was an
intellectual process rather than an emotional event. The converts'
motives for writing (apologia and apologetics) and their intended
audience (Protestant) led them to stress this major difference. But
there is a striking similarity: both evangelical Protestants and Roman
Catholics experienced "heart religion." The Church satisfied the wants

of the heart as well as the wants of reason in its uniformity of teaching, its polity, and its piety. Conversion to Catholicism was an affective and an intellectual experience, which was the climax of a gradual process of religious development: it was a matter of mind and heart.

BIBLIOGRAPHY

I. Primary Works: Personal Narratives

Barber, Daniel. Catholic Worship and Piety Explained and Recommended,
    in sundry letters, to a very near friend, and others. By
    Daniel Barber, A. M. And not so long since a Minister of the
    Protestant Episcopal Church in Claremont, State of New
    Hampshire. Washington City: E. DeKrafft Press, 1821.

Blyth, Stephen Cleveland. A Narrative of the Conversion of Stephen
    Cleveland Blyth, to the Faith of the Catholic, Apostolic
    and Roman Church, to Which Is Annexed, A Brief Refutation of
    the Current Objections to Many Articles of Catholic Faith
    and Discipline. Montreal: Nahum Mower, 1822.

Blythe, Stephen Cleveland. An Apology for the Conversion of Stephen
    Cleveland Blythe, to the Faith of the Catholic, Apostolic
    and Roman Church. Respectfully Addressed to Protestants
    of Every Denomination. New York: Printed by Joseph Desnoues,
    1815.

Brownson, Orestes A. The Convert; Or, Leaves From My Experience.
    New York: D. & J. Sadlier, 1857.

Hecker, Isaac T. Questions of the Soul. New York: D. Appleton &
    Co., 1855.

Hewit, Augustine F. "How I Became a Catholic." The Catholic World 46
    (1887):32-43.

Huntington, Joshua. Gropings After Truth; A Life Journey from New
    England Congregationalism to the One Catholic and Apostolic
    Church. New York: The Catholic Publication Society, 1868.

Ives, Levi Silliman. The Trials of a Mind in its Progress to Catholi-
    cism: A Letter to His Old Friends. Boston: Patrick
    Donahue, 1854.

Richards, William. On the Road to Rome, and How Two Brothers Got
    There. New York: Benzinger Brothers, 1895.

Stoddard, Charles Warren. A Troubled Heart and How It Was Comforted
    At Last. Notre Dame, Ind.: "Ave Maria" Office, 1895.

Thayer, John. An Account of the Conversion of the Reverend Mr. John
Thayer, Lately a Protestant Minister, at Boston in North-
America, Who embraced the Roman Catholic religion at Rome,
on the 25th of May, 1783; Written by Himself. 5th ed.
Baltimore: William Goddard, 1788.

Walworth, Clarence E. The Oxford Movement in America; or Glimpses of
Life in an Anglican Seminary. New York: The Catholic
Book Exchange, 1895; reprint ed., New York: United
States Catholic Historical Society, 1974.

Whitcher, B. W. Story of a Convert, as Told to His Former Parishioners.
New York: P. O'Shea, 1875.

II. Works Cited

Barber, Daniel. The History of My Own Times. Washington City:
S. C. Ustick, 1827.

Brownson, Orestes A. The American Republic: Its Constitution,
Tendencies, and Destiny. New York: P. O'Shea, 1866.

_____. Conversations on Liberalism and the Church. New York:
D. & J. Sadlier, 1870.

_____. New Views of Christianity, Society, and the Church. Boston:
C. C. Little and J. Brown, 1836.

_____. The Spirit-Rapper; An Autobiography. Boston: Little,
Brown & Co., 1854.

_____. The Works of Orestes A. Brownson. 20 vols. Edited by
Henry F. Brownson. Detroit: H. F. Brownson, 1887-1907.

Buck, J. R. A Convert Pastor's Autobiography. Huntington, Ind.:
Our Sunday Visitor, 1942.

Burnett, Peter Hardeman. The Path Which Led a Protestant Lawyer to
the Catholic Church. New York: Benzinger Brothers, 1859.

Hecker, Isaac T. Aspirations of Nature. New York: J. B. Kirker,
1857.

_____. The Church and the Age. New York: The Catholic Book
Exchange, 1896.

Oertel, J. J. M. The Reasons of J. J. M. Oertel, late a Lutheran
minister, for becoming a Catholic. New York: Patrick
Kavanaugh, 1840.

Richards, Henry Livingston. Fifty Years in the Church. St. Paul, Minn.: The Catholic Truth Society of America, 1902.

_____. Forty Years in the Church. St. Paul, Minn.: The Catholic Truth Society of America, 1892.

_____. A. Loyal Life. St. Louis: B. Herder, 1913.

Sargent, Leonard. Pictures and Persons. Washington: St. Anselm's Priory, 1931.

Seton, Elizabeth. Memoirs of Mrs. S****, Written by herself, A Fragment of Real History. Elizabethtown, N.J.: Isaac A. Kollock, 1817.

Starr, Eliza Allen. The Life and Letters of Eliza Allen Starr. Edited by James J. McGovern. Chicago: The Lakeside Press, 1905.

Stoddard, Charles Warren. Hawaiian Life. Chicago: F. T. Neely, 1894.

_____. In the Footprints of the Padres. San Francisco: A. M. Robertson, 1902.

_____. The Island of Tranquil Delights, a South Sea Idyl, and Others. Boston: H. B. Turner, 1904.

_____. The Lepers of Molokai. Notre Dame: "Ave Maria" Press, 1885.

_____. Poems of Charles Warren Stoddard. Collected by Ina Coolbrith. London: John Lane, 1917.

_____. South-Sea Idyls. Boston: J. R. Osgood, 1873.

Stoddard, John Lawson. Rebuilding a Lost Faith. New York: F. J. Kennedy, 1923.

Stone, James Kent. An Awakening and What Followed. Notre Dame: The Ave Maria Press, 1920.

_____. An Invitation Heeded: Reason for Return to Catholic Unity. 2nd ed. New York: The Catholic Publication Society, 1870.

Walworth, Clarence E. Early Ritualism in America: Reminiscenses of Edgar P. Wadhams. New York: Christian Press Association Publishing Co., 1911.

"History of a Conversion." The Catholic World 45 (1887):708-710.

"The History of a Conversion." The Catholic World 49 (1889):547-552.

"The History of a Conversion." The Catholic World 50 (1889):260-262.

"History of a Conversion." The Catholic World 50 (1890):839-840.

"How a Ritualist Became a Catholic." The Catholic World 46 (1887): 272-275.

"The Story of a Colored Man's Conversion." The Catholic World 47 (1888):562-565.

"The Story of a Conversion." The Catholic World 45 (1887):562-564.

"Story of a Conversion." The Catholic World 46 (1888):559-562.

"Story of a Conversion." The Catholic World 46 (1888):708-712.

"Story of a Conversion." The Catholic World 47 (1888):128-132.

"Story of a Conversion." The Catholic World 47 (1888):271-274.

"Story of a Conversion." The Catholic World 47 (1888):418-422.

"A Young Girl's Conversion." The Catholic World 46 (1888):843-846.

III. Secondary Sources

A. Biographical Studies of Narrative Authors

Brownson, Henry F. Orestes A. Brownson's Early Life: From 1803-1844. Detroit: H. F. Brownson, 1898.

_____. Orestes A. Brownson's Middle Life: From 1845-1855. Detroit: H. F. Brownson, 1899.

_____. Orestes A. Brownson's Later Life: From 1855-1876. Detroit: H. F. Brownson, 1900.

Elliott, Walter. The Life of Father Hecker. New York: The Columbia Press, 1891; reprint ed., New York: Arno Press, 1972.

Gibson, Laurita. Some Anglo-American Converts to Catholicism Prior to 1829. Washington: The Catholic University of America, 1943.

Holden, Vincent F. The Yankee Paul: Isaac Thomas Hecker. Milwaukee: The Bruce Publishing Co., 1958.

The Huntington Family in America: A Geneological Memoir of the Known Descendents of Simon Huntington from 1633 to 1915. Hartford, Conn.: Huntington Family Association, 1915.

Malone, Michael Taylor. "Levi Silliman Ives: Priest, Tractarian, and Roman Catholic Convert." Ph.D. dissertation, Duke University, 1970.

Maynard, Theodore. Orestes Brownson: Yankee, Radical, Catholic. New York: The Macmillan Co., 1943.

Merritt, Percival. Sketches of the Three Earliest Roman Catholic Priests in Boston. The Colonial Society of Massachusetts, Vol. 25; reprint ed., Cambridge: John Wilson and Son, 1923.

O'Grady, John. Levi Silliman Ives: Pioneer Leader in Catholic Charities. New York: P. J. Kenedy & Sons, 1933.

Richards, J. Havens. A Loyal Life: A Biography of Henry Livingston Richards with Selections from His Letters and A Sketch of the Catholic Movement in America. St. Louis: B. Herder, 1913.

Ryan, Thomas R. Orestes A. Brownson: A Definitive Biography. Huntington, Ind.: Our Sunday Visitor, 1976.

Schlesinger, Arthur M., Jr. Orestes A. Brownson: A Pilgrim's Progress. Boston: Little, Brown and Co., 1939.

Sveino, Per. Orestes A. Brownson's Road to Catholicism. New York: Humanities Press, 1970.

Walworth, E. H. Life Sketches of Father Walworth. Albany: J. B. Lyon Co., 1907.

Capps, Donald. "Orestes Brownson: The Psychology of Religious Affiliation." Journal for the Scientific Study of Religion 7 (1968):197-209.

Clarke, Richard H. "A Noted Pioneer Convert of New England: Rev. John Thayer, 1758-1815." American Catholic Quarterly Review 29 (1904):138-166.

Connolly, Arthur T. "Historical Sketch of the Rev. John Thayer, Boston's First Native-Born Priest." United States Catholic Historical Magazine 2 (1889):261-273.

Elliott, W. "Father Walworth: A Character Sketch." The Catholic World 73 (1901):320-337.

Hecker, Isaac T. "Dr. Brownson and Catholicity (Conclusion)." The Catholic World 46 (1887):222-235.

_____. "Dr. Brownson and Bishop Fitzpatrick." The Catholic
World 45 (1887):1-7.

_____. "Dr. Brownson and the Workingmen's Party Fifty Years
Ago." The Catholic World 45 (1887):200-208.

_____. "Dr. Brownson in Boston." The Catholic World 45 (1887):
466-472.

_____. "Dr. Brownson's Road to the Church." The Catholic World
46 (1887):1-11.

McAvoy, Thomas T. "Orestes A. Brownson and American History."
Catholic Historical Review 40 (1954):262-265.

O'Keefe, Henry E. "Very Rev. Augustine F. Hewit, C. S. P."
American Catholic Quarterly Review 28 (1903):535-542.

Catholic Encyclopedia. S. V. "Barber, Daniel," "Brownson, Orestes
Augustus," "Ives, Levi Silliman," "Stoddard, Charles
Warren."

David, Brother. American Catholic Convert Authors: A Bio-Bibligraphy.
Detroit: Walter Romig & Co., 1944.

Dictionary of American Biography. S. V. "Brownson, Orestes A.,"
"Hecker, Isaac T.," "Stoddard, Charles Warren," "Thayer,
John," "Walworth, Clarence E."

Dictionary of Catholic Biography, 1961 ed. S. V. "Barber, Daniel,"
"Brownson, Orestes A.," "Hewit, Augustine F.," "Ives, Levi
Silliman," "Stoddard, Charles Warren," "Thayer, John,"
"Walworth, Clarence E."

New Catholic Encyclopedia. S. V. "Barber, Daniel," "Brownson, Orestes
Augustus," "Hecker, Isaac T.," "Hewit, Augustine F.," "Ives,
Levi Silliman," "Stoddard, Charles Warren," "Thayer, John,"
"Walworth, Clarence E."

Who Was Who in America: Historical Volume 1607-1896, 1963 ed.
S. V. "Whitcher, France Miriam Berry."

B. Other Biographical and Autobiographical Works

Augustine of Hippo, Confessions. Translated by Vernon J. Bourke.
Washington: The Catholic University of America Press, 1953.

Bunyan, John. Grace Abounding to the Chief of Sinners and the Pilgrim's
Progress from World to that which is to come. Edited by
Roger Sharrock. London: Oxford University Press, 1966.

415

Cartwright, Peter. _Autobiography of Peter Cartwright_. Introduction,
    Bibliography, and Index by Charles L. Wallis. New York:
    Abingdon Press, 1956.

Finney, Charles G. _Memoirs of Rev. Charles G. Finney, Written by
    Himself_. New York: A. S. Barnes & Co., 1876.

Fox, George. _The Journal of George Fox_. Edited by John L. Nickolls.
    Cambridge: Cambridge University Press, 1952.

Guilday, Peter. _The Life and Times of John Carroll_. Westminster, Md.:
    The Newman Press, 1954.

Hewit, Augustine F. _Memoir of the Life of the Rev. Francis A. Baker_.
    New York, 1859; 7th ed. New York: The Catholic Publication
    Society, 1887.

Kunitz, Stanley J. and Haycraft, Howard. _American Authors 1600-1900:
    A Biographical Dictionary of American Literature_. New York:
    The H. W. Wilson Co., 1938.

Mead, Sidney E. _Nathaniel William Taylor 1786-1858. A Connecticut
    Liberal_. Chicago: University of Chicago Press, 1942.

Rowland, Kate Mason. _The Life of Charles Carroll of Carrollton,
    1737-1832 with His Correspondence and Public Papers_, 2 vols.
    New York: G. P. Putnam's Sons, 1898.

Stone, Barton Warren. _The Biography of Eld. Barton Warren Stone,
    Written by Himself: with Additions and Reflections by
    Elder John Rogers_. Cincinatti, 1847; reprint ed., New York:
    Arno Press, 1972.

Walsh, James J. "Doctor Jedediah Vincent Huntington and the Oxford
    Movement in America: I. To the Time of His Conversion;
    II. After His Conversion." _Records of the American Catholic
    Historical Society of Philadelphia_ 16 (1905):241-267;
    416-442.

Catholic Encyclopedia. S. V. "Huntington, Jedediah V."

Dictionary of American Biography. S. V. "Burnett, Peter H.,"
    "Huntington, Jedediah V.," "Starr, Eliza Allen," "Stone,
    James Kent," "Whitcher, Frances Miriam Berry."

Dictionary of Catholic Biography, 1961 ed. S. V. "Burnett, Peter
    H.," "Huntington, Jedediah V.," "Stone, James Kent."

The National Cyclopedia of American Biography, 1896 ed. S. V. "Whitcher,
    Frances Miriam Berry."

New Catholic Encyclopedia. S. V. "Huntington, Jedediah V."

C. General Studies of American Religious History

Ahlstrom, Sydney E. A Religious History of the American People.
New Haven: Yale University Press, 1972.

Gaustad, Edwin Scott. Historical Atlas of Religion in America. New
York: Harper & Row, 1962.

_____. A Religious History of America. New York: Harper & Row,
1974.

Hudson, Winthrop S. Religion in America. New York: Scribners,
1965.

Mead, Sidney E. The Lively Experiment: The Shaping of Christianity
in America. New York: Harper & Row, 1963.

Wilson, John. Religion in American Society: The Effective Presence
Englewood Cliffs: Prentice-Hall, 1978.

D. Studies in American Protestantism

Addison, James Thayer. The Episcopal Church in the United States
1789-1931. New York: Charles Scribner's Sons, 1951;
reprint ed., New York: Archon Books, 1969.

Barnes, Gilbert H. The Anti-Slavery Impulse, 1830-1844. New York:
D. Appleton-Century Co., 1933.

Billington, Ray Allen. The Protestant Crusade 1800-1860: A Study
of the Origins of Nativism. New York: Rinehart, 1938.

Boles, John B. The Great Revival, 1787-1805: The Origins of the
Southern Evangelical Mind. Lexington: The University
of Kentucky Press, 1972.

Bodo, John R. The Protestant Clergy and Public Issues, 1812-1848.
Princeton: Princeton University Press, 1954.

Bruce, Dickson D., Jr. And They All Sang Hallelujah: Plain
Folks Camp Meeting Religion. Knoxville: The University
of Tennessee Press, 1974.

Burgess, George. List of Persons Admitted to the Order of Deacons in
the Protestant Episcopal Church in the United States of
America, From A.D. 1785, to A.D. 1857, both inclusive.
Boston: A. Williams & Co., 1875.

Cole, Charles C., Jr. The Social Ideas of the Northern Evangelists, 1826-1860. New York: Octogon Books, 1966.

Canonical Forms and Requisites for Persons Seeking Holy Orders in the Protestant Episcopal Church. Prepared by the Standing Committee of the Diocese of Ohio. Cincinatti: Robert Clarke & Co., 1872.

Cross, Whitney Rogers. The Burned-Over District: The Social and Intellectual History of Enthusiastic Religion in Western New York, 1800-1850. Ithaca: Cornell University Press, 1950; reprint ed., New York: Harper & Row, 1965.

DeMille, George E. The Catholic Movement in the American Episcopal Church. Philadelphia: Church Historical Society, 1941; reprint ed., New Brunswick: Vogt Printing Co., 1950.

Edwards, Jonathan. The Works of Jonathan Edwards. Edited by C. C. Goen. Vol. 4: The Great Awakening. New Haven: Yale University Press, 1972.

Finney, Charles Grandison. Lectures on Revivals of Religion. Edited by William G. McLoughlin. Cambridge, Mass.: The Belknap Press of Harvard University Press, 1960.

Fostor, Charles I. An Errand of Mercy: The Evangelical United Front, 1790-1837. Chapel Hill: University of South Carolina Press, 1960.

Gaustad, Edwin Scott, ed. The Rise of Adventism: Religion and Society in Mid-Nineteenth Century America. New York: Harper & Row, 1974.

Goddard, Harold Clarke. Studies in New England Transcendentalism. New York: Columbia University Press, 1908; reprint ed., New York: Humanities Press, 1969.

Griffin, Clifford S. Their Brothers' Keepers: Moral Stewardship in the United States, 1800-1865. New Brunswick: Rutgers University Press, 1960.

Haller, William. The Rise of Puritanism. New York: Harper & Row, 1938.

Handlin, Oscar. The Uprooted: The Epic Story of the Great Migration that Made the American People. Boston: Little Brown & Co., 1951.

Hudson, Winthrop S. American Protestantism. Chicago: University of Chicago Press, 1961.

Johnson, Charles A. The Frontier Camp Meeting: Religion's Harvest
  Time. Dallas: Southern Methodist University Press, 1955.

Journal of the Proceedings of the Bishops, Clergy, and Laity of the
  Protestant Episcopal Church in the United States of America
  Assembled in a General Convention, Held in St. Andrew's
  Church in the City of Philadelphia From October 2nd,
  to October 22d, inclusive, in the Year of Our Lord 1844.
  With an Appendix Containing the Constitution and Canons,
  A List of Clergy, etc. New York: James A. Sparks, 1845.

Journal of the Proceedings of the Bishops, Clergy, and Laity of the
  Protestant Episcopal Church in the United States of
  America Assembled in a General Convention, Held in
  St. John's Chapel, in the City of New York, From October
  6th, to October 28th, inclusive, in the year of Our Lord
  1847. With an Appendix Containing the Constitution and
  Canons. A List of Clergy, etc. New York: Daniel Dana, Jr.,
  1847.

Journal of the Proceedings of the Bishops, Clergy, and Laity of the
  Protestant Episcopal Church in the United States of
  America Assembled in General Convention, Held in Christ
  Church, in the City of Cincinnatti, From October 2d to
  October 16th, inclusive, in the Years of Our Lord, 1850.
  With an Appendix Containing the Constitution and Canons,
  A List of the Clergy, etc. Philadelphia: King & Baird,
  Printers, 1851.

Journal of the Proceedings of the Bishops, Clergy, and Laity of the
  Protestant Episcopal Church in the United States of America
  Assembled in a General Convention, Held in Trinity Church
  and St. John's Chapel, in the City of New York, From
  October 5th to October 26th, Inclusive. In the Year of
  Our Lord 1853. With an Appendix Containing the Constitution
  and Canons, A List of Clergy, etc. Philadelphia: King &
  Baird, Printers, 1854.

Journal of the Proceedings of the Eleventh Annual Convention of the
  Protestant Episcopal Church in the Diocese of Western New
  York, Held in Trinity Church, Geneva, on Wednesday, August 16th
  and Thursday, August 17th, A.D. 1848. To Which is Prefixed
  a List of the Clergy of the Diocese. Utica: H. H. Curtiss,
  1848.

Journal of the Proceedings of the Twelfth Annual Convention of the
  Protestant Episcopal Church in the Diocese of Western New
  York, Held in Trinity Church, Geneva, on Wednesday, August 15th
  and Thursday, August 16th, A.D. 1849. To Which is Prefixed
  A List of Clergy of the Diocese. Utica: H. H. Curtiss, 1849.

Journal of the Proceedings of the Fifteenth Annual Convention
    of the Protestant Episcopal Church in the Diocese of
    Western New York, Held in St. Paul's Church, Syracuse,
    on Wednesday, August 18th, and Thursday, August 19th,
    A.D. 1852. To Which is Prefixed a List of the Clergy
    of the Diocese. Utica: Curtiss & White, 1852.

Journal of the Proceedings of the Sixteenth Annual Convention of the
    Protestant Episcopal Church in the Diocese of Western
    New York, Held in St. Paul's Church, Buffalo, on Wednesday,
    August 17th and Thursday, August 18th, A.D. 1853. To
    Which is Prefixed A List of the Clergy of the Diocese.
    Utica: Curtiss & White, 1853.

Journal of the Proceedings of the Seventeenth Annual Convention of
    the Protestant Episcopal Church in the Diocese of Western
    New York, Held in Trinity Church, Utica on Wednesday,
    August 16th and Thursday, August 17th, A.D. 1854. To
    Which is Prefixed A List of Clergy of the Diocese. Utica:
    Curtiss & White, 1854.

McLoughlin, William G. "Revivalism." In The Rise of Adventism,
    pp. 119-153. Edited by Edwin Scott Gaustad. New York:
    Harper & Row, 1974.

Manross, William Wilson. A History of the American Episcopal Church.
    New York: Morehouse-Gorham Co., 1959.

Mijakawa, T. Scott. Protestants and Pioneers: Individualism and
    Conformity on the American Frontier. Chicago: University of
    Chicago Press, 1964.

Miller, Perry. The Life of the Mind in America. New York: Harcourt,
    Brace & World, 1965.

Miller, Perry, ed. The Transcendentalists. Cambridge: Harvard
    University Press, 1967.

Morgan, Edmund Sears. Visible Saints: The History of a Puritan
    Idea. New York: New York University Press, 1963.

Parker, Theodore. A Discourse of Matters Pertaining to Religion.
    Boston, 1842; reprint ed., New York: Arno Press, 1972.

Smith, Timothy L. Revivalism and Social Reform in Mid-Nineteenth
    Century America. Nashville: Abingdon Press, 1957.

Sweet, William Warren, ed. The Baptists, 1783-1840. Chicago:
    University of Chicago Press, 1931.

_____. The Methodists, A Collection of Source Materials. Chicago:
    University of Chicago Press, 1946.

Tyler, Alice Felt. Freedom's Ferment: Phases of American Social History to 1860. Minneapolis: University of Minnesota Press, 1944.

Turk, Milton Haight. Hobart: The Story of a Hundred Years, 1822-1922. Geneva, N.Y.: W. F. Humphrey, 1921.

Vaughan, Alden T., ed. The Puritan Tradition in America 1620-1730. Columbia: University of South Carolina Press, 1972.

Ward, William George. Ideal of a Christian Church. 2nd ed. London: J. Tooney, 1844.

Ward, Wilfred. William George Ward and the Oxford Movement. London and New York: Macmillan, 1889.

Weisberger, Bernand A. They Gathered at the River: The Story of the Great Revivalists and Their Impact upon Religion in America. Boston: Little, Brown & Co., 1958.

Mead, Sidney E. "Denominationalism: The Shape of Protestantism in America." Church History 23 (1954):291-320.

E.   Studies in American Catholicism and Related Works

Cross, Robert D. The Emergence of Liberal Catholicism in America. Cambridge: Harvard University Press, 1958.

Curtis, Georgina Pell. Some Roads to Rome in America. St. Louis: B. Herder, 1909.

Dolan, Jay P. Catholic Revivalism and the American Experience. Notre Dame: University of Notre Dame Press, 1978.

_____. Catholic Revivalism and the Immigrant Church: New York's Irish and German Catholics, 1815-1865. Baltimore: Johns Hopkins University Press, 1975.

Ellis, John Tracy. American Catholicism. 2nd ed. Chicago: The University of Chicago Press, 1969.

Foik, Paul J. Pioneer Catholic Journalism. New York: The United States Catholic Historical Society, 1930.

Gleason, Philip, ed. Contemporary Catholicism in the United States. Notre Dame: University of Notre Dame Press, 1969.

Gorman, Robert. Catholic Apologetical Literature in the United States (1784-1858). Washington: The Catholic University of America Press, 1939.

Herberg, Will. "Religion and Culture in Present-Day America."
In Roman Catholicism and the American Way of Life,
pp. 4-19. Edited by Thomas T. McAvoy. Notre Dame:
University of Notre Dame Press, 1960.

Mannix, Edward J. The American Convert Movement. New York: The
Devin-Adair Co., 1923.

McAvoy, Thomas T. A History of the Catholic Church in the United
States. Notre Dame: University of Notre Dame Press, 1969.

Malone, George K. The True Church: A Study of the Apologetics of
Orestes Augustus Brownson. Mundelein, Ill.: St. Mary of
the Lake Seminary, 1957.

Merwick, Donna. Boston Priests, 1848-1910: A Study of Social and
Intellectual Change. Cambridge: Harvard University Press,
1973.

Moehler, John Adam. Symbolism, or Expositions of the Doctrinal
Differences between Catholics and Protestants, as Evidenced
by Their Symbolical Writings. 5th ed. Translated by
James Burton Robinson. New York: Benzinger Brothers,
1906.

Mueller, Michael. The Catholic Dogma: Out of the Church There Is
No Salvation. New York: Benzinger Brothers, 1888.

The National Pastorals of the American Hierarchy, 1792-1919. Edited
by Peter Guilday. Washington: National Catholic Welfare
Council, 1923.

O'Brien, John J. The Renewal of American Catholicism. New York:
Paulist Press, 1972.

O'Neill, Scannell. Converts to Rome in America. Detroit: n.p., 1921.

Riley, Arthur J. Catholicism in New England to 1788. Washington:
The Catholic University of America Press, 1936.

Shannon, James P. "The Irish Catholic Immigration." In Roman
Catholicism and the American Way of Life, pp. 204-210.
Edited by Thomas T. McAvoy. Notre Dame: Notre Dame
University Press, 1960.

Shaughnessy, Gerald. Has the Immigrant Kept the Faith? A Study of
Immigration and Catholic Growth in the United States, 1790-
1920. New York: The Macmillan Co., 1825; reprint ed.,
New York: Arno Press, 1969.

A Survey of Catholic Book Publishing in the United States, 1831-1900.
Washington: The Catholic University of America Photoduplication
Service, 1960.

Wright, Willard E. "The Native American Catholic, the Immigrant, and Immigration." In Roman Catholicism and the American Way of Life, pp. 211-224. Edited by Thomas T. McAvoy. Notre Dame: Notre Dame University Press, 1960.

Yuhaus, Cassion J. Compelled to Speak. Westminster, Md.: Newman Press, 1967.

Chinnici, Joseph P. "Organization of the Spiritual Life: American Catholic Doctrinal Works, 1791-1866." Theological Studies 40 (1979):229-255.

Clarke, Richard H. "Our Converts." American Catholic Quarterly Review 18 (1893):539-561; 19 (1894):112-138.

Elliott, Walter. "Half-Converts." The Catholic World 63 (1896): 429-434.

_____. "The Human Environment of the Catholic Faith." The Catholic World 43 (1886):463-470.

Hennesey, James. "Dimensions of American Catholic Experience." Catholic Mind 73 (1975):18-26.

Hewit, A. F. "Pure vs. Diluted Catholicism." American Catholic Quarterly Review 20 (1895):460-485.

Keane, J. J. "The Reunion of Christendom," American Catholic Quarterly Review 13 (1888):304-314.

Lentz, F. G. "The Conversion of the American People." The Catholic World 55 (1892):884-887.

"Mr. Witcher's [sic] Lecture." Union & Advertiser (Rochester, New York), 13 February 1871.

"The Philosophy of Conversion." The Catholic World 4 (1868):459-471.

Preston, Thomas S. "American Catholicity," American Catholic Quarterly Review 16 (1891):396-408.

Shea, John Gilmary. "Converts--Their Influence and Work in this Country." American Catholic Quarterly Review 8 (1883):509-529.

Walworth, Clarence A. "Reminiscences of a Catholic Crisis in England Fifty Years Ago." The Catholic World 69 (1889):396-406.

Young, Alfred. "A Plea for Erring Brethren," The Catholic World 50 (1889):351-366.

423

New Catholic Encyclopedia. S. V. "United States of America,"
by J. T. Ellis.

F. Studies in Spiritual Autobiography

Abrams, M. H. Natural Supernaturalism: Tradition and Revolution in
Romantic Literature. New York: W. W. Norton & Co., 1971.

Bottrall, Margaret. Every Man a Phoenix: Studies in Seventeenth-
century Autobiography. London: John Murray, 1958.

Ebner, Ivan Dean. "Seventeenth-century British Autobiography:
The Impact of Religious Commitment." Ph.D. dissertation,
Stanford University, 1965.

McGiffert, Michael, ed. God's Plot: The Paradoxes of Puritan
Piety, Being the Autobiography and Journal of Thomas
Shephard. Amherst: The University of Massachusetts
Press, 1972.

Misch, George. A History of Autobiography in Antiquity. 2 vols.
Cambridge: Harvard University Press, 1951.

Pascal, Roy. Design and Truth in Autobiography. Cambridge: Harvard
University Press, 1960.

Peyre, Henri. Literature and Sincerity. New Haven: Yale University
Press, 1963.

Scholes, Robert, and Kellogg, Robert. The Nature of Narrative.
New York: Oxford University Press, 1966.

Shea, Daniel B. Spiritual Autobiography in Early America. Princeton:
Princeton University Press, 1968.

Trilling, Lionel. Sincerity and Authenticity. Cambridge: Harvard
University Press, 1972.

Watkins, Owen. The Puritan Experience: Studies in Spiritual Autobiography. New York: Shocken Books, 1972.

Wright, Luella M. The Literary Life of the Early Friends: 1650-1725.
New York: Columbia University Press, 1932; reprint ed.,
New York: AMS Press, 1966.

Weintraub, Karl J. "Autobiography and Historical Consciousness,"
Critical Inquiry 1 (1975):821-878.

Wolff, Cynthia G. "Literary Reflections of the Puritan Character."
Journal of the History of Ideas 29 (1968):

Bibliotheca Americana: A Dictionary of Books Relating to America,
1934 ed. S. V. "Thayer (John)."

Fullerton, B. F. Selective Bibliography of American Literature 1775-
1900. New York: William Farquhar Payson, 1932.

Kaplan, Louis. A Bibliography of American Autobiographies. Madison:
The University of Wisconsin Press, 1961.

G. Related Topics

Berger, Peter L. The Sacred Canopy: Elements of a Sociological
Theory of Religion. New York: Doubleday & Co., 1967.

Chadwick, Owen. The Reformation. Baltimore: Penguin Books, 1964.

Clark, E. T. The Psychology of Religious Awakening. New York:
Macmillan, 1929.

Coe, George A. The Psychology of Religion. Chicago: University
of Chicago Press, 1916.

Garrison, Winfred E. "Characteristics of American Organized Religion."
The Annals of the American Academy of Political and Social
Science 256 (1948):14-24.

Geertz, Clifford. Islam Observed: Religious Development in Morocco
and Indonesia. New Haven: Yale University Press, 1968.

_____. "Religion as a Cultural System." In Antropological
Approaches to the Study of Religion, pp. 204-215. Edited
by Michael Banton. London: Tavistock, 1969.

Gennep, Arnold Van. The Rites of Passage. Chicago: University
of Chicago Press, 1960.

Herberg, Will. Protestant--Catholic--Jew: An Essay in American
Religious Sociology. Rev. ed., New York: Doubleday & Co.,
1960.

Hofstadter, Richard. Anti-Intellectualism in American Life. New
York: Knopf, 1963.

James, William. The Varieties of Religious Experience. New York:
Longmans, Green & Co., 1902; reprint ed., New York: Collier
Books, 1961.

Lonergan, Bernard. <u>Method in Theology</u>. New York: Herder and Herder, 1972.

Moberg, David O. <u>The Church as a Social Institution: The Sociology of American Religion</u>. Englewood Cliffs: Prentice Hall, 1962.

Starbuck, Edwin. <u>The Psychology of Religion</u>. New York: C. Scribner's Sons, 1899.

Smith, Wilfred Cantwell. <u>Faith and Belief</u>. Princeton: Princeton University Press, 1979.

Turner, Victor W. "Betwixt and Between: <u>The Liminal Period in Rites de Passage</u>." In <u>Symposium on New Approaches in the Study of Religion: Proceedings of the American Ethnological Society, 1964</u>, pp. 4-20. Edited by June Helm. Seattle: University of Washington Press, 1964.

Turner, Victor W. <u>The Ritual Process: Structure and Anti-Structure</u>. Chicago: Aldine, 1969.

Wilson, Bryan. <u>Religious Sects</u>. New York: McGraw Hill Book Co., 1970.

Starbuck, Edwin. "A Study of Conversion." <u>American Journal of Psychology</u> 9 (1897-1898):268-308.

Turner, Victor W. "Passages, Margins, and Poverty: Religious Symbols of Communitas." <u>Worship</u> 46 (1972):390-412; 482-494.

Zetterberg, Hans L. "The Religious Conversion as a Change of Social Roles." <u>Sociology and Social Research</u> 26 (1952): 159-166.

The Heritage of
American Catholicisim

1. EDWARD R. KANTOWICZ, EDITOR
   MODERN AMERICAN CATHOLICISM, 1900-1965:
   SELECTED HISTORICAL ESSAYS
   New York 1988

2. DOLORES LIPTAK, R.S.M., EDITOR
   A CHURCH OF MANY CULTURES:
   SELECTED HISTORICAL ESSAYS ON ETHNIC AMERICAN CATHOLICISIM
   New York 1988

3. TIMOTHY J. MEAGHER, EDITOR
   URBAN AMERICAN CATHOLICISM:
   THE CULTURE AND IDENTITY OF THE AMERICAN CATHOLIC PEOPLE
   New York 1988

4. BRIAN MITCHELL, EDITOR
   BUILDING THE AMERICAN CATHOLIC CITY:
   PARISHES AND INSTITUTIONS
   New York 1988

5. MICHAEL J. PERKO, S.J., EDITOR
   ENLIGHTENING THE NEXT GENERATION:
   CATHOLICS AND THEIR SCHOOLS, 1830-1980
   New York 1988

6. WILLIAM PORTIER, EDITOR
   THE ENCULTURATION OF AMERICAN CATHOLICISM, 1820-1900:
   SELECTED HISTORICAL ESSAYS
   New York 1988